CONDEMNED

CONDEMNED

THE TRANSPORTED MEN, WOMEN AND CHILDREN WHO BUILT BRITAIN'S EMPIRE

Graham Seal

YALE UNIVERSITY PRESS
NEW HAVEN AND LONDON

For information about this and other Yale University Press publications, please contact:
U.S. Office: sales.press@yale.edu   yalebooks.com
Europe Office: sales@yaleup.co.uk   yalebooks.co.uk

Set in Adobe Garamond Pro by IDSUK (DataConnection) Ltd
Printed in Great Britain by TJ Books, Padstow, Cornwall

Library of Congress Control Number: 2020946717

ISBN 978-0-300-24648-3

A catalogue record for this book is available from the British Library.

10 9 8 7 6 5 4 3 2 1

In memory of
Jack 'Rasher' Bainton (1928–1993)

CONTENTS

List of Plates ix
Acknowledgements xi
Notes on Usage xii
Map of Convict Transportation xv

INTRODUCTION: EMPIRE OF CHAINS 1

1 A HISTORY WITH MANY LINKS 5

2 KIDNAPPERS, SPIRITS AND SOUL DRIVERS 14
Ill-disposed Children—Virtuous Maids—'So Cold a Blood'—Scots Rebels and
the Mystery of the Irish Children—England's Slaves—Spirited to the
New World

3 TRAITORS AND DECEIVERS 32
The Counterfeit Lady—Ominous Presages—The Woes of Squire Jeaffreson—
Divine Providence in Jamaica—Barbadozed—The Neck Verse

4 THE BODY TRADE 49
Master of the Trade—A Most Infamous Character—The Real Moll Flanders—
That Miserable Woman—The Wayward Apprentice—Indian Peter's Revenge—
Betty Spriggs Writes Home

CONTENTS

5 A RACE OF CONVICTS 68

Ben Franklin's Rattlesnakes—The Slaves of Lundy—A Genius of the Female Sex—Poor Unhappy Felons—James Revel's Fairy Tale—The Secret Transports— 'Tore All to Pieces'

6 THIS SOLITARY WASTE 91

The Governor's Instructions—Damned Whores and Floating Brothels—Prince of Pickpockets—Death or Liberty—The Fortunes of Sarah Bird—'I Believe I am at This Time in a Pregnant Condition'

7 CRUEL TYRANNY 113

'I Have Been Cruley Used'—Sons of Freedom—Heroes and Villains—Fleeing Hell's Gate—The Flogging Tree—'Not Even the Hair on Your Head is Your Own'—Warriors in Chains

8 THE DEVIL'S ISLES 143

Unspeakable Iniquity—Dark Island—A Devil's Choice—Across the Black Water—Rudrapah's Tale

9 ONE VAST CHARNEL HOUSE 169

Artful Dodgers—The Outskirts of Habitable Creation—See a Female Factory Once—The Charnel House—The Hero of Van Diemen's Land—The Mysteries of Mina—The End of the System?

10 RIVER OF TEARS 199

A Rats' Nest—The Children's Friends—The Last Rebels—Seeds of Empire

11 THE END OF THE CHAIN? 224

Timeline 229
Notes 235
Select Bibliography 258
Index 270

PLATES

1. Convicts being taken from Newgate Prison to Blackfriars, 1760. Anonymous collage, record number 4919. © London Metropolitan Archives.

2. *View near Woolwich in Kent shewing* [sic] *the Employment of the Convicts from the Hulks, c.* 1800. Printed for Bowles & Carver. State Library of New South Wales.

3. *Government Gaol Gang: Views in New South Wales and Van Diemens Land: Australian scrap book*, Augustus Earl, 1830. State Library of New South Wales.

4. Convicts washing. *Illustrated London News*, 21 February 1846, p. 125 (ZPER 34/8).

5. 'The London Convict Maid', *c.* 1830. National Library of Australia.

6. *Political electricity; or, an historical & prophetical print*, 1770. Library of Congress.

7. 'Indian Peter' (Peter Williamson), artist unknown. *Grand Magazine*, June 1759. National Portrait Gallery, London.

8. Convicts leaving England for Australia. Rex Nan Kivell Collection, National Library of Australia.

9. *Convictos en la Nueva Olanda* [Convicts in New Holland], Juan Ravenet, 1793 (84). State Library of New South Wales.

10. The 'Vinegar Hill' rising, artist unknown, *c.* 1804. National Library of Australia.

11. Convicts working the treadmill, artist unknown. *Gentleman's Magazine*, 1822, vol. 92, part 2, pp. 8–9. Mitchell Library, State Library of New South Wales.

12. A flogging in Van Diemen's Land (Tasmania), artist unknown, *c.* 1830. Archives Office Tasmania, PH30/1/2720B.

13. Convicts at Singapore Prison. J.F.A. McNair, *Prisoners Their Own Warders: A Record of the Convict Prison at Singapore in the Straits Settlements Established 1825*, 1899. National Archives UK.

14. A heavily ironed prisoner at Singapore Prison. J.F.A. McNair, *Prisoners Their Own Warders: A Record of the Convict Prison at Singapore in the Straits Settlements Established 1825*, 1899. National Archives UK.

15. Prisoners working a treadmill, Rangoon, Burma, *c.* 1890s. Photograph by Watts & Skeen, 189-. Wellcome Collection. Attribution 4.0 International (CC BY 4.0).

16. English children bound for a Fairbridge farm in Molong, New South Wales, 1938. Molong Historical Society, New South Wales.

17. A boy ploughing at Dr Barnardo's Industrial Farm, Russell, Manitoba, *c.* 1900. Photographer unknown. National Archives, Canada.

18. Barefoot boys from the British child migration scheme working a forge at Fairbridge Farm School, Pinjarra, Western Australia, 1942. State Library of Western Australia.

ACKNOWLEDGEMENTS

Thanks are due to many people, named and unnamed. In the former category I am grateful for welcome forms of help and support from Maureen Seal, Kylie Seal-Pollard for editing and my agent, Sarah McKenzie; at Yale University Press in London: Julian Loose, Marika Lysandrou, Richard Mason and staff. In the latter group I am grateful for the perceptive comments of the anonymous reviewers and readers of the manuscript at various stages of its evolution.

NOTES ON USAGE

LEGISLATION

Over the centuries covered by this book, England, Ireland and Scotland did not exist in their current forms. Nor did Britain or the United Kingdom. Each country had its own lawmaking and judicial systems that evolved their own transportation legislation, interpretations and processes. Even when obliged to adopt or adapt 'English' or 'British' legislation from Westminster, Scottish and Irish courts could apply that law in accordance with their own traditions and perceptions. Commanders of military operations against rebels might also be given the right to transport prisoners. At different times, usually depending on political situations, these disparities produced a variety of legal and other outcomes for those transported, whether they were convicts, abductees, rebels, or just unlucky.

To a significant, though not sole extent, these political and legal realities contributed to the slapdash evolution of the transportation system and the production of many different outcomes for affected individuals at different times and places and, often, their various financial, family or other circumstances.

Each human story in this book is the result of a different interaction between these various legal processes. The lived experience for transportees was a variation of the same trauma – they were severed from home, family, friends and country, and placed into some form of bondage in the public, private or combined service of empire. This book is mainly about how just a few of the hundreds of thousands responded to such coercive circumstances and their many possible consequences, good and bad.

CALENDARS AND DATES

From 1752 Britain adopted the Gregorian calendar. Like most official impositions, this development was resisted in some places, with the 'old' Julian calendar dates still being used, in some cases for many years in certain jurisdictions and colonies. This can lead to some complexities in dating documents. Unless otherwise noted, dates given are as they appear in primary sources.

Titles and dates given for legislation referred to use in the year of the relevant sovereign's reign. For statutes enacted before 1793, the calendar year of the commencement of the relevant parliamentary session enacting the bill is given. This standard legal practice may lead to different dates being cited compared with other published histories.

PLACE NAMES

Place names have also changed over the period. What we now know as Sydney, for instance, was variously referred to as 'Botany Bay' (inaccurately), 'Sydney Cove' or 'Port Jackson' by administrators, travellers, journalists and convicts. Many places previously within the British empire have now reverted to their traditional names or been given new ones. This book generally uses the place name given in relevant primary sources, unless this is likely to cause confusion.

MONEY VALUES

Calculating the present-day purchasing power of historical sums is a complex task and the results are not necessarily helpful in understanding historical values, particularly in relation to varying costs of living and other variables. (See https://www.measuringworth.com/calculators/ppoweruk.)

Where required, an approximate figure only is given.

'SLAVES'

While the complexities, politics and emotions involved in the historical iniquity of black chattel slavery are beyond the scope of this book, that experience has resonances with the story of *Condemned*. In historical debates over the transportation system, in the media of the day, in government reports and inquiries and in the accounts of some transportees, their situation is described as 'slavery'. Many were also treated as slaves and suffered slave-like conditions of labour, abuse and coercion. But their sufferings were time-limited, some of their rights were, in theory at least, protected, and their bodies – and those of their descendants – were not the property of an individual who might have the power of life and death over them.

Other than the relatively few black chattel slaves who were transported for insurrection, mainly between the Caribbean colonies, transportees in colonial America, the West Indies and elsewhere in the empire were not 'slaves' – even though they might be sold as bonded labour – as their servitude was intended only for the period of their judicial sentence. Transportees in Australia were never sold, had legal rights which they sometimes successfully exercised, and laboured only for the terms of their sentences. Many suffered badly, but they were not chattel slaves.

However, in many cases, transportees believed and stated that they *were* slaves, were frequently treated *like* slaves, and were often described *as* slaves by observers, including some with a close knowledge of their situations. Despite these contemporary observations and perspectives, the condemned people whose stories are told in this book were most definitely *not* slaves and attempts to portray them as such are pernicious and false, as shown by many historians.

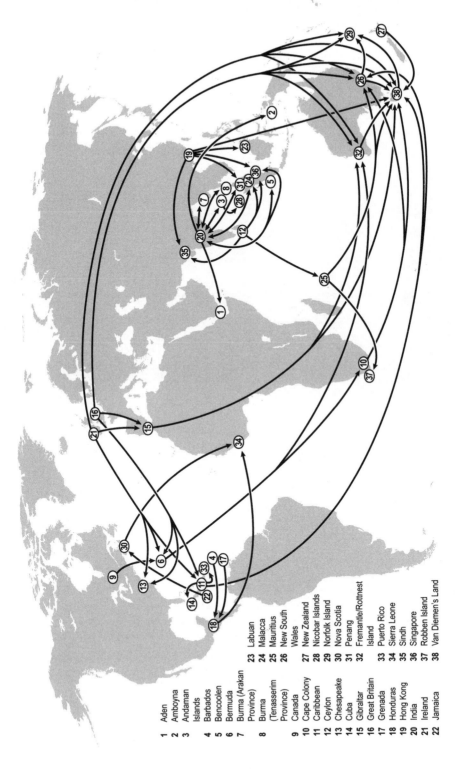

1	Aden	**23**	Labuan
2	Amboyna	**24**	Malacca
3	Andaman Islands	**25**	Mauritius
4	Barbados	**26**	New South Wales
5	Bencoolen	**27**	New Zealand
6	Bermuda	**28**	Nicobar Islands
7	Burma (Arakan Province)	**29**	Norfolk Island
8	Burma (Tenasserim Province)	**30**	Nova Scotia
		31	Penang
9	Canada	**32**	Fremantle/Rottnest Island
10	Cape Colony	**33**	Puerto Rico
11	Caribbean	**34**	Sierra Leone
12	Ceylon	**35**	Sindh
13	Chesapeake	**36**	Singapore
14	Cuba	**37**	Robben Island
15	Gibraltar	**38**	Van Diemen's Land
16	Great Britain		
17	Grenada		
18	Honduras		
19	Hong Kong		
20	India		
21	Ireland		
22	Jamaica		

Map of Convict Transportation

INTRODUCTION
Empire of Chains

In 1806 the *Venus*, a forty-five-ton ship, set sail from Sydney, New South Wales, in the direction of Van Diemen's Land, a penal settlement known today as Tasmania. The *Venus* carried crucial cargo for the few free migrants who had settled there: supplies, workers and convicts who would be put to hard labour.

The first mate, American whaler Ben Kelly, had a thin, whiskery face scarred by smallpox; a prominent scar disfigured the second mate's cheek; a 'mulatto' seaman wore his hair tied up and heavy rings distended his ears. An unnamed Malay cook, two cabin boys, a soldier and several seamen rounded out the crew. The ship's captain, Samuel Chace,[1] was a hard man – and trouble lay ahead.

Two of those aboard the brig were women. Middle-aged Kitty Hegarty was 'much inclined to smile' and had a loud, hoarse voice. Charlotte Badger was fat and bad-tempered. She had arrived in Australia in 1801 when she was just twenty-three years old, finishing a seven-year sentence for stealing her master's goods.

At first Charlotte was an inmate at the notorious Female Factory at Parramatta. Modelled on the English workhouses, this 'female establishment' was, supposedly, a place of useful labour and necessary punishment.[2] Its inmates were regulated and cared for according to official dictates and their own needs.[3] It was not unknown for women in the Factory – 'very nice young women' – to marry an elderly man and go to live with him on an isolated bush farm. The reason was simple. If a convict woman married a free man, she became free herself.

Charlotte, however, lacked the conventional physical attractions that might lure even an old husband. She was assigned as a servant to the wife of a local free settler. But after a few years she was returned to the Factory, expecting a child. Like most convict women who fell pregnant out of wedlock, Charlotte refused to name

1

the father. It might have been a soldier, another convict, or perhaps a settler, as enforced sex between female servants and the males who effectively owned them was not uncommon.[4] Whatever had befallen Charlotte, she once again found herself voyaging, now with her infant, 'beyond the seas'.[5]

Bad weather kept the *Venus* at Twofold Bay on the south coast of New South Wales for over a month. Captain Chace had to go ashore for business, leaving Ben Kelly in command. The ship was well provisioned with food and grog and there was not a lot to do. When Chace returned, he found the party in full swing. He reportedly ordered the two women flogged, but the crew refused, so he did the job himself. He then had the revellers chained up and told Kelly he would be dismissed as soon as the *Venus* landed. But next morning, after the captain calmed down and Kelly sobered up, Chace released the mate as he was needed to navigate the ship.

After what must have been a tense eight-day voyage across the treacherous Bass Strait, the *Venus* arrived in the Tamar Estuary. Chace went ashore with official despatches, returning next morning to see his vessel sailing out to sea. The *Venus* had been hijacked. Those loyal to the captain, threatened by muskets and cutlass, had been forced off the ship. It was a 'piratical capture', as the press put it.[5]

Nothing more was heard until news of a ship much like the *Venus* came from the other side of the Pacific. Kelly and the mutineers had reached Chile, but Charlotte was not with them. She and her child, together with several others, were landed in New Zealand's Bay of Islands before the *Venus* continued her piratical voyage. What happened next has been much mythologised, with claims that Charlotte lived with the Maori for years; that she ended up in Tonga or that she went to America with the captain of a whaleship.

It seems that Charlotte remained among the Maori for no more than a few months. She was taken off by an American whaleship and returned to Sydney via Norfolk Island. There are no records of an accompanying child, but a woman identified as Charlotte later married and gave birth to a daughter in New South Wales. Was this the fugitive pirate woman? Probably, though no record of her death has yet been uncovered. Nor any evidence that she was ever charged with piracy.[6] Whatever happened, or did not, Charlotte is today remembered as the first female *Pakeha* to settle New Zealand.[7]

Charlotte Badger is one of many ghosts in the empire of chains, appearing corporeally in the records and newspapers of the day, yet melting into myth when we try to seek her out centuries later. Her fleeting story is one of many hundreds of thousands that might be told of those condemned to suffer Britain's transportation system.

Over four centuries Britain evolved an impressively effective way to rid itself of those considered undesirable, including criminals, the poor, the rebellious and the simply inconvenient, deploying their labour and skills to its various colonial outposts, beginning with the Americas but later including the Straits settlements, Africa, India, Burma, as well as numerous islands in the Indian Ocean, the Caribbean and the Pacific. Not only were people transported from Britain to all these and other destinations, but tens of thousands more were re-transported within these colonies and between them.[8] While the numbers involved were dwarfed by those of black slaves, 'the Transported' – whether convicted criminals or otherwise – were a crucial element of empire expansion. Every habitable continent in the world received at least some transportees – North America, South America, Africa, the Indian subcontinent, other parts of Asia, Europe and, most notoriously, Australia, the smallest continent but the largest island.

In *Condemned* I set out to highlight the human and cultural dimensions of transportation rather than the system's official history. Whether they were sentenced, kidnapped, arbitrarily captured, or unwittingly migrated, this is the story of men, women and children condemned to exile 'beyond the seas'. It is a broad chronicle told through many small stories, forming a collective biography of cutpurses, cutthroats, artful dodgers, highwaymen, con artists, ruined apprentices, 'nymphs of the pave', ladies and gentlemen of fortune, deserters, rebels, and 'natives' of Britain's many colonial holdings.

These people left relatively few documents, whether reminiscences, statements, letters or diaries. Their ghosts can sometimes be traced through detailed official records. But not all jurisdictions and business enterprises necessarily kept good files. Others have been lost. In this book I aim to recover, as far as possible, the voices of the transported as they have come down to us in diaries, letters and incidental sources. Reports of investigations and inquiries also provide valuable information, especially when they include first-person evidence. The work of the large legions of family historians has also been of value in retrieving the minutiae of the everyday lives of individuals and families, often treasured in private rather than public sources. Together, these sources reveal that, despite legal and official regulations, not only convicted criminals were transported. And, while legislators usually directed certain procedures and outcomes for those who were transported, what was supposed to happen to them often did not – and what was not supposed to happen all too frequently did.

Condemned also attempts to explore the covert underculture of convictism – its attitudes, values, language, customs, myths, songs, poems, heroes and villains. This has to be retrieved from folk tradition, police and prison records, the chance survival of ephemeral documents and the surviving artefacts of convictism, including tattoos, arts and crafts and some archaeological evidence. Convict experience and expression were complemented by a strong public and popular interest in transportation that produced a lively street literature of ballads and chapbooks and also fed on a continual rumble of discontent – at home and in the colonies – from thinkers, some politicians and concerned middle-class observers. Opposition to transportation began early and, boosted by the popular interest in crime, its consequences and its characters, made the subject a running sore for the empire over many centuries.

Eventually, the system did end, leaving indelible traces in the colonial past. But there are no neat scissor-cuts in history. The jagged vestiges of transportation link us back to what might and might not have happened to the condemned. These include the burgeoning interest in convict ancestors, the extensive preservation of convict heritage sites and the rise in tourist visits to the cold stone remains of prisons. The abusive child migration programs that succeeded the system must also be counted in the legacy of Britain's empire of chains.

1

A HISTORY WITH MANY LINKS

. . . this enterprise will be for the manifold imploymente of numbers of idle men, and for breeding of many sufficient, and for utteraunce of the greate quantitie of the commodities of our realme.

Richard Hakluyt, *Discourse of Western Planting*, 1584

From earliest times, societies developed methods of expelling those considered criminal or otherwise undesirable. This often took the form of outlawry, a process through which individuals could be ejected from a community. Sometimes the ejection might be temporary, as in the case of Norse practice. More likely outlawry was intended to be permanent and increasingly came to mean that the outlaw's goods and property, if any, were forfeit to the Crown and he (as it usually was) could be hunted down and killed without legal sanction. This approach, in one form or another, persisted into the medieval period and well into the nineteenth century in some parts of the British empire.[1] It did not involve transportation, though it evolved into another form of official social and political ejection that required individuals to take themselves beyond the realm. Medieval banishment usually involved a person voluntarily going abroad as an alternative to execution. Not a difficult choice to make. Most of those banished were in the upper echelons of medieval society, nobles, aristocrats and gentry who had fallen foul of monarchs, lords or later, parliaments, through political or economic intrigues and power plays. But by the fourteenth century it was the lower orders who were causing most concern to officialdom, with legislation against nightwalkers, vagabonds and beggars often enacted.[2] In the following century, an Act dealing with vagrants and beggars decreed that 'Vagabonds, idle and suspected persons' were to be clapped in the stocks for three days and nights on bread and water, then ejected from the town. If they could work, beggars were to return to their 'hundred', or district where they had recently lived or in which they had been born.[3]

This was followed in 1530, during the reign of Henry VIII, with legislation that substituted whipping for the stocks and introduced licenced begging. Seventeen years later, another Vagrancy Act decreed that idle persons were to be given to masters and compelled to work for them, effectively as slaves.[4] Masters were able to beat, chain and otherwise compel these unfortunates to work for them for a period of two years. Vagabonds bound under this legislation could also be bought and sold. Boys and girls could be declared 'apprentices' and worked until they turned twenty-four in the case of boys and twenty in the case of girls. Escape attempts might extend the period of servitude. To be classified as 'idle', individuals did not apparently need to have committed a crime or to have been subject to any judicial process. This legislation was repealed in 1549, in favour of a return to the 1530 provisions. But despite this, the connection between poverty and its consequences, with remedies of punishment, bondage and coercion, was firmly established in law and in the minds of those who made it.

A further step in the process of criminalizing poverty occurred in the Vagabonds Act of 1572, which directed that public funds could be used to move the homeless to places where they might find work.[5] This Act also threw the cost of maintaining vagrants onto the parish and introduced some relief measures. But undesirables could still be whipped and even burned through the ear. As a polemical pamphlet of the 1570s put it, these miscreants were a large and motley crew, including 'Dauncers, Fydlers and Minstrels, Diceplayers, Maskers, Fencers, Bearewardes, Theeves, Common Players in Enterludes, Cutpurses, Cosiners, Maisterlesse servauntes, Jugglers, Roges, sturdye Beggers, &c.'

A generation later, an Order by the Privy Council to the Justices of the Peace of Middlesex described the activities of:

> . . . a great number of dissolute, loose and insolent people harboured and main-tained in such and like noysom and disorderly howses, as namely poor cottages and habitacions of beggars and people without trade, stables, ins, alehowses,

tavernes, garden howses converted to dwellings, ordinaries, dicying howses, bowling allies and brothell howses. The most part of which pestering those parts of the citty with disorder and uncleannes are either apt to breed contagion and sicknes, or otherwize serve for the resort and refuge of masterless men and other idle and evill dispozed persons, and are the cause of cozenages, thefts, and other dishonest conversacion and may also be used to cover dangerous practizes.[6]

The privy councillors concisely stated the many objections to such persons – they were unruly, dirty, diseased, idle and criminal. Primarily, they were 'masterless' and so – worryingly for social order – 'without constraint or command'.

But the problems these laws were designed to eradicate kept growing and governments and other interested parties began to seriously search for more coercive solutions to vagrancy and challenges to the political order. A view emerged that these issues should be treated as crimes, and so, along with felonies, amenable to legal punishment. While this might remove beggars and rogues from the streets and taverns, it meant that they had to be gaoled together with thieves, murderers, rapists and other criminals, at mounting expense to the always-strained public purse. Even with a draconian death-sentencing policy, not enough of the condemned could be disposed of to make a serious dent on the problem. Perhaps they could be sent somewhere else to perform some useful task?

The beginnings of this solution were tenuous. In 1577 some condemned men were sent to assist Martin Frobisher's second voyage to find a northwest passage, though they were dismissed before the expedition departed. Seven years later, the great maritime historian Richard Hakluyt wrote a *Discourse of Western Planting* in which he suggested that criminals – who included the poor – 'sturdy vagabonds' and 'the fry of wandering beggars of England that grow up idly, and . . . burdensome to this realm', could be sent overseas to provide labour for developing colonies. This would clear the highways, byways and prisons of their unwanted and expensive denizens.

Although others had made similar proposals before,[7] Hakluyt's argument was cleverly designed to appeal to Elizabeth I, particularly his suggestion that the enterprise would be 'a great bridle to the Indies of the Kinge of Spaine'. As well as discomfiting the Catholic Spaniards, trade would flourish, Her Majesty's income from customs duties would increase and new lands would be appropriated before rivals could stake their claims. Western voyages and discoveries would be advantageous in many other ways, including spreading the Gospel, or at least the Protestant version of it. This would also have another benefit: '. . . this enterprise will be for the manifold imploymente of numbers of idle men, and for breeding of many sufficient, and for utteraunce of the greate quantitie of the commodities of our realme'.[8] The need for procreation to establish populations sufficient to produce and consume for the benefit of trade and commerce would remain a pillar of coerced empire migration into the twentieth century.

The Reformation added another class of miscreants to the list of those who might potentially be ejected. Conflicts between Roman Catholic and Protestants produced governments of differing religious persuasions, with unpleasant consequences for those who refused to change their faiths. The official murdering of religious believers, known as 'martyring', was gradually wound back, largely on the grounds that it was cheaper as well as politically and theologically desirable for 'the multitude of such seditious and dangerous people'[9] to be out of the country. Those found guilty of such offences were given the option of banishment rather than the usual death by burning or dismemberment. From 1585, Jesuit priests could be banished instead of martyred and five years later Roman Catholics who refused to attend Anglican services, as well as dissenting Protestants, were granted the same indulgence.

At this time, famine and unemployment caused by the enclosure of common lands brought widespread distress and social unrest. In 1597 Parliament passed an Act that provided for penal transportation, theoretically to the colonies to be established in America. Those condemned to death might escape that fate by agreeing to be transported and to then work in bonded service.[10] A Royal Decree on the continuing issue of vagabondage was issued by James I in 1603. It identified the East and West Indies, Newfoundland and mainland Europe as likely locations for those to be banished. But transportation as a form of colonial labour supply did not become the practice – legally, at least – until 1615. Then, the Privy Council ordered that any persons, with the exception of those found guilty of wilful murder, rape, witchcraft, burglary, or who had been sentenced for robbery or felony, might be dispatched to work the new colonies of the West Indies and America. However, those convicted of the more heinous capital offences might be pardoned and sent abroad. Seventeen pardoned convicts were given to the East India Company for this purpose, and they most likely went to Virginia.[11]

The legal basis for transportation of the poor, the criminal, the rebellious and the faithful – of whichever persuasion – was now in place, if only in piecemeal and shaky form.[12] Complementing the efforts of legislators was the intellectual conversation about colonization and labour first proposed by Richard Hakluyt a quarter of a century earlier. The idea was abroad. The fledgling colony of Virginia was quick to take it up. Just a few years after its foundation, the settlers requested James I to send convicts under sentence of death to work their fields. It seems that few, if any, arrived, officially at least, though from 1618 London's Old Bailey was increasingly transporting pardoned capital offenders as well as those convicted of lesser crimes. There was an attempt around 1613 to send criminals to Robben Island, off what is now today South Africa, though this was abandoned due to conflict with the Dutch. But by 1615 those guilty of misdemeanours and pardoned felons could be forced to work in colonies as long as they paid for their passage and did not return to Britain before the expiry of their sentences, on pain of death.[13] Some went to the Caribbean islands in the 1620s, and in 1635 eight men and eight women were to be transported to Guyana.[14] From around the same time, the state-supported workhouses, known generally as 'Bridewells', also began transporting inmates convicted of various petty crimes, providing another source of colonial labour.[15]

As well as the indigent and the criminal, another group of troublemakers could also be dealt with through transportation. In overviewing the early centuries of the trade, a historian of violence observed that: 'The first deportees, the vagabonds and beggars of the sixteenth century, made way in the seventeenth for prisoners of war, Irish Catholics, and pirates.'[16] By the seventeenth and eighteenth centuries this was an established rationale, complemented by an official willingness to bend and even break the law in pursuit of these ends, despite opposition from reformers, politicians and concerned citizens. Rebels would again be a significant cohort in Australian transportation and also within the broader empire.[17] This could also include the endemic bandits who raided across the English–Scottish borders. Known variously as 'Reivers' and, later, 'moss troopers', these hereditary gangs based on family and clan were a perennial thorn in the side of successive monarchs. In 1666 earlier legislation against these marauders was renewed and extended. The new Act provided for 'preventing of Thefte and Rapine upon the Northerne Border of England' removed clergy from offenders and sanctioned transportation 'into any of His Majestyes Dominions in America there to remaine and not to returne'.[18]

As this ramshackle regime of coercion and control wobbled into the beginnings of a system,[19] enmeshing more and more human lives in its creaking machinery, it continued to be a convenient means of ejecting the unwanted and of providing labour, skills and markets for a growing empire.[20] It would become the engine that powered Britain's rise to global domination. The system would be increasingly refined as Britain gained control of more and more territories around the world, beginning with the lands nearest to them. At the end of the twelfth century, Ireland was invaded by Anglo-Normans. While Ireland was rarely thought of as a colony, the usually negative attitudes of the English government towards its subjects across the Irish Sea would fester through the succeeding centuries as new possessions were added to what became a glittering array of global assets.

England began to seriously aspire to planting new colonies in 1578 when Elizabeth I gave Humphrey Gilbert the right to take over any lands not already occupied by another Christian power. Five years later, Gilbert claimed Newfoundland. Two years after that, Walter Raleigh was instrumental in the founding of the ill-fated Roanoke settlement, and the first enduring North American colony was established at Jamestown in 1607, followed by the other early American colonies. Caribbean islands were intermittently occupied and settled from the 1620s, while the sugar-rich Jamaica was taken from Spain in 1655. Charles I gained the Moroccan enclave of Tangier as a wedding dowry in 1661. This constantly besieged hell-hole also served well as a destination for ejected malcontents from England and Scotland and even Algonquin prisoners of the 1676–7 war in New England,[21] until it passed into Moroccan rule in 1684. There were also early, mostly ill-fated, English and Scots incursions into the north-eastern coast of South America from early in the seventeenth century. The first successful settlement began in 1652 under the leadership of Francis Willoughby in what is now Guyana.[22]

The 1717 Transportation Act[23] allowed for transportation of those who had not been pardoned of capital offences. This substantially increased the available pool of colonial workers just as the empire required them. In the eighteenth century,

Britain acquired, by one means or another, Gibraltar and some Canadian provinces. Georgia was established in the 1730s and from the 1790s parts of Africa fell to British domination, including Sierra Leone, Cape Colony, Natal and Gambia. The process continued into the following century. Ceylon, now Sri Lanka, became a colony in 1802, and Burma (now, intermittently, Myanmar) in the mid-nineteenth century. Hong Kong was named a Crown colony in the 1840s and Malaya came under British control in 1896. Many of these possessions would play greater or smaller roles in the history of transportation. Whatever their role, they formed part of the expanding network of an empire that reached the peak of its extent and power towards the end of the nineteenth century.

These acquisitions were, variously, of economic, strategic, political and economic value. Sometimes all of those. The jewel of the imperial Crown was India. The British were involved with the subcontinent and its diverse peoples from the beginning of the seventeenth century and gradually extended their influence over the following decades. But it was not until their surging East India Company (EIC) took the capital of Mysore in 1799 that British interests became dominant and then expanded throughout the following century.[24] After the Indian Mutiny – or First War of Independence – in 1857–9, the British government began direct rule. Although India was never officially a colony, it played an important role in the use of internal transportation for the labour demands of British Asia and for maintaining imperial economic and political hegemony in that large part of the world.

Further south, Australia would be the location of the last great phase of empire transportation. In desperation, the continent was colonized in 1788, with a number of complementary punitive, strategic and commercial aspirations. The Australian experience, initially in the east and later in the west, perhaps most perfectly represents the role and function of transportation within the empire. Unlike previous operations, it was established by government and initially run by the navy and the army. It was the result of a deliberate policy of using convict labour and skills to establish a viable colonial community and to protect British interests against potential threats from any other power with Antipodean designs. The Australian experience of the system was not the barely regulated and commercial free-for-all of the earlier era, but a government-initiated and controlled operation. Detailed records were kept, and these provide deep insights into the human aspects of transportation. Not that official control improved the lot of many convicts. In many ways the scale and intensity of oppressive cruelty that many suffered in the Australian colonies is even more extreme than the casual brutalities of the earlier period of Atlantic transportation.

As transportation of those from these disparate social groups and locations wound down towards the end of the nineteenth century, a parallel activity evolved. It began with the dispatching of juvenile offenders to Australia with the laudable aim of providing them with the skills and opportunities needed to make better lives for themselves. At first, these were state-sponsored schemes and continued to be so, alongside a growing industry of private charitable organizations that sent orphaned and unwanted children to many parts of the empire in the hope of saving them from the horrors of industrialism and the cities 'of dreadful night'. These bodies increased in number, sending more and more boys and girls, some as young as five, to the ends of empire to be trained in farm schools and religious institutions. As with troublesome and abducted children transported to America by the aldermen of London in the seventeenth century, these boys and girls were effectively criminalized. The abuse and mistreatment suffered by many was implicitly sanctioned by the existence of the transportation system and drew directly from its methods of oppression and punishment. These practices and their attendant abuses continued to the 1980s, from around which time they were increasingly revealed, leading to momentous legal, civil and reputational damage for some of the world's oldest and most powerful organizations, as well as personal consequences for those victimized within them.

The complex history of British empire transportation – penal or otherwise – extends well back in time and continues to have consequences and resonances of one kind or another today. It also intersects with many aspects of human endeavour. In the consequential discourses of social relations and the evolution of what is often called 'civilization', the coerced movement of men, women and children, criminal or not, has ramifications for issues of class, crime, the law, penal reform, race, gender relations and human rights. Economically, the transported provided labour, growing populations and local markets. The natural resources of those colonies also often produced goods that could be traded throughout the empire and beyond, including, among other commodities, tobacco from America, sugar from the Caribbean and wool from Australia.

As well as these practical, social, political and economic advantages, transportation to, within and around the empire provided a climate of acquiescence within which the convenient fiction of a shared empire 'family' could be extended and maintained. Transportation was a concrete projection of the great and thriving entity of mercantile imperialism. Along with trade and migration, the seaways that carried human beings to distant places of penance were visible evidence of the links that forged the empire and kept it strong. Even after American independence, these connections continued. Canadians were transported to New South Wales, Americans to Van Diemen's Land, Britons from Bermuda to Western Australia. Escape attempts from Australia saw convicts reach New Zealand, South America, Japan, China and North America. Indians were sent to the Straits colonies and to the Andaman Islands.

The empire of chains was held together by many links, along which bonded humans passed from freedom to imprisonment and, sometimes, back again.

2

KIDNAPPERS, SPIRITS AND SOUL DRIVERS

A thing not known amongst the cruel Turks, to sell and enslave those of their own country and religion, much less the innocent.

Marcellus Rivers and Oxenbridge Foyle, 1659

In the minds of seventeenth- and eighteenth-century authorities and colonists, and in many of the legislative and social structures in Britain and the New World colonies, transportees were just another form of bonded labour. They were bought and sold in the same way and performed much of the same types of work. As black chattel slavery took over the bulk of the labour supply in the American and other Atlantic colonies, the much smaller numbers of convicts and servants were lost in the larger misery. Long before then, the legal and commercial practices that would become the transportation system had begun. Some of its first victims would be children.

ILL-DISPOSED CHILDREN

Founded in a headlong rush for land, riches and freedom from religious persecution, the American colonies were otherwise diverse in the religious and political attitudes and social values of their settlers.[1] One thing they did have in common was a shortage of skills and labour. Jamestown, shakily established in 1607, was only four years later petitioning King James I to send over capitally convicted labour. Officially, at least, it seems that none arrived for another seven years. In the interim, the British authorities began to construct what would become a global system of coercion and misery that fuelled the empire for centuries to come. Those guilty only of misdemeanours could now be transported, as well as reprieved felons – murderers, rapists, housebreakers and the like – as long as they paid for their own passages and did not return to Britain before serving their full sentences, on pain of death.

In 1617 John Browne, felon, was reprieved from execution in the county of Kent. He was an early beneficiary of the king's 'singular Clemency and mercy' as well as other 'diverse weighty Considerations'. These considerations included the wish that Browne 'be rather Corrected than destroyed' and that in being transported he might 'yield a profitable Service to the Common wealth in parts abroad'. He was 'to be delivered unto Sir Thomas Smith (Smythe) Governor of the East Indie Company or his Assignees, to be Conveyed into the East Indies or other parts beyond the Seas where he shall direct, with all convenient speed, and not to return again upon the pain before specified'.[2] Reprieve in accordance with royal mercy[3] made the king look benevolent, avoided yet more bodies in expensive prisons, contributed to the 'Common wealth' abroad, and even held hope of rehabilitation.

A 1603 royal decree on vagabondage had identified the East and West Indies, Newfoundland and continental Europe as likely destinations for the unwanted. London's Old Bailey was transporting people from at least 1618, though not, it seems, in large numbers.[4] As the judicial system became more draconian, juries were often left with only the choice of a lethal conviction or acquittal.[5] Penal transportation provided an alternative that courts were happy to adopt and one that led to a swift rise in the number of convicts transported.

The innocent were also being transported. In his will, London alderman Anthony Abdy, carefully dividing his considerable wealth between family, servants and charity, gave 'the sume of one hundred and Twenty pounds to be disposed and bestowed by my Executors upon twenty poore Boyes and Girles to be taken up out of the Streets of London as vagrants for the Cloathing and transporting of them either to Virginia New England or any other of the Western Plantations there to be placed'.[6] The alderman's intentions were presumably charitable rather than punitive, but by then the notion of ridding the country of unwanted souls – for whatever reasons – with a view to providing colonial labour was well established. A free-enterprise arrangement of bondage evolved in which private interests shouldered the costs of transportation and recouped these – with profit – by selling off individuals unable to pay for their passage to the highest bidders.

In some cases there was a willingness to dip into the public purse to fund the removal of perceived problems. The City of London, suffering from a 'superfluous multitude' of unwanted and troublesome children, 'appointed' one hundred of them to be taken to Virginia in 1620,[7] 'there to be bound apprentices, upon very beneficial conditions'. So anxious was the City to rid itself of this innocent excess that 500 shillings were granted 'for their passage and outfit'. It seems that some of the children were reluctant to go to an unknown land across dangerous seas. The City petitioned the Board of Trades and Plantations for a ruling to overcome what was, even then, a dramatic infringement of personal liberty. The argument made by the London authorities was based on the redemption 'of the ill-disposed children' from the sin of existing. They argued that the children 'under severe masters in Virginia may be brought to goodness'. But without official sanction, the City was unable to deliver the children to the Virginia Company for transportation against their will, desiring a 'higher authority to get over the difficulty.[8] Of course, a way was found to get around the 'difficulty' and to rid the City of what it considered to be its youthful burden. And so it was with all aspects of transportation. With or without the support of the law, valuable, preferably young bodies would be procured for the needs of the New World.

It was not long before this side of the business began to boom. Despite ongoing government attempts at regulation over the next sixty years, children continued to be abducted. In 1698 a newspaper, the *Flying Post*, reported on around two hundred boys being held aboard a ship in the River Thames, awaiting transportation to the colonies. One boy told the reporter his story:

> A person gave him a letter to carry to a certain house by the waterside, for which he paid him part in hand and promised to pay him the rest when he returned. But he was no sooner entered the house when he was obliged to swear that he had no parents alive and was sent aboard the said ship where there were about two hundred of different ages, some eight, some nine, and others eleven, but the oldest not above twelve.[9]

The trade continued to flourish in Scotland as well as England. Throughout the 1740s hundreds of children were said to have disappeared from the Aberdeen area alone, as traders, authorities and New World planters took advantage of the poor, the orphaned and the plain unlucky.[10]

The ill-favoured included those who did not fit in. As well as children, sturdy beggars, strolling players and their troublesome like, 'Egyptians', as Roma people were then known,[11] were transported. With their nomadic lifestyle and distinctive dress, they were always easy targets. They were banished from England as early as 1531 and a few years later, in 1544. These unfortunates were sent to continental Europe, but as the empire established its foundations and banishment evolved into transportation, the Americas provided new destinations. In 1665 an Edinburgh merchant, George Hutcheson, and his business partners were empowered by the Privy Council to transport loose and dissolute persons, including 'Egyptians', to Barbados and Jamaica.[12] A similar privilege was granted to an Edinburgh syndicate in 1669.[13] Nearly fifty years later, in 1715, nine male and female Gypsies were sent to Virginia.[14] What, if any, crimes these people had committed, was usually unclear. Magistrates were generally allowed to round up vagabonds and anyone else deemed to be masterless or idle and have them delivered to waiting ships bound for the New World.[15] Others went willingly.

VIRTUOUS MAIDS

As early as 1619 Sir Edwin Sandys, of the Virginia Company then overseeing the Virginian plantations, suggested 'that a fit hundred might be sent of women, maids young and uncorrupt to make wives to the inhabitants'. The Company was concerned that the planters were only interested in braving disease and the indigenous inhabitants of the New World long enough to make their fortunes, whereupon they planned to return to Britain and live at ease. Sandys thought that 'For the remedying of that mischief and of the establishing a perpetuity of the plantation he advised to send them over one hundred young maids to become wives, that wives, children and families might make them less movable, and settle them together with their posterity in that soil.'[16] Willing 'maids' and some widows were found and embarked for Virginia in three shiploads over the next few years. The Company recorded that 'There hath been especial care had in the choice of them for there hath not any one of them been received but upon good commendations.' Of course, the baggage had to be paid for. The Company's costs were high in running the scheme and providing the women with necessities for their voyage. The bride price was set at over 120 pounds weight of best leaf tobacco, later raised to 150 pounds, due to loss of value in shipping the leaf to England. As well as gaining a wife, the husbands with sufficient funds to purchase them received benefits from the Company.

Despite the commercial realities involved, this was not a coercive arrangement. The women came of their own free will, some having relations already in Virginia. They were generally well educated and adept in the household skills required for a woman of that era, and came from middle-class and even gentry backgrounds. Anne Rickard from the parish of St James Clerkenwell in London was a respected widow in her community, a woman of 'honest life and conversation', as the church-wardens wrote in their testimonial of her good character. She was 'minded and purposed to dwell elsewhere' and, for whatever reasons, wished to leave her old life behind and begin a new one. Similar intentions perhaps motivated the other widows, while the younger 'maids' seem to have often been ready for adventure in largely undiscovered lands. The English economy was weak at this time, forcing young men to defer marriage. Without a husband, young women faced the possibility of a difficult life, economically and socially. A chancy sea passage to a frontier colony may have been worth the risk, particularly given the superior economic possibilities for married women available through the Virginian property and inheritance system. For whatever their reasons, 139 women voyaged there from England between 1619 and 1621.[17]

The Company was keen for the venture to succeed. Its Virginia agents were instructed:

... to be fathers to them in this business, not enforcing them to marry against their wills; neither send we them to be servants but in case of extremities, for we would have their condition as much better as multitudes may be allured thereby to come unto you. And you may assure such men as marry these women, that

18

the first servants sent over by the Company shall be consigned to them, it being our intent to preserve families and proper married men, before single persons.[18]

The emphasis on family and marriage was intended to ensure a stable community of colonists. Many women previously arriving in the colony had been scoured from England's streets and gaols and simply let loose on their arrival. The Company and its investors wanted no repeat of the crime and debauchery that reportedly followed. And the scheme was a success. By Christmas 1621 all the women were married. They went on to lead lives entwined with the history of Virginia. Some certainly perished in the 1622 Indian[19] attack on the settlers. Some were later involved in legal actions of various kinds, while others simply made quiet contributions to the colonization of America.

Not all voluntary female parties were so successfully integrated into the aspiring respectable colonial society. Other groups of women arrivals were said to have 'fornicated when they were supposed to remain celibate, they slandered gentlemen and gentlewomen, and they brawled with those with whom they had a quarrel'.[20] But whatever their activities these bold women came to America, as far as we know, of their own free will. They were not 'transportees', yet the concept of collecting and despatching women en masse to the colonies for population growth and social stability in conjunction with coerced labour was now firmly established. The need for marriageable women, willing and unwilling, would feature in various guises throughout the history of transportation, as the British government sought to people, and so preserve, its expanding empire.[21]

'SO COLD A BLOOD'

Justice Hitcham was merciful. He granted Elizabeth Wynn and Magdalene Dutton a temporary reprieve. Elizabeth's baby was delivered several days before her trial and she was too weak to walk into court unaided. Magdalene's baby would be born a few months after her trial. The two women had been arrested independently in 1632 and 1633 respectively and had conceived by unnamed fathers while in prison. Both women were found guilty of their several robberies and sentenced to death. Hitcham allowed Elizabeth's execution to be delayed until her health improved. Magdalene would not have to die until a month after the birth of her child.

Elizabeth and Magdalene awaited their ends in Southwark gaol, but they were not resigned to their judicial fates. About the time they had been condemned to hang, they petitioned King Charles I for a pardon. In accordance with the established procedure for such pleas, the trial judge was consulted about the fitness of the women to receive the royal mercy. Hitcham thought the women should have already been despatched and wanted to know what the Sheriff, Sir Richard Evelyn, had been doing all this time. So did the king. Evelyn was charged in the Star Chamber for defying the royal prerogative and, effectively, reprieving Elizabeth and Magdalene beyond the date decreed by Hitcham. Luckily for Sir Richard, there were extenuating circumstances – Magdalene's baby had still not arrived when she made her petition, he had been ill, his deputy was running things, another prisoner involved with the petition for pardon had highly placed connections and was seeking a reprieve, making the deputy reluctant to do anything terminal in case he offended someone powerful, and so on. In the end, Evelyn was let off with a reprimand for negligence and poor management.

But what would happen to the new mothers? Technically, they were to be dealt with according to their original sentence. But the merciful Hitcham considered that too much time had now passed since then, and to send them to the gallows 'upon so cold a blood' would be a most unusual circumstance. Accordingly, he would not stand against any 'gracious and princely compassion' the king might care to show. And he did, after a fashion.

Perhaps influenced by the fecundity of the convicted women, King Charles, or more likely one of his advisors, had a smart idea. The convicted women would be spared death but were to be transported with five other women and seven men. At this time the usual destination of these breeding pairs would have been Virginia or Bermuda. But a struggling Company for the Plantation of Guyana,[22] supported by the Duke of Buckingham, a favourite of Charles I, was in need of labour and progeny in their South American investment. Elizabeth and Magdalene, probably together with their babies, were to become the property of colonial speculators. Unfortunately – or perhaps not – the records have no more to tell us.[23] We do not know if the fourteen, or more, ever sailed for the swamps of Guyana, and the enterprise attempting to exploit the South American colony disappeared into the deep mire of failed speculations.

Elizabeth and Magdalene, together with their companions, were the victims of a capricious process in which the prerogatives of royalty and the state, of law and the judicial system, as well as commercial greed, were bound together. They were merely human assets, their bodies available for deployment through ensnarement in the penal process. As the empire was expanding, the notion of peopling it with the convicted or otherwise condemned was much in the air. An Act effectively enslaving convicted criminals was drafted in 1621 although, fortunately, not presented to Parliament, and by 1640 able-bodied paupers were being poached from London's poorhouses to tend Thomas Verney's plantation in Barbados.[24]

SCOTS REBELS AND THE MYSTERY OF THE IRISH CHILDREN

It was not only the unwanted poor, Gypsies, juveniles and criminals who could be conveniently removed by transportation. From its beginnings, the system was also valuable for ridding the state of those who openly defied its power, for whatever reasons. The Covenanters of Scotland's Protestant faith considered they had several very good reasons to resist.

In 1638 a National Covenant was signed by those who rejected English efforts to force the Scottish church to follow English church belief and governance. There had been similar 'bands' in the sixteenth century, but the attempt of Charles I and William Laud, Archbishop of Canterbury, to impose the English form of worship was strenuously resisted. 'Covenanters', as those who signed the agreement and those who followed their ideals became known, would be continually at odds with religious and political factions in England, Scotland and Ireland until the restoration of Charles II. They would be suppressed and oppressed, forced to maintain their beliefs through underground networks and clandestine, open-air services called 'conventicles'. Those caught attending the particular form of holy writ preached at these events were liable to transportation, and worse. Covenanters were also ruinously fined for refusing to attend the official services of the state-sanctioned church.

Despite these troubles the Covenanters remained a significant force in English as well as Irish politics and maintained a repressive control of Scotland's Catholic minority. In 1643 they convinced the English parliament to accept the establishment of a Presbyterian state church in England and Ireland, as well as Scotland, in return for their support against the Royalists in the first Civil War. But after this first bout of bloodletting ended, the agreement was not honoured. The Covenanters swapped sides and fought for Charles I in the second Civil War and later for Charles II. Unfortunately for them, the Parliamentary forces were victorious at the Battle of Preston in 1648 and Oliver Cromwell's invasion of Scotland in 1650–1 destroyed the Covenanter hold.

The geographic extent and long duration of the English civil wars were the result of the deeply divided nature of British society, religion and politics leading up to the hostilities and persisting long afterwards. After the execution of Charles I in January 1649, the Scots rallied, some reluctantly, to support Charles II in trying to regain the English throne. One faction attempted a failed invasion of England which was avenged by Cromwell's forces at the Battle of Dunbar in 1650. In the aftermath of this bloody defeat English troops occupied Edinburgh and captured a large number of Scots rebels. As in 1648, many would be transported.[25]

By all accounts, these prisoners of war were poorly treated. More died during a forced march south and in captivity than were killed in the bloody battle. Around 2,000 who survived malnutrition, mistreatment, cold and disease were to be transported to Ireland,[26] though not the hardy highlanders.[27] They may have been the 150 Scots rebels transported and sold in Boston for twenty pounds each.[28] The traders who contracted for this voyage paid only five pounds for each prisoner. When they arrived aboard the *Unity* in December 1650 most of the Scots went to the ironworks, another group of twenty or so went to the sawmill, and the rest were sold off individually to local buyers. Their sentences were for seven years.

More Scots rebels were transported to Virginia, Maine and Massachusetts after the Battle of Worcester in 1651.[29] Around 500 went to Barbados in 1654 where they formed the basis of a poor white underclass that still exists, often known pejoratively as 'Red Legs'. Overall, between 1649 and 1655 thousands of losers in both Scottish and English conflicts were sent to Barbados.[30]

At the Restoration of 1660, Charles II followed his father's desire for a Scottish Episcopalian church led by a bishop and there was more oppression, interspersed with negotiations and further resistance. Scots Covenanters were sent to America in 1666 in the wake of the failed Battle of Rullion Green that ended the Pentland Rising.[31] Another rising in 1679 was also defeated at Bothwell Bridge, leading to a more extreme response from the Covenanters and the beginning of what they called 'the Killing Time', during which Covenanters were severely persecuted and many transported. Resistance refocused around the Sanquhar Declaration in 1680 but ended in 1688 with the Glorious Revolution when the Presbyterian Church was restored in Scotland.

While the convulsions of state and church wracked Britain, men and women were killed and transported for refusing to bend their conflicting beliefs. While the momentous matters of politics were fought out people were still committing crimes, being apprehended, tried and sentenced to be sent across the seas. In January 1666 Robert Armestrong, aka Hethersgill, and Anthony Pott were 'indyttet and accused of divers and sundrie poynts of thift and vyrs capittall crymes'. They were to be sent to Barbados 'or vry remoit paice And their to be sold as slaves and never to returne to any of his majesties Dominiones vnder the paine of daith . . .'[32] Anywhere would do, and don't come back. Many did not, whether their transgressions were criminal or political.

The lives and labours of the Scots – rebels or criminals – transported to America and elsewhere were hard. But many learned trades and skills during their indentured time and went on after their release to become prosperous and respected mainstays of their colonial communities. They married, produced children, squabbled with their neighbours, fought and drank with the 'indians.' Some received land grants, others purchased property and became solid members of their communities.[33] But they did not all forget their rebellious attitudes. William Furbush declined to accept English authority and, with his wife, refused to attend church. In 1681 he called court officials 'Divills and Hell hounds', receiving twenty lashes for his outburst. His wife attacked a constable who came to confiscate property while Furbush 'tooke up a dreadful weapon and sayd that he would dy before his goods should be carried away'.[34]

Another Scot, Alexander Maxwell, abused 'his master and his wife' and was flogged on thirty occasions. His master was given permission to sell him off in Virginia if there was any more trouble. Fortunately for Maxwell, there was none, and he joined the Scots community in York, Maine on his release. His violent temper would often get the better of him, but he managed to become a successful tavern keeper, fought off several Native American attacks and willed his property for the building of a Scottish church.[35]

Despite these injustices and hardships, many would prosper in the New World. By 1730, around three generations of Scots had been transported. Roderick Gordon, a ship's surgeon and resident of Virginia, compared their lot with that of their countrymen still at home. He thought it a pity 'that thousands of my country people should be starving at home, when they may live here in peace and plenty, as a great many who have been transported for a punishment have found pleasure, profit, and ease and would rather undergo any hardship than be forced back on their own country'.[36]

The civil wars also provided opportunities for Cromwell to exile other trouble-some elements.[37] Penruddock's failed rising against Cromwell in 1655 saw Cornishmen transported to the West Indies. When the Civil War expanded into Ireland during the 1650s, large numbers of Irish were transported to the Americas, especially to the Leeward Islands.[38] The price they paid for defying English domi-nation was great and the benefits to the growing empire even greater.

While these political processes were becoming an established aspect of trans-portation, so the Atlantic body trade grew apace as a commercial enterprise. As well as relieving the English state of the considerable costs involved in sending large numbers across the seas, this system conveniently removed political irritants. There was little or no attempt to dress these banishments up in any legal process. In 1656 the Council of State would simply order that 'lewd and dangerous persons' should be transported to 'the English plantations in America'.[39] The transported rebels were ejected wholesale from their homelands and dumped in America or the West Indies as indentured labourers, for sale to the highest bidders, or simply put to work in local industries and infrastructure. By now the system had become something of a free-for-all. Governments of whatever persuasion were using it to rid themselves of political enemies. Entrepreneurs were making fortunes and colonists were purchasing relatively cheap labour over which they had absolute power, once again including children.

In 1655 Henry Cromwell, son of Oliver and then Major-General of the Parliamentarian Army in Ireland, had a clever idea. He wanted to gather a thousand Irish girls and a thousand Irish boys between the ages of twelve and fourteen and send them from Kinsale and Galway to Jamaica. This would be 'for their own good', even though he knew it would involve force. The plan was discussed at the highest levels of state but was only partly implemented. Nevertheless, it has generated a persistent myth that more than 100,000 Irish children were torn from their parents to be sold in the colonies of the New World. Like 'fake news', this has become a 'fact', stated in many books and especially on the World Wide Web.[40] It is often accompanied by another claim that two years earlier a Boston tobacco merchant named David Selleck was given a warrant to transport 400 Irish children to New England and Virginia. *An Act for transportation of poor Irish children to England and the plantations* was drafted and Selleck's inaptly named ships, *Providence* and *Goodfellow*, sailed for Kinsale.

But somewhere between the granting of the original warrant, for which Selleck had lobbied, and the proclamation of the Act, something had changed. Instead of children, Selleck and his partner, Mr Leader, were now authorized to procure 250 Irish women over the age of twelve and under forty-five, together with 300 men over twelve and under fifty. Adults were likely to bring a higher price in the colonies, reducing the risk of Selleck and Leader's investment. They were officially advised of the best place to find the 'rogues, vagabonds, idlers and wanderers' they sought (County Cork) and carefully reminded that they were liable for 'all charge of providing for them and conducting them to the waterside and maintaining them well from the time of their receiving them'. The Commonwealth was 'to be freed of all charge therein'.[41]

A few orphaned or otherwise unlucky children made destitute through the incursions of the English troops were probably picked up in Selleck and Leader's dragnet. They would have been sold as indentured servants along with the adults subsequently landed in Virginia and New England. Effectively, these unlucky people were kidnapped in a legal sleight of hand that suited the government and ensured Selleck and Leader's profits. As well as forcibly taking their victims, the transporters would 'elude and deceive poor people by false pretences' and even offer money to take husbands or wives away with them. So blatant did this form of kidnap for profit become that transportation from Ireland was ended, officially at least, in March 1657. But people were still being sent 'beyond the seas' from England.

ENGLAND'S SLAVES

Marcellus Rivers and Oxenbridge Foyle, gentlemen, were two of more than seventy Royalist rebels from the Penruddock rising transported to Barbados in 1656. They had fought with the wrong army and simply been sold into forced labour by Cromwell's main financier. Plantation slavery was well established by this time and the planters were not particular about the exact legal status of their workers – slave, indentured labourer or convict. They were all treated in much the same way, especially when it came to tending the fields. Ten to twelve-hour days were standard, with overseers using harsh punishment to enforce obedience and productivity. Sunday was the only day of rest. Observers at the time likened the working conditions to those of galley slaves, an unremitting regime of backbreaking effort conducted at a uniform pace decreed by the planter.

Rivers and Foyle were the prime movers of a petition to Parliament complaining about this treatment. The perception of convict and indentured labour as a form of slavery was commonplace, both in England and in America. In Barbados, planters short of labour thought nothing of writing home to request prisoners be sent over to till their fields.[42] In their petition, smuggled to England for publication, Rivers and Foyle called themselves and their unfortunate companions 'England's slaves' and 'England's merchandise'. Their story was compelling, even at that time.

After being imprisoned at Exeter, even though 'many of them never saw Salisbury, nor bore arms in their lives' and underwent no legal process, let alone a trial, the men languished for a year. Then without warning, they were 'snatched out of their prisons' and driven under guard in carts through the city. After further movements, they sailed from Plymouth and arrived at Barbados nearly six weeks later, 'four thousand and five hundred miles distant from their native country, wives, children, parents, friends, and whatever is near and dear unto them'. They had been aboard their ship for two weeks before departure and throughout the voyage were 'all the way locked up under decks, (and guards) amongst horses, that their souls, through heat and steam, under the tropic, fainted in them; and they never till they came to the island knew whither they were going.'

Bad as this experience was, there was worse to come. After landing in Barbados in May 1656, the master sold 'the generality of them to most inhuman and barbarous persons, for one thousand five-hundred-and-fifty-pound weight of sugar a-piece, more or less'. These men became the 'goods and chattels' of a couple of London aldermen and a captain of Plymouth. The oldest among the prisoners was seventy-six, but he was not spared 'grinding at the mills and attending at the furnaces, or digging in this scorching island; having nought to feed on (notwithstanding their hard labour) but potatoe roots, nor to drink, but water with such roots washed in it, besides the bread and tears of their own afflictions.' They were hawked from one master to another in the same way that horses were sold, slept 'in sties worse than hogs in England' and were whipped at will.

The petitioners asked the court 'to question by what authority so great a breach is made upon the free people of England, they having never seen the faces of these their pretended owners, merchants that deal in slaves and souls of men, nor ever heard of their names before Mr. Cole made affidavit in the office of Barbadoes, that he sold them as their goods'. They wanted to know where their enslavers derived their mandate 'for the sale and slavery of your poor petitioners'. The court was asked to 'take course to curb the unlimited power under which the petitioners and others suffer; that neither you nor any of their brethren, upon these miserable terms, may come into this miserable place of torment. A thing not known amongst the cruel Turks, to sell and enslave those of their own country and religion, much less the innocent.'[43]

The plight of Rivers and Foyle and their unfortunate companions caused an uproar among the public and in Parliament. Although they were technically indentured servants rather than chattel slaves or felons, their interpretation of their condition was accepted by most and contributed to the view that colonial transportation was a system that enslaved English people, an affront to the popular notion of the 'freeborn Englishman'.[44] Widespread popular opposition to transportation stems largely from this period.[45]

Oxenbridge Foyle seems to be lost to history, but we know that Marcellus Rivers returned to England. He took the opportunity of the restoration of the monarchy in 1660 to bring a case against the previously well-connected planters and slavers who had trafficked him and his companions, reducing them to 'Barbados merchandize'. Rivers and his companions were but just a few of the human commodities in the market.

SPIRITED TO THE NEW WORLD

One reason for the growth of opposition to transportation was the practice of 'spiriting'. Beneath the legal and more or less legal arrangements for satisfying the colonial labour demand ran a murky but organized stream operated by people known as 'Spirits'. Often women, Spirits specialized in enticing young males and females to alehouses where they were inebriated and taken against their will aboard ships for passage to Barbados or elsewhere in the colonies. Children were also taken, and the practice had become serious enough by the mid-1640s for London to lay down ordinances against 'Inveigling, purloining, carrying and Stealing away Boys, Maides and other persons and transporting them Beyond Seas'. A similar measure was passed by Bristol in 1654 when kidnapping was common throughout the country, reaching what an alarmed public perceived as a major threat. Even soldiers in Cromwell's own regiment were involved in one plot to send people to Jamaica.[46] If it was good enough for their leaders to profit from the transportation business, why not them? The money was good. A young woman kidnapped in this way in 1654 fetched forty shillings for her enticer. A stolen adult male brought another Spirit a handsome three pounds.[47]

Supernatural terminology also evolved at the receiving end of the body trade. When a shipload of convicts or indentured servants arrived in the American colonies, their human cargo was offered for sale in the port. Those individuals who, for whatever reason, did not find a buyer, were herded together and driven inland like cattle in the hope that they could be sold off in the smaller settlements and farms behind the advancing frontier. The term 'soul drivers' would come to be used for those men who trafficked these human caravans. John Harrower, an indentured servant, described what had become common practice in Virginia more than a century later:

This day severalls [*sic*] came on board to purchase servts. Indentures and among them there was two Soul drivers. They are men who make it their bussines to go on board all ships who have in either Servants or Convicts and buy sometimes the whole and sometimes a parcell of them as they can agree, and then they drive them through the Country like a parcell of Sheep untill they can sell them to advantage, but all went away without buying any.[48]

Another convict in the same period confirmed the similarity to livestock sales. William Green and his transported companions were chained together and 'drove in lots like oxen or sheep'. Prospective purchasers examined the convicts' teeth and limbs 'as the dealers in horses do those animals'.[49]

Long before John Harrower and William Green were being treated like animals, others were being sold for cattle or corn. Will Downing and Phillip Welch stood before the Salem Quarterly Court of 26 June 1661. They were there for 'absolutely refusing to serve' their master, Samuel Symonds, any longer. Seven years earlier, Symonds agreed to pay the master of the ship *Goodfellow* '26li. [pounds] in merchantable corn or live cattle' due before the end of the following October for the two young men kidnapped from their beds in their own country. They were neither convicts nor indentured servants and were almost certainly sold illegally into servitude. Nevertheless, Downing and Welch had worked their master's fields ever since. And Symonds insisted that he had paid good value for them to do so for nine years, not seven.

One Sunday evening in March 1661 Downing and Welch joined the Symonds family in the parlour for prayer, as usual. Before the family and their servants began to worship, Welch declared to his master 'We will worke with you, or for you, noe longer.' Symonds sarcastically enquired that if they were not working what would they do – 'play?'

Downing and Welch stood their ground. They had served Symonds and his family for the seven years they believed to be their penance for simply being in the wrong place at the time Cromwell's soldiers were scouring their area for victims. Symonds told them that they were obliged to work for him unless they ran away, a crime with severe punishment. They did not wish to flee; instead they pleaded 'If you will free us, we will plant your corne, & mende your fences, & if you will pay us as other men, but we will not worke with you upon the same termes, or conditions as before.'

This must have been a memorable moment in the life of the family and its servants. All had been living and working cheek by jowl and praying regularly together for seven years. There was some talk about business difficulties as Symonds sought to make his servants see what he considered to be sense. His wife backed him up, saying that this was not a good time to bring up the subject of money. But the young men remained adamant. When their master asked them to begin prayers together, they refused. Next morning Symonds summoned the local constable to his home, demanding that the rebellious servants be 'secured'. The constable wondered whether it was necessary for the men to be taken away, but Symonds insisted a warrant be served on them and that they should be paraded before the court. Which they duly were.

Now Downing and Welch had a chance to state their case: 'We were brought out of or owne Country, contrary to our owne wills & minds, & sold here unto Mr. Symonds, by ye master of the Ship, Mr. Dill, but what Agreement was made betweene Mr. Symonds & ye Said master, was neuer Acted by our Consent or knowledge, yet notwithstanding we haue indeauored to do him ye best seruice wee Could these seuen Compleat yeeres . . .'

Welch and Downing considered they had already served their time, and more, because the usual practice of transport shipmasters was to sell their stolen human cargoes in Barbados for only four years of servitude. But now for seven years the two men had laboured on Samuel Symonds' ten acres of corn 'And for our seruice, we haue noe Callings nor wages, but meat & Cloths.'

For his part, Symonds testified that he had made a bargain with the shipmaster and he had the 'covenant', or contract, to prove it. There was a supporting deposition from the shipmaster who said he had sold Symonds 'two of the Irish youths I brought over by order of the State of England'.

Some other servants gave evidence. One man who had been kidnapped and transported with Downing and Welch described how they had all been rounded up against their will 'weeping and Crying, because they were stollen from theyr frends'. Some of Symonds' own servants testified to the resentment of Welch and Downing against their situation and their determination to be free. Welch reportedly said at one point that if Symonds would give him the same share of his estate as he would give his own children, then he would continue to serve.

The intensely personal nature of the relationships between master, family and servants in the Symonds household is clear in these testimonies. But the court, rightly or not, found the arrangement was legal and decreed that Downing and Welch should continue to serve until May 1663. An appeal was notified immediately but the two men agreed to work for Symonds until a date for the hearing could be set. He was bound to give them leave to attend.[50]

Whether this appeal was ever heard is not known. Possibly the full nine years were served before it could be and Downing and Welch were finally unbound. Then they could sell their labour and start the families they wished for in the New World. For those sent in chains to that world, many destinies awaited.

3

TRAITORS AND DECEIVERS

... for want of a Governour we are ruled by a Council, some of whom have been perhaps transported Criminals ...

Aphra Behn, *The Widdow Ranter*, 1690

While transported Irish boys were struggling for whatever rights they thought they had in America, religious dissenters in Britain were suffering for their beliefs. In Bristol in 1664 the crew of the *Mary Fortune* declared: 'Cursed is he who parteth man and wife.' They were refusing to obey the Conventicle Act which, in this case, was being used to transport Quakers accused of assembling to observe their faith. The sailors expressed their pity for the Quakers: 'their Cry, and the Cry of their Family and Friends, are entered into the Ears of the Lord, and he hath smitten us to the very Heart'.[1]

The Conventicle Act of 1664 was one of a number of legal structures enacted to discourage the growth of religious nonconformism of any kind, not only Covenanters, and to safeguard the established Church. Three convictions under several of these Acts led to transportation. While this was the official position, as in many other circumstances, these laws might be flouted. They were on this occasion, and on others, as everyday people expressed strong sympathy for tolerance, as well as a popular dislike of repressive legislation.

Nevertheless, once again in the 1670s and 1680s, men and women of the Scottish Covenanters were banished to New Jersey and the Caribbean colonies. They were all branded and the men's ears were sliced off. Their treatment was severe, even by the standards of the era. In November 1679 over 250 were summarily

32

taken from prison and loaded like cattle into a transport. 'The barbarity exercised upon them in the ship cannot be expressed,' wrote one historian. There was so little room beneath decks that most of the prisoners had to stand up to allow the sick and dying a space on the filthy boards. Those standing were so closely packed that they hardly moved and 'were almost stilled for want of air', often fainting. The sailors stole what food and water they were supposed to be given according to the compact struck by the master with the government. Many were forced to drink their urine and 'it may be nauseous to remark, that, when they were about to throw their excrements over board, the seamen were so malicious as to cast them back upon them'.[2] Even without these reported cruelties, the perils of a transportation voyage to the Americas included body lice, disease, scurvy, robbery, rape and violence.

Mention of the pinchgut master's contractual obligations indicates that transportation of human bodies – however obtained – to the colonies was now a major trade, if a chaotic one. Seeking guidance, the Council of Trades made representations about the issue in the late 1690s to the wise heads of the king in Council. The king's men handed the problem straight back to the merchants, ordering them to 'consider and report how and to what places convicts pardoned on condition of transportation may be best disposed of, or what punishment might be more proper for such convicts in lieu of transportation'.[3] This tart response concisely captured the nub of the problem – if transportation was not available, what was the state to do with the ever-increasing numbers of pardoned felons and rebels filling its gaols?

By 1670 the random free-for-all that the system was becoming led to a bill to end transportation without trial. This would later become the Habeus Corpus Act of 1679. The requirement to bring any accused before a properly constituted court is one of the most important pieces of legislation ever made, but its initial effect was to legalize the existing practice of pardoning convicted criminals if they consented to be sent across the seas for an agreed period.[4] When those exiled from their homeland did arrive in their places of condemnation they often found colonial variations of the same divisive conflicts that put them in chains. Even those trying to carry on trade by using transported convicts for labour found themselves mired in politics, war and chicanery in the New World.

THE COUNTERFEIT LADY

Beneath the follies and machinations of rebels and merchants, those with a taste for the better things in life, but without the means to enjoy them, exercised the arts of deception. Many found these twisted life paths led them aboard a heaving transport ship bound for years of hard labour – and who knew what else – in the new colonies.

The woman who became known as 'the German Princess' began life in Canterbury, Kent, probably in 1642.[5] From an early age she combined amorous relationships, embezzlement and theft to a prodigious degree. Mary Moders, better known as Mary Carleton, specialized in relationships with middle- and upper-class men of substance, young and old, all ending with her disappearance, along with their wealth, or whatever was left of it. In 1663 during the course of one imposture, Mary married John Carleton, neglecting to mention her existing marriage. Not for the first time, she was charged with bigamy and in prison became such a celebrity that she was visited by the diarist Samuel Pepys, who also seems to have fallen under her spell. She used her glamour again at her trial, reportedly arguing her defence at the Old Bailey so effectively that, in her own words, she was 'acquitted by publique proclamation'. If the words of a pamphlet on the trial are anything to go by, Mary's claim was no boast. Referring to her first husband, a shoemaker and a bricklayer witness who had claimed to be her husband, she declaimed:

> My Lord, they brand me for marrying of a Shoo-make, and another sad piece of Mortality, a Brick-layer. My lord, My Soul abhorreth such a thought, and never was accomodated with such Condiscention, to move in so low an Orb. My Lord, by all that I can observe of the Persons that appear against me, they may be divided into two sorts; the one of them come against me for want of Wit, the other for want of Money.[6]

Pepys was also happy at her acquittal, but her most recent husband was not. Fooled and scandalized, John Carleton now attacked the 'pretended Germane Lady' in a public pamphlet, setting off a paper war of accusations and counter-accusations, including some of Mary's. All this served only to raise the crafty deceiver even higher in public estimation. She even played herself in a stage production witnessed by Pepys. Some lines from Mary's epilogue nicely encapsulate her philosophy of life:

I've passed one trial, but it is my fear
I shall receive a rigid sentence here:
You think me a bold cheat, put case 'twere so,
Which of you are not? Now you'd swear I know.
But do not, lest that you deserve to be
Censur'd worse than you can censure me,
The world's a cheat, and we that move in it,
In our degrees, do exercise our wit;
And better 'tis to get a glorious name,
However got, than live by common fame.[7]

Mary cleverly exploited her notoriety as far as she could, pursuing her serial relationships and frauds for some years, until arrested for stealing. The 'princess' was found guilty and transported to Jamaica in 1671. According to a pamphlet on her final brush with the law, Mary was transported along with twenty-five others who then plotted to murder the captain and take the ship. She was promised a third of the haul but decided to inform on the plotters. They were put in irons and she was rewarded with her freedom when the ship reached Jamaica.

Port Royal was a roistering town of desperate pirates and wealthy planters, each group trading off the other in an alcoholic haze produced by 'kill devil', the potent local rum. Mary's freedom meant that she needed to work for a living and she wasted no time putting her trade skills to good use among the rougher classes. By her own account, she was 'treated like my self, I mean a Princess' and found a good number of her old underworld acquaintances were also serving time on the island. And the pickings were good. Drunken freebooters, flush with their share of plunder, were easily swindled by the enterprising Mary, memorably described by one of her chroniclers as 'A stout frigate . . . or else she never could have endured so many batteries and assaults. A woman of unexampled modesty, if she may be her own herald. But she was as common as a barber's chair: no sooner was one out, but another was in. Cunning, crafty, subtle, and hot in the pursuit of her intended designs.'[8]

Despite the business success that her 'cunning' ensured, the draining climate did not suit the Princess and she fell ill. Recovering, Mary decided to return to England as she 'trusted to much of the King's mercy for the good she had done in saving the whole ship's company alive, that she ventured to come over again'. She sailed home in the same ship on which she had arrived, this time without incident. But the service she provided in betraying her companions won Mary no favours for breaking the law against returning from banishment before serving the full sentence. At her trial in London the judge asked why she had come back:

> . . . to which she answered that she had somewhat [something] that troubled her conscience about treachery which she had a great desire to discover, and til she had made it known to the government, she could not be at quiet; and upon that account she thus transgressed the law of her being transported, only to make those things known which lay so much upon her, til she had made a discovery of it.[9]

Mary declined to reveal what these matters might be and the judge eventually decided to try her only on the charge of return from banishment, of which she was swiftly found guilty. The guileful reprobate tried to 'plead the belly', but twelve gentlewomen testified that she was not pregnant. On the day of her execution, 22 January 1673, 'she appeared rather more gay and brisk than ever before' and went to the gallows professing her Catholic faith and with a picture of her estranged husband, John Carleton, pinned to her sleeve. As she went to her final performance, Mary told the waiting crowd that she had been a very vain woman and expected to pay for that sin. Nevertheless, still proud, she declared 'that though the world had condemned her, she had much to say for herself; that she prayed God to forgive her, as she did her enemies; and a little more to the same effect. After which she was turned off, in the thirty-eighth year of her age, and in the same month she was born in.'

The repentant deceiver was buried in St Martin's churchyard and given a final poetic send-off by an anonymous wit:

The German princess here, against her will,
Lies underneath, and yet oh, strange! lies still.[10]

The playwright Aphra Behn provided a more sympathetic epitaph in the epilogue to her play *The Dutch Lover*, published shortly after Mary's execution:

Whilst sad experience our eyes convinces,
That damn'd their Playes which hang'd the German Princess:
And we with ornament set off a Play
Like her drest fine for Execution-day.
And faith I think with as small hopes to live;
Unless kind Gallants the same grace you'd give
Our Comedie as Her; beg a Reprive.[11]

Mary remained a celebrity, with street ballads and accounts of her adventures still being published and republished half a century after her execution.[12] Her raffish life, brief transportation and ill-judged return highlight the haphazard nature of the system and the often random fates of those caught within it, whether at home or abroad.[13] Her insinuation that she had secret knowledge of some 'treachery' against the government was not taken seriously. But treason elsewhere in the growing empire was very serious, at home or abroad.

OMINOUS PRESAGES

In the year 1675 the people of Virginia witnessed 'three prodigies in that country, which from th' attending disasters, were look'd upon as ominous presages'. Each night for a week or more a comet 'streaming like a horse taile westwards' was seen crossing the sky to disappear towards the northwest. Giant flocks of pigeons darkened the sky and broke tree branches with the weight of their nesting. The last time this had been seen was in the 1640s when 'th' Indians committed the last massacre'. Then the ground erupted with swarms of large flies that ate the new tree growth and disappeared as mysteriously as they had arisen.[14] For the superstitious communities of the colonies these portents signalled strange and momentous events of some kind.[15] Their fears were realized the following year.

The conditions of frontier life in Virginia and the other American colonies were still difficult even seventy years or so after the founding of Jamestown. Although the resistance of Native American peoples of the region had been largely overcome, there was still frequent conflict and bloodshed as settlement, trade and white interests thrust ever deeper into the traditional lands and their resources. There was also trouble and dissension within and among the dominant class of planters, the main owners of transported convicts and indentured labourers, stemming from the same political and social fissures that split Britain during this period.

The complicated orgy of bloodletting in Virginia known as 'Bacon's Rebellion' originated in a dispute with Native Americans but soon developed into a power struggle between the governor and Nathaniel Bacon, the recently arrived black sheep of a wealthy English family. Short-lived but extremely violent, what was effectively a civil war led to the burning of Jamestown by Bacon's supporters. Bacon died of dysentery a few months later, though fighting between the opposing factions intensified as the loyalists of the governor killed, captured and hanged many of Bacon's traitors. Two rebel leaders changed sides and by the time the king's relief force and investigating commission arrived, the violence was mostly over. Among those rebels still resisting were slaves, indentured servants and probably some transportees who hoped to keep the liberty they had won as part of Bacon's forces.

The exact causes and consequences of this event are still much debated by historians. Taxes, control of the colony's trade by England and broad unhappiness with what many consider the inequitable development of Virginia were major factors. Bacon's Rebellion resulted in the consolidation of power by the elite plantation owners, many of whom were Catholic royalists who opposed the Protestant Cromwell and had fled to the Americas. At the time of the trouble, Virginia was moving from a dependence on indentured servants for labour to African slaves. While the number of convicts transported to Virginia in the seventeenth century is estimated to be less than 3,000,[16] they were part of a coerced labouring underclass together with slaves and indentured servants. Thirteen years before Bacon ignited the short but bloody period of looting and hanging that bears his name, transported ex-soldiers from Cromwell's army plotted a mutiny in collaboration with African slaves. They were betrayed by an indentured servant.[17]

The intriguing adventuress, writer and occasional spy, Aphra Behn, wrote a highly romanticized play based on Bacon's Rebellion. While casting Bacon as an honour-driven hero of classical proportions, the depiction of Virginian society was mostly negative. Transportees who had completed their period of service were portrayed as having gained great wealth and so taken over the civic and legal institutions: 'This Country wants nothing but to be peopled with a well-born Race, to make it one of the best Colonies in the World; but for want of a Governour we are ruled by a Council, some of whom have been perhaps transported Criminals, who having acquired great Estates, are now become your Honour and Right Worshipful, and possess all Places of Authority . . .'[18]

It is not clear that the well-travelled Behn was ever in Virginia,[19] but her words probably reflect a popular perception of the time. Some transportees certainly prospered in the colonies, though their masters were far more likely to benefit.

THE WOES OF SQUIRE JEAFFRESON

It was Easter Eve, 1685. The clanking of chains dragging along London's cobbled streets soon attracted a crowd to jeer at the heavily guarded convicts being escorted from Newgate Prison to London Bridge. At the head of the parade was Christopher Jeaffreson, a country squire from Cambridgeshire. The thirty-seven barefooted 'malefactors' were his property, bound for many years of hard labour in his St Kitts (St Christopher) sugar plantations. Despite their 'hard and desperate case', the prisoners were not daunted by their situation, or purged of their love of mischief. More than one well-dressed idler whose curiosity took him too close to the carnival was rapidly stripped of hat and wig, much to the uproarious delight of the gawping mob. Jeaffreson was relieved to finally get his workers to the river, from where they could be loaded aboard ship for the long voyage to the Caribbean. It had been a long, hard road to reach this point in his efforts to revive the family holdings in the 'Indies'.

Conveniently located in the Leeward Islands on the route from Europe to the American colonies, St Kitts had been sighted by Christopher Columbus on his second voyage in 1493. There were numerous other European sightings and landings as exploration, trade and war filled the Atlantic Ocean with ships of many nations. The first English settlements were in the 1620s. St Kitts was occupied by both the French and the English, who often fought over it, causing some English planters to abandon their holdings. After one such episode, the Jeaffreson family plantation passed out of their control until the 1670s when Christopher Jeaffreson returned and found his family's property in a poor state and set about developing it into a sugar plantation, which he saw as 'a certain gaine'.

He desperately needed skilled artisans, especially carpenters and masons, to build his sugar domain. He also needed labour. His bond servants had 'gone free' and African slaves were expensive and troublesome. He wanted 'any sorte of men, and one or two women if they can be found'.[20] Taking matters into his own hands, Jeaffreson resolved to find a group of convicts selected according to his needs and those of other planters, all of whom were desperate for labourers. It was a decision he would live to regret.

Back in London, Jeaffreson entered into a lengthy saga in which he discovered the intricacies and deceptions of the convict trade. The colonists of the Caribbean were continually lobbying the Lords of Trade in England for artisans and labourers to protect the islands from attack by the Spanish or French and to develop their economies and social structures.[21] At least, that was what they said. There was some truth in these arguments, but the primary aim of the planters was to develop their private holdings and enrich themselves. This was the complex brew of money, politics and vested interests that Jeaffreson and his associates needed to navigate.

In 1682 he petitioned the Lords of the Committee for Foreign Plantations for 300 convict workers and received their lordships' approval. Believing his mission was essentially accomplished, he thought he only needed to make arrangements for the convicts, from London and Middlesex gaols, to be conveyed to St Kitts. But he was woefully naïve. An official approval was exactly that: a piece of paper that gave Jeaffreson the right to obtain and transport convicts – if he could obtain them. As he soon discovered, there were simply not that many available and there were other obstacles. Certain fees were required to grease certain palms. Forty-five to fifty-five shillings per convict would need to be paid to the chief gaoler of Newgate. An undisclosed but significant portion of this money went to the Recorder of London, some to those in charge of the other London prisons from which the convicts had been taken to be assembled at Newgate. Then there were sums and gratuities for 'under-gaolers and turnkeys'. Such exactions were not official, of course, but without them nothing happened.

Squire Jeaffreson was coming to understand the monetary manipulations and realities of an economic structure that depended on expensive patronage and perquisites. In those days official posts were frequently purchased by those wishing to occupy them, and they were not cheap. The higher up the ladder the post, the more expensive it was. Those who occupied them had to recoup their initial outlay, make a living, apportion something for themselves, cover the costs of this and that. 'Anyhow the fees must be paid. "No fee no convict" was law at the Old Bailey, even as "no song no supper" was law at the social table.'

The increasingly desperate planter pushed on but found that his 300 convicts – should they become available – had been given by the court to the agent for the rival island of Jamaica and he would have to wait until the next batch were dragged from the gaols. He persisted, and in 1684 was successful in transporting nearly thirty men and women to St Kitts. But his battles against the London authorities continued, with obstacle after obstacle being placed in his path.

And so it was that he came to be herding his manacled 'malefactors' through the streets of London. The convicts were to be barged down the Thames to the ship waiting to carry them to their labours. Jeaffreson was protecting his considerable investment in these transportees. Not only had he paid a lot for them in money, time and energy – if any escaped he would be liable to 'heavy forfeiture'.

The convicts were at last successfully despatched and Christopher once again thought his troubles were over. But that was not to be. When the labour force arrived at St Kitts, his partners in the deal, the governor and one of the island's prominent planters, cherry-picked the most able of the transportees for their own needs and those of other planters, leaving Jeaffreson with the infirm, weak and aged. Not only that, but they cheated him on the sugar shipment he was supposed to receive in England to cover the costs of purchasing, accommodating and trans-porting the 'malefactors'. According to his numerous outraged letters to St Kitts on the subject, he received nothing.[22]

Squire Jeaffreson's troubles provide a detailed insight into the manoeuvring, machinations and money involved in the seventeenth-century transportation trade. It was an industry in human lives that operated from the very top of society down through the aristocracy, the civil servants, the courts, the gaols, private contractors and colonial planters. This public-private partnership was built on the demand for labour provided by the state through its criminal codes and processes. Like any system of demand, this one required a steady supply of raw materials. Criminals were one reliable source of bodies, traitors were another.

DIVINE PROVIDENCE IN JAMAICA

Bad language drove God-fearing John Coad to treason. The Puritan carpenter was called out with the Somerset Militia when the Duke of Monmouth and fewer than a hundred followers sailed from Holland to Lyme Regis in 1685, intent on taking the throne from the Catholic James II. Offended by the 'hellish oaths and ribaldry' of his companions and anxious to serve the Protestant rather than the Roman cause, Coad deserted to Monmouth's ragged army of peasants. Badly wounded at the battle of Philip's Norton in June of that year, Coad was lucky to escape death but was taken and brought before the dreaded 'hanging judge' Jeffreys at the notorious Bloody Assizes. As well as illegal and cruel, Jeffreys' justice was a form of chaotic revenge. Wealthy leaders of Monmouth's army were allowed to bribe their way to freedom whereas the less well-off were convicted and sentenced in droves to death or transportation.[23] Sentenced to execution, Coad managed to substitute himself for another man in a group of 200 rebels being assembled for transportation to Jamaica. He thanked his God profusely:

> O wonderful providence of God wherein all the attributes of God were concerned for a poor worm who is no way profitable. I was wounded, but Mercy healed; I was caft down, but Mercy took me up; I was in prifon, but Mercy delivered me; I flood before the bloody Popifh Judge, the mercilefs monfter Jefferies, but God in mercy was with me and held me up faithful was he that promifed that he would never leave nor forfake me; I was caft in the fnare and left for dead by men, but Mercy lengthened out my life.[24]

John Coad's gratitude to his God flowed over. Although bound with cords, 'Mercy cut them afunder', the Almighty freed him from the hand of his enemies, and 'Free grace, love, mercy, faithfulnefs, wifdom, and power fet all thefe wheels of providence on worke for the deliverance of fuch an unworthy creature. O the love and grace and mercy of God, 'tis higher than the heavens, 'tis broader than the fea, 'tis unmeafurable . . .' If he had known the suffering that awaited him, Coad may not have been quite so grateful to be spared the noose. The Duke of Monmouth himself was literally butchered in a dreadfully botched execution. The outraged crowd in attendance threatened to tear the inept axeman limb from limb and he had to be hurried away under protection. The many Protestants in the crowd sorrowfully dipped their handkerchiefs in Monmouth's martyred blood.[25]

John Coad's pain was less severe but more prolonged. The 800 rebels who escaped execution were casually given to the king's favourites to do with as they wished.[26] They were to be transported to the West Indies as slaves, then sold off there to the highest bidders. Judge Jeffreys calculated that each rebel would be worth around ten to fifteen pounds. Very good profits for those lucky enough to get in on the deal. The men were bound for the Caribbean where they would serve for ten years. The journey out was a voyage through hell. Ninety-nine prisoners were bound under armed guard below decks in a room too small for them to lie down without covering each other. A pot on the floor was the only toilet provided 'by which means the fhip was foon infedled with grievous and contagious difeafes, as, the fmall pox, fever, calenture [heat-induced delirium], and the plague, with frightful blotches'.

Fortunately, the convict ships had a fast passage. Even so, twenty-two of those with Coad died and he estimated that over 20 per cent of those who departed England were 'flung to the sharks'. The transports were badly treated, even after they helped save the ship when she lost the mainstay – 'when the danger was over, his heart was quickly hardened againft us and so remained to the laft'. Many of the surviving transports were so emaciated from poor diet and the insanitary conditions that they arrived as 'mere skeletons'. The merchant deemed it necessary to fatten them up for sale.

After nearly seven weeks the surviving rebels reached Port Royal in Jamaica in late November 1685. Here the local people took pity on the 'poor miscreants'.

They were given biscuits, butter, fried fish and fresh water, and allowed to walk about the town in daylight. John Coad gave praise 'for a multitude of mercies'. He was fortunate in being appointed to a master who shared his faith and was told he could work off the debt owed for new clothes and for an artificially low purchase price of only twelve shillings rather than the usual thirty shillings paid for transported individuals. Then he would be free of servitude, if not of his ten-year sentence.

But then Coad fell ill, his body unable to cope with the sudden infusion of quality fresh food: 'my Doctor left me for a dead man, my Mafter fold the clothes which he had made for me, and all hope of life was paft'. Again, the Lord came to Coad's aid. He recovered and was sent to a kind Christian master and eventually established himself as a carpenter on his plantation; sometimes Coad was hired out to others, allowing him to earn money for himself. After four years the transports were entitled to apply for their liberty. Coad and some others went to the Justice of the Peace in Port Royal to arrange this but were told that they were too useful to be freed.

Following this disappointment, the island was shaken by earthquakes and riven by French raiders, who destroyed crops and abducted the black slaves. Despite his faith, Coad considered his situation hopeless after hearing a sermon he thought was calculated to worsen rather than lighten the load that he and his companions had to bear, leaving them with 'no redress, remedy, or hope, from Mafters, Magiftrates, nor Minifters'. There was one brighter moment, however, when he returned to his servitude to find that 'our heathenish overseer' had died. Nevertheless, 'All human hopes of freedom from our bondage being cut off', he found solace in the Book of Isaiah: 'But thus faith the Lord, Even the captives of the mighty will be taken away, and the prey of the terrible fhall be delivered.'

Finally, they were. The Protestant William of Orange took the throne in early 1689, displacing the Catholic James II – a 'glorious revolution', Coad wrote. Determined to seek his freedom when the new governor arrived, the signs were not good. The word among the prisoners was that the governor had other rebels seeking liberty whipped. Coad's situation seemed as hopeless as ever. Eventually he was able to present a petition to the governor's guard. The prisoners waited anxiously at the gate. Through a window they could see the governor walking to and fro as he considered their plea. After what seemed a very long time he called for the men and 'received us very kindly, with a compliment of a fmall bow'. The governor told them he had received orders to free all the rebels and allow them to return home.

There was jubilation in the streets – but a little too much. Coad had to convince his newly freed rebel companions to keep the peace. There would be some months of delay before they could sail for England, due mainly to the commercial manoeu- vrings of the merchants. By now, some of Coad's companions were in a poor state for the approaching winter voyage across the Atlantic. He himself was fortunate enough to have ten pounds in his pocket, his wages from being allowed to work for himself during the last year.

They eventually sailed in September 1689, but it would be a long voyage home. On 5 November, as Coad celebrated with the captain, 'the wonderful deliverance we had on that day from the powder plot', a gale blew up and raged for days. The ship's steering gear was broken but he was able to use his skills as a carpenter to repair the tiller. Their troubles were not over, though, for French privateers were on the prowl in the same waters. Fortunately, the same storm drove their enemies into harbour, giving Coad and his companions a clear passage to Plymouth. But just as they approached the harbour, the seas blew up again and they were saved from disaster only by a naval ship coming to press the sailors into military service. The day was 24 November, exactly five years since Coad first reached Jamaica: 'So that our perilous times were by the inconceivable, wonderful mercy, and good Providence of our God by one half of what was intended by our enemies cut fhort.'

John Coad reached his home on 4 December and 'found my Wife and 3 Sons living, but in a poor low condition'.[27] The rebel had returned. The faith that impelled Coad to join the losing side in the Civil War had also sustained him through the subsequent ordeal of vengeful retribution and transportation, deliv- ering him back to hearth and home.

BARBADOZED

Despite his sufferings, John Coad was comparatively lucky. Monmouth's rebels were transported variously to the Leeward Islands[28] and, probably, to Virginia. Henry Pitman and his brother were among 300 or so sent to Barbados. They had been 'Barbadozed', a popular term of the time describing what had become a common experience.

Henry Pitman was to serve his ten years in a place where, if possible, conditions were even more unbearable than Jamaica. Nine died aboard the transport ship. Pitman was 'consigned' to a master who virtually starved him and refused to allow him to practise his faith. When this master went broke, Pitman was sold off to another, along with all his other goods. The penalty for attempting escape was thirty-nine public lashes and an hour in the pillory, followed by branding on the forehead with the letters 'F T', meaning 'Fugitive Traitor'. When Pitman's brother died he resolved to risk this punishment, fleeing in a leaky boat with seven other convicts in May 1685. Five of the other fugitives were, like Pitman, 'Sufferers on the account of the Duke of Monmouth'.

After surviving bad weather, the escapees landed on the island of Curaçao where they encountered a group of privateers, legalized pirates, who invited the convicts to join them. Pitman and his companions refused, whereupon the privateers burned their boat and stole their belongings in the hope of giving them no option but to join. Pitman's faith and morality sustained him. He 'chose rather to trust Divine Providence on that desolate and uninhabitable island than to partake or be any ways concerned with them in their piracy: having confidence in myself, that GOD, who had so wonderfully and miraculously preserved us on the sea and brought us to this island, would, in like manner, deliver us hence, if we continued faithful to Him.' Four of the privateers joined the convicts and they waited together on the island for relief. The ship that eventually turned up was another privateer. But this one was bound for Providence Island with a prize ship. Henry Pitman was fêted by the captain and allowed to go with them. But they would not take his companions, who were left behind with ample supplies to sustain them.

Pitman eventually made his way to New York. Here he accidentally met with an old Barbados acquaintance who told him that after their escape Pitman and his companions were believed to have drowned at sea. From New York, Pitman boarded a vessel and eventually made his way through the Netherlands to Southampton. He travelled in disguise as discovery would have resulted in his execution. When he arrived home, he was happily surprised to find that his family had 'procured my Pardon; and joyfully received me, as one risen from the dead.'[29]

Henry Pitman's story and that of John Coad were perhaps rare happy endings for transported rebels. Both suffered greatly and Pitman also lost his brother. But, sustained by their faith and being determined characters, they won through in the end. Coad's story would form the basis of the novel *Captain Blood* (1922) by Rafael Sabatini, later made into a famous film.[30] Others who dared defy the powers of the land were not so fortunate. In the same year that the Duke of Monmouth failed, so did his supporter in the north, Archibald Campbell, 9th Earl of Argyll. Almost 200 of Argyll's men were transported to Jamaica and 100 to New Jersey.[31]

The old religious and political troubles between the English, Scots, Welsh and Irish periodically erupted in attempts to restore a Catholic monarch to the English throne. The series of risings usually known as the Jacobite Revolts began with the 'Glorious Revolution' of 1688 when the Protestant William of Orange deposed the Catholic James II of England. Supporters of the Jacobite cause mounted four failed rebellions, until the fifth ended in the defeat of Charles Edward Stuart, 'Bonnie Prince Charlie', at Culloden in 1746. Over 500 Scots survivors of that bloody battle are thought to have been transported. One lucky group of 150 were sent aboard *The Veteran* in May 1747, bound for sale in Antigua, Barbados, St Kitts and Nevis. Their ship was captured by the French, who were sympathetic to the Jacobite cause and set the Scots prisoners free on the French island of Martinique.[32] By the end of the American War of Independence it is calculated that around 7,000 Scots had been transported since 1615.[33]

THE NECK VERSE

But it was not traitors, however defined and condemned, who would become the major staples of the transportation trade. Early in the eighteenth century a process that allowed some first offenders guilty of specified capital crimes to claim immunity from the death sentence was significantly amended. Originating in the Middle Ages, 'benefit of clergy' was a church right that allowed male offenders to be punished according to religious rather than secular law. The right was established by the offender reading a section of the Bible, usually the 'neck verse', the 51st Psalm, beginning 'O God, have mercy upon me . . .' Over time this right was gradually extended to women, and anyone who was able to read the set biblical passage might claim the privilege. The practice was abandoned in 1706 and benefit of clergy could be sought by anyone who had not been charged with a small number of excluded capital offences, including murder, rape, highway robbery and various other forms of theft.

When the Transportation Act passed into law in 1718, the increasing numbers of people spared execution through benefit of clergy were among those already filling overcrowded prisons that had passed their limited holding capacities. These prisoners were mostly sentenced to hard labour as there were few sentencing alternatives. But the Transportation Act allowed judges to transport felons, a punishment considered more fitting for whatever crimes the 'clergyable' had committed. Judges relished this new opportunity and began sending men, women and sometimes children across the seas. But it seems that no one had given much thought to the practicalities of moving the burgeoning population of the convicted from Britain all the way across the Atlantic Ocean.

4

THE BODY TRADE

. . . if you have any Bowels of Compassion left show it by sending me some Relief . . .

Betty Spriggs, writing to her father from Baltimore, 1746

By 1719 the British government was in trouble. As courts wielded the new powers of the Transportation Act, numbers of the convicted awaiting a voyage to America grew rapidly. An industry soon evolved around the new economics of bondage. The major players were the government and those who provided shipping, together with a range of services needed to move large groups of people from foul prisons around Britain to convict ships waiting to take them to the colonies. Within this ecology a host of others also took their share, including gaolers, blacksmiths, carters and petty officials in regional and central court systems. In America, it depended on 'factors' who were the agents for ensuring the sale of transportees to those who were to become their masters. Astute businessmen quickly perceived an opportunity to solve the government's dilemma, at a price.

MASTER OF THE TRADE

First among them was an especially shrewd slave and tobacco trader named Jonathan Forward. He had already taken a load of more than 130 convicts to Maryland in 1717. Now he carried around forty to the same destination free of charge. He sold them there to recoup his costs, then approached the government back in Britain with an offer to take their many remaining human problems off their hands for just three pounds a head. He could not offer such a good deal on those to be ejected

49

from Wales and Ireland, regrettably, due to the extra distance, the trouble, the danger, the expense. For those, he would have to charge five pounds each.

Even at these rates it seems that Forward was undercutting his competitors. Although the government was reluctant to encourage such a trade, they were even more reluctant to pay for it themselves. So, with the endorsement of the main sponsor of the Transportation Act, Forward was made 'Contractor for Transports to the Government'.[1] More important than the impressive title was the fact that he now had a strong grip on the flesh business of the British Isles and a monopoly on those to be transported from the City of London.

Forward's success with what we would today call 'lobbying' the government was aided by his location in Britain's capital city. The thirty-three-year-old Londoner operated his business from a house in Fenchurch Street, which gave him insider knowledge of the government and his industry. He was known to buy up the bankrupt businesses of other tobacco traders and was also involved in litigation when one of his ships was impounded and his Maryland assets, valued at what was then a stunning £2,000, were confiscated. While the legal wrangling proceeded, Forward used a slave ship from his fleet to carry on with business. It is estimated that the British government paid out over £86,000[2] in what were effectively bounties on the heads of felons between 1718 and 1772 when the system was abolished. Jonathan Forward dominated the first twenty years or so of this business and greatly increased his already substantial fortune.

His money was not gained without dangers, both for his business and those unfortunate enough to sail aboard some of his vessels. In 1718 Forward's *Eagle* was carrying over one hundred convicts to the colonial plantations when she was attacked and boarded off the Virginia Capes by pirates under the command of Captain Richard Worley, notorious along the coast of New York and Pennsylvania. The pirates struck the chains from the convicts in the hold and locked some of them on the captain and his men. With the newly freed felons manning the *Eagle*, 'the two ships went a pirating together'. But not for long. After a few days they 'were met by several ships of force'. A desperate fight followed in which the pirates were routed and 'one in particular was cut to pieces after an obstinate resistance'. The two vessels were taken to Carolina, 'where about 50 of the felons and pyrates were executed, and the rest sold for slaves'.[3]

Despite the risks, many others operated in the trade between Britain and the American colonies. Sometimes, like Forward, they appeared as tobacco merchants, sometimes as transportation providers, sometimes as slavers. Often, they were all three. Bodies were simply another commodity to be bought cheaply, delivered to market and sold as dearly as possible. The trick to staying in business was to cross-subsidize. When the tobacco trade was down, entrepreneurs focused on convicts or slaves, the same ships being used for both. Only a year after his appointment as 'Contractor for Transports', Forward was petitioning the government for an increase in the convict bounty, citing hard times in the tobacco industry.

To negotiate the vagaries of the trade it was necessary for merchants to maintain factors in America. These were needed wherever convicts and other goods were loaded and offloaded. Forward had a network of such men who kept him informed of what was going on in terms of business, and who politically and generally looked after his interests. Sometimes, like the occasional shipmaster in his service, they swindled him. This was part of the cost of doing business.

Other expenses for Forward were legal fees, disputations and distractions. In 1725 he sued the Lord Lieutenant of Lincolnshire in relation to a transportation contract. Two years earlier he was called to the Old Bailey as a witness for William Blewit, who had been charged with returning from transportation. Blewit claimed he had been instrumental in preventing a mutiny on one of Forward's ships bound for the Leeward Islands 'and saved the Ship's Crew and Cargoe'. Forward testified that he knew nothing of this, though Blewit had certainly been landed on the island of Nevis 'and was come back'. The sentence was 'Death'.[4] Business continued as usual.

As well as payment from the authorities for carrying bodies across the ocean,[5] traders like Forward could also benefit from those with sufficient means to pay for their passage. In the 1730s a habitual criminal named George Sutton was transported to Virginia. He was landed near Hobbs Hole and 'having carry'd Money out with him, and wanting for nothing, he travell'd from thence [to] Williamsburg, and so to Philadelphia'. He then took a ship straight back to Dover, resumed his life of crime and ended it on the gallows in 1737.[6] There were others who were transported first-class.

From a well-to-do background, Henry Justice was a graduate of Cambridge University who pursued a successful career in the law at London's Middle Temple.

But he had an unusual problem. The short, fat and pox-pitted barrister[7] was addicted to books.[8] In 1736 he was arrested and tried for stealing sixty volumes – many of great rarity and value in English, Latin, French and Italian – from Cambridge University library. Stealing books was a niche criminal enterprise in eighteenth-century Britain, usually perpetrated by uneducated thieves looking for a quick profit. But Justice was not, apparently, interested in the monetary value of his spoils, he was in love with the objects themselves. He was also a member of the supposedly respectable upper classes. His trial at the Old Bailey was a sensational event. The prosecution was handled by two senior law officers, a full jury was empanelled and the published proceedings of the trial were eagerly awaited by a curious public. Upon being found guilty, Justice made a tearful plea to be burnt on the hand and for punishment 'at Home', rather than transportation. His entreaties were futile and he was transported for seven years.[9]

But Henry Justice was no common criminal. His standing and contacts saw him taken sedately to the transportation vessel in the coach of Jonathan Forward, the trafficker in flesh. On the voyage to Virginia, Justice was accommodated in the captain's cabin.[10] Having paid for his freedom, Justice was able to avoid any unpleasant consequences of his crime and was soon reported to be back in England. Disgraced, he finished his life in Holland, a centre of the book trade, reputedly with an extensive library of manuscripts and books.

Jonathan Forward retired in 1739, a very rich man.[11] Some idea of the very substantial amounts paid to him through the official processes can be seen in an order from Prime Minister Walpole to arrange payment for transporting sixty-six 'malefactors' from Newgate and elsewhere in the country to 'His Ma[jesties] plantations in America'. Forward was given £264[12] for the job, pursuant to providing security and undertaking not to bring any further charges to the Crown.[13] And he picked up the proceeds of their sale.

With government monies of this value, the transportation business continued to thrive, although resistance to it grew in the colonies. Pennsylvania attempted to place a prohibitive tax on the importation of convicts who had committed 'heinous crimes' as early as 1722.[14] Other colonies were no more successful in their opposition. Maryland and Virginia enacted several pieces of anti-transportation legislation from the 1720s, but it continued unabated.

A MOST INFAMOUS CHARACTER

It was not only traders like Jonathan Forward who were turning transportation to their advantage. Some of those who were being shipped abroad found ways to make it pay. In 1720 William Riddlesden, Esquire and lawyer of the Middle Temple, found himself sailing to America for a term of transportation. Although this was not his first sentence of banishment, it was the first time he had actually set sail for the colonies. His first offence was stealing the communion plate from a chapel in Whitehall, for which crime he was convicted and sentenced to death. Obtaining a royal pardon and, in accordance with the usual practice at the time, he agreed to transport himself within six months. But he never left.

This time, he had fallen foul of the self-styled 'Thief taker General' and master criminal, Jonathan Wild, who occasionally employed Riddlesden for his legal work. Wild fitted the lawyer up with a felony in late 1720. With his previous record, the trial did not go well and this time Riddlesden did leave England. But he did not travel as a common convict. He arrived at Annapolis in Maryland in May 1721 with a cargo of goods to trade and an expensive mistress with 'rich Silk Cloathes and a Gold Striking Watch', and began living like a wealthy man. The couple moved to Philadelphia where Riddlesden hoped to make an even better living than he was enjoying in Annapolis where he wasted most of his time 'jollily carousing with some of his Associates', mostly transported convicts who had paid their way out of chains.[15] He opened up shop as a seller of tallow and soap, with a sideline in providing legal advice. He was refused a licence to practise in the colony and moved to Boston to try again, though now without his female companion. Tiring of her partner's failure to continue the lifestyle they had originally established, she returned to England.

By 1721 or 1722,[16] the crafty lawyer was himself back in England, an illegal returnee from transportation. Here, he found another female companion and, calling himself Cornwallis, put his legal knowledge to use in trying to obtain a pardon for a 'William Riddlesden'. Assuming another identity with the aim of winning himself a legal pardon was just a little too clever, it seems, and the resourceful returnee was identified and arrested. In accordance with the law on returned transports, he was sentenced to death but escaped the gallows and was again sent to America in 1723.[17]

Riddlesden's sudden name change during his American sojourn was a calculated move. While in Maryland he had taken up impersonating the descendants of the pioneering Cornwallis family, illegally selling off land in the counties of the Eastern Shore.[18] He was also notoriously busy pursuing his English interests. When Benjamin Franklin first visited London, he inadvertently presented a letter from Riddlesden as his official letter of introduction. The official receiver immediately recognized the writer's notorious name and gave Franklin the cold shoulder.[19]

During his next sojourn in Maryland, Riddlesden continued his previous activities and apparently forged the deeds to some property using his Cornwallis alias. But he was brought to book in the Lower House of the Maryland Assembly in October 1724 where he was described as 'a Convict, of a most infamous Character'. The following March, and now using the name William Vanhaesdonk Riddlesden, he was commanded to surrender himself for trial within eighteen months. He had still not done so by November 1725, though he was given an extension.[20] It is unlikely that William Riddlesden, under any of his numerous aliases, ever attended the Maryland Assembly. He moved to the colony of Delaware and by 1727 he was dead.

The departed shyster's will revealed his holding of 27,200 acres of land and personal assets in Maryland and in England. These he left to his wife Rebeccah (née Fisher) and his stepchildren, who appear to have sold them. Four years later William Riddlesden's legal and commercial manoeuvres were still causing trouble when the will was contested.[21] By then, colourful though his life had been, the swindler was mostly forgotten as other even more lurid creatures were enmeshed in the net of transportation.

THE REAL MOLL FLANDERS

It was quickly apparent to anyone who wished to look that the Transportation Act opened up an array of sometimes dubious business opportunities. And not only for the merchants. As William Riddlesden's story shows, there was some room in the system for enterprising convicts to profit. The writer Daniel Defoe rapidly presented the public with what has turned out to be an enduring tale of just such a person. He called her Moll Flanders.

The eponymous novel is presented as the autobiography of an intriguingly colourful adventuress. A summary of the tale is given in the book's subtitle:

The Fortunes and Misfortunes of the Famous Moll Flanders, &c. Who was Born in Newgate, and during a Life of continu'd Variety for Threescore Years, besides her Childhood, was Twelve Year a Whore, five times a Wife (whereof once to her own Brother), Twelve Year a Thief, Eight Year a Transported Felon in Virginia, at last grew Rich, liv'd Honest, and died a Penitent.

Through a complicated plot Moll, under various names, marries or has liaisons with an amazing number of men and gives birth to a bewildering number of children on both sides of the Atlantic. Ultimately, a long way through a life ill-spent, the conniving, hard-hearted heroine repents in Newgate Prison. Inside, she rediscovers the love of her life and is transported to Virginia. There, she is reunited with her mother and her son (born from an unwitting marriage to her half-brother during her previous sojourn in the colony), receives her rightful inheritance and is set up for life. She confesses her sins to her forgiving husband and they return, wealthy, to England to live out their lives 'in sincere penitence for the wicked lives we have led'.

Defoe used the story to make critical points about the many failings of the transportation system – in which he was once an investor – as well as the foibles of human nature. But his lengthy fiction was based on the possibly real life of a flamboyant woman known – among other names – as Moll King. Defoe seems to have become aware of this Moll when she was serving time in Newgate Prison in 1721. By then she was a notorious prostitute, madam and pickpocket involved, like so many others in the city, with the 'thief taker', corrupt law officer and master criminal, Jonathan Wild.

Her life story to that point, or at least a version of it, was recounted shortly after her death in a popular pamphlet called *The Life and Character of Moll King, Late Mistress of King's Coffee House in Covent Garden*. According to the anonymous author, Moll was born in poor circumstances in St Giles-in-the-Fields, London, probably in 1696.[22] She went into service but soon became tired of domestic servitude and began selling fruit, and herself, in the streets. After years of various criminal activities, she was caught purloining a lady's gold watch in Soho and sentenced to death. She managed to avoid the gallows by successfully 'pleading the belly' and in 1720 was transported to Annapolis. The resourceful Moll soon returned to England and to her previous professional relationship with Jonathan Wild. His influence seems to have discouraged the transportation agent who prosecuted her from coming to court to confirm her identity. On this occasion Moll got off, though she might have later been transported to America a second time under her real name of Adkins. This would explain her absence from the records for some years.

But wherever she had been, or not, Moll now reappeared as the mistress of a notorious London coffee house owned with her husband, Tom King. As well as serving food and drink, the establishment served sex. The enterprise thrived and expanded, soon becoming a notorious rendezvous for night walkers, strumpets and their clients, including the great and even the noble of the city. Moll was also said to run a loan-sharking business for rich and poor, allegedly at preferential interest rates for the lower ranks of society.

Moll was in trouble with the law again in 1739 when she was fined a massive £200 for keeping a disorderly house, plus three months' prison time. In later life, Moll prospered, owning considerable property in London. After a long illness, she died in 1747 leaving a substantial fortune. Her epitaph, said to have been composed by one of her 'favourite customers' was pithy:

> Here lies my Love, who often drove,
> Wheelbarrows in the Street;
> From which low State to Billingsgate,
> With wickedness replete.
> She sold a dish, of stinking fish,
> With Oaths and Imprecations;
> And swore her Ware, was better Far,
> Than any in the Nation,
> From thence she came to be in fame,
> Among the Rogues and Whores;
> But now she's gone to her long home,
> To settle all her scores.[23]

Whatever the nature of the Moll Flanders/Moll King confection of fact and fiction, Defoe's book and Moll King's purported low life signalled the start of a growing public fascination with transportation, its processes and its horrors. Banishment across the seas was not now something that only happened to unsuccessful rebels as a consequence of war. All sorts of people were being whisked off for all sorts of crimes, great and small. As the number of allegedly first-hand accounts of convicts began to appear in the streets of major British cities and towns, so there was a mounting body of progressive opinion opposed to the entire project. Not just in the American colonies where discomfort with transportation had always existed awkwardly alongside the need for labour, but also among the lettered classes. This trend would remain strong into the late eighteenth and early nineteenth centuries when a large segment of a whole new continent became available to receive the unwanted battalions of the criminal, the poor and – still – the politically trouble-some. Before those developments the empire would expand and refine a coercive system in which the state not only colluded but played the primary role in the rolling drama of transportation. And there were other players on the stage.

THAT MISERABLE WOMAN

It was a dreadful story that Susanna(h) Buckler told Lieutenant Governor Lawrence Armstrong of Annapolis Royal, Nova Scotia, one spring day in 1736. With her husband Andrew Buckler, owner of the brigantine *Baltimore*, she had sailed from Dublin the previous October, bound for Maryland. On 15 December their ship was beset with foul weather and blown off course, coming at last to rest in Chebogue Harbour in Nova Scotia. All aboard died, other than Mrs Buckler and two sailors. The three of them were still breathing, just, when Susannah Buckler was kidnapped by indigenous Mi'kmaq who also stole the *Baltimore*'s valuable cargo, gold and silver, altogether worth over £13,000. Managing to escape, Mrs Buckler was rescued by a French-descended man of the Pubnico colony. Together with another man, a surveyor for the Crown, the shipwrecked survivor was brought to Annapolis Royal.

Aghast at these indignities suffered by a lady of quality and fearing for the fate of those wrecked with her, Armstrong despatched a ship to search for any survivors. He also provided Mrs Buckler with money and letters of introduction. The fortunate survivor went on her way and Armstrong at first congratulated himself on having done the right thing for an unfortunate lady in such distress. But several weeks later he received a letter from Barbados. It was from a Mrs Susan Buckler asking for news of her husband and his ship, the *Baltimore*. Belatedly realizing he had been duped, Armstrong set about tracking the deceitful 'Mrs. Buckler' down and warning others about her:

> I see Mrs. Buckler makes great complaint of the savages of Cape Sables and the losses she has suffered. Nothing could be more fabulous than her statements. It is fortunate for her that no one remains on the Baltimore to enlighten you as to the truth. I think this woman is a wicked adventuress, and is perhaps guilty of dreadful crimes on this occasion. For is it possible that she alone could endure all the fatigues and ills which have caused the death of all the crew?[24]

The *Baltimore* was recovered and sailed back to Annapolis Royal. Documents found aboard the ship showed she had sailed from Dublin. The valuable cargo she carried was in fact a consignment of convicts. Armstrong wrote to Governor Belcher of Massachusetts of his now confirmed suspicions about 'that miserable woman', of her story of a convict rising and her survival of a 'most barbrous massacre'. Inquiries were made and, eventually, the imposter was identified as a thief and prostitute known as Mrs Matthews. She was among the cargo of transportees aboard the *Baltimore* and had used her wits to survive and escape whatever horrors had taken place on the vessel. But it was too late. By the time the true story came out, Mrs Matthews had sailed from Boston for London. She was never seen again. The hulk of the *Baltimore*, stripped of her gear by the mutineers and the local Pubnico folk, lay at Annapolis Royal for six or seven years until she was burned at sea.

'Susan Buckler's' story illustrates the possibilities for women prepared to take advantage of the opportunities offered by the transportation system, in this case a convict shipboard mutiny. Criminal though she was, Mrs Matthews deployed considerable skill and daring in her deceptions. She was clearly no victim, but a predator, one of a type that would often appear in the transportation system.[25] She,

Moll King and many other women were inevitable participants in the body trade. Not only its victims or its profiteers, they nevertheless turned their situations to their own advantage. In King's case, her manipulations ended on the gallows, though Mrs Matthews, or whatever her real name might have been, disappeared back into the great underclass that spawned her and millions more. We do not know what her ultimate fate might have been. Perhaps, even probably, more crime. A woman of her wits and experience was sure to find her way through the thickets of eighteenth-century criminality, possibly to prosper and perhaps even die respectable. Some men certainly did.

THE WAYWARD APPRENTICE

It was at the Black Lion Inn near the church of St Clement Danes that young Anthony Lamb was ruined. Just twenty-one years of age, the bright lad was almost at the end of his apprenticeship to a London maker of mathematical instruments and could look forward to a secure future as a master of fine metal craft and engraving. But, like so many other naive apprentices, he fell in with bad company. Very bad company.

In 1724 the thief and escapee, Jack Sheppard, was a celebrated London criminal. Around the same age as Lamb, Sheppard came to know the apprentice instrument maker during his own time as a very unreliable apprentice. One night in the boozy fug of the Black Lion he recognized the apprentice and invited him to drink with his unsavoury but colourful friends. Flattered by this attention, Lamb soon fell in with Sheppard's mob. Their highly embroidered accounts of their daring exploits outside the law captivated the apprentice and it was not long before he sought to impress their tellers with something that might be of interest to them. His master had a wealthy tailor lodging in his house. Lamb would leave the door to the tailor's room open on the night of 16 June, allowing his new friends to rob the man. Lamb was as good as his unwise word. Around 2 a.m. Sheppard's mob crept through the open door. They quietly collected the promised loot, slipping away into the thick London night with over £300 and a large haul of expensive clothing.

Lamb's poor choice of acquaintances had not gone unnoticed at his place of work. As soon as the theft was discovered his master sent for the constable. He came promptly, dragging the apprentice out of bed by his hair and threatening him with far worse. The frightened young man confessed. Sheppard and his gang had gone to ground, quickly disposing of the loot, so Lamb was left to face retribution alone. He spent almost a month in the foulness of Newgate Prison until he was led in chains through the streets to the Old Bailey for trial. Here, the miserable youth confessed. He was acquitted by the jury of the serious charge of burglary and fortunately found guilty only of a felony to the value of thirty-nine shillings. This was presumably a recognition of his youth and previous good character as it allowed him to claim the right of 'benefit of clergy'. At that time it was the custom for courts to transport those who successfully claimed this benefit. Anthony Lamb was transported for seven years.

It was another three months before Lamb briefly breathed cleaner air than that of Newgate. In October he went aboard Jonathan Forward's eponymous frigate. Chained together in groups of six, the convicts spent most of the voyage below decks where the stench was as bad as that in Newgate. Among the other 142 male and female convicts aboard the *Forward* were some other members of Sheppard's gang. Sheppard himself would be riotously but messily hanged for his other many crimes the following month. No doubt, Anthony and his companions were thankful to have avoided the same fate; or perhaps they were just glad to hear that the man who ruined so many had now been 'topped'.

Or they might not have heard about it until much later. At this time a voyage to America usually took three months. It was not a pleasant cruise. Death rates were high and diseases, including smallpox, commonplace. Some declared they would rather have been hanged than sent on another transport ship. When they finally landed, the men would be told to shave and the women to dress in their best clothes. It is unlikely that these preparations would have disguised the distinctive odour emitted by all disembarking prisoners, but the goods needed to be packaged for sale. Spruced up, the convicts were taken in chains to be auctioned off to planters. Ten pounds for a fit man; eight or nine for a woman, and up to twenty-five pounds for a tradesman.

The *Forward* berthed at Annapolis in December 1724. Anthony Lamb was ejected along with her whole cargo of misery – then disappeared for six years. If he was lucky enough to have had his passage paid, possibly by his master who seems to have been an uncle, Lamb might have operated in the colonies much as a free man, as long as he did not return to England before the expiry of his sentence. There is no record of any planter purchasing him or indication of where he was or what he was doing. Like so many others, he might have vanished forever.

But suddenly he returns to the light in New York, then a city scattered mainly at the southern end of Manhattan Island. He was set up in business as a maker and supplier of mathematical instruments. Advertising in the *Pennsylvania Gazette* from November 1730, he made the most of his rare skills and nothing of his criminal past:

ANTHONY LAMB, Mathematical Instrument-maker, from London, now living in New York, near the New Dock, at the sign of the Compass and Quadrant, makes and sells all sorts of Instruments for Sea or Land, as Compasses, Quadrants, Forestaffs, Nocturnals, Sectors, Protractors, all sorts of Scales, Gaugin-Rods, and Rules, in Wood, Ivory, Brass or Silver, also any other small Work by Wholesale or Retale [*sic*].

Lamb was targeting the busy sea trade of the Middle Colonies as well as surveyors and cartographers. He did well. In May 1731 he was named a freeman of New York. The privileges of this respectable status were the right to follow his trade. His obligations were loyalty to the monarch and payment of all his taxes and fees. The following year he married Cornelia Ham, of Dutch descent, and they eventually produced two daughters and a son, John.

In 1735 Lamb became 'Overseer of Fire Engines', a paid post he held for some years. He continued to have connections with the municipal authorities and in 1738 enlisted in the militia as a private. He was quickly becoming the most noted follower of his trade in the expanding city, at the forefront of new inventions and developments in instruments for measuring distances and the angles of the sun and other heavenly bodies. His son John entered the business in or around 1750 and it became 'Anthony Lamb & Son'.

Three years later a newspaper advertisement appeared: 'Run away from the subscriber, in New-York, on Friday the 6th Instant, a well-set negro wench, named Jane.' The fugitive was said to be wearing a green waistcoat and a blue petticoat 'and is supposed to be harbour'd by some of her own colour in or about this City'. Anyone who returned her to her master would receive 'Twenty Shillings, and all reasonable charges'. Her master was Anthony Lamb. The once transported felon was now a slave owner, his respectability and relative affluence confirmed.

Always restless and ambitious, John left the family business in 1760. The following year both he and his father became candidates for the New York Assembly. John later served in the War of Independence, eventually becoming a general and a sometime commandant at West Point.

Anthony Lamb survived the British occupation of New York City by alternatively fleeing and returning. Despite the likely loss of business feared by most of his peers should the revolution succeed, Lamb was a staunch supporter of the Continental Army. His business premises burned down at least twice. Aged eighty, he at last returned to what was left of the city, one now depopulated and largely in ruins. Too old to begin again, Lamb was nevertheless a respected and respectable man. As his biographer put it, 'The indiscretions of his youth were acknowledged but never shadowed his career.'[26] His obituary of December 1784 acknowledged his life and achievements: 'He was an affectionate husband, tender parent, steady friend, obliging neighbor, and was distinguished by his philanthropy. He left behind many friends and no enemies – His *Standing Monument* is a GOOD NAME.'[27] The transported convict had indeed made good in the New World, his skills and character redeeming one youthful mistake. He became the best of citizens and, as another of his death notices had it, 'a steady friend to the liberties of America'.[28]

Others who came after the fallen instrument maker's apprentice might also find redemption. In August 1805 the traveller Robert Sutcliff was in Frederick-Town, Maryland. Here he heard about a recently deceased man named Smith. Transported from England in early life, Smith 'had lived and wrought with the black slaves' and had taken a wife from among them. After serving his sentence, he had amassed a considerable fortune. Some of which went to the children of his black wife, though the largest share went to his white offspring. Smith eventually became the principal stockholder of the Columbia Bank.[29]

INDIAN PETER'S REVENGE

Children continued to be among the victims of the transportation trade. In 1728 twelve-year-old James Annesley was kidnapped in Dublin. Thrown onto the streets three years earlier due to his parents' separation, young Annesley had been fending for himself ever since. After his father's death, his uncle was determined to inherit the family's vast estates and five aristocratic titles. Annesley was kidnapped by thugs in his uncle's service and delivered aboard a ship bound for Delaware. He laboured there for twelve years as an indentured servant, all the time proclaiming his rights and trying to escape. At the third attempt, in 1740, he was successful, returning to Ireland to claim his birthright. A sensational trial followed, the outcome of which favoured Annesley. But his uncle's appeal tied the estate up for many years and both Annesley and his wicked relative died before the case was settled.[30] This sensational story may have been the basis of Robert Louis Stevenson's *Kidnapped* and several other fictions. But a lesser-known tale would later be told by another abductee.

One winter's day in 1743 thirteen-year-old[31] Peter Williamson played with his friends on the quay in Aberdeen harbour. Being of 'a stout and robust constitution' he attracted the interest of two seamen. They were in the pay of some local merchants whose profits came from 'stealing young children from their parents, and selling them as slaves in the plantations abroad'. Young Peter was 'cajoled' aboard a vessel moored in the harbour where he joined other children kidnapped in the same way. With them he spent a month below decks being diverted by music and games while the ship gradually filled its complement of 'unhappy youths'. They then set sail for America.

Twelve weeks later near Cape May, their ship went aground in a 'hard gale' and 'to the great terror and affright of the ship's company, in a short time, was almost full of water'. The captain and crew launched a small boat and pulled for the shore, leaving their captive cargo to their fates. 'The cries, the shrieks, and tears of a parcel of infants, had no effect on, or caused the least remorse in the breasts of these merciless wretches,' Williamson recalled. The foundered ship and its wailing children lay on the sandbank all the following night, battered by the winds but holding together. Around ten the next morning the gale weakened and the captain sent some of the crew back to the stricken ship to bring his valuable human cargo ashore. Here, the children and sailors managed to survive for three weeks until picked up by a vessel bound for Philadelphia. The captain wasted no time getting his charges fit for disposal and then driving them 'through the country like cattle to a Smithfield market' to fairs where they were 'exposed to sale ... as so many brute beasts', realizing a healthy sixteen shillings a head.

Williamson would never see any of his companions again, as they were all sold off to different masters. He was lucky enough to be purchased for seven years by Hugh Wilson, who had himself been kidnapped in the same way while young. Like many others in America, Wilson had prospered in life by taking advantage of abducted and otherwise indentured labour. He was, 'contrary to many other of his calling, a humane, worthy, honest man' who treated young Williamson much like the son he did not have. The kidnapped youth was spared the brutality that many others in his situation suffered. He described the planters as 'generally of an idle disposition, not caring to fatigue themselves with work'. Instead, they purchased human energy. Harsh labour with little rest or proper clothing was the dismal expectation of most plantation workers, whether indentured or convict. If they escaped and were caught, as many were, they were made to serve an extra week for every day they had been fugitives, an extra month for every week and for every month an extra year. The recaptured servants were also liable for the cost of their own 'wanted' advertisements and associated costs in tracking them down and bringing them back. This 'often protracts their slavery four or five years longer'. For many, it was too much: 'after groaning for some time under the yoke of tyranny and oppression, with only a distant prospect of relief' they put an end to their bondage and their lives.

After four years of very different treatment, Williamson wished to get an education, and his master was happy to allow him to attend school each winter for five years. Wilson died when Williamson was seventeen, leaving the young man a substantial legacy, together with his best horse, saddle and clothing. He travelled around for a few years, expanding his skills and education. In his early twenties Williamson felt it was time to settle down. He had enough money to set up as a farmer and to marry the daughter of a well-to-do planter. Life was good. But then, his frontier farm was attacked by Cherokee Indians and he was once again abducted and made hostage. He escaped, but on returning to his relations found that his wife had died during his enforced absence. With nothing more to lose, Williamson enlisted to fight in the French and Indian War. He was promoted to an officer but then captured by the French, who eventually exchanged him for prisoners held by the British. After many hardships he returned from Quebec to Britain, often supporting himself by dressing as a 'red Indian' and demonstrating Cherokee customs, or at least his version of what he had seen during his captivity and subsequent experiences in the wars.

Williamson began to make his way north to Scotland in the hope of reuniting with his relations and to take revenge on the Aberdeen merchants and magistrates who had him abducted. Arriving penniless in the northern English town of York, his story attracted enough local sympathy to fund the writing and publication of his memoirs. The profits from this enterprise allowed him to continue to Aberdeen to pursue his case. In these attempts he rattled the cage of the vested interests who had been profiting from the kidnapping and transportation trade for decades. He called them 'monsters of impiety', comparing their actions to the barbarities of the 'Indians' he luridly described in his book. Williamson set himself up as a crusader against the kidnapping business, becoming a self-taught expert on the subject as he pursued his case, naming and shaming, as well as seeking restitution. Now 'new enemies started up, who, as if the abettors of those who laid the snare for me when a child, now contrived a new species of captivity for me, when I was a man'.

The Aberdeen abductors charged Williamson with libel and arranged for copies of his book to be seized and publicly burned by the hangman. He was then forced to sign a recantation of his accusations, fined, and ejected from the city. Travelling to Edinburgh, he was fortunate enough to gain the assistance of lawyers who took on his case. Returning to the Aberdeen court, and now with a slew of witnesses, Peter succeeded in gaining a judgement in his favour as well as compensation from the merchants. After some unsuccessful legal manoeuvring against the judgement, the merchants were further exposed and Williamson's claims vindicated. He was awarded an even more substantial amount in damages and costs, enabling him to establish himself in Edinburgh as a man of substance. He wrote in a later edition of his memoirs: 'Thus ended this process of oppression, carried on by a poor man against the magistracy of one of the most opulent and most respectable boroughs in Scotland'.[32]

Peter Williamson went on to become a well-known Edinburgh individual who established Edinburgh's first postal system. He continued to trade on his colonial adventures, becoming a wealthy businessman and publican. He died in 1799, according to some sources, of alcoholism.[33]

BETTY SPRIGGS WRITES HOME

In September 1756 the convict Betty Spriggs sent a letter home from a holding near Baltimore to her 'dear Father' in England. She acknowledged her 'former bad Conduct' but described her sufferings as being out of proportion to her crimes: 'I am sure you'll pitty your Destress Daughter. What we unfortunat English People suffer here is beyond the probility of you in England to Conceive.'

Betty was one of an 'unhappy Number' forced to toil most of the day and night and called a 'Bitch' for not working hard enough. She was 'tied up and whipp'd to that Degree that you'd not serve an Annimal', starved, going almost naked with no shoes or stockings and being forced to sleep on the hard ground with only a blanket. She was treated worse than the black slaves – 'nay many Neagroes are better used'. Betty begged her father 'if you have any Bowels of Compassion left show it by sending me some Relief, Clothing is the principal thing wanting.' They could be sent to her at a holding near Baltimore.[34]

We will never know if Betty Spriggs received the clothing she needed so badly. But the torments described in her letter are well documented in relation to the experience of male transports and indentured servants, and there is ample evidence from other sources of the hard lot of indentured or transported women in the colonies. Their trials began even before they left Britain. Female transports were separated from their children prior to embarkation. When they arrived at their destination they were sold off to the highest bidder and put to work at the kind of drudgery described by Betty Spriggs. They were vulnerable to unwanted sexual advances from masters and their family and from other convicts and servant slaves. Women who sought comfort or even love might have relations with black male slaves. If they gave birth they were guilty of 'bastardy and miscegenation'. Their children were known as 'mullatoes' and were confiscated to become the property of the woman's master until the age of thirty-one. If the bastards were white they remained in the ownership of the master until the age of twenty-one for males and sixteen for females. Or they could simply be sold. Punishment for the mother was usually an increase in her sentence. Suicide was not uncommon.[35]

Whatever 'bad conduct' Betty Spriggs had perpetrated and whatever her fate might have been, other women transports displayed agency and spirit in their careers. At least they did according to the popular pamphlets, ballads and other not necessarily reliable accounts of their adventures. While these sources are mostly commercial sensationalizations, the women who starred in them were the brazen celebrities of their day, notorious but well-regarded in the streets and drinking dens. 'Susannah Buckler' became notorious, carrying out her deceptions with aplomb and then slyly disappearing into history's undergrowth. She was neither the first nor the last woman to practise successful impostures, deploying native wit and boldness to con their way through difficult lives.

The many other women transported to the Americas remained mostly anonymous, lost in the fog of history. What happened, for instance, to 'fresh coloured' and smallpox-scarred Hannah Boyer? She was a 'Convict Servant Woman' described as a 'robust, masculine wench' in the wanted notice for her second escape attempt in 1752. Only six months earlier her previous owner, Catharine Jennings, offered a reward of twenty shillings for her recapture. That is all we know of twenty-three-year-old Hannah, except that she had no shoes or stockings.[36] Young women were in demand as workers in Maryland where, unlike male convicts or slaves, they were not subject to taxes, reducing the planters' costs. Nevertheless, women often worked and lived like slaves, and it was often stated that they were no better, or even more badly treated.[37] Whatever the bonded experiences of these women, once free, 'many were anxious to turn their backs on the past and their precarious and isolated experience as servants, to blend into the population without notice, to put down roots and, in time, to become the focal point of new, American-born families and kin networks'.[38]

Con men like William Riddlesden, determined avengers like 'Indian Peter' and successes like Anthony Lamb were figures in the tawdry but rich story of eighteenth-century transportation. All lived out their varied lives as a consequence of the extensive industry of which Jonathan Forward was only the most prominent trader. But the long tale was only beginning. Many more men, women and children would endure the Atlantic passage to face uncertain fates in the colonies of the New World.

5

A RACE OF CONVICTS

Sir, they are a race of convicts, and ought to be thankful for anything we allow them short of hanging.

Samuel Johnson[1]

Samuel Johnson's reported perspective of Americans was inaccurate but reflected a popular view of the colonies as a sink of criminals ejected from the British Isles. It was not surprising that the general public saw transportation in these terms. The trials of those sentenced to banishment were often widely reported in the press of the day, as well as in street ballads and booklets. Illustrators turned out graphic images of the miseries associated with transportation, while its benefits and evils were debated by politicians and other public figures. As well as those being sent over the water, there was thought to be a steady stream of convicts returning to Britain before the expiration of their sentences. One or two of these were enterprising enough to publish accounts of their adventures, real and imagined, though most simply returned to the lives of crime that saw them transported in the first place. Many were caught again and suffered the consequences. This was a rich field for publishers to feed a public excited to read, hear and sing of escapes, miseries, female deceivers and a cavalcade of colourful chancers who sometimes managed to get the better of the system, though more often succumbed to it.

BEN FRANKLIN'S RATTLESNAKES

Public interest in convict transportation took various forms. As well as a burgeoning industry in the titillation of the masses with street ballads and pamphlets that told the allegedly true tales of the underworld, its colourful characters and their right-eous fates, there was also serious concern in better-heeled circles about its effective-ness and its consequences. Even official statements could add to the bad odour of transportation and those who tried to escape its grip.

In 1718 'His EXCELLENCY, Samuel Shute, Esq; Captain General and GOVERNOUR in Chief in and over His Majesty's Province of the Massachusetts-Bay in New-England, &c.' issued a proclamation notifying 'sundry Felons trans-ported from Great Britain have Deserted and Broke loose from their Confinement on Board the Willing Mind Briganteen, John Brown Master, and the Ship Happy Return, Peter Harvey Master, and have committed many Robberies, and other Enormities in the Places whether they are fled'. The seven men included 'John Simonds, A thin slender Man of about Twenty-eight Years of Age, his Face thin and fretted with the Small Pox', and James Barret, 'A lusty black Man with streight black Hair, a loose grey Coat, and Tarpaulin Cap, Aged about Thirty Years'. One of the men had 'a shot Hole thro' his Leg', which must have slowed the fugitives down. The convicts were the property of Boston ship merchants Daniel Oliver and William Welsteed and the proclamation forbade anyone 'entertaining or concealing the said Felons', promising fifty shillings reward for the apprehension of each man.[2]

Opposition to transportation was often fuelled by such real or perceived threats to public order and private security. They arose almost as soon as the system began, growing louder over time. In 1751 the statesman, journalist and arch-satirist Benjamin Franklin penned a letter to the *Pennsylvania Gazette*. Franklin was commenting on the news that the British government had refused to allow the American colonies to make their own laws governing 'the importation of Convicts from Great Britain'. It was suggested by the British that the convicts would not only provide labour but – somehow – would also be transformed into hard-working and upstanding citizens.

In words laced with his signature sarcasm, Franklin suggested the American rattlesnake might be an appropriate payment to Mother England for the benefits her transported convicts were said to bring to the colonies. Just as the convicts might change their character when transported to America, so might the rattle-snakes when transplanted to the British climate. Franklin proposed to have the snakes 'carefully distributed in St. James's Park, in the Spring-Gardens and other

Places of Pleasure about London; in the Gardens of all the Nobility and Gentry throughout the Nation; but particularly in the Gardens of the Prime Ministers, the Lords of Trade and Members of Parliament; for to them we are most particularly obliged'.

Franklin sounded the note that would be heard wherever transportation was in force or proposed: If 'all the Newgates and Dungeons in Britain are emptied into the Colonies', it might satisfy 'publick utility' and private interests and concerns would just have to put up with it because:

> Our Mother knows what is best for us. What is a little Housebreaking, Shoplifting, or Highway Robbing; what is a Son now and then corrupted and hang'd, a Daughter debauch'd and pox'd, a Wife stabb'd, a Husband's Throat cut, or a Child's Brains beat out with an Axe, compar'd with this 'Improvement and well peopling of the Colonies!'

Finally, Franklin argued that the rattlesnakes would be much less risky for the British than were 'Human Serpents' transported to the colonies: 'For the Rattle Snake gives Warning before he attempts his Mischief; which the Convict does not.'[3]

This reaction was sharpened by news of several gruesome murders committed in the colonies around the same time by transported convicts. In March 1751 Jeremiah Swift, an educated twenty-one-year-old from Essex, had been in Maryland for about a year when he hacked one of his master's young sons to death with a hoe. He then murdered the boy's sister with an axe, as well as savagely injuring another brother. Sparing three young children, he fled but was soon caught, quickly found guilty, then hanged in chains.

Other crimes by transports were reported in the colonial and British press, providing fuel for Franklin's incendiary prose.[4] The same year that Jeremiah Swift took an axe to his master's children, another convict servant also picked up an axe with deadly intent. He broke into his master's house determined to kill his mistress. But, seeing 'how d—nd innocent she looked' in sleep, he changed his mind. Laying his hand on a block, he sliced it off with a blow of the axe. Picking up the severed object with his other hand, he threw it at his now-awakened mistress, saying, 'Now make me work if you can'. According to the press, he then earned a living begging in Pennsylvania, pretending to have lost his hand by accident.[5]

As the colonies stumbled towards what was to be the great liberating war with Britain, others raised their voices. J. Hector St John de Crevecoeur echoed Franklin's theme, asking his famous question 'What then is the American, this new man?' In the course of answering his own question he wrote:

> What a strange compliment has our mother country paid to two of the finest provinces in America! England has entertained in that respect very mistaken ideas; what was intended as a punishment, is become the good fortune of several; many of those who have been transported as felons, are now rich, and strangers to the stings of those wants that urged them to violations of the law: they are become industrious, exemplary, and useful citizens.[6]

Despite the eloquence and passion of Franklin's view and a sizeable body of similar opinion in the colonies and in Britain, the transport system continued without pause, as did its exploitation. The extreme vagueness and malleability of the transportation laws allowed one enterprising English scoundrel to turn convicts into his private 'slaves'.

THE SLAVES OF LUNDY

Thomas Benson was born into a substantial merchant family in Devon in 1708. He inherited some ships and resources upon his father's death and embarked on a career of legitimate trading supplemented by piracy and smuggling. By the late 1740s Benson was in a position to lease the island of Lundy, around ten miles off the Devon coast, for sixty pounds a year. This enabled him to land tobacco from America and smuggle it onto the mainland, avoiding the duty payable.

Benson also obtained a government contract to transport convicts to Maryland. He had a clever scheme in mind. Instead of taking the convicts across the Atlantic Ocean to the American colony, for which the government paid him twenty pounds a head, he simply offloaded them on Lundy. Here they were forced to work on improvements to the island's infrastructure and assist with the tobacco-smuggling operation. The convicts were boarded in the castle keep and worked around the island in chains. A group of seven or eight managed to escape and reach the mainland in the island's boat, vanishing into oblivion.[7] But their unfortunate companions remained to labour on the island.

It was a scheme of criminal genius and worked like a charm – until Benson unwisely took some house guests to Lundy, including the Sheriff of Somerset, to show off his enterprise. The Sheriff was not impressed with Benson's claim that he was only obliged to transport convicts off mainland Britain and not all the expensive way to the Americas. He was prosecuted, but unsuccessfully. So imprecise and contradictory were the laws governing transportation that his feeble excuse was accepted.

To this point Benson appeared not to have been much more scheming than many other traders of the time. But he would eventually distinguish himself as a criminal exploiter of the worst kind. His plan was devious and audacious. Deep in debt, Benson now planned a bold insurance scam. He indemnified his oldest and leakiest ship, the *Nightingale*, together with its cargo and crew, for as much as the insurance company would bear. Suborning his upright but needy Captain Lancey and a crew of sea-going desperadoes, Benson had them ready the *Nightingale* for sea in the summer of 1752. Her cargo was an unremarkable mix of salt, cloth, pewter and cutlery, along with a mysterious 'hogshead of dry goods'.

In addition, there were twelve men and three women, all in chains, the men in pairs and the women together. Brought down from Exeter Gaol, the miserable convicts were bound for transportation to Maryland. From Bristol they sailed straight to Lundy where most of the cargo was illegally unloaded and the crew bribed to keep quiet about their part in this act and in what was to follow.

After a couple of nights trans-shipping the cargo to the island, an operation kept concealed from the convicts, the *Nightingale* was put to sea. About eighty kilometres west they encountered the *Charming Nancy* out of Philadelphia. After the customary exchange of pleasantries, the American ship continued on her way and Lancey initiated the next stage of the scheme.

The ship's boat was readied and two sailors were ordered to break open the hogshead of dried goods. It was filled with small barrels of tar and oakum soaked in tar. The black tar was spread around in the hold and a hole cut between that area and the bread room or pantry. A hole was drilled below the waterline and stopped with a marlinspike. A lighted candle was then pushed through the hole into the hold where it ignited the tar. And then the marlinspike was pulled out. The *Nightingale* was afire.

The crew then pretended to put out the fire, making as much noise as possible to attract the attention of the *Charming Nancy*. While all this was taking place, the hapless convicts remained in chains. Lancey loudly accused them of starting the fire and moved them towards the waiting ship's boat. Everyone clambered into the lifeboat, the convicts protesting their innocence. By now the American ship had sighted the smoke and swung around to pick up the *Nightingale's* boat. A few hours later another ship took them aboard and brought them all safely ashore at Clovelly. From here, Lancey was able to quickly return to Benson's house.

Surprised by this unexpectedly early return of his co-conspirators, willing and otherwise, Benson insisted that the captain and the crew sign affidavits attesting that the fiery fate of the *Nightingale* was an accident. But it was in vain. One of the crew drank too much and boasted of the deed in Barnstaple one market day where plenty of eager ears heard the true story. One of Benson's rivals bribed the sailor to confess. Lancey was arrested and the crew began to turn themselves in to the authorities. Eventually the captain and one of the sailors were examined by the Judge of the Admiralty, as was the custom then. Lancey refused to give evidence against Benson, despite being promised clemency. The two men were committed for trial.

Meanwhile, Benson attempted to ensure through various legal and financial ploys that the true story did not come out in court and so reveal the extent of his debt. None of these were successful and he was eventually judged to owe over £8,000, an enormous sum in those days. Unable to pay, his property was seized and in December he fled to Portugal where he had family business connections.

Lancey and two of the crew were tried at the Court of the Admiralty in February 1754. The unlucky captain was found guilty and sentenced to death. He seems to have accepted his fate without rancour for any of his co-conspirators, even Benson. He prayed ceaselessly for two days leading up to his execution and 'to his last hour, behaved with a steadiness and composure, very seldom seen on the like solemn occasion'.[8] Lancey was hanged at Wapping on 17 June 1754. Benson revived his business in Portugal, courtesy of his captain's misplaced loyalty. Threatened with extradition, he fled to Spain. But his crimes were soon forgotten as Britain went to war with France once again and Benson returned to Portugal where he lived until his death in 1772.

The fate of the island convict colony is unknown. Research into initials carved into the walls of what is now known as 'Benson's Cave', quarried into shale beneath the castle keep, provides only the barest hints of who these people were. They seem to have been transported from Exeter in two groups, the first in 1749 and the second group on the *Nightingale* a few years later. It is assumed the authorities arranged for the men and women to continue their interrupted voyage to Maryland to serve out whatever remained of their original sentences.

The economics of the transportation trade were compelling enough for Benson to construct his elaborate scheme. His offshore labour needs diverted a few from transportation to the Americas, but that trade continued to flourish until after the War of Independence. Some of its victims even managed to prosper.

A GENIUS OF THE FEMALE SEX

The young noblewoman was charming. Well dressed and well decked out in expensive clothes and jewels, Princess Susanna Caroline Matilda turned many a South Carolina gentleman's head in the early 1770s. Receiving the hospitality of the finest homes of the colony and their wealthy owners, the princess glided through what passed for high society at that time and place with the appropriate aplomb for someone claiming to be the sister of Queen Charlotte, wife of George III. Those who kissed her graciously extended hand were promised promotion, honours, even governments. Of course, these privileges required serious amounts of cash, which the besotted gentry of the colony delivered into the same hands their lips had gratefully grazed.

It was all too good to be true. Queen Charlotte had no sister and news eventually arrived from Maryland identifying the princess as an escaped convict, real name Sarah Wilson and very much a commoner. A Staffordshire bailiff's daughter born in 1754, Sarah made a dishonest living in town and country by impersonating the well-to-do and the noble, and by obtaining goods and money through her accomplished pretences. In 1767 she was tried for the theft of clothes from a London shop and sentenced to transportation for seven years.[9]

Sarah Wilson, felon, arrived in Maryland in the autumn of 1771, where, as the *London Magazine* later described it, 'she was exposed to sale and purchased'[10] by a Mr W. Devall of Bush Creek, Frederick County. But not for long. Sarah soon fled to Virginia, apparently in possession of some jewels and some fine clothes, together with a miniature portrait of Queen Charlotte, a valuable prop to give her deception credibility. She travelled from one gentleman's house to another through North Carolina to South Carolina under a new identity as none other than the queen's sister. Devall advertised for the fugitive, empowering an attorney named Michael Dalton to search for her from Philadelphia to Charlestown. For anyone who did apprehend her, there was a payment of 'five pistoles, besides all costs and charges'.[11]

During this time the enterprising Sarah cut a swathe through the colonial gentry, fleecing them blind, often for considerable amounts of money. Her progress was noted by the press as she travelled through the colonies under a variety of evermore elaborate pseudonyms, including 'her Serene Highness Caroline Augusta Harriot', bearing among other titles, 'Marchioness of Waldegrave'. She seems to have picked up her assumed names and their noble associations from stories in the press, creatively manipulating them for the naivety of her victims. With a repertoire of such personas, Sarah generated a considerable personal mythology that has obfuscated the historical record. The accomplished imposter and confidence trickster was then reportedly apprehended at gunpoint and 'reduced to her former slavery'.[12]

But there is no record of Sarah ever being charged for her escape and impersonation. It was said that two years after her return to Bush Creek, she took advantage of her owner's absence fighting the War of Independence to escape once again. In a fairy-tale ending to that story, Sarah was said to have later married a British Light Dragoons officer. As with much of the imposter's extensive mythology,[13] there are different versions of what happened next. Some say she disappeared. Others that, somehow, she managed to retain the money she gained by her earlier false pretences and established her husband in business after the war. She supposedly bore him many children and lived respectably in the Bowery, New York.[14] In reality, she died in Maine in 1780.[15]

Whatever the truth of this imposter's follies and fate, she was, as a contemporary newspaper put it, 'the most surprising genius of the female sex that was ever obliged to visit America'.[16] As the historians who have studied Sarah's story, together with those of other colonial fraudsters, note: 'These women were heroines of their own narratives – inventing and reinventing themselves as necessity and whim dictated, performing the carefully judged persona to a chosen audience.'[17] Sarah Wilson, fake noblewoman, not only escaped her bondage and the full consequences of her crimes, but also managed to elude history. Others transported to the American colonies would also engineer escapes of a different kind.

POOR UNHAPPY FELONS

An unknown number of convicts transported to the Americas returned to Britain before the expiry of their sentences. If they had no credible proof that they had been freed through purchase, gift or other legal means, they risked execution. Many who might have contemplated escape from the colonies were deterred, but some were more determined.

Other returnees received the death sentence, though there were ways around that sense of finality. It was sometimes possible to gain a royal pardon if a special case could be made.

Although not revealing he was a returned convict, highwayman and burglar, John Poulter wrote an account of his life and crimes that was a sensational bestseller of the mid-eighteenth century. Poulter pulled no punches, he named names and revealed the alleged existence of a vast criminal sub-culture that operated in Britain's murky underworld. He also gave instructions on how to return from transportation. The trick was to have a friend or accomplice purchase the convict's freedom from the merchant or ship's captain. At that time the going rate was around ten pounds, perhaps less. In return the payer received a signed note that left them 'free to go unmolested when the Ships arrive between the Capes of Virginia, where they pleafe'. If they later wished to return to England, there were ships aplenty on which no paying passenger, convict or not, would be refused passage. And there was always the possibility of working a passage back to Britain if insufficient funds were at hand.

But Poulter neglected the large legal issue faced by those who returned before the expiry of their original sentence, even if they possessed some documentation. Demonstrating the old adage that 'there is no honour among thieves', *The Discoveries of John Poulter* named a woman pickpocket who had managed to bribe her way out of transportation before her ship left the 'Transport Hole' at Bristol. Elizabeth Connor, convicted and sentenced in or around 1748, never left England. Others may have managed the same trick. By whatever means they avoided or ameliorated their sentences, the system leaked like the proverbial sieve and Poulter was keen to further ingratiate himself with the authorities by offering advice on how they could 'prevent any Convict coming back before their limited Time is out'. His solution was for all those intending to go aboard homeward-bound ships to be publicly registered and to have a certificate from the governor proving they were neither indented or a convict. Shipmasters and merchants were to be subject to fines if they freed anyone for money.[18] There is no evidence that Poulter's suggestions were ever taken up. His extraordinary memoir of betrayal was concocted while he was negotiating a pardon for his own return from America. He was hanged.

Poulter's book contributed to the notion that transportation was failing as a punishment if it were so easy to avoid. The truth of his writing is difficult to validate, and it seems likely that much was contrived for the purpose of earning him a pardon for his latter-day crimes. Historians differ on how frequently convicts still under sentence returned from the American colonies.[19] Some certainly did, and were caught.[20] We will never know how many others did successfully abscond and fade into places far distant from their old haunts and accomplices and so manage to avoid detection and prosecution.[21] But one or two can tell their stories down the centuries.

'An unfortunate youth of tender years', Maurice Salisbury came from a poor but respectable Somerset family. Described as 'a sober, quiet Youth, very tractable and diligent in Business, not given to Idleness, or Wickedness', young Maurice fell into bad company and bad ways, 'seduced by the evil Counsel and Conversation of some of his Companions'. He stole rings and money from his employer's maid and was eventually caught and tried at Dorchester Assizes in March 1750. Sentenced to seven years' transportation, a local gentleman made representations 'that he might be sent Abroad with a Master of a Ship, that might use him as kindly as might be, and that he might not be sold for a Slave'. The owner of the transport ship complied, and Maurice was put under the charge of the ship's Master who 'kept him on Board, not as a common Convict Transport'. The boy worked as a sailor and cook aboard the *Catharine* during the two-month voyage to Virginia. The cargo was unloaded and Maurice remained with the ship until the following August, when the *Catharine* returned with a full cargo of tobacco.

Safely back in Appledore, the Master began sending Maurice ashore to run his errands. Barefoot and in peril of being identified as a returned transport, the youth complained of overwork. He was 'met with rough Language, and was told, that as he was a Convict Transport, he must submit to any Thing without murmuring, or it might be the worse for him'. Maurice considered his situation and decided that 'Under these Circumstances, upon Reflection, he did not choose to live; as they had not made a Slave of him Abroad, he had Resolution enough not to be made one at Home'. He 'took French leave' and walked to London, where he had a brother living. Here, the escapee worked for some months as a tailor until he was suddenly arrested for stealing. Acquitted at the Old Bailey, he was nevertheless discovered as a returned transport and consigned to Newgate. At his trial, the charge that had seen him transported was brought up and he was sentenced to death. On 1 June the convicted penitent, resigned 'to the justice of his Fate', was taken in a cart, together with another returned transport, to the place of execution. 'After the Executioner had tied the Ropes to the fatal Tree', there were prayers for the condemned men's' souls. Maurice 'behaved very decently, and shewed great Marks of Contrition, weeping heartily'. His companion, a more desperate character, behaved 'not quite so well' before the cart was pulled from under them. Maurice Salisbury was just twenty years old.[22]

Joseph Derbin bore the brand of the thief on one hand. He was transported for seven years in 1763 for stealing clothes, and it was not the first time. Less than a year later he was defending himself at the Old Bailey after being caught stealing a watch, more clothes and having in his possession 'Twelve pick-lock keys'. Derbin confessed he was a returned transport but argued in his defence that 'the question is, Whether or no I lose my freedom of being a free subject of either this kingdom, or any of his Majesty's plantations. In purchasing my freedom, I think I have a right to be here; my friends paid my passage; here is the copy of the paper they granted me.' He produced the document:

On Board the Neptune, Captain Somervell,

June 17th, 1763.
Joseph Derbin is a freeman. Any Magistrate may grant him a pass by destroying this. Witness my hand,
David Ross.

Derbin explained that David Ross was the convict consignee in Maryland and that the paper pass had been given by Colonel William Harrison, Justice of the Peace for Charles County. But the judge was unwilling to accept the legality of the colonial paper: 'You can't be so weak as to imagine they have power to reverse the sentence you received here,' he said, and promptly condemned the man to death.[23]

John Read (aka John Miller and David Miller), transported felon, was taken in London with a loaded pistol by one of Sir Henry Fielding's men in 1770. He was convicted of returning before his sentence had expired and sentenced to death. Surprisingly, he thanked the jury, saying 'he would rather die than live a transport, as no man knew the misery of such a state, but those who felt it; which, to him, he said, was so intolerable, that being disappointed, in several efforts he made, to escape from his slavery and bondage, he attempted to hang himself, which, he said, he was fully determined to do, had he not succeeded in his last escape.' On the gallows he addressed the crowd in similar terms, stating that he was 'very happy in leaving this world, and died in peace, good will, and forgiveness with all mankind'.[24]

Tried and sentenced in 1772, nineteen-year-old Alice Walker's experience was very different. Convicted in London for stealing a canvas bag and twelve pounds in cash from a lovelorn wagoner, she was transported to Rappahannock for seven years. There she was purchased by prominent planters, the Sampson brothers. The Sampsons used both slaves and convicts to perform their labour, a good few of whom appeared in advertisements for runaways. In 1773 Alice Walker became one of them. In company with two men, one of whose names she used, she was described as 'a low, well set woman, about 20 years of age', with sandy-coloured hair. She wore a brown gown, a red petticoat and sported four red silk handkerchiefs.[25] Alice and her companions eluded capture and she, unwisely, returned to England, where she was fairly soon apprehended and tried at the Old Bailey. Sentenced to death, the jury recommended mercy if she agreed to be re-transported for fourteen years. Although the records fall silent at this point, it seems likely that Alice Walker took the offer and went back to America.[26]

The transatlantic adventures of another returnee, Richard Kibble, highlighted the random nature of the system. Convicted of various crimes, he was transported to Virginia in 1738, escaped and returned home, only to be apprehended, tried, convicted and transported yet again. So adept was Kibble at cheating the executioner that when he was finally hanged he was said to have been transported four or even five times.[27]

These were not the only varied outcomes of the transportation system. So poorly thought through was the process that it was possible for a transported felon to arrive in America but to find no buyer. What happened then? The shipmaster would not take the convict unless paid, a highly unlikely prospect, and the convict was not allowed to return until his or her sentence had been served. The luckless transport was simply dumped and left to survive if possible.

In 1771 James Hancock was convicted of stealing a man's watch. He was duly transported for seven years where, by his own account:

I went from here on board one of his majesty's vessels, to Virginia to Leeds town; I am a watch-maker; not getting any work there, I went to Philadelphia to get business; I got there on Friday, and was to go to work on Monday; there was a man that went over in the same vessel there, that was known to be a convict; he save himself [sic] impeached me as being a convict; I did not know before that a convict was not admitted there. I was then drove to the necessity to return, having no money nor friends.

His sentence was 'Death. Recommended',[28] meaning mercy was likely, though not guaranteed, to be forthcoming.

JAMES REVEL'S FAIRY TALE

Returnees were just one element of the public fascination with the transportation system. The experiences of convicts in the colonies were featured in personal accounts like John Poulter's book, as well as early newspapers and magazines. They were also an important segment of the booming street-ballad business. Purporting to tell true stories of transported felons, these crudely printed sheets of paper were sold cheaply on British street corners to a public anxious for lurid tales of the miseries suffered in the colonies. They were also equally popular in the colonies; Benjamin Franklin even composed and hawked several in his youth.[29]

One popular production of this type, 'The Lads of Virginia', begins with the stock ballad situation of the fallen apprentice led astray by wine, women and song. He goes robbing on the highway to maintain an expensive lifestyle but 'By that I got lagged to Virginia'. He is transported and 'sold for a slave in Virginia'. In England the transport could 'Rest my bones down on dry feathers', while in Virginia 'I lay like a hog' and:

> My bones are quite rotten, my feet are quite sore,
> I'm parched with the fever and am at death's door . . .

and:

> Old England! Old England! I shall never see you more . . .
> But if ever I live to see seven years more
> Then I'll bid adieu to Virginia.[30]

In the imaginary of the street ballad, it happened to women as well. A broadside of the late seventeenth and early eighteenth centuries titled 'The Trepanned (ensnared) Maiden' or 'The Distressed Damsel' presented a litany of misery for its fictional protagonist 'That lately was betray'd / And sent to Virginy O'. For five years she serves 'Under Mafter Guy' and, like Betty Spriggs, is starved, poorly clothed and must sleep on straw. She carries loads of wood upon her back, nurses babies and complains that 'No reft that I can have, Whilft I am here a Slave'. She pines to return to England and to rest from her ceaseless labours.[31] It is not clear whether the damsel is an indentured servant or a convict, but in any case she is not in Virginia of her own free will and conditions were much the same, regardless of the legal status of the condemned.

Sometimes the balladists varied the plot. Around the middle of the eighteenth century and later, a lengthy publication recounting *The Poor Unhappy Felon's Sorrowful Account* was sold on the streets of Britain. It was allegedly the story of James Revel's fourteen years' transportation to Virginia. Apprenticed to a 'Tinman' (tinsmith), like many before and after, Revel fell into bad company, ran away and took to robbery with a gang of thieves. His parents were devastated but his master eventually 'got me home again/And used me well in hopes I might reclaim' (reform). Despite promising his parents and master that he would give up his wicked ways, he returned to his old friends in crime and wild living. One night the gang was captured. Three were hung and Revel was transported along with a 'wicked lousy crew' of ruffians. Five died on the voyage, which ended 'when after sailing seven weeks and more/We at Virginia all were put ashore'. Here, the convicts were cleaned up:

> Our faces shav'd, comb'd out wigs and hair,
> That we in decent order might appear,
> Against the planters did come us to view,
> How well they lik'd this fresh transported crew.

They were lined up separately, the male and female convicts being displayed to their potential purchasers. They were asked their trade, paraded around so their limbs could be felt for quality:

> Some view'd our teeth to see if they were good,
> And fit to chow our hard and homely food.

Eventually, Revel is sold to 'a grim old man', himself an ex-transportee, who has him chained again and taken a hundred cold miles up the Rappahannock River. When they arrive, Revel's 'European clothes' are taken from him, replaced with a canvas shirt, trousers and 'a hop-sack frock, in which I was a slave'. No shoes, stockings or hat. Revel is made to work from dawn to sunset in the tobacco fields along with black slaves and other transports:

> We and the negroes both alike did fare,
> Of work and food we had an equal share;

They work for six days a week and on the Sunday must till their own fields to feed themselves. Escape is a dangerous possibility:

> But if we offer once to run away,
> For every hour we must serve a day,
> For every day a week, they're so severe,
> Every week a month, and every month a year.

After some time, the convict becomes ill, though he is still forced to work 'while I could stand/ Or hold the hoe within my feeble hand'. He receives better treatment from the 'poor negro slaves' than from his 'brutal and inhuman master'. Enduring all this, Revel eventually seeks holy deliverance from the Lord. He repents of his 'former wicked ways' and is restored to health.

In the twelfth year of his sentence, Revel's master dies and he is purchased by another planter from Jamestown. On hearing his new possession's tale, his kindly master does not use him as a slave but as a servant, offering to pay his passage back to England if he behaves well for the remainder of his sentence:

> Thus did I live in plenty, peace, and ease,
> Having none but my master to please . . .

During this time Revel is often aggrieved to see the conditions in which the transports are 'like horses made to trudge and slave'. His fortunes have turned and he now enjoys a life of comparative comfort. True to his word, his master sends him back to England after two years. He is reunited with his aged parents in an affecting scene of contrition and redemption:

The Lord unto me so much grace will give,
To work for you both whilst I do live . . .

This epic fairy-tale rendition of a transport's experience ends with the stern moral warning typical of the street literature of convictism:

My countrymen take warning e'er it be too late,
Lest you should share my hard unhappy fate,
Altho' but little crimes you here have done,
Think on seven or fourteen years to come;

Forc'd from your country for to go
Among the negroes to work at the hoe,
In different countries void of relief
Sold for a slave because you prov'd a thief.

Young men all with speed your lives amend,
Take my advice as one that was your friend,
For tho' so light of it you do make here,
Hard is your lot if you do once get there.

It is most likely that this ballad of James Revel's experiences was a composite of a number of stories, as well as several fictional tropes,[32] but it does feature authentic details of seventeenth-century transportation to Virginia within its stock template of unhappy transports, of which there were a great many being purveyed throughout Britain. 'James Revel' may simply have been an appealing name on which to hang the tale. The existence of this and similar publications reflected the strong public interest in transportation and the early reprocessing of the lived experience into narratives calculated to appeal to the masses – and to warn them of the dire consequences of crime. The perceptions and prejudices surrounding transportation were both created and sustained by the proliferating popular literature of the seventeenth and early eighteenth centuries. Those notions of suffering, brutality and the occasional Hollywood ending would continue into the street ballads of the late eighteenth century, including James Revel's story. It was still being sold, told and sung in Australia during the nineteenth century, the details suitably altered for geography and circumstances.

THE SECRET TRANSPORTS

In 1779 Duncan Campbell was called before a special House of Commons committee on convict transportation. Campbell had been twenty years in the business of contracting with the government to transport felons to the American colonies. For most of those years he had received five pounds per convict to cover his expenses. He would then sell the foul-smelling convicts to the highest bidders in Maryland and Virginia. Such was the fate of those without the means to buy their way out of servitude. This was not only possible but, according to Campbell, 'many convicts who had money bought off their servitude, and their punishment was only banishment for the term prescribed'.

The 'overseer of convicts' estimated that over a seven-year average he had transported around 500 people each year. Around one-seventh of the men died during the two-month voyage, but only about half that number of women, mainly from smallpox and less so from gaol fever. Campbell attributed the higher female survival rate to 'their constitutions being less impaired, and to their sobriety'. He was unabashedly direct about the profits to be made from the body business. Of those that were sold, the prices he received were for 'common male convicts, not artificers, on an average for £10 a piece; females at about £8 or £9; those who were of useful trades, such as carpenters and blacksmiths, from £15 to £25; the old and infirm he used to dispose of to those humane people who chose to take them, but with some he was obliged to give premiums.'

Although the overseer referred to 'convicts' in his evidence before British politicians, the distinctions were lost when transports arrived in the colonies as commercial assets. Indentured servants and convicts were dealt with in the same manner once they reached the American colonies. In July 1767 the transport *Thornton* docked in Annapolis. *The Maryland Gazette* carried an advertisement for 'One Hundred and Fifty-two Seven Years SERVANTS', including tradesmen, farmers' several boys, 'and many notable Women'. The advertisement continued:

'These Servants will be exposed to sale aboard the said ship.' Directly beneath appeared the official disease clearance of the local naval officer, confirming no cases of 'Small-Pox, Jail-Fever, Yellow Fever, Flux or any such dangerous distemper' [spelling modernized] of the 'One Hundred and Fifty-two Convicts'. The men, women and children aboard the *Thornton* were transported convicts with sentences of seven years, not indentured servants, as mentioned elsewhere in the non-commercial context of a local news item on the same page, where the arrivals were referred to as 'his majesty's Seven Years paffengers'. It was better marketing to advertise the human cargo as servants for the gentlemen who would be carried to and from the ship in 'Proper boats, well manned' to purchase their labour needs for the next seven years.[33]

Campbell observed that the trade became uneconomical after the revolt of the American colonies. It might be possible to land a hundred or so each in Florida or Georgia, but none in Canada. He did not say so, but the strong implication was that there was no longer a financial incentive for the private sector to be involved in transporting convicts. That, at least, seems to have been the feeling of the House of Commons Special Committee on Transportation to which he was giving evidence. The committee 'thought proper, therefore, to examine how far transportation might be practicable to other parts of the world'.[34]

The body trader's evidence suggested that there might still be some limited opportunities to send British felons to America after the War of Independence. Although Britain lost its colonies there, some assumed that transportation would continue to that part of the world. Two entrepreneurs, George Moore in England and George Salmon in Maryland, decided to resume the stalled trade to the Americas in the belief that there were good profits to be taken. The British government, eager to find a safety valve for its increasing burden of criminals, gladly pledged £500 towards the enterprise.

In October 1783 the *Swift* set sail with a cargo of convicts bound, officially at least, for Nova Scotia. This was the ship's second attempt to transport convicts to the Americas. The first voyage in August ended almost before it began in a convict mutiny based to some degree at least on the rumour that their destination was the dreaded penal settlement in West Africa, known as Cape Castle. The *Swift* had a less troubled second voyage with those of her original consignment who had not taken advantage of the opportunity to flee. But the real trouble began when she arrived in Maryland just before Christmas.

The American end of the deal, Salmon, had advised his English partner, Moore, that it would be best to claim that the *Swift* and her convicts were not bound for Baltimore but Nova Scotia. Although Salmon was convinced there was a market for convicts in his colony, he was also aware that there was considerable resistance to the idea of taking Britain's castoffs. But the plot was blown before *Swift* arrived. When she did, the Baltimore colonists were not inclined to deal. Despite this, some of the convicts were sold off with five-year indentures and for less than anticipated. But then a shipment of indentured Irish workers arrived and the labour demand faded away. The *Swift* spent a hard winter in the harbour, her remaining cargo soon sickening and plotting escape. Although the bulk of the convicts were sold, the enterprise was not a financial success. Salmon decided to quit the arrangement and wrote to Moore. But the over-optimistic English partner had already despatched another shipload of human goods.

One hundred and fifty-seven men and twenty-two women sailed aboard the *Mercury* in April 1784. Only Moore and the captain knew they were bound for Maryland and, for a second time, they wanted to keep it quiet. Once again there was a mutiny. After six days of drunkenness and bloody threats to the captain and officers, the mutineers sailed back to Torbay. Many escaped before a conveniently passing Royal Navy ship restored law and order. While the escapees were being rounded up by authorities as far afield as London, the *Mercury* was repaired and set out once again in May. She was turned away at Baltimore and forced to find another market for her cargo of condemned. But no recently independent American colony would take them and so she headed south to a fever-ridden slice of jungle known as Honduras Bay.

Established by freebooters in the early seventeenth century, Honduras Bay had long been a sink of pirates, shipwrecked sailors and fugitives under constant threat of attack by the Spanish, the remnants of the indigenous Maya, or anyone else who thought there might be something worth taking or recovering. By the time the *Mercury* arrived, desperate to land her human freight, it had at least been recognized as an official British colony and boasted an economy of sorts, based on exporting timber. The tiny settlement was in the process of reconstructing itself after an attack by Spain in 1779. The eighty-six convicts aboard the *Mercury* greatly outnumbered the white settlers. They were not wanted. With nowhere else to go, the master, sailors and convicts on the *Mercury* began a crude settlement of their own, to the increased displeasure of the men of Honduras Bay. After months of conflict between the locals and the luckless lost souls of the *Mercury* a resolution of sorts evolved. The convicts were gradually incorporated into the local labour force.[35]

In 1785 there was another attempt, again by the desperate George Moore, to transport convicts to Honduras Bay. The shipment ended up in Mosquito Shore, as another of the free-booting Honduran colonies was known. A small group was landed from the *Fair American* in the midst of another of the regular conflicts with Spain. The fate of these convicts remains unknown.

That was the effective end of British convict transportation to America.[36] Salmon and Moore lost large amounts of money and it was clear to all interested parties that Britain would need to find another place to banish its unwanted. They were many and mounting.

A makeshift plan to hold the multitudes bursting out of British gaols was conceived. Old and usually rotting ships were decommissioned and anchored in the Thames, the Medway and at Portsmouth, becoming floating prisons that quickly gained a reputation for squalor and the full range of human miseries. The 'hulks', as they were quickly dubbed, would remain in use for the remaining history of transportation. But they were not a solution to the pressing problem of where to convey the condemned. Various suggestions and schemes were considered by the government. India was the logical option, but it was feared the French would invade. Perhaps Canada? The French were a problem there as well, and now the newly liberated Americans were likely to have an interest in the vast lands to their north. Africa? Too many disasters. One in particular.

'TORE ALL TO PIECES'

The magnificently named 'Company of Merchants Trading to Africa' possessed a number of slave forts along the Gold Coast. The company preferred slaves to convicts for security reasons and also because they thought the sight of whites in chains would undermine the authority of the company over their enslaved Africans.

Desperate to establish new penal colonies after the loss of America, the British government found a clever but devious way around this problem. They simply made the convicts bound for Africa members of new army regiments to be known as the 101st and 102nd Independent Companies of Foot. An ambitious and as it turned out, murderous, regimental commander named Captain Kenneth Mackenzie, assisted by George Katenkamp, raised the more than 200 men needed to fill the ranks of these two companies. That solved the administrative issues, but there was a practical obstacle. As no army officers were willing to go to Africa, a lethal destination for both people and careers, so Mackenzie and his men were not told their destination until the last moment before departure.

Mackenzie was furious but had to obey orders. The first convict soldiers under the command of Mackenzie and Katenkamp left for Africa in June 1781. Katenkamp died before the regiments reached Cape Coast Castle. When they did settle in their quarters, the governor asked them to attack a neighbouring Dutch fortress. The attack was a spectacular disaster, revealing Mackenzie as a poor leader and, according to at least one officer, a coward.

And it went further downhill from there. At odds with his surviving officers and the governor, Mackenzie deprived his charges of supplies and clothing, resulting in illness and a growing reservoir of resentment towards him. He also pursued a disciplinary policy that was harsh even by the rough standards of the time, including floggings. There were mutinies and desertions, usually punished fearfully by imprisoning those involved in 'slave holes', tiny cells with no light and little air. Mackenzie, short of officers, unwisely placed some of the convict soldiers under the command of a convict named William Murray. Eventually, Mackenzie accused Murray of plotting a mutiny and sentenced him to death without trial. In a particularly sadistic execution, Mackenzie had Murray lashed across the muzzle of a nine-pounder cannon, forcing another convict to fire it at gunpoint. As one of those unfortunate enough to help collect the body parts observed: the dead man was 'tore all to pieces, all but his head, and his shoulders, and legs, and he had his arms on him'.[37]

Such behaviour was too much, even for the tolerated infamies of transportation. Convicted of wilful murder in 1784, Mackenzie was himself sentenced to death, but his connections gained him a pardon the following year. The companies of convicts left behind were disbanded and the ex-'soldiers' were made indentured servants to the company.

This catastrophe further curdled the reputation of Africa as a reasonable destination for transported convicts. But the idea was still firmly planted in the British popular mind. Even as preparations were well advanced for the experiment at Botany Bay, there were rumours that convicts in urban prisons were to be sent to Africa while country convicts would go to New South Wales: 'The policy of this distinction is obvious – the country convicts are supposed to be fittest for agriculture, &c.; while the villains of London are thought to be most proper to be sent to Africa.'[38]

But it was not to be. Other than a brief flirtation with the island of Cuba, the options available to an increasingly desperate British government gradually narrowed to just one.

6

THIS SOLITARY WASTE

Thieves, robbers and villains they'll send them away
To become a new people at Botany Bay

Street ballad, late 1780s[1]

Transportation to Australia began when the First Fleet of around 800 convicts and 600 naval officers, marines, sailors and administrators, some with families, sailed from England in May 1787. They landed at Botany Bay on the east coast of the continent in 1788. The bay was unsuitable for colonization, so the fleet sailed a little further north and established a penal settlement at what would become Sydney. Well over 160,000 convicts would be sent to New South Wales, Van Diemen's Land and Western Australia between 1788 and 1868. Many more were internally re-transported from other empire possessions and thousands of Aboriginal people were also banished through the 'system', as convictism was by then generally known. The human stories from this forced mass migration range from the grotesquely brutal to the redemptive, with almost infinite variations of good and bad in between. The first years of settlement saw the full catalogue of human depravity from stealing scarce food supplies to murder. Men and women convicts were hanged, relations with the local indigenous people rapidly deteriorated into a guerrilla resistance and the colonists came perilously close to starvation. All this, and much of what came later, originated in a few sheets of paper.

THE GOVERNOR'S INSTRUCTIONS

In April 1787 perhaps the world's most remarkable national foundation document was drawn up and 'Given at Our Court at St. James'. It was a set of instructions from King George III through the Privy Council to the 'well beloved Arthur Phillip Esq. Our Captain General and Governor in Chief' of 'Our Territory called New South Wales'.[2] Phillip was to lead a fleet of eleven ships carrying 'about 600 Male, and 180 Female Convicts now under sentence or order of Transportation' to a barely known destination at the other end of the earth called 'Botany Bay'. The convicts, together with their marine guards and a clutch of administrators, were firstly to secure themselves against the 'Natives' (originally 'Savages', deleted) and then 'proceed to the Cultivation of the Land, distributing the Convicts for that purpose in such manner, and under such Inspectors or Overseers and under such Regulations as may appear to You to be necessary and best calculated for procuring Supplies of Grain and Ground Provisions'. The convicts were to work the soil to produce sufficient food for themselves and their families, as well as the military and civil establishments. They were also to grow enough excess food for 'a further number of Convicts which you may expect will shortly follow you from hence'.

The framers of these directives were concerned about the imbalance between the sexes and advised that women should also be sent to the satellite settlements of Norfolk Island and elsewhere.[3] Not only that, but whenever the captains of Phillip's ships happened to land at inhabited islands, they were to 'take on board any of the women who may be disposed to accompany them to the said settlements'. The instructions sought here to head off an obvious danger with this arrangement: 'Take special care, that the Officers who may happen to be employed upon this Service, do not upon any account, exercise any compulsive measures, or make use of fallacious pretences for bringing away any of the said Woman from the places of their present Residence.'

Phillip was also ordered to secure what was effectively the east coast of Australia and adjacent islands for Britain and to generally ensure the development of a viable colony, rather than a gaol. Nowhere in this concise set of instructions is any mention made of punishment, incarceration or other penal control of the transported. Their function, and that of the many who were to follow, was simply to cultivate the land and establish a viable society based on an export economy, the most promising product at that time being flax. Trade was to operate along the already established sea links of the East India Company, as well as with China and the vast region nowadays generally referred to as South Asia. When their sentences expired, convicts, their wives and children, if any, were to be granted land for cultivation free of rent and taxes. What they grew was, for ten years, their own produce, with the exception of any timber suitable for naval use, on which the government had first rights.[4]

This foundational document focused, and hopefully resolved, the British government's attempts to find a new transportation destination after the loss of the Americas. Few British possessions had not been suggested, and some tried, but none successfully. Botany Bay, briefly reconnoitred by James Cook eighteen years earlier, was the last resort. And while what would become modern Australia was a place to send convicted felons, it was primarily a colony, intended to quickly take its place in the empire's network of trade, resource appropriation and labour supply. Felons were expected to partner, procreate and even prosper as they increasingly cultivated the vast new land and sent its resource riches back along the imperial seaways, adding value all the time. In these ways they would atone for their crimes.

On these flimsy hopes and the ten pages of hastily drafted and redrafted orders, was erected a nation. Its founding fathers, mothers, sons and daughters were predominantly felons. But, initially their punishment was not to rot inside prison walls but to somehow build a new society in which their descendants would flourish. Like many a grand colonial scheme before it, the Australian experiment began with high hopes and lofty aspirations. But it would be generations before these even began to be realized. The realities of simply surviving in the unforgiving environment spawned one of history's most brutal regimes of penance, pain and punishment. The flogging and the hanging began almost immediately.

On a Thursday morning in early February 1788, Governor Phillip called his flock of convicts and their gaolers together. He was not happy. He had tried their characters and 'was now thoroughly convinced there were many amongst them incorrigible' and that 'nothing but severity would have any effect upon them, to induce them to behave properly'. This particularly included attempts to enter the women's tents at night. Offenders would be fired on by the marines. Those who did not work would not eat and stealing the most trifling article of stock or provisions should be punished with death. Despite his 'feelings towards his fellow creatures', Phillip declared that he would not hesitate to ensure justice against wrongdoers. The governor and his officers and retinue of officials then retired for 'a cold collation under a large tent erected for that purpose to which the general officers only were invited'. The excluded convicts, soldiers and sailors did have some slight consolation. The mutton slaughtered for the meal the previous day heaved with maggots in the oppressive heat of the Australian summer.[5]

Three weeks later Thomas Barrett, forger and engraver, was the first to encounter Phillip's justice.[6] With three other convicts he had robbed the government stores of butter, peas and pork.[7] They were tried by a court of officers and three were condemned to die before sunset that same evening, 27 February.[8] Brought to the hanging tree in chains, two of the men were respited for twenty-four hours, while Barrett climbed up to the noose alone. He showed no fear until actually on the ladder, whereupon 'he turn'd very pale & seem'd very much shock'd'. But there was a hitch. Despite the careful preparations made for the First Fleet, no one had thought to appoint an official hangman. The convicts assembled to witness Phillip's justice were reluctant to oblige. But one of their number, who had apparently agreed previously to take on the job, was compelled to do his duty under threat of being shot. The condemned man 'then exhorted all of them to take warning by his unhappy fate & so la[u]nched into Eternity; the Body hung an hour & was then buried in a grave dug very near the Gallows'.[9]

Grim though this scene must have been, there was worse to come. Only two days later another four convicts were quickly condemned for stealing food and sentenced to hang later that evening. As the four men waited beneath the hanging tree with nooses around their necks, Phillip reprieved one with a flogging. Another, James Freeman, was then made an offer difficult to refuse. Freeman would be given a conditional pardon if he would agree to become the colony's public executioner. As the chief medical officer of the First Fleet, John White wrote: 'after some little pause, he reluctantly accepted',[10] and became the colony's Jack Ketch. He hanged twenty-year-old John Bennett on 2 May. In November 1789 Mary Davis became the first woman executed in the colony. She was convicted of stealing clothes and other goods from a convict house. Another nineteen executions of convicts and civilians, as well as marines, are recorded in the colony between 1788 and 1792, all presumably carried out by Freeman.

As the rough justice of the colony depleted its numbers, so did the indigenous Gadigal people. Less than a year after the First Fleet deposited its cargo of felons at Port Jackson an unidentified convict woman wrote home. She was unhappy but hoped for better times:

> I take the first opportunity that has been given us to acquaint you with our disconsolate situation in this solitary waste of the creation. Our passage, you may have heard by the first ships, was tolerably favourable; but the inconveniences since suffered for want of shelter, bedding, &c., are not to be imagined by any stranger . . . Notwithstanding all our presents, the savages still continue to do us all the injury they can, which makes the soldiers' duty very hard, and much dissatisfaction among the officers. I know not how many of our people have been killed.

Although Phillip was under instructions to deal fairly with the 'natives', it was not long before a guerrilla resistance contributed to the mounting problems of the colony. This would continue across the continent in one form or another until well into the twentieth century and would sometimes be punished through the mechanisms of transportation.

DAMNED WHORES AND FLOATING BROTHELS

Life in the colony was particularly hard for the female convicts. One unnamed woman wrote home before the end of the first grim year. She had to send the letter privately, as the military were censoring convict mail:

> As for the distresses of the women, they are past description, as they are deprived of tea and other things they were indulged in in the voyage by the seamen, and as they are all totally unprovided with clothes, those who have young children are quite wretched. Besides this, though a number of marriages have taken place, several women, who became pregnant on the voyage, and are since left by

their partners, who have returned to England, are not likely even here to form any fresh connections.[11]

The women convicts of the First Fleet's *Lady Penrhyn* went ashore at Sydney Cove on 6 February 1788. Most had seven- or fourteen-year terms and there were a few 'lifers' among them. Arthur Bowes Smythe, the surgeon aboard the former slave ship that had brought them to this wild place, thought that 'there was never a more abandon'd set of wretches collected in one place ... The greater part of them are so totally abandoned & callous'd to all sense of shame & even common decency that it frequently becomes indispensably necessary to inflict Corporal punishment upon them ...'[12]

Bowes Smythe was certainly glad to see the women leave the ship: 'we had the long wish'd for pleasure of seeing the last of them,' he wrote. The *Lady Penrhyn's* lumbering voyage from England had been tedious and troubled with illness, lack of food and indiscipline. Many of the women suffered from venereal disease as, no doubt, did many of the men, though that was rarely mentioned. Although attempts were made to keep the sexes separate, cohabitation between the all-female convicts, the crew and the soldiers quickly became commonplace. In April 1787, a month or so before they set sail for Botany Bay, five women were chained up for having relations with crewmen. During the voyage seventy-year-old Elizabeth Beckford died of 'dropsy', or oedema, her bloated corpse buried at sea. She was not the last. Jane Parkinson died after the ship left the Cape of Good Hope.

By the time the *Lady Penrhyn* finally anchored in the great body of water that would become known as Sydney Harbour, the 101 women and more than 70 male crew and marines had been cooped up on the thirty-by-eight-metre vessel, in some cases, for up to thirteen months. The women were flogged, chained, punished with thumb screws and shaven. According to Bowes Smythe, 'The Men Convicts got to them very soon after they landed, & it is beyond my abilities to give a just discription [*sic*] of the Scene of Debauchery & Riot that ensued during the night.'

That, at least, is the story that has been handed down over the years and embellished by subsequent generations.[13] But there is only one report of the event and that from someone who was on a ship in the harbour and could not possibly have seen what was happening, or not happening, ashore. In all the accounts of those who were on land at the time, none mentioned such a graphic event as convicts copulating crazily in a violent tempest. Historians have mostly concluded that there was no orgy.[14] But in the eyes of many, there should have been one, because it is an apt image for a nation founded in crime and infamy.

A Second Fleet arrived in June 1790, bringing little relief and more mouths to feed. The convicts aboard this armada of misery were in worse condition than most of the First Fleet survivors. Another unidentified convict woman wrote: 'Oh! if you had but seen the shocking sight of the poor creatures that came out in the three ships it would make your heart bleed; they were almost dead, very few could stand, and they were obliged to fling them as you would goods, and hoist them out of the ships, they were so feeble; and they died ten or twelve of a day when they first landed . . .'[15] The settlement's chaplain was unable to go below decks on one transport because the smell of death and putrefaction was so offensive.[16]

The *Lady Juliana* (*Julian*) was the first transport to carry only female convicts, over 220 of them. She arrived as part of the Second Fleet after a shockingly lengthy voyage of more than 300 days, following over seven months in port preparing to sail, more than enough time for those on board to get to know each other very well. According to the main eyewitness, many did. Steward John Nicol wrote that when the ship got to sea, 'every man on board took a wife from among the convicts, they nothing loath'. Nicol also struck up a relationship with a convict woman, as did the ship's surgeon.

Some historians have subscribed to the theory that the *Lady Juliana* was 'a floating brothel'.[17] Others point out that the women were free to make whatever relationships they chose and that there is no evidence of coercion or commerce in their arrangements.[18] Relatively few transported women had records of prostitution, despite the views of some contemporaries, most floridly expressed in Ralph Clark's misogynistic view of the Second Fleet women as 'those damned whores'. Almost all surviving records are from the point of view of respectable males who generally saw working-class women as morally degenerate because they often needed to live in de facto relationships. Not the same as prostitution, of course, but subtlety and precision were not prominent qualities of Georgian and Victorian social observations.

The Third Fleet began arriving shortly after the Second and the convict route from Britain to Australia was firmly established. There were frequently similar claims made about illicit sexual relations aboard convict ships, consensual or not. These certainly took place, though much amplified by gossip stemming from the prejudices of the time. Perceptions and misperceptions like this would continue throughout the colonial era. They became a potent element in the notion of 'the convict stain' and, despite the efforts of historians to present a more balanced view, are still strong elements of the mythology of convictism, stemming from the first landing of convicts.

Even as the colony gradually clawed its way out of immediate danger of extinction, the misery continued. So did the floggings and the hangings. There was no shortage of offences for which a convict might receive a death sentence, a scourging of up to many hundreds of lashes, or a sentence of labouring in irons on the work gangs that built the roads, bridges and buildings that formed the colony's rudimentary infrastructure. Sometimes all three punishments were inflicted. Death sentences were often transmuted to severe whippings, followed by further suffering on the 'ironed gangs'. As if all this wretchedness were not enough, there was still trouble on the ships before convicts even reached their distant prisons.

Aboard the *Speedy*, carrying a cargo of more than fifty female convicts to New South Wales in 1799–1800, Anna King kept a diary. She was outward bound with her husband, Philip Gidley King RN, travelling to eventually replace Governor Hunter. The Kings travelled in the most commodious quarters of the ship. The convicts were confined in the hold during bad weather, which was frequent, and spent long periods of the five-month voyage 'wet as drowned rats'. Despite these conditions, Anna King reported that the convicts were 'all very well, and very happy – now they are got used to it'. Several, including children, would die. One woman, Mary Butler, went mad before her death and burial off Trinidad. Five days later, Anna reported 'a great outcry amongst the ladies that they had seen Mary Butler's spirit amongst them in the night'.

Nevertheless, boredom and the burden of her ageing and gouty husband, drove Anna to her pen and notebook. She was at first sympathetic towards the women, but by Christmas had changed her mind – 'What hardened depraved creatures the greater part of them are,' she wrote, after an incident involving 'one of the boys' and a convict woman. The captain's favoured disciplinary technique was 'pumping', presumably subjecting the guilty party to a severe dousing beneath the ship's pumps and quite possibly a form of waterboarding. The convict woman had a fear of this punishment and had been heard to say she would rather jump overboard than suffer it. And she did. Quick action by the captain and crew and her voluminous skirts maintaining her afloat kept her alive – just. The doctor fully resurrected the nearly drowned woman by forcing a glass of red wine mixed with three teaspoons of ground pepper down her throat. She recovered and resolved to live a better life.

After further storms, accidents, illnesses, a fire and another death, the *Speedy* reached Port Jackson on 13 April. Anna King concluded her chronicle writing that she was 'very happy – to put my foot once more on dry land – and I hope never to take another voyage after arriving again in England – for I am quite sick of the seas'.[19]

Anna would go on to help establish the 'Female Orphan Institution' to cater for the large numbers of orphaned children in the colony. As well as the expense of maintaining boys and girls without parents, officials and some members of the public worried about the lack of stable family formation in the colony. There were any number of charitable schemes and institutions founded during the penal era to ameliorate this perceived problem. It was allied to the perception that convict women, and some free women, were morally dubious, if not seriously depraved, and unsuitable to be wives and mothers. And, in any case, there were simply not enough women in the colony to promote familial and social stability.[20] Among the male majority were some very colourful curiosities.

PRINCE OF PICKPOCKETS

The elegant figure addressing the bench of the Old Bailey in September 1790 was not a solicitor defending a client. He was the accused, pleading eloquently for his life. His name was George Barrington, known as 'the 'prince of pickpockets', a title that barely did him justice, so expansive was his criminality. Many of his deceptions and thefts depended on his manners and his mouth, and today he displayed his facility with both. The trial had proceeded to the point where the prisoner was asked if he wished to say anything. He did. A lot:

May it please your lordship, and you gentlemen of the jury, to favour me with your attention for a little time. The situation of every person who has the misfortune to stand here is extremely distressing and awkward; mine is so in a peculiar degree: if I am totally silent, it may be considered perhaps as a proof of guilt; and if I presume to offer those arguments which present themselves to my mind, in my defence, they may not perhaps be favoured with that attention which they might deserve; you by no means distrust the candour and sense of the jury; and therefore I beg leave to proceed to state the circumstances of the case as they occur to me . . .

And so, the diatribe went on for a considerable time as the great thief gave a largely irrelevant but florid review of his case and of the prosecutor. He concluded:

Gentlemen of the Jury, the thought of death may appal [*sic*] the rich and prosperous, but on the other hand the unfortunate cannot have much to fear from it, yet the tenderness of nature cannot be quite subdued by the utmost degree of human resolution, and I cannot be insensible to the woes which must be felt by an affectionate companion, and an infant offspring; and there is, besides, a principle in human nature, stronger even than the fear of death, and which can hardly fail to operate some time or other in life, I mean the desire of good fame: Under that laudable influence, gentlemen, if I am acquitted, I will quickly retire to some distant land, where my name and misfortunes will be alike unknown; where harmless manners shall shield me from the imputation of guilt, and where prejudice will not be liable to misrepresentation: and I do now assure you, gentlemen of the jury, that I feel a cheering hope, even at this awful moment, that the rest of my life will be so conducted, as to make me as much an object of esteem and applause, as I am now the unhappy object of censure and suspicion.

It was characteristic of the flamboyant Barrington that he could not resist playing to the audience in the theatre of the court. He was not on trial for larceny. Instead, it was the theft of a substantial gold pocket watch, well within the range of Barrington's many previous thefts and deceptions. The judge summed up and 'The jury instantly found him GUILTY'.

Now the judge gave vent to his feelings:

Mr. Barrington, Hitherto I have conducted myself towards you on this trial, as if I had never seen you before; but now, when nothing I can say can prejudice the Jury, I must say that you have been treated with much more favour than you deserve. This ought to have been a capital indictment, and it ought to have reached your life, and public justice very much calls for such a sacrifice; for if ever there was a man in the world that abused and prostituted great talents to the most unworthy and shameful purposes, you are that man; and you have done it against all warning, against the example of your own case, and of a thousand other cases that have occurred; and I am afraid, that now, as the punishment does not reach your life, I cannot entertain the least hope that you will in any manner reform; but that you must be a shameful spectacle at your latter end.

The illustrious Barrington, true to form, 'bowed and retired'. A few days later he was arraigned for sentence. He was to be 'transported for the term of seven years to parts beyond the seas'. The garrulous conman had to have the last word, or words:

My Lord, I had a few words to say why sentence of death should not be passed upon me; I had much to say, though I shall say but little on the occasion: Notwithstanding I have the best opinion of his Lordship's candour, and have no wish or pleasure in casting a reflection on any person whatever; but I cannot help observing that it is the strange lot of some persons through life, that with the best wishes, the best endeavours, and the best intentions, they are not able to escape the envenomed tooth of calumny; whatever they say or do is so twisted and perverted from the reality, that they will meet with censure and misfortune, where perhaps they were entitled to success and praise. The world, my Lord, has given me credit for much more abilities than I am conscious of possessing; but the world should also consider that the greatest abilities may be so obstructed by the mercenary nature of some unfeeling minds, as to tender them entirely useless to the possessor. Where was the generous and powerful man that would come forward and say, you have some abilities which might be of service to yourself and to others, but you have much to struggle with, I feel for your situation, and will place you in a condition to try the sincerity of your intentions; and as long as you act with diligence and fidelity you shall not want for countenance and protection? But, my Lord, the die is cast! I am prepared to meet the sentence of the Court with respectful resignation, and the painful lot assigned me, I hope, with becoming resolution.

Again, the prince of pickpockets bowed and retired, his course now set for New South Wales and penance for the life of crime he had led for many years.[21]

George Barrington, real name probably Waldron, from County Kildare, often managed to elude punishment for his crimes, so well did he play the role of gentleman thief among London's elite. In the 1770s he was celebrated by the press and it became a form of social cachet to be robbed by the great pickpocket. He notoriously relieved the Russian Count Orlov of a diamond-encrusted silver snuffbox, said to be worth £30,000, an unimaginable sum for most people at the time. Barrington was caught and made to return his booty, and so Orlov refused to prosecute.

But in 1777 Barrington was sent to the Woolwich hulks for three years' hard labour. His way with words earned him a pardon in less than a year. Almost immediately he was again tried for theft. At the trial he performed the first of the courtroom speeches that became his speciality, though he received another five years on the hulks. He appealed for a remission after four years and was released on condition that he went into exile. For a short time he operated in Scotland and Ireland but was apprehended again in London at the end of 1782 and charged with breaking the terms of his pardon. His usual speech claimed he was ignorant of having been exiled for life. He also argued that he was too ill to be sent back to the hulks. The silver tongue failed to convince the court of his innocence, but he was spared a return to the hulks and was sent instead to Newgate Prison to serve out his original five-year sentence. He was out again in 1784 and up to his old tricks. There were several appearances before the courts, in all of which he succeeded in escaping retribution.

Until now. Notwithstanding a high-powered legal defence and another lengthy speech, the amazing Barrington was brought to book. Neither his smooth talk, his connections nor his money could extricate him from this latest predicament. The persistent thief and refined confidence trickster was to spend seven years at hard labour in a frontier hellhole where, he allegedly lamented, the natives had no pockets for him to pick. What would the nefarious gentleman make of this change in his fortunes?

After months at sea, during which the captain ordered him ironed in extra-heavy chains, Barrington entered into the penal desperation of New South Wales. His fate, like that of most convicts, was to labour for the survival and development of the colony. Yet, little more than a year after his arrival, the pickpocket's talents and abilities saw him freed, soon to become a superintendent of the convicts he had once sweated among and, later, chief constable of the main secondary settlement of Parramatta. Governor Hunter granted him land and he purchased more, prospering as a famer and a more or less reformed character. Pardoned in 1796 and pensioned off the government service four years later, Barrington's behaviour became increasingly erratic, even for New South Wales. The prince of pickpockets was declared insane and died in 1804, ending his colourful life in an Antipodean world turned upside down, where master criminals became the keepers of convicts and the thieves of other people's property became wealthy proprietors.

Not surprisingly, Barrington's legend lived on. Like many folk heroes, he was said by some to have lived to a ripe old age. His almost certainly faked but raffish memoirs were frequently reprinted and he still featured in newspapers even a century and a half after his death. He was also, inaccurately, credited with some often-quoted lines that have passed into the folklore of transportation and convictism. At the opening of the colony's first theatre in 1796 he is supposed to have delivered this verse:

From distant climes, o'er widespread seas we come,
Though not with much éclat, or beat of drum.
True patriots all, for be it understood,
We left our country, for our country's good.[22]

Many other stories were told about him. One yarn had it that there was a party at the home of a wealthy Sydney merchant during Barrington's time in the colony. The gossip-worthy pickpocket came up as a topic during conversation. The merchant's wife and hostess of the event firmly proclaimed that she did not believe the outlandish yarns about the smooth-talking Barrington and his thieving skills. A couple of days after the party a gentleman called asking to speak with the hostess's husband. He was away, so the hostess showed off her array of expensive jewels while they waited. But the husband did not return as expected and the man said he would try again another day. As he left, the debonair visitor put his hand in his coat and drew out the hostess's gold earrings and necklace. He bowed, saying 'I think these are yours, madam. Kindly tell your husband that Mr Barrington called.'[23]

George Barrington used his considerable wiles to prosper in the strange new world of Australia. His intelligence, cultivated graces and cunning propelled him sinuously to the top of what passed for society in that time and place. By contrast, less endowed convicts sought to take advantage of the rudimentary state of authority through violence.

DEATH OR LIBERTY!

Philip Cunningham spat the defiant rallying cry of Irish rebellion at Major George Johnston on a March morning in 1804. They stood on a hill between troops of the New South Wales Corps and the ragged band of escaped convicts following Cunningham to promised freedom. The next few moments would decide the fates of two to three hundred rebels.

A journey of many years led Cunningham to this moment of reckoning. Born in County Kerry, he was a publican and stonemason in Tipperary when he joined the rolling revolt against the English known as the 1798 Rebellion. This bloody episode was the most organized, to that time, of all the insurrections that convulsed Ireland for centuries. Cunningham was an effective leader of the United Irish network, responsible for recruiting and various acts of violence against British troops and bases. He was betrayed and captured in 1799, escaping execution on a legal issue and transported for life to New South Wales, one among the roughly 400 other United Irishmen condemned to the same distant gulag.

Many of these men accompanied Cunningham on the *Anne* where, on 29 July 1800, the convicts mutinied. While the prisoners' quarters were having their regular fumigation of vinegar and gunpowder, Captain Stewart was taken. 'I was seized by the throat by a convict, vociferating death or liberty,' he later testified. About thirty convicts rushed onto the deck, tearing iron bars from the ship and a cutlass from a guard. This group was quickly overcome by the guards and Stewart managed to free himself from his captor and return to the deck. He ordered the crew to arm themselves as the *Anne*'s mate and gunner were still held by the convicts below. One convict was killed and two wounded but, in the melee, the two sailors were rescued.

Among the now-subdued convicts on deck was one of the mutiny's ringleaders. According to Stewart, Marcus Sheehy 'confessed his guilt and was, by the sentence of all the officers immediately shot, in the presence of the convicts'. Another convict was given 250 lashes – 'and thus ended this disagreeable affair', Stewart concluded.[24] He and the mate were subsequently tried by a naval court but were both honourably acquitted.

Philip Cunningham either played a small part in this desperate affair or was clever enough to melt into the ranks of the remaining convicts. The *Anne* reached her destination at Sydney Cove without further incident, but retribution awaited the surviving mutineers. They were sent straight to the most feared penal settlement of Norfolk Island. But Cunningham was fortunate. His skills as a mason were in desperate demand in the growing settlement of Sydney, where he was soon returned and then assigned to the prison farm at Castle Hill. Here, his abilities saw him rise quickly to become the overseer of government stonemasons.

But he was still a prisoner and, like most, wanted to escape. With another convict who had been with him on the *Anne*, Cunningham made a bid for freedom in October 1802. The plan was to make their way from Castle Hill to Sydney and to stow away aboard a French ship in the harbour. They only made it as far as the nearby settlement of Parramatta, where they were both apprehended. For their efforts both men received a relatively lenient one hundred lashes.

Now Cunningham seemed to settle down to his situation. By New South Wales standards he had a plum job and was able to follow his trade with minimal supervision. He used his spare time and skills to build himself a stone house. But in February 1804 news of the failed uprising in Dublin led by Robert Emmett reached New South Wales. Since the rising of 1798, many more rebels had arrived in the penal colony, fuelling fears that they might revolt against the authorities. At 7 p.m. on Sunday 4 March those fears were realized.

The rising was signalled by the firing of a house at Castle Hill. Under Cunningham's leadership, the convicts ransacked other houses for weapons. Then the newly aroused rebel gathered them together for a fiery speech. Together they would take the local settlements, arm themselves, and then march to the Hawkesbury River to be joined by others, making a convict army of over 1,000 men. The combined force would return to Castle Hill the next morning and go on to capture the government administrative centre of Parramatta. After planting a tree of liberty there, the rebels would march to Sydney and take ships back home. Little thought was given to the likelihood of government forces coming between Cunningham's rhetoric and his men's dream of freedom. The rebel leader concluded with a rallying cry of 'Now, my boys, Liberty or Death!' and the rag-tag army followed him to a nearby hill. Here, the convicts divided into raiding and recruiting parties.

By now, news of the feared rising had reached Parramatta and Sydney. Governor King declared martial law and the New South Wales Corps was turned out under Major Johnston, who marched his troops to Parramatta, arriving at the government barracks around dawn. Johnston was now joined by armed free settlers of the district, fearful of what might happen to them if the convicts triumphed. He divided his forces in two and, at the head of one party, marched rapidly to face the convicts. When he reached the hill where they had camped, the convicts had retreated towards the Hawkesbury River. The day was very hot and while the foot soldiers struggled along the road, Johnson and a trooper rode ahead. After an eighteen-kilometre ride, they finally caught up with the 250 convicts.

The convicts invited him to join them, but Johnston called out that he was already within pistol shot so it was safe for the rebel leaders to come out to him. Eventually, Philip Cunningham and another ringleader emerged from the crowd. Johnston said he did not want violence and would bring a Catholic priest to speak with the convicts. They replied with a brief statement of their terms: 'Death or Liberty, and a ship to take us home'.

Johnston's hot and weary soldiers were now beginning to arrive, including the priest. Johnston brought him up to the convict ranks and asked them to surrender.

Cunningham and his comrade appeared again and delivered a repeat of their demands unaware that their expected reinforcements had been betrayed to the authorities and would never arrive. Just then the second party of soldiers arrived, drawing the attention of the convicts to this new threat. Seizing the moment, Johnston drew a pistol concealed in his sash and pointed it at Cunningham's head, threatening to 'blow his soul to hell'. His trooper did the same with the other man and the two leaders were disarmed and escorted back to the soldiers.

Johnston now had the upper hand. 'Cut them to ribbons', he commanded, and his men opened fire. A scattered volley was returned by the convicts, but they were no match for even the notoriously unsoldierly New South Wales Corps and they soon scattered into the bush. Nine died there, three more later on. Many were wounded and captured. The soldiers pursued the fleeing rebels until nightfall and eventually rounded up most of them. Other groups of convicts were pursued by settlers and over 300 were captured or surrendered within a few days of the brief battle. Most were sent back to work with nothing but a reprimand.

But not Philip Cunningham. Exactly what happened to him is still a mystery. In one story he was killed or fatally wounded by a New South Wales Corps officer during the surrender negotiations. According to another story, he escaped but was soon captured and summarily hanged, his body gibbeted as a warning to any others who might contemplate a rising. According to the newspaper report of the affair:

> Philip Cunningham the Principal leader, who was carried among the wounded to Hawkesbury being still alive, and very properly considered by Major Johnston as a proper object to make an immediate example of, by virtue of the Martial Law that then existed, and the discretionary power given him by His Excellency, and after taking the opinion of the Officers about him, directed him to be publicly executed on the Stair case of the Public Store, which he had boasted in his march he was going to plunder.[25]

Punishment of many of the other rebels was almost as summary and swift. Ten were quickly tried, found guilty and hanged over three days, two in chains. Two were reprieved and 'Five others received Corporal Punishment; and about thirty were ordered to the different Gaol gangs until they can be otherwise disposed of.'[26] Others were flogged or sent to hard labour in the dangerous mines at Coal River, ending the hopeless rising of the Irish[27] convicts.

Cunningham is now mostly forgotten, but he led a group of Roman Catholics and Protestants who tried to take over the system in which they were trapped. The revolt had much to do with the Irish political situation, but was also a local rising against the injustice, oppression and cruelty that had already come to characterize the military–penal system of New South Wales.

THE FORTUNES OF SARAH BIRD

One of the human consequences of transportation was the way it threw individuals from different backgrounds together into the same situation. Lives became entangled through need, passion, commerce and violence. One extraordinary story traversed all these imperatives.

Sarah Bird was in her mid-twenties when she stole some handkerchiefs and other linen from her employer in Westminster. Just four foot six inches tall, with dark hair and grey eyes, she was transported for seven years, arriving in Sydney in 1796. Sarah was an enterprising young woman who traded sugar, tea, tobacco, needles and other requisites during the six-month voyage and then in the colony, where she received very high prices, as she boasted in her letter home:

> I have sold my petticoats at two guineas each and my long black cloak at ten guineas which shows that black silk sells well here; the edging that I gave 1 shilling and eight pence per yard in England I got 5 shillings for it here. I have sold all the worst of my cloaths as wearing apparel bring a good price.
>
> I bought a roll of tobacco at Rio Janeiro at 54lb weight, which cost me 20 shillings which I was cheated out of: I could have got 12 shillings a pound for it here. I likewise bought a cwt of sugar there and also many other articles. Rum sells for 1 shilling and sixpence per gallon there, and here at times 2 shillings.[28]

In the letter she also told her family that she had already purchased a house, three suckling pigs, ducks, geese, turkeys, a goat and a dog. Ever the entrepreneur, she turned part of her new home into a licensed public house. The 'Three Jolly Settlers' was the first legal pub in Australia and a woman was the licensee.

Sarah was a colonial success story, her unpromising circumstances being transformed by the opportunities offered during her voyage and within the growing settlement of New South Wales. She offered advice and encouragement to anyone who was minded to emigrate, as they were 'liable to make a fortune'. For herself, she wrote: 'I really believe with the assistance of god, by the time I have paid the forfeit, according to the laws of my country, I shall acquire a little money to return home with, which I have not the smallest doubt of, and to be a comfort to you at the latter end of your days.' Sarah told her family that she lived alone in the colony 'and did not do as the rest of the women did on the passage, which was, every one of them that could, had a husband'. But within a few years Sarah Bird did have a common-law husband,[29] and then her troubles began.

John Morris (aka John Morris Stephens) was a thief transported for seven years on the First Fleet. He was a harness-maker in his early twenties and soon in trouble after his arrival. He was flogged for stealing and made to work in the iron gang of which he had been the assistant overseer. Over the next few years Morris killed and attempted to kill several men, though he managed to avoid serious punishment for these and other crimes, apart from burning, or branding, of the hand and some gaol time.

In the upside-down society of early Sydney, things were not as they might have been elsewhere. Somehow this violent man won Sarah Bird over and by 1801 they were living together. It was not long before he convinced her, or coerced her, to leave the promising 'Three Jolly Settlers' and move to the outlying Hawkesbury River to open a new inn, with himself as publican. They lived there for several years, during which time Sarah gave birth to two daughters. The business went broke and it was not long before Morris was in trouble again. He was arrested for attempted murder and confined 'owing to his desperate character and conduct'. Early one morning he spoke to his gaoler, then, 'suddenly drawing from his sleeve a knife 7 inches in the blade several times stabbed him in the chest then rushing from the prison burst violently into the house of Sarah Bird, with whom he had for many years cohabited, then in bed, and with the same instrument made a horrible and ghastly incision across her throat from ear to ear'.[30] Sarah managed to ward off further blows, though the blade sliced through the sinews of her left arm. Her screams brought constables and neighbours, who subdued the raving Morris. He was sentenced to death, though once again reprieved, he was sent to Norfolk Island.

The rest of John Morris's days followed his established downward spiral, with frequent violence and punishment, though not as severe as that he received on Norfolk Island.

> It was confirmed that Wilson had ordered that Morris' head be shaved; on the way to the triangle, Wilson had repeatedly beaten the prisoner with a metal tipped stick until his body was welted, before the flagellator was called upon to administer 100 lashes. After the flogging, Captain Wilson directed that salt water be thrown over the lacerated prisoner, and then commenced to beat him again with his stick until Morris was double ironed using hot rivets that burnt his skin.[31]

Ill-treatment of this kind was common on Norfolk Island and elsewhere, but Wilson seems to have had a personal motive for this intimate abuse. It is possible that he was related to a man killed by Morris some years earlier. Surviving yet again, Morris was free by 1814,[32] living in Sydney and working as a saddler.

Meanwhile the fortunes of Sarah and her daughters moved in the opposite direction. In 1821 Ann Bird married into the wealthy family who ran the *Sydney Gazette* newspaper. When Ann's husband died, she inherited control of the business and became Australia's first female press proprietor. As a respectable member of one of the colony's elite families, Sarah lived well, while her dark former partner struggled to make a living and probably died in 1836. Sarah Bird never did return to England. She died in 1871, aged seventy-four. Improbably, she and John Morris had together made their diverse convict contributions to the development of New South Wales.

'I BELIEVE I AM AT THIS TIME IN A PREGNANT CONDITION'

The *Janus* left Cork in December 1819 with a cargo of 105 women, about a third of them Irish Catholics. There were twenty-six children and some passengers, including the priests Philip Connelly and John Therry. Governor Macquarie contentedly reported the safe arrival of the transport *Janus* in May 1820. Although the ship's surgeon superintendent died on the voyage, prisoners and passengers arrived in good health. But six weeks later, one of the *Janus* women, Mary Long from Lancaster, complained that she had been impregnated by Captain Mowat. Lydia Esden,[33] also of the *Janus*, with a conviction for passing forged currency, had the same complaint, though she blamed the chief mate, John Hedges.

Macquarie wasted no time assembling a bench of magistrates to investigate.[34] It turned out that few of the convict women aboard the *Janus* did not arrive pregnant, and that cohabitation between them and the crew was as frequent as it was with the officers. Witnesses were called. Some said they had seen no evidence of impropriety. But Connelly and Therry stated that there had been relationships between the sailors and the female convicts from the start of the voyage. And it was not just the sailors, the women 'were as determined to communicate with the sailors as they themselves were'. In response to a complaint from the priests, new locks had been placed on the convicts' quarters when the ship reached Rio de Janeiro. But these were deemed to be ineffective in preventing continuing intercourse.

Mowat defended himself strongly, claiming that Father Connelly was trying 'to represent as blameless all those of his own persuasion'. Attention turned to the role of the surgeon, Dr Creagh, who was also implicated in the alleged wrongdoing. A part of his role was to maintain proper relations aboard the ship, which, according to Mowat, he failed to do.

There were clearly a number of tensions aboard the *Janus* that run through the accounts given to the magistrates. But the evidence of Lydia Esden and Mary Long was convincing. Mary testified that she did the captain's washing and mending and 'When I have not been confined in the Prison during the night, I have passed my time in the Captain's Cabin. I believe I am at this time in a pregnant Condition. I charge Captain Mowat with the cause of my being in this Condition.' Lydia was even more damning, describing how she:

... passed much of my time in his (Hedges') Cabin during the voyage. The Surgeon knew of my going up and down, and of the other women, too, and did not peremptorily order us to our Prison, but only to be more Circumspect, and not to do it openly, lest the Priests should know of it; for that his living depended on his Character. He said he would have a woman in his Cabin, if it was not for the Priests.[35]

Not surprisingly, the bench concluded that we 'are of the opinion that Prostitution did prevail on board the said Ship throughout the Voyage from England to this Territory; that due exertions were not made on the part of the Captain and officers to prevent the same; and that the matter of Charge, as against the Captain and Officers of the said Ship individually in that respect, is true and well founded in fact.'

Despite this finding there seems to have been no consequences for the men involved. The *Janus* sailed away the following July to go whaling off New Zealand, with Mowat still in command. She eventually returned to England without revisiting Sydney.

Lydia Esden was a person of some means, probably due to her involvement with forgery and uttering, the legal term for putting forged money into circulation. Before leaving England, she withdrew the then substantial sum of five pounds from her account to see her through the voyage and whatever settlement in a new country might entail.[36] She later married a publican and lived a fair life with several husbands as a keeper of country pubs and wife of a policeman. Lydia had six children and survived an attempted rape. She died at Goulburn, New South Wales, in 1859, another convict pioneer.[37] What happened to Mary Long remains a mystery.

The first few decades of convictism in Australia continued many of the themes established during the previous centuries. As well as those found guilty of crimes and sentenced to penal servitude, others were capriciously cast into bondage. Women, children and 'others', particularly the Irish, were victimized. Convicts, of course, continued to provide colonial labour, markets and populations, and governments would find transportation convenient for dealing with perceived social problems and political dissent, at home and abroad. Transportation was a legal mechanism now well suited for suppressing the resistance of indigenous people. But the most chilling development was the official apparatus of coercion and control that evolved, together with its attendant brutalities. In Australia the British instituted a regime of bureaucracy, incarceration, punishment and oppression that crushed many, benefited some, and provoked others to defiance, bloody resistance and escape.

7

CRUEL TYRANNY

Then sound your golden trumpets, play on your tuneful notes,
The Cyprus brig is sailing, how proudly now she floats.
May fortune help the Noble lads, and keep them ever free
From Gags, and Cats, and Chains, and Traps, and Cruel Tyranny.

'The Cyprus Brig', 1830s[1]

Convicts found many ways to exploit their circumstances – sometimes to significant benefit for themselves and, more broadly, to the new society whose citizens they had inadvertently become. Many simply defied the system through violence, indiscipline and escape. A few of the better educated sought to assert the rights they believed were still theirs after being transported for pursuing them. In whichever of the many places of condemnation within the penal system of New South Wales, most suffered for their resistance. Those who sought to prosper often succeeded, but not without significant tribulations.

Ever present within this rough order were the Irish. Their numbers were great and their circumstances various, but a great many bore the English Protestant establishment ill will. While insurrection ended with the 'Vinegar Hill' disaster, many other modes of resistance were widely practised. This disaffection runs through the decades of convictism, right up to its final years and beyond. Convict mutinies, escapes and bushranging were not exclusively Irish activities, but those transported from Erin's green isle were well represented wherever there was friction with colonial authority. A few of these men became heroes, their real and fabled deeds celebrated in song and story, contributing to the underculture of convictism, the clandestine milieu of oath-taking, plotting conspiracy, sedition or just straightforward crime.

Some took personal stands against the system with nothing but a strong will, body and mind, even while in the service of empire.

'I HAVE BEEN CRULEY USED'

In 1820 ex-Private Michael Keane (Kain), drum and fife player late of His Majesty's 59th Regiment, landed at Sydney Cove aboard the *Seaflower*. He came from India.[2] His sentence was for life. What had he done to deserve spending the rest of his life as a convict?

It began when the twenty-five-year-old Irishman enlisted in the British Army in 1805. He fell in with bad companions and was soon being regularly flogged for staying out of barracks, petty thievery and insubordination. For his first punishment 'I received seventy-five lashess on the britche'. The next time he was given one hundred lashes, again on the buttocks. In 1807, after getting drunk one night, he was struck by the drum-major and hit him back with a fire poker. Sentenced to 300 lashes he seems to have been lucky to endure only 'one hundered and fifty on the bak and britch'.

Michael Keane then lived a harsh life as a soldier in constant trouble with his comrades and officers. While still in Ireland he was court martialled for being absent from his guard post, receiving 175 lashes, though originally sentenced to 300 lashes. He sailed with his regiment to the West Indies where he fought the French in Martinique: 'I underwent a good dail of hardship there for three months in the field, three days and nights without eating any thing only the duice of sugear cane.' After stealing rum, flour and beef from a native, Keane was tied to a tree and given 250 lashes. A few hours later he was in battle and was wounded in the knee.

In 1810 Keane again fought the French and Dutch on Guadalupe and other islands. Accused of drunkenness by a sergeant, Keane was flayed with 400 lashes. He was wounded twice in engagements and eventually went into hospital at Guadalupe in 1811. Caught outside the hospital grounds without a pass, Keane was sentenced to a mammoth flogging of 900 strokes, though he received a mere 700. In 1813 a dispute led to Keane striking a sergeant with a bayonet and abusing the sergeant-major. A court martial awarded him 800 stripes, of which he bore 700.

But despite his record, by 1814 the well-whipped soldier had been promoted to sergeant and drum-major himself, though the elevation did not alter his habits. After a boozy day and night at a Guadalupe tavern he stole a ring from a native woman and was again court martialled. Reduced to the ranks, Keane only received a light 300 cuts this time. There were another 200 lashes for drunkenness and abusing a sergeant and then, in 1815 Keane was discharged and returned to England. But without the means to support himself he soon re-enlisted in a regiment bound for Bengal. It did not take long for the old pattern to reappear. On the voyage to India he was, as he usually claimed, wrongfully accused of drunkenness and threats then sentenced to 300 lashes, receiving 225.

After months of fighting, Keane took to 'desarting' – again and again. On the first three occasions he suffered 900 lashes. The fourth time he was thrown into solitary confinement for ninety-three days with no pay. Then he deserted once more but was recognized in Calcutta, arrested and court martialled. Perhaps exasperated with their battle-hardened but recalcitrant soldier, the army sentenced him to transportation and he was 'sent to this countary for life'. He landed in Sydney in May 1820 'wheare the mother of misfortuane kep close to me, and still remains a companion of mine'. He received fifty lashes for stopping out of barracks and, after refusing to submit to the authority and corrupt perquisites of an overseer, spent fourteen days in solitary. When he got out he 'went to wheare I had my cloths and I came to the Dog and Duck on the Brickfield Hill where I remained drinking until six o'clock in the evening and then came to the Barracks'. Keane went to work the next day but was soon arrested and tried for stealing and sent to the Newcastle area for two years, ending up in a lime-burning gang:

> . . . and then I begone my hardship at that place. I never dun any work in my
> life before, I did not no how to get on, I was sick and I was sent to the Hospital,
> and the place the Dacter put me was in the dead house, wheare I remaind for
> five days upon halfe pound a bread and one pint of grual a day. I was almost
> dead in this place for the two years that I was at Newcastle I underwent a grate
> dail of hardship – through starvation neakedness and solitary confinement

sometimes on the bar for 7 days and some times in the cells for 14 and 21 days at a time without any kind of covering only on the coald flagg stone withaut any kind of clothing.

While he was at Newcastle, convict Keane 'received one thausand faure hundererd and 75 lashess, and one hundered and 23 days in the cells upon a pound a bread a day . . .' Then it was back to Sydney and then to 'joyne a gang up the country'. True to his character, he was soon in trouble again and was sentenced to Port Macquarie where, after two years, he was brought 'all most to deaths door through flogging and starvation'. During this time 'I recavid one thausand 5 hundred and 25 lashess, and 28 days in the cells on bread and water.'

Transferred back to Sydney once again, the thoroughly flogged offender's drunkenness earned him four painful days on the treadmill. Then, wrongly accused again of theft, he was sent to the iron gang to work in chains for three months. But here 'I could not stop through the tyranny of the overseer and half starved'. He absconded and received fourteen days on the treadmill after recapture.

Michael Keane summed up his defiant life of soldiering, petty crime, drunkenness and flogging:

> I have been cruley used in this countary, through tyrints of overseers and constobles that was at Newcastle and Port Macquarie that I was under; and now for life in the countary, after been 15 years in the army, foure time wounded in the field of Battle, and now poor and miserable and despised by every one above me. The corproal punshment that I recavid sence the 5th June, 1805 untill the 26th September 1826, is sevean thousand two hundered and fifty lashess, and three hundered and foure days in the solitary cells between the army and been a prisoner.

The extraordinary suffering of this man did not destroy him. His health was broken but not his spirit or his identity. This 'Botany Bay hero', as he wryly called himself, finished his life story with the clear affirmation that 'I still remain, the same Michael Keane, Altho' not so well in health and strenth, as I would wish to have beane.'[3]

Horrific though Michael Keane's many punishments were, they differed only in magnitude from the experiences of many condemned to New South Wales. Another convict, anonymous but educated, wrote of his experiences after arriving in New South Wales in 1827. He had been assigned up country to a master who was difficult to please and set to work for which he had no experience or skills. He learned to hew wood, burn off the bush, shear sheep and later became a servant, a less laborious occupation. The writer speaks of lack of food and the harsh physical conditions of bondage. 'Tea, sugar and tobacco are called indulgences, and rest with the discretion of the master, who seldom forgets to use his power like a giant.'

He claims that 'the slightest offence provokes flogging'. He sees men sent to the iron gang to labour, 'half famished'. Others are bound up and given fifty or seventy-five lashes. The settlers lash and torture their 'slaves' for insolence and 'it is useless to murmur, for complaint is crime in this dreadful spot'. The masters are 'petty kings' and exercise their power in 'truly diabolical' ways. 'We all feel a tenfold degradation here: we feel that we are slaves to paltry tyrants who seem as if they were born to add to the stings and tortures of a wretched criminal.'[4]

The perception of convicts as slaves was not restricted to those suffering the system but was also in the minds of those who kept them there. In company with the lieutenant-governor of Van Diemen's Land, the Quaker missionary James Backhouse visited the penitentiary in February 1832. The lieutenant-governor spoke to several newly arrived convicts: '. . . he alluded to the degraded state into which they had brought themselves by their crimes; this he justly compared to a state of slavery . . .'[5] Little surprise that convicts made desperate bids for freedom from Van Diemen's Land.

SONS OF FREEDOM

The stench from the ship was 'unbearable'. But the samurai disguised as a fisherman had no choice but to board the strange vessel that appeared near Mugi on Shikoku Island in January 1830. Japan was closed to foreign shipping and the local authorities were anxious to know what had just arrived on their shores.

The secret samurai took careful note of what he saw and heard. The ship was crewed by a rag-tag bunch of foreigners with long noses, strange gaudy clothing and a small object they stuck in their mouths, lit and inhaled. They had a dog that the samurai thought did not look like food and were clearly in some distress, pleading for water and firewood, though not food.[6] An alcoholic drink was offered, though the samurai declined and went back to report to his commander. After considerable discussion, the Japanese decided that the men on the strange ship were pirates and should be destroyed.

In fact, the men were escaped convicts. They had mutinied aboard the brig *Cyprus* in Recherche Bay, Van Diemen's Land, five months earlier. The overcrowded brig was carrying around thirty ironed prisoners to the dreaded Macquarie Harbour penal station, but they became storm-bound for a week during which the convicts plotted a mutiny. Four were able to seize the ship. They unchained their fellow transports and then sent ashore any who did not want to join them, along with the soldiers, sailors and civilian passengers. Forty-four were cast away on the beach and later rescued through the bravery of one of the convicts marooned with them. One of them was a convict named William Pobjoy, who had deserted the mutineers in favour of the castaways. He would play a crucial role near the end of an epic tale.

The eighteen convicts still aboard the *Cyprus* sailed boldly into the Pacific Ocean for a life of piracy and plunder. Their only experienced sailor was a man who named himself after a free-flying bird, William Swallow. His real name was William Walker, though he had a long list of other criminal aliases and a colourful record. Born in 1792, Walker was transported for stealing, arriving in Van Diemen's Land in 1829. The records describe him as nearing five foot nine inches in height, with brown hair, blue eyes and a small scar across his nose and chin. He was married with three children.[7] He escaped back to England, where he was eventually recaptured and tried under an alias, escaping a likely death sentence for returning from transportation. Back in Van Diemen's Land, he again attempted to escape, for which crime he was being sent to Macquarie Harbour aboard the *Cyprus*.

Now William Swallow and his companions were praying for the Japanese to stop firing on their bedraggled vessel. They had been given a few days to leave but a lack of wind prevented their departure. This delay gave the Japanese time to confirm that the ship was British, and so a legitimate target. Their warning 'hail of cannon and musketoon balls' became a fusillade of cannon balls aimed at the waterline. Two smashed into the ship. There was nothing for William Swallow and the other convicts to do but pray. Their prayers were answered when the Japanese decided to help them out with some advice about the weather and winds, allowing them to set sail and drift away to sea. After dusk the Japanese heard the strains of 'a strange pipe and singing' from the *Cyprus* as it floated away to China.[8]

Without much experience as navigators they managed to reach China, losing only one man overboard. Three more departed the crew and in February 1830 the remaining mutineers scuttled the *Cyprus* and took to the ship's boat with the aim of pretending they were shipwrecked sailors. The authorities in Canton believed their lies and the convicts scattered. Some headed for America never to be heard from again, but Swallow and three others sailed for England.

While they were in transit, news of the mutiny on the *Cyprus* reached Canton and one of the convicts who had remained there confessed to the crime. A fast ship carried the news to England and when Swallow and his accomplices arrived there six days later the authorities were waiting. Swallow managed to escape but was recaptured. Not only did he tell convincing lies about how the other fugitives had forced him to sail the *Cyprus*, but Pobjoy was now in London and prepared to testify against them. Two of Swallow's accomplices were hanged but he escaped the noose by convincing the court that he had acted under intimidation and navigated the ship to save himself. He was found not guilty of piracy and sentenced to serve out the remainder of his sentence. For the third time he sailed to Van Diemen's Land and arrived at the destination of his original voyage – two years late. He died in 1834 at another notorious prison a few years after returning to penal servitude. William Walker alias, among other names, William Swallow, was laid to rest in an unmarked grave on the Isle of the Dead, the Port Arthur cemetery.

The sensational story of the mutiny and subsequent voyage of the *Cyprus* inspired a defiant ballad that vividly put across the prisoner's point of view and added another item to the clandestine traditions of convict underculture:

Come all you sons of Freedom, a chorus join with me,
I'll sing a song of heroes, and glorious liberty.
Some lads condemned from England sail'd to Van Diemen's Shore,
Their Country, friends and parents, perhaps never to see more.

Unlike the official view of the escape, the convicts knew Bill Swallow and his runaway mates had indeed made it to Japan:

> . . . For Navigating smartly Bill Swallow was the man,
> Who laid a course out neatly to take us to Japan.

These triumphant verses of convict revenge concluded:

> Then sound your golden trumpets, play on your tuneful notes,
> The Cyprus brig is sailing, how proudly now she floats.
> May fortune help the Noble lads, and keep them ever free
> From Gags, and Cats, and Chains, and Traps, and Cruel Tyranny.[9]

Even as late as the 1960s an elderly Tasmanian could sing a version of this ballad to a visiting folklorist and it can still occasionally be heard today performed by revival folk singers. It was one of many similar ballads in the underground repertoire of convicts.

HEROES AND VILLAINS

'If you stir an inch I will blow your brains out.' With this command, Sergeant of Police Moore arrested a most wanted bushranger at the Traveller's Inn on the Parramatta River on 30 May 1832. The notorious John Troy and his accomplices had been drinking at the inn for several hours, long enough for the publican to have a message smuggled to the police. The startled Troy was pinioned by a law-abiding drinker as he yelled a warning to his mates in another room. They fled and he went quietly into handcuffs.[10] It was a great day for the authorities but a dark one for the resistant underground of felonry.

Johnny Troy's history and curious transnational afterlife[11] began when he was transported from Dublin aboard the *Asia* in 1825. An eighteen-year-old weaver with faded blue eyes and light brown hair, Troy was 'boated' for seven years after being found guilty of burglary and robbery. Transportation had no reforming effect on the young man, and he was soon in trouble again, serving two years on the *Phoenix* hulk for robbery. This was followed by four or five years of continual defiance and retribution. Troy became a 'bolter', a convict who escaped from road gangs and took to the wilderness to lead the life, commit the crimes and suffer the death of the bushranger.

In 1829 Troy was re-transported to the cruelties of Moreton Bay, arriving in the middle of a cholera outbreak. Disease was the least of the dangers faced by prisoners. Overseers murdered fellow prisoners with impunity, some starved to death, and many were flogged mercilessly. Even the sick were not safe. The most notorious commandant at the penal settlement, Captain Logan, was said to have once had all the cripples in the hospital flogged, some in crutches, merely at his whim.[12]

Troy survived Moreton Bay and returned to Sydney in late 1831. He soon absconded to swell the ranks of the many escaped convicts ranging the bush around the outskirts of the settlement. These armed gangs robbed travellers of money, food, clothing and anything else they fancied. If they had a grudge against any unfortunate, they gave them a thrashing as well, or worse. Troy was captured in 1832 but acquitted, immediately resuming his criminal activities until he was betrayed and arrested by Sergeant Moore.

Tried with two accomplices, a procession of prosecution witnesses ensured a swift guilty verdict against the bushrangers. They were sentenced to death, but one was later reprieved. On 18 August 1832 Troy and his accomplice walked up the stairs of the scaffold erected in Sydney Gaol. Troy addressed the large crowd of spectators, saying that he had 'committed many offences and deserved to suffer death; and he would rather now resign himself to that fate, as the will of God, than go for life to a penal settlement'. After some further religious exhortations from the Catholic clergy present, 'The executioners were some time adjusting the ropes, in their usual bungling manner, which being ended, the fatal bolt was withdrawn, and the wretched culprits, after some convulsive struggling, were ushered into eternity.'[13]

The standard method of disposing of executed bushrangers was to box them in a cheap coffin and send them to the cemetery in a 'Public Nuisance' cart, usually employed in collecting decaying refuse from the streets. But Johnny Troy's mortal remains, along with those of the man executed with him, Michael Smith, suffered no such indignity. Friends of the bushrangers took the bodies for an Irish wake and provided decent coffins. Later, no doubt fuelled by the alcohol traditionally consumed at such events, the mourners laid the bushrangers' bodies outside the house of a man named Donohoe who had informed against Smith. The red hand-kerchief Smith and Troy apparently held between them as they died was thrown at the man's door, a menacing gesture strongly hinting at future vengeance. Matters soon became clamorous and 'The police were obliged to interfere, and the mob, after giving Donohoe three groans, proceeded peaceably to the church yard, where the bodies were consigned to the grave.'[14] A large crowd of convicts and some free settlers followed the coffins to their final resting place.

Sustained though Troy's escapes and crimes were, they could have been matched by any number of other turbulent convict bolters. What inspired his elevation to folk hero is unclear, but he was highly regarded by his contemporaries and by those who came after him. In the annals of convictism, Johnny Troy's name appears in a poem by the humorously defiant Francis MacNamara, and in several ballads. It is the name of a hero. To convicts, this man's exploits were worthy of celebration and remembrance. MacNamara's most sustained and biting work is a satire known as 'The Convict's Tour to Hell' in which Frank dreams he has died and travels to the lower regions. Here in Hell he finds all the floggers, tyrants and other convict *bêtes noires* suffering eternal torment. The convict is told that he does not belong with these tortured souls suffering for their earthly deeds, but in heaven. When Frank reaches the gates of heaven and asks for entrance, Saint Peter questions him: 'Pray, who in heaven do you know?' Frank replies with the names of some noted bushrangers:

Well, I know brave Donohue,
Young Troy, and Jenkins too,
And many others whom floggers mangled,
And lastly by Jack Ketch were strangled . . .

St Peter immediately asks Jesus to 'Let him in/For he is thoroughly purged from sin.'[15]

But in spite of this peer adulation, Troy disappeared from Australian history and memory altogether, only to turn up, even more enigmatically, in a folk song circu-lating in nineteenth-century America. Unknown in Australia, where it nevertheless originated, this ballad catalogues the bushranger's real and imagined deeds and insists on his worthiness:

> Come all ye daring bushrangers and outlaws of the land,
> Who scorn to live in slavery or wear the convict's brand,
> I'll tell to you the story of the most heroic boy:
> All the country knew him by the name of Johnny Troy.

In the manner of Robin Hoods around the world, Troy refuses to rob a needy old man and even gives him fifty pounds to 'help you on your way'. In some versions of the ballad he is explicitly a friend of the dispossessed:

> The poor I'll serve both night and day, the rich I will annoy;
> The people round know me right well, they call me Johnny Troy.[16]

In its stereotypical contours the story of this convict bushranger and his transnational legend is a small insight into the convict *mentalité*. Its heroes are those who resist, their crimes seen as acts of defiance and justifiable revenge against the iniquities of the system and its tyrannical rulers.

The forcing together of so many people into a one-size-fits-all crucible of brutalization and misery brewed a distinctive, frequently oppositional and always potentially subversive culture. The transported came from diverse social, regional and economic backgrounds, forming many different constituencies within their shared constraints and concerns. The poor – generally defined at the time as the indigent, the idle and the unsavoury – were one very large group. They shaded into the various classes of more or less professional, often hereditary, criminals with a breathtaking range of dark skills and obviously difficult relationships with the keepers of law and order, as well as the keeper of prisons. Those unhappy with the politics or the economics of their situation, and prepared to do something about it, formed a smaller but significant convict constituency. The rest were made up of the unlucky, the foolish and the misguided.

Some members of these groups already belonged to closed communities and sub-cultures, whether urban underworlds, resistant and often clandestine organizations, the many constituencies of displaced disaffected rural labourers, Welsh Rebecca rioters[17] and the Irish among others. When transported together or meeting up later, old ties and shared interests were either preserved or revived. The difference, of course, was that these bonds were now constricted within a penal organization dedicated to their eradication.

The other difference was that, regardless of their backgrounds, convicts were subjected to the same processes of arrest, trial, sentence, imprisonment, transportation and directed labour upon arrival at their new abodes. There was both a diversity of origins, values, attitudes, status, education and a similarity of shared experience in the social dynamics of the convict experience. These forces collided, colluded and conflicted in a unique half-world created through and within the government-initiated and controlled 'system'.

This underground had its own language, customs, attitudes, beliefs, prejudices, and a shared body of lore, song and story, transmitted through whispers and in secretively shared manuscripts.[18] These expressions and practices were anti-authoritarian and fiercely egalitarian, their shibboleths the easily targeted floggers, commandants and random brutalizers. Because this culture was largely oral, unofficial and subversive, it was rarely visible, and so, little documented. Few traces have survived, and we can only catch the odd echo in fragments of convict verse and song and through the occasional authentic convict narratives extant. A generation after the cessation of transportation we also hear it in the bitter cadences of bushranger Ned Kelly's 'Jerilderie Letter' in which he rages against the 'tyrants' of the system that broke his convict father.[19]

Convicts were also members of the larger society and consumers of its products, including broadside ballads and related forms of street literature. Publishers in Britain catered to the public interest in transportation – its human suffering, its exotic geographic appeal and opposition to it. Their underlying function was to confirm class, racial and political structures appropriate to maintaining British, and therefore, imperial, loyalty. But their very popularity and broad working-class dissemination also made them available to lyrical reworking and ironic performance within the largely oral convict culture.[20]

Songs on other topics could also be subversive. James Porter, leader of a noted escape from Macquarie Harbour, sang 'The Grand Conversation on Napoleon' as part of the plot to steal the *Frederick*.[21] This song is notable for its pro-Napoleon sentiments and apparent criticism of British treatment of the dictator, and was still part of oral tradition into the twentieth century:[22]

It was over that wild beaten track, a friend of bold Buonaparte,
Did pace the sands and lofty rocks of St. Helena's shore.
The wind it blew a hurricane, the lightning's flash around did
     dart.

The sea gulls were shrieking and the waves around did roar;
Ah ! hush, rude winds, the stranger cried, awhile I range the
     dreary spot,

Where last a gallant hero his envied eyes did close,
But while his valued limbs do rot, his name will never be forgot,
This grand conversation on Napoleon arose.

Ah England! he cried, did you persecute that hero bold.
Much better had you slain him on the plains of Waterloo;
Napoleon he was a friend to heroes all, both young and old,
He caus'd the money for to fly wherever he did go;
When plans were ranging night and day, the bold commander
     to betray . . .[23]

The anti-authoritarian defiance came largely from the long and tragic Irish rebel tradition. But there were also the disaffections of the Scots and the Welsh, as well as a steady stream of English rick-burners, animal maimers and machine breakers.[24] These victims of enclosure and the rural distress of the post-Napoleonic War era, and before, were joined by increasingly sophisticated attempts at working-class organization in the form of pioneer unionists and the more fully formed, mass reform movement of Chartism.[25]

But resistant attitudes were not restricted to overtly rebellious Luddites, Swing rioters and Welsh Rebeccaites. The large numbers transported from professional criminal classes also had a lengthy tradition of illegal activity. This may not have had the aim of changing the political structure, but it contained individuals with little incentive to support the status quo and with, rightly or wrongly, a potent aversion to authority in any form, particularly when it forced you to sometimes fatal toil and flogged you, literally, to the bone. Criminals had an existing ethos as a necessary dimension of their calling. They also had a shared secret language, known variously as 'the flash', 'kiddy' language or, more broadly, as 'cant', a cryptolect providing a sense of shared identity and a means of keeping their secrets safe from the flagellators.[26]

Individual members of these constituencies suffered more than others, but ill treatment and harsh conditions engendered a sense of shared torment that further cohered the various groups that constituted the convict culture. This is not to suggest an underlying communal solidity of 'honour among thieves'. The readiness with which convicts betrayed and, when invited, executed each other, gives ample evidence that there was no such honour, although informing against others was one of the worst sins a convict could commit.

Of course, individuals made their own choices about their actions once in the colony. Some achieved rehabilitation, some pursued the unprecedented new opportunities available, often with spectacular success. Others simply achieved solid, more or less respectable lives. But many persisted with the familiar patterns of crime and fraternized with others like them. They would come to be known as the 'old lags', the reprobates, recidivists and hopeless cases who turned up year after year, if not more frequently, on charge sheets and flogging trees for infractions large and small. Other than their imprints in official documents, these individuals left few records of their hard times. A few managed to bequeath their vivid stories to posterity.

FLEEING HELL'S GATE

Tattooed, scarred and blind in one eye, James Porter was about twenty-three years old when he was convicted of stealing silks and furs. He was sent to Van Diemen's Land for life in 1823. By then, he had been to sea for seven or eight years, sailing mostly in South American waters, a location that would play a major role in his escape a few years later from 'Hell's Gate'. This was the name given to the treacherous narrow sea channel to Sarah Island, the penal station in the forbidding Macquarie Harbour. Designed to hold the most desperate convicts and reoffenders, floggings, hard labour in irons and solitary confinement were everyday realities as convicts felled timber for a shipbuilding industry that the government hoped to establish. Escape attempts were routine. At one point, out of around 200 convicts on the island, about half were missing, believed to have escaped. Many were never seen again.

Complementing the infernal associations of 'Hell's Gate', some convicts, presumably those with a superior education, also knew Macquarie Harbour as 'Pluto', or 'Pluto's Land', a reference to the Roman god of the underworld, or Hell. A twenty-two-year-old convict named John Thompson scribbled some lines of verse that described the conditions in a place more feared than Port Arthur:

> Before the morn has warm'd the east
> Each man must early rise
> To labour all the day like beast
> Till darkness clouds the skies.

Their labours were rowing through the dangerous waters of Macquarie Harbour, felling timber and bringing the great logs back from the bush in rafts, rain or shine, light or dark. Lack of food gnawed their stomachs:

> And thus in grief afflicted sore
> They stretch their limbs and die,
> Their wither'd flesh by birds is tore
> And scattered through the sky.

Many were flogged at the triangle:

> Three posts triangle firmly stand
> Deep stained with human gore
> A picture frame for Pluto's land

Where poor men's flesh is tore.

Where men are bound both hand and foot

Fast to the fatal wood,

From mangled flesh that's basely cut

Runs streams of British blood . . .[27]

After eleven years of this misery and despair, Sarah Island was closed. In the transition, the usual security arrangements were slackened and Porter, with a group of other prisoners, overwhelmed two soldiers left on board the just-completed brig, *Frederick*. One of the convicts could navigate and some, including Porter, could sail. With fine weather and a good wind, they sighted the South American coast after little more than six weeks at sea. They abandoned the leaking *Frederick* and posed as shipwrecked sailors, a common ploy by convicts escaping aboard stolen vessels, and were picked up by the authorities, who thought they were pirates and threatened to shoot them all.

According to Porter's account, he gave the Chileans a spirited response:

> . . . we as sailors shipwrecked and in distress expected when we made this port to be treated in a Christian like manner not as though we were dogs; is this the way you would have treated us [in] 1818 when the british [*sic*] Tars were fighting for your independence and bleeding in your cause against the old Spaniards – and if we were Pirates do you suppose we should be so weak as to cringe to your Tyranny, never (!) I also wish you to understand that if we were shot england will know of it and will be revenged – you will find us in the same mind tomorrow we are in now, and should you put your threat into execution tomorrow we will teach you Spaniards how to die.

After an unlucky identification from a British naval officer who had previously sailed with Porter, the convicts were taken back to their quarters. But one of their number was absent. They soon worked out that a persistent malcontent in their group named Cheshire had betrayed them in return for the Chileans sparing his life. The men decided to tell their captors the truth, including Cheshire during the confession, to make sure they all hanged together. The eloquent Porter was spokesman: 'I told him the whole of the circumstance, but also stated that we would rather have died than given him any satisfaction but our motive in so doing was that Cheshire should not escape but share the same fate as us.' The governor agreed and then released them, keeping Cheshire in custody for his own safety as he knew the other convicts would kill him if they had the chance. Besides, his carpentry skills were useful.

Porter and his companions integrated into the Chilean community, establishing relationships with local women and making their living using the skills they had brought to, or learned at, Macquarie Harbour. But the authorities eventually rearrested them with a view to handing them over to the British: 'I then gave up all hope of ever regaining my liberty, we had been Confined above 7 months Chained two and two like dogs.'

Porter managed to get himself separated from his manacled companion, but 'they put me on a pair of Bar irons, the Bar placed across my instep so that I could not stride or step more than 4 or 6 inches at a time'. Assisted by a woman of his acquaintance, he obtained a knife and file, eventually managing to grind through his manacles. Using the change of guards as his cover, he shook off his irons and jumped barefoot from a springing plank to the top of the twelve-foot prison wall and made off through the darkened streets of the town, across the river in a stolen canoe and into the country. He was at liberty for a few uncomfortable days until, suffering from dysentery, he was captured. There were more escape attempts, torture and death threats, and Porter reached the point where he no longer cared whether he lived or died. But he survived and was eventually taken with his companions in a British ship back to England. Their true identities as escapees revealed, Porter and his companions were transported once again to Van Diemen's Land.

On the return voyage Porter was, falsely he claimed, accused by Cheshire and another of the *Frederick* convicts of fomenting a mutiny: 'I was seized by the soldiers lashed to the gratin and a powerfull black fellow flogged me across the back, lines and every other part of the body until my head sank on my breast with exhaustion, as for the quantity of lashes I received I cannot say, for I would not give them the satisfaction to seringe [*sic* 'cringe'?] to their cruel torture, until nature gave way and I was senseless.'

Chained together with the other bleeding accused conspirators, Porter 'craved for death'. After three weeks of this treatment the surgeon had the fettered and starving men released and the truth, or at least Porter's version of it, came out. Cheshire, 'the monster in human shape', was confined below until they reached Hobart in March 1837. As the convicts were taken off the ship, Porter managed to get close to the treacherous Cheshire: 'I seized him by the throat and hurled him over my hip and would have throttled him but was prevented by the police.'

Tried in heavy irons, Porter and his accomplices were found guilty and sentenced to death. They escaped only on a legal technicality and Porter spent almost the next two and a half years ironed in Hobart Gaol. He was then sent to Norfolk Island, 'wer Tyranny and Cruelty was in its vigour'.[28] After a brief attempt at rehabilitation under the humane commandant, Captain Maconochie, Porter was later sent back to the mainland. In May 1847 he was part of a group who escaped from Newcastle on the brig *Sir John Byng*. James Porter had survived more than two decades of floggings, beatings, torture and hard labour in heavy irons during numerous extended imprisonments in Australia, England, Chile and on the high seas. Neither he nor the *Sir John Byng* were ever heard of again.[29]

THE FLOGGING TREE

Thomas Brooks, as he preferred to call himself, arrived in New South Wales for seven years in 1818. Once a handloom weaver and canal boatman, his first wife died and he took up with others less interested in work than 'swag', or money, illegally obtained. His first impressions of Sydney were relatively favourable. Determined to bow to the demands of the system in the hope of early release, he thought that the convicts he mixed with there were punished severely 'but afterwards experience opened my eyes as to what a convict's life really was'.[30]

The 'new chum' was 'eventually leased or *sold* to a settler' and, finding bush life did not suit him, attempted to escape. He was captured and sent to the penal station of Newcastle to work in the coal mines, where he wrote: 'My hardships now began'. Also known as Coal River, Newcastle was a feared place of punishment where 'I had hard work, was badly fed, and the free use of the lash at this place was a standing caution to be careful how I conducted myself.' Brooks escaped, hoping to reach Sydney and get aboard a ship bound for England. He was taken after only two days and sent back to Newcastle for his punishment. Seventy-five lashes with the 'cat', a nine-thonged whip that exponentially increased the amount of pain inflicted on its victims:

> They tied me up – having bared my back, and the cruel whip descended. The first blow made me feel sick in stomach and heart. I resolved not to betray my feelings. Again and again the nine thongs came twisting and gloating with my flesh; and as the instrument of torture was made to do duty continuously, I felt the blood running down my back, and there was this query in my thoughts, 'of what use is life?'

He was then sent to Port Macquarie, another penal settlement with an even worse reputation than Newcastle. Brooks toiled here without incident for two years, but then 'another of the longing fits came on for home' and he absconded. Caught after a few days in the bush, he was given one hundred lashes and made to work wearing extra-heavy leg irons. Uncowed, Brooks took part in a group escape, but this too ended badly. He was then sentenced to death. However, in one of the few instances of good luck in the life of Thomas Brooks, the newly arrived governor granted reprieves to all those awaiting hanging. But even this piece of good fortune led to more suffering. He was sent to a new penal settlement at Moreton Bay, near modern-day Brisbane.

Together with other convicts, Brooks was ironed with 16-pound chains and made to clear the bush. One of the men with him, named Macarthy, was ill and unable to work. But the overseer said he was malingering. He received a hundred lashes the next morning and was sent back to work. Unable to do so, he was given another hundred lashes the next morning and again told to work. He could not and was again taken to be flogged on the third morning – 'they gave him, while he shrieked for mercy, another hundred, making three hundred in three days . . . they fleyed his back till it was one mass of wounds. His spirit was broken. Life was despised.' Somehow, Macarthy later managed to slip his shackles and escape into the bush. He was never heard of again.

The lesson was not lost on the now hardened lifer: 'This little incident taught me I had come to a spot where they were not very particular how they kept the spirits in subjection, and I hoped by hard work and attention yet to be extricated from my misery.' Brooks managed to keep a low profile, even as others suffered all around him. He saw one of his companions flogged, then left tied to a fence, his raw bleeding back further tormented by the biting of fierce mosquitoes. Others were viciously and capriciously flogged for trivial offences. After a few months, Brooks and another convict decided they had suffered enough and attempted to escape. They were recaptured and given one hundred lashes each. Brooks had the weight of his leg irons increased to twenty-four pounds but managed to work on as a bullock driver.

He suffered another hundred lashes on a trumped-up accusation of escaping. 'The fire used to flash from my eyes while I was taking the floggings, and it seemed as if the very hell of agony had fastened on me. A boiling sensation of pain, as if I was being scorched with a red hot iron was the sensation towards the close . . .' He became known as a 'brick', a convict who would not submit to the system, no matter how often he was flogged. His back was cut to ribbons and he was in constant pain as men were cruelly abused and murdered all around him. Sometimes the convicts murdered themselves:

Working one day on the line of road which was then being constructed, there was a prisoner named Tom Allen, and a Scotch boy by his side. I call the last named a boy, as he was so young, though he had apparently grown up. I give the scene exactly as it occurred.

'I am tired of my life,' said Tom Allen.

'So am I,' answered the boy.

'I will kill you, if you like,' responded Tom, 'then they will hang me, and there will be an end to both of us.'

'Do so,' spoke the boy.

Tom raised the pick he was using, struck the boy on the head, from the effects of which blow he fell. Tom drew the pick from the head of the boy, placed his foot upon the head, and dealt another blow – the boy's life was gone. As Tom finished his bloody deed, he exclaimed, 'So, we are now both dead men.'

Tom Allen was taken to Sydney. After the formulas of the law had been observed, as much as they used to be in those days, he was hanged. He sought to lose his life, and they rewarded him in the way he wished.

Brooks and eight others tried a mass breakout next. With old knives they hacked through the rivets on their manacles, the only weak point on the irons. With the same tools they cut the bars on the dormitory window and began to pass through. But the alarm was given and they were caught: 'The usual 100 were given to all who had been concerned in this futile attempt.' The weight of their irons was increased once again and they were sent to work on the gaol-gang.

With another man, known only as Charley, Brooks attempted liberty once again. With a better plan and some supplies, they made good time through the bush until they needed to swim across a stretch of sea water. Brooks could not swim. Charley struck out for the other shore but when Brooks tried to cross he lost most of his supplies and cooking equipment. After three days he was nearing death when a group of Aborigines helped him recover his cooking utensils and knife, in return for the axe he was also carrying. They took him to a place where he could safely cross the water and he lived off the land, again with the assistance of Aboriginal people, making his way towards Sydney and freedom.

A few days later he came across Charley, weak, ill and dying of hunger. Brooks tended his unfaithful companion for nine days until the patient was able to move. They struggled through the bush, with Brooks helping Charley ford creeks and forage for food. They made it to Port Macquarie, where Brooks had friends who would shelter the fugitives. They were greeted and made comfortable. They told their story and relaxed in the security of fellow convicts. For a day and a night. Then the authorities arrived – 'our *friends* had sold us – to gain favour with the officials.' Brooks and Charley were taken to Sydney where they received 150 lashes each, which Brooks considered a 'blessing'. Charley went to Norfolk Island and Brooks was returned to Moreton Bay.

His next bid for freedom was a solo effort. From what he had learned through previous failures, Brooks succeeded in reaching Sydney after seven weeks. He was there for three months, beginning to arrange passage on a ship. But then he was recognized and taken. For some reason, 'they only gave me one hundred lashes' and although 'That fiendish "cat" did duty once more, and my poor backed [*sic*] was bared to the bones', he considered himself fortunate once again and did as he was told for the next nine months.

But then the desire for 'home' overtook him again and he made his last escape. He fell in with a group of soldiers, who arrested him. He was sentenced to 300 lashes, one hundred each morning for three successive days. 'The first hundred I took very comfortably,' he recalled, but the second hundred 'made me like a madman', though he did not cry out. On the third morning they tied him up again:

> My back and sides, my every part, were gnawn by excruciating agony, the bones being [*sic*] bared, and the old wounds of the previous mornings gaping ghastly, and giving forth a bloody gore. They flogged on – fifty had been counted – my tongue was swollen, and I gnawed a leaden button with such symptoms of madness in my soul, though the sharp sensation of wringing pain had ceased, that if I had not had some hard substance in my mouth I should have bitten my tongue in twain.

After another seventy strokes he lost count and passed out until he heard the count of eighty-five. Still he had not screamed:

> . . . then I heard the word 'cast him off', and the voice of him who had said thus greeted me with 'you b- you will not holloa', and he spit on the ground savagely.
>
> 'Have I had my punishment sir?'
>
> 'No – you are fifteen short.'
>
> 'Then please give them to me now. I don't want them hanging over my head. I shall be sure to get them at some time.'
>
> 'Take him away,' said the same voice.

As Brooks recovered in the hospital, 'all idea of escape seemed to go out of my mind. I did give it up. I own I was beaten; and if I had not been "a tough customer" I could not have kept up the desire and the attempts so long.'

The system had broken yet another man. Brooks now toiled without incident for three years until a humane commandant, Captain Fynes, ordered his shackles struck off: 'God bless Captain Fines [*sic*]. I walked from his presence without the everlasting clanking of the irons, which had not only galled my legs, but planted wormwood in my soul.' Brooks soon received his ticket-of-leave, allowing him to work for himself. He accumulated some money and attempted to have his brother brought to Australia. But the man was too old for the hard voyage. Without family, Brooks served another five years on a ticket-of-leave until he received his 'final freedom'. Emancipated at last, Thomas Brooks had been a convict for twenty-seven years.

'Old Tom the Lifer' as he called himself', now worked hard and did well. He drank well also and counted himself fortunate to have survived the brutalities and oppressions of the system. But freedom brought its troubles, too. Saved from an Aboriginal attack by an indigenous woman named Susey, he spent the last years of his lost life with her. 'Susey cooks and washes – has gone with me one hundred miles up the country, and ever proved faithful. She likes a glass of grog, and so do I; but we jog along very comfortably together, and if we quarrel, why, like sensible people, we try to make it up as soon as possible.' Thomas Brooks was content with his limited lot:

All these past six years my life has not much varied. A bark [h]umpie, tea and damper, 21 fresh or salt meat, as the occasion may be, and a quiet pipe while Susey looks on, is about the height of my enjoyment. I have no rent to pay – no taxes to injure me, plenty of wood to burn, and good water to drink. Mine is not one of the most enviable positions in the world, but I tell you what, if you had suffered twenty-one years as a slave, and six years as a ticket-of-leave man, had been obliged to live on 'hominy' for months as I have, and had your back torn with those hellish thongs until you felt as if your life was departing, I guess the contrast would take a favourable side for my picture . . .

Reminiscing in his seventies, Old Tom compared the convict's lot with that of black slaves. He pointed to the contradiction in a society that outlawed chattel slavery yet could devise and perpetuate the convict system that he and tens of thousands more had suffered: 'For our slavery there was no balm. Those who believed in the freedom of men had cast us out; and those who were incapable of reflection must have seen the impassable gulph between the stains of our bondage and the free position of honest liberty.'

And he told the emblematic story of the flogging tree: 'I knew that old tree in the Valley, which was burned a few weeks back, when it had its seasons of spring-tide and autumn. It did not die a natural death. It's [*sic*] life was whipped out of it.' He recalled the screams of 'men enduring mortal agony' as men were tortured in the early mornings, sometimes with a crowd of other convicts, 'so that they might learn how tremendous that power was which held their liberty'. The flagellators 'flogged that tree to death. It was of noble growth, and its trunk was so large, that when an offender was made a "spread eagle" of, his body did not cover it. The lashes went against the bark of the tree, reaching over the bared backs, until the bark was entirely whipped away; and then it died. They flogged at that tree long after its life had departed.'

Many locals knew the tree and its grim history and it was a well-known waymarker. Brooks had mixed feelings: 'Were it not that the remembrance of sad cruelty practised were better obliterated, I could have wished the old tree had been spared, with its thousands of indentations, worn by the whip, in flogging human beings.'

At the end, Tom the Lifer frankly declared he had been well and truly punished for his dishonesties: 'I have not endeavoured, by lying, to make myself other than I am, but whomsoever shall read these lines, and trace the avenging hand of justice for dishonesty, will acknowledge that I have suffered enough for my misdeeds.' Like many other transports, Thomas Brooks raged against the brutalities of the penal system he found in New South Wales. Like many others, he was finally beaten down by that regime of oppression, yet, by his own account, endured to find a kind of redemption.

'NOT EVEN THE HAIR ON YOUR HEAD IS YOUR OWN'

Thomas Brooks reached New South Wales with no agenda other than survival. Like most, he was simply a convicted criminal. But there were those who were transported for their political actions and made to suffer for them in the colony. In April 1834 the Dorset farm labourer James Brine was confined below decks of an overcrowded ship bound for New South Wales 'with a number of the most degraded and wretched criminals'. There was fighting over the limited and poor food the grasping ship's master provided and not enough room to lie down at full length. The 'noxious state of the atmosphere, and the badness and saltness of the provisions, induced disease and suffering which it is impossible to describe'. Brine and the trade unionists being exiled with him were further tormented by 'the agonizing reflection that we had done nothing deserving this punishment, and the conscious-ness that our families, thus suddenly deprived of their protectors, and a stigma affixed to their names, would probably be thrown unpitied and friendless upon the world'. Their only comfort was that they were sailing with most of the other men sentenced to seven years' transportation for the crime of swearing an oath.

Wages for agricultural workers in southern England were dropping fast through the 1820s. The introduction of mechanical threshing machines quickly made many manual tasks obsolete. Faced with starvation, farm labourers rose in a spon-taneous and uncoordinated rebellion known as the 'Swing Riots' in August 1830. The insurrection was a serious shock to the established order and was quickly and brutally put down with many gaoled, executed or transported. In the aftermath of these disturbances the formation of a union by a group of Dorset agricultural workers was seen by the local authorities as another threat to social order. While the organization of a union was no longer illegal, the taking of secret oaths was an offence. New union members were blindfolded while they swore allegiance on the Bible. The blindfold was removed to reveal a macabre painting of a large human skeleton holding a scythe in one hand and an hourglass in the other. These clan-destine actions in and around the town of Tolpuddle were enough for the arrest and trial of brothers George and James Loveless, father and son Thomas and John Standfield, James Brine and James Hammett. All except Hammett were devout Methodists.

The voyage to Sydney took 111 days. They arrived on 17 August and were marched to Hyde Park Barracks. The unionists were soon separated, while James Brine was 'to proceed to his master'. He was assigned up country to a private farm, travelling the lengthy distance by steamboat and on foot. He was robbed along the way by bushrangers and arrived exhausted at the farm with nothing but the old clothes he wore and having eaten only one meal in three days.

Taken before the master, Brine was asked where his belongings were, but his encounter with the bushrangers was not believed. The master called him a liar and promised him a 'D–d good flogging' in the morning. '"You are one of the Dorsetshire machine-breakers," said he; "but you are caught at last."' Brine recalled: 'He gave me nothing to eat until the following day. In the morning I was employed to dig post-holes, and during the day he came and asked how I was getting on. I told him I was doing as well as I could, but was unable to do much through weakness, and that having walked so far without shoes, my feet were so cut and sore I could not put them to the spade.' The master told him to make no further complaints and that if he asked for anything over the following six months, he would be severely treated. Brine went without clothes or bedding and slept on the ground. He found a piece of iron hoop 'and wrapped it round my foot to tread upon, and for six months, until I became due'.

Brine then spent seventeen days up to his chest in water, dipping sheep. He caught a bad cold and asked his master for something to cover himself with at night, even a piece of horsecloth. 'I will give you nothing until you are due for it,' he replied. 'What would your masters in England have to cover them if you had not been sent here? I understand it was your intention to have murdered, burnt, and destroyed everything before you, and you are sent over here to be severely punished, and no mercy shall be shown you. If you ask me for anything before the six months is expired, I will flog you as often as I like.'

The master then asked Brine to explain the plans he and his comrades had for the trade union they attempted to form, in return for a possible 'ticket of indulgence'. Brine said that the union was not a violent organization. Dissatisfied with this answer, the master said, 'You d–d convict, if you persist in this obstinacy and insolence I will severely punish you! Don't you know that not even the hair on your head is your own. Go to your hut or I will kick you.' The master was the local magistrate.

Back in England the Tolpuddle men were popular heroes, but their families were suffering. Their applications for parish relief were refused because the local landowners still feared the power of organized labour. In a letter to supporters, the martyrs' wives wrote: 'Tolpuddle have for many years been noticed for tyranny and oppression and cruelty and now the union is broke up here'. Fortunately, the issue was the object of intense political agitation. Funds for the support of the families were donated.[31]

The Tolpuddle Martyrs were conditionally pardoned in 1835 and received full pardons in 1836. They returned to England where all except one continued to fight for what was then considered the radical cause of universal male suffrage, the right of every adult to vote and other significant political reforms. Eventually, still harassed, most emigrated with their families to Ontario, Canada, where they began new lives. Holding their politics as strongly as their faith, today they are remembered as heroes of the early trade union movement.

Brine and the Tolpuddle men did not belong to the criminal constituency of convictism – the intergenerational criminals' confederacies and hardened 'hulkers'. Their struggle for a better life was part of the long decline of rural England and its people following the expensive defeat of Napoleon at Waterloo, the return of soldiers to a depressed economy and labour market, and through the displacements inflicted by new technology. They were God-fearing, hard-working when they could be, generally honest and socially respectable. Their affront to the privileges of embedded wealth and power was, within the rudimentary structures available to them, political rather than criminal. Although they were not agricultural machine breakers, Luddite industrial saboteurs or Welsh Rebeccas destroying tollgates, they were part of a cohort of mostly English agrarian malcontents, transported to the Antipodes. Together with Chartists, Irish nationalists and even rebels from Canada, they formed a body of transported political prisoners equivalent to those exiled to the Americas in the seventeenth and eighteenth centuries.

WARRIORS IN CHAINS

While so many convict lives were transformed, for better or worse, through the effects of transportation, so were indigenous lives. As the colonizing intentions of the newcomers became obvious to Aboriginal groups around the country, so a guerrilla resistance developed. These were localized wars of small raiding parties harrying outlying settlers and travellers. There were various leaders at different times and places. One in particular would be probably the first indigenous Australian to be transported, though he would not be the last. Another was transported from New Zealand.

From 1805 an Aboriginal man in his twenties known to the settlers as 'Musquito' (Muskito' Muskitoe) declared, in excellent English, his intention to violently resist British incursions on his people's traditional lands north of the settlement of Sydney.[32] He was deemed to be responsible for killing a settler along the Hawkesbury River[33] and, following an arrest order, was captured by other Aboriginal people hostile to him. Along with another resister known as 'Bulldog', Musquito was transported – 'exiled' officially – to Norfolk Island for eight years. Bulldog was returned to Sydney but Musquito remained on the island, working mainly as a charcoal burner. At the end of this term he was transferred to Van Diemen's Land and set free, his skills as a tracker helping to run down the bushranger Michael Howe in 1818.

After this, Musquito took to the bush himself, disappointed in years of unhonoured promises that he would be allowed to return to his own people. He joined local indigenous groups in their struggles against the colonists. Captured by an Aboriginal boy in late 1824, the fighter was subjected to an improper trial for murder based on unsafe evidence and hanged in Hobart in February 1825.[34]

Musquito was only one of many other indigenous people transported within the Australian penal settlements, mostly for crimes related to resistance and rebellion, particularly in Western Australia. Their fates were mostly unhappy, the oppressions of the convict system sharpened by the racism of officials and non-indigenous convicts.[35] Even New Zealand, largely immune to transportation, was not averse to imposing it on the Maori people.

Te Umuroa was a resistance fighter born around the 1820s. He joined other Maori in attacks on settlers in New Zealand's Wellington district and was captured in August 1846.[36] Court martialled rather than being tried as prisoners of war, Te Umuroa and his companions pleaded guilty and were convicted of rebellion and possession of firearms. Their sentence was to be transported for life, firstly to Van Diemen's Land and then on to Norfolk Island.

In full traditional dress, Te Umuroa with five other Maori rebels landed at Hobart in November 1846. The novelty of this situation excited the local community and press. Acting Lieutenant-Governor La Trobe decided to keep the men in the colony at the Darlington probation station. Here they were housed on Maria Island together, away from the main body of prisoners and treated as celebrities, visited by the press and having their portraits painted. There was a well-founded concern that the Maori had been unfairly treated and that their military trial was not legal. After Te Umuroa died of tuberculosis in 1847 the legality of the trial was questioned by administrators in Australia and in Britain, leading to the release of the surviving Maori prisoners and their return to Auckland. Te Umuroa was buried on Darlington Island but in 1988 his remains were returned to New Zealand where he was reinterred at Roma on the Wanganui River.

Te Umuroa was among more than a hundred sailors, soldiers, bolters from the Australian penal settlements and others transported from New Zealand to Van Diemen's Land between 1843 and 1853. Around half of these were soldiers, many of whom had deserted rather than face the Maori warriors fiercely defending their land. At least one was a woman. Margaret Reardon was transported for seven years for perjuring herself in a murder trial. She left a husband behind who was later executed for murdering a military officer. Margaret later remarried and lived a respectable life to a good age in the colony of Victoria.

Other indigenous people also felt the sting of whips and the chafing of chains. For decades, Australian colonial governments regulated a trade in Pacific Islander lives and labour that remains a controversial issue to this day. Technically, many of the tens of thousands brought from numerous Pacific Islands to till the sugar fields of Queensland in accordance with the Pacific Islanders Protection Acts of 1872 and 1875 were indentured labourers. They agreed to work under contractual arrangements that would see them returned to their homes at the end of the agreed period. But so great was the demand for labour that the trade quickly became notorious for the kidnapping of islanders who were forced to work against their will, a business known as 'blackbirding'.[37] Indigenous Australians were also the targets of this trade.

Blackbirding was an amalgam of indentured labour, transportation and slavery. The first attempt to bring island workers to Australia was in the 1840s when over sixty men from Vanuatu and New Caledonia were shipped to the south coast of New South Wales. This experiment failed but set a precedent for obtaining cheap labour for the booming northern sugar industry from the 1860s. When traders could not entice enough islanders to come to Queensland under contract, they resorted to the same techniques used to supply the trade in transported convicts to Britain's New World colonies two centuries earlier.

Known colloquially as 'kanakas' or even 'sugar slaves', it is thought that around 60,000 Pacific Islanders were forced or cajoled into Australia to work mainly in the Queensland sugar-cane industry where they were often badly treated and poorly paid. The trade began in the 1860s and lasted until 1904 when those who had been indentured and their descendants were summarily deported in accordance with the Immigration Restriction Act (the 'White Australia Policy'). Several thousand islanders remained in Australia, forming the basis of their 20,000 or more descendants who now live mainly in North Queensland. On those islands where people were taken, they are still mourned.[38]

Transportation was the essential mainspring of the empire. Originally conceived as a solution to the perceived problem of Britain's indigent and dangerous unwanted, the system reached its peak of convenience and utility within the colonialism of the eighteenth and nineteenth centuries. Australia was a vital link in this chain. The island continent was ideally located for its penal and imperial roles. But it was only the most striking site of punishment in the Southern Hemisphere.

8

THE DEVIL'S ISLES

The end is considered sufficiently advantageous to justify the means.

The Straits Times, 1846[1]

The man who would one day give the world his theory of evolution reached the Indian Ocean island of Mauritius aboard the *Beagle* in 1836. Between 1814 and 1837 around 1,500 Indians, as well as political prisoners from Ceylon (Sri Lanka), were sent to Mauritius,[2] once known as the Isle de France. Charles Darwin gave a glowing report of what he saw there:

> The various races of men walking in the streets afford the most interesting spectacle in Port Louis. Convicts from India are banished here for life; at present there are about 800, and they are employed in various public works. Before seeing these people, I had no idea that the inhabitants of India were such noble-looking figures. Their skin is extremely dark, and many of the older men had large mustaches and beards of a snow-white colour; this, together with the fire of their expression, gave them quite an imposing aspect. The greater number had been banished for murder and the worst crimes; others for causes which can scarcely be considered as moral faults, such as for not obeying, from superstitious motives, the English laws.

Darwin compared these unfortunates favourably with the convicts he had recently seen in Australia. He thought that 'These men are generally quiet and well-conducted; from their outward conduct, their cleanliness and faithful observance of their strange religious rites, it was impossible to look at them with the same eyes as on our wretched convicts in New South Wales.'[3] While Darwin's romanticizing of the exotic was a common imperial affectation of the British middle and upper classes, it suggests that Mauritius was a relatively pleasant place to be serving time. If so, it was in stark contrast to other island prisons.

Islands have always been favoured locations for exile and incarceration. Their advantages for these purposes are obvious – difficulty of access and egress preventing escape. Islands are also natural panopticons, allowing total surveillance of prisoners by gaolers. Islands also engender a sense of isolation and close off, or severely restrict, the possibilities for communication with those outside the captive population. These natural and psychological features account for the large numbers of penal institutions established on usually forbidding patches of rock surrounded by sea,[4] or places approximating the same natural features. As a world maritime power, Britain had many such places at its disposal. Prisoners could be transported to them from the home country, as well as shuttled between them, depending on labour needs. The Bahamas were targeted for 'peopling immediately' in 1752 with the 'Multitude of Vagabonds that infect the Streets and Roads in and about London'.[5] In 1853 British Guiana (Guyana) began receiving convicts transported from the British West Indies colonies.[6] The East India Company shipped Indian convicts from Bombay and European convicts from Madras to Mauritius, Singapore, the 'Isle of France', Penang, Prince of Wales Island and even to New South Wales.[7] Upon some islands were built prisons noted for heinousness and brutality. Van Diemen's Land and Norfolk Island were foremost in Australia's list of infamy, though others also harboured dark realities.

UNSPEAKABLE INIQUITY

Discovered in the early sixteenth century, Bermuda or 'the Bermudas' remained a small uninhabited island archipelago in the North Atlantic for over a hundred years. Long before convicts were transported there it was known to sailors as 'the isle of devils'. In 1609 the Virginia Company ship *Sea Venture(r)*, en route to the new colony in America, was deliberately wrecked on reefs to the east of the island to save those aboard. This was effectively the start of a turbulent history in which

1. Convicts being taken from Newgate Prison to Blackfriars, from where they were transported, 1760. These prisoners were usually paraded through the streets in a group and could be subjected to abuse and assault from gawping crowds.

2. Convicts from the Medway River prison hulks (pictured in the background) labouring onshore in Kent, c. 1800. Prisoners held on the hulks were usually sent ashore during the day to labour on public or military works. Much the same pattern was followed in hulks throughout the empire, including in Gibraltar, Bermuda and Australia.

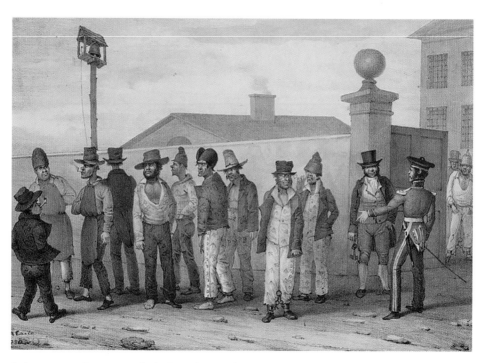

3. A convict work gang outside the barracks in Sydney. Convicts were issued a variety of uniforms, as seen here. Those marked 'PB' refer to the police barracks, delineating them as prisoners and preventing them from selling their clothing to civilians. The men wearing the broad arrow uniform are mostly manacled at the ankle.

4. Convicts washing on a very tidy hulk, 1846. Most accounts of conditions aboard the hulks emphasize overcrowding, squalor and poor treatment of prisoners. There were investigations and reported improvements; perhaps this was drawn after one such?

5. One of many broadside ballads about transportation sold throughout Britain in the seventeenth and eighteenth centuries. In one form or another, 'The London Convict Maid' and ballads like it were distributed and sung widely.

6. This satirical cartoon from 1770 shows lords, esquires and attorneys in chains, boarding ship for transport from England to Georgia. It reflects the popular fascination with transportation, as well as opposition to it.

7. 'Indian Peter' (Peter Williamson) in his version of traditional Delaware dress. Williamson sustained himself in Britain wearing this garb and telling tales of his American adventures. The proceeds allowed him to take legal action in Aberdeen seeking restitution for his childhood kidnapping to America.

8. Despite the images of gallows and hulks in the background, this is a romantic treatment of convicts leaving England for Australia. Convictism and penal Australia were popular topics in Britain throughout the transportation period.

9. Two well-dressed convicts in New Holland, 1793, depicted by a visiting Spanish artist. Unless charged with new crimes, convicts in early colonial Australia were not necessarily confined and were expected to contribute to the growth of the economy by growing their own food, or even a surplus, and sometimes establishing businesses.

10. The 'Vinegar Hill' rising, when convicts broke out of their Castle Hill quarters and marched on Sydney, 1804. Most of the rebels were Irish Catholics. Convict 'mutinies' and insurrections were a constant fear in colonial Australia and were ruthlessly suppressed when they occurred.

11. Convicts working the treadmill, probably in Sydney. With high risks of accident or death, this was one of the most dreaded punishments. This machine combined punishment with productive labour, the ideal of penal thinking at the time.

12. A flogging in Van Diemen's Land, c. 1830. Convicts might also be flogged spreadeagled around a convenient tree or on the 'triangle', a three-sided wooden frame across which the victim was stretched, increasing the severity of the punishment.

13. Convicts were mustered each month in Singapore Prison during Major J.F.A. McNair's tenure, a surveillance technique also used in New South Wales.

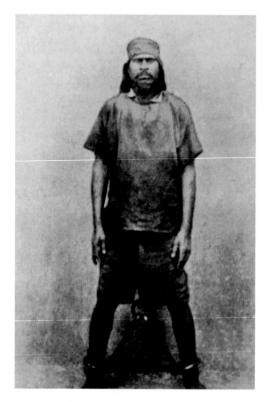

14. A heavily ironed prisoner at Singapore Prison. This unidentified man is a convict of the fifth class, 'a "punishment class" for troublesome characters'. He is also one of the 'Section A' convicts, a category for refractory prisoners who were shackled in the heaviest chains and put to hard labour.

15. Convicts working a large treadmill in Rangoon Prison during the 1890s. Treadmills large and small were deployed in penal establishments throughout the empire.

16. English children bound for a Fairbridge farm in Molong, New South Wales, 1938. Obviously posed, this image was one of many produced by migration societies depicting happy children lugging new suitcases to better lives in the empire.

17. A boy ploughing at Dr Barnardo's Industrial Farm, Russell, Manitoba, *c.* 1900. In 2010, the photo was reproduced on a Canadian postage stamp commemorating Home Children emigration.

18. Barefoot boys from the British child migration scheme working a forge at Fairbridge Farm School, Pinjarra, 1942. Perhaps their feet were fireproof?

transportation played a small but significant part. While Bermuda was never an official penal colony, its important role in empire defence strategy led to a need for labour to erect and maintain the fortifications and docks that supported colonial interests and activities.

Slaves were brought to Bermuda from the 1620s and the British government took control from the commercial Somers Isles Company in 1684. Slavery itself was not abolished until 1834 and, from 1823, had been supplemented with the labour of transported convicts. Shackled for the first two years of their sentences, these unfortunates cut limestone blocks in humid heat and spent their nights in cramped, fetid and morally abandoned conditions aboard the hulks, generally considered to be far worse than those elsewhere.[8] Bermuda's Royal Naval Dockyard was built largely by the labour of 9,000 or more British and Irish convicts, as well as a few military prisoners from Canada, transported between 1823 and 1863. Bermuda was of high strategic significance for the British naval presence in the Atlantic after the War of Independence, and the beautiful islands quickly became notorious for harsh and dangerous conditions, including outbreaks of yellow fever and accidents.

A thriving clandestine industry in forging coins operated on the hulks, supporting a variety of criminal activities and gambling, through which individuals were able to improve – or not – the abysmal conditions of their captivity. Mexican silver dollars as well as English shillings and other coinage were manufactured and distributed through criminal networks that may have included guards and officers. A local newspaper observed in 1830 that 'The coins counterfeited are Spanish Dollars and tenpennies, English half crowns and shillings. The shillings are remarkable [sic] well executed, but may be easily detected, being thicker, and of a darker colour than the good coin, they have a greasy feel, which the good have not.'[9] The considerable skills and resourcefulness needed to make, conceal and distribute such items is evidence of convict resourcefulness. These shady talents were also put to more respectable activities in the manufacture of handmade objects, including dominoes, jewellery, dice and other objects carved from locally available materials such as coral, flowstone and mother of pearl.[10]

In 1837 an epidemic of yellow fever killed a large number of convicts.[11] But the dead were soon replenished from the living prisoners of Britain and elsewhere in the empire. Bermuda was the destination for a small number of convicts transported from British North America. Eight arrived from Canada in 1838 and twenty-three came from Nova Scotia ten years later. In the 1840s one very high-profile political prisoner arrived. He would come to believe that 'The Devil is in this place'. Sentenced to fourteen years transportation for treason, together with other Young Ireland leaders, the prominent nationalist John Mitchel was held aboard one of the notorious Bermuda hulks, the *Dromedary*. By then, the place was well established within the empire of chains and would remain so for more than a decade.

Between 1847 and 1850 a committee of inquiry into conditions on the Bermuda hulks led to the eventual abandonment of the hulk system in Britain and Ireland, though it lasted for another decade in Bermuda. From one such floating prison, John Mitchel described the situation that the inquiry was trying to investigate:

> Each hulk, each mess or ward, is a normal school of unspeakable iniquity: and young boys who come out, as many surely do, not utterly desperate and incurable villains, are sure to become so very soon under such training. I hear enough to make me aware that the established etiquette among them (for there is a peculiar good breeding for hulks as for drawing rooms) is to cram as much brutal obscenity and stupid blasphemy into their common speech as it will hold – and that a man is respected and influential among his messmates in direct proportion to the atrocity of his language and behaviour.[12]

Money was in ample supply, with high-stakes gambling commonplace and convicts with trade skills able to earn well from working for the Bermudans, and by stealing, which was endemic: 'If any of them were to discover a scruple about stealing, or decline or neglect to steal when he might, I find it would be resented as an offence against the laws and usages of the commonwealth, and punished accordingly. In short, evil is their recognized good – and the most loathsome extremities of depravity in mind and body are their summum bonum.'

The well-educated political prisoner considered these places to be nurseries of vice and crime: 'Think of a boy of twelve or fourteen years, who has been driven by want or induced by example to commit a theft, and sent to school at Bermuda for half his lifetime, in order to reform him!' It enraged Mitchel even more to 'think of the crowd of starved Irish, old and young, who have taken sheep or poultry to keep their perishing families alive in the Famine, sent out to Bermuda to live in a style of comfort they never knew before even in their dreams, and to be initiated into mysteries and profound depths of corruption that their mother tongue had no name for'. He described a shipload of Irish famine victims, aged between twelve and sixty. 'They were all about three-quarters starved, and so miserably reduced by hunger and hardship, that they have been dying off very fast from dysentery.'

Mitchel wrote of 'many hundreds of poor convicts', some in chains, being marched in gangs to work the quarries: 'They walk, as I fancy, with a drooping gait and carriage. Their eyes, it is said, are greatly injured by the glare of the white rocks, and many of them grow "moon-blind," as they call it, so that they stumble over stones as they walk.' Mitchel complained that 'the clank of chains is seldom out of my ears'. Nor was the sound of the lash. Any who answered back to their gaolers, or 'gave cheek', were flogged.[13] Following another flagellation in November 1848, Mitchel documented the gory and sadistic aftermath:

The laceration is finished. The gangs are sent out to their work after being mustered to witness the example: the troops who were drawn up on the pier have marched home to their barracks: quarter-masters and guards have washed the blood-gouts from their arms and faces, and arranged their dress again: the three torn carcases have been carried down half-dead to the several hospital-rooms. Though shut up in my cell all the time, I heard the horrid screams of one man plainly. After being lashed in the Medway, they had all been carried to this ship, with blankets thrown over their bloody backs: and the first of them, after receiving a dozen blows with miserable shrieks, grew weak and swooned; the scourging stopped for about ten minutes while the surgeon used means to revive him – and then he had the remainder of his allowance. He was then carried groaning out of this ship into the Coromandel, instantly stripped again, and cross scarified with another twenty lashes. The other two men took their punishment throughout in silence – but I heard one of them shout once fiercely to the quarter-master, 'Don't cut below the mark, d--- you!'[14]

The 'mark' was the regulation area above the buttocks which floggers were not officially allowed to scourge. They frequently did.

But Mitchel also came to learn another side to the story, what he called the 'profession' of 'hulking'. Many convicts had never been so well fed or housed in their lives. The commander told Mitchel that, once they had recovered from the pleasant shock, they wrote home to 'tell their half-starved friends how well a felon is fed, what can be more natural than that famished Honesty should be tempted to put itself in the way of being sent to so plentiful a country?' The commander also claimed that he had prisoners in the hulk who had been imprisoned before and that 'it is not uncommon to find families who have hulked for three or four generations. Hulking, as a profession, is as yet confined to England – that it will become a more favourite line of business there, as the poverty of the English poor shall grow more inveterate, cannot be doubted.'

Mitchel's close contact with the system eventually enabled him to glimpse something of the convict underworld. He described a vast clandestine network of chains, stretching from Spike Island in Cork Harbour, Ireland, to Gibraltar and to Australia:

> There are now about two thousand convicts at Bermuda – about a thousand at Spike Island; how many may be at Gibraltar and Australia, not to speak of the several depots for them in England, I know not; but on the whole there is an immense and rapidly growing convict community distributed in all these earthly hells, maintained in much comfort, with everything handsome about them, at the cost of the hard-working and ill-fed, and even harder working and worse-fed people of England, Scotland, and Ireland. That there is a limit to all this, one may easily see.[15]

The Irish nationalist was inside the belly of the British empire system. He understood its brutalities, its contradictions and its rationale. Convictism was the inevitable unofficial obverse of a global imperial institution. At the top of the social order were the government, officials, penal authorities, the military, merchants, traders and armies of administrators necessary to run such an extensive enterprise and its attendant bureaucracy. At the bottom were the poor, indigent, criminal, rebellious and otherwise troublesome individuals. The upper and lower spheres depended on each other for their continued existence in a twisted chain of mutual dependency. Mitchel's middle-class status led him to conclude that 'all our robbers, burglars, and forgers' should be hanged because they were a drain on the public purse and the taxes of the honest and hard-working people 'keep up the "convict service", just as they keep up the navy and the excise men'.[16]

From 1848, Bermudan convicts began to be transferred off the island. The following year Mitchel was among almost 300 sent on the *Neptune* to the Cape colony. Most on board had accepted the British government's offer of a reduced sentence for agreeing to settle there, but the government had neglected to obtain the approval of the colonists. The *Neptune* was refused entry and after a five-month hiatus at Cape Town, eventually ended up in Tasmania. The convicts who had accepted the government's resettlement offer were given pardons, but not the traitor Mitchel. He was only granted a ticket-of-leave, allowing him a smaller degree of freedom. Nevertheless, his wife was able to join him and while he languished further, the legend of his political martyrdom grew and was celebrated, charted and to some extent created through a number of ballads of the type commonly composed for such heroes by the street press.

These ballads, and many more on the fates of other Irish nationalists, were inspired by largely commercial motives as comments on the issues of the day. But the balladeers knew their audiences. These songs were taken up and sung in Irish communities around the world, often adapted to the views and local conditions.[17] Like the broader ballads of transportation produced and circulated since the seventeenth century,[18] they came to form a vital stratum in the global underculture of Irish resistance to English and British rule. 'John Mitchel's Address' was a spirited lyric that was especially popular and was still being sung a century or more after the events it depicts:

When I received my sentence upon that holy ground,
Where numbers of my countrymen assembled all around,
I was offered my liberty if I'd forsake the cause,
I'd sooner die ten thousand deaths than forsake my Irish boys.

In 1853 the Irish politician and journalist P.J. Smyth, correspondent for the *New York Tribune*, arrived in Hobart to report for his newspaper. That, at least, was the cover story. Smyth also had a secret mission. With the support of Irish-American sympathizers, he helped Mitchel escape to Sydney and finally, to New York. When news of the patriot's getaway from Van Diemen's Land reached Britain, 'John Mitchel's Escape' told the joyful tale in six jubilant verses:

> . . . no longer a felon in chains he is bound,
>
> Amy peace and prosperity always surround
>
> That hero, John Mitchel, wherever he goes.

The freed felon went on to a tumultuous career in journalism and politics in America and Ireland, espousing abolition and often criticizing the pope. He supported the Confederacy in the Civil War but then quarrelled with Jefferson Davis and returned to New York to edit a Democratic newspaper, through which he attacked the government and was imprisoned yet again. In 1875 he was elected to the British Parliament several times as the member for Tipperary but was unable to take up his seat because he had been a convicted felon. His return to Ireland and involvement in politics generated 'John Mitchel's Return', its chorus cheekily commenting on the official refusal to recognize his legitimacy as a member of parliament:

> To the British House of Commons
>
> Don't you think it is a sin?
>
> I've been sent from Tipperary,
>
> But they won't let me in.[19]

A subsequent by-election saw Mitchel contest and win the seat, but he died before again being ruled ineligible, his seat subsequently awarded to the Conservative candidate.

Bermuda continued to be one of many troubled islands within the empire's chain of colonial possessions. It was often ranked with Norfolk Island in the annals of convict infamy, though it hardly needed any magnification of its miseries. Anthony Trollope, the famed English novelist, was a reluctant visitor in the late

1850s. At that time, around 1,000 of the 1,500 convicts then working on the island's fortifications were housed in the appalling hulks so chillingly described by John Mitchel. In a short story Trollope later wrote, he observed that 'Bermuda, as all the world knows, is a British colony at which we maintain a convict establishment. Most of our outlying convict establishments have been sent back upon our hands from our colonies, but here one is still maintained.' He described the strong military fortifications and 'some six thousand white people and some six thousand black people, eating, drinking, sleeping, and dying'. The whites were chained, while the blacks were free. There was little contact between the prisoners and the Bermudans. Escape, while not impossible, was very likely to be the end of any of the 'Poor wretches! who braved it'.[20]

In 1859 the chaplain in charge, Reverend J.M. Guilding, described the conditions on these notoriously unhygienic and overcrowded floating prisons. This, and other evidence from Guilding, was quoted by the 4th Earl of Carnarvon, during a campaign in the House of Lords to abolish the hulks, as they had been elsewhere in the empire: 'It is my painful conviction, after some years' experience of the matter, that the great majority of the prisoners confined in the hulks become incurably corrupted, and that they leave them, in most cases, more reckless and hardened in sin than they were upon reception.' The earl proceeded to give a graphic description of the Bermuda hulks:

Few are aware of the extent of suffering to which a prisoner is exposed on board the hulks, or the horrible nature of the associations by which he is surrounded. There is no safety for life, no supervision over the bad, no protection to the good. The hulks are unfit for a tropical climate. They are productive of sins of such foul impurity and unnatural crime that one even shudders to mention them. In the close and stifling nights of summer the heat between decks is so oppressive as to make the stench intolerable, and to cause the miserable inmates frequently to strip off every vestige of clothing and gasp at the port-holes for a breath of air. A mob law, and tyranny of the strong over the weak, exists below, which makes the well-disposed live in constant misery and terror; and when the passions of these lawless and desperate men are excited by quarrels among themselves the most deadly and murderous affrays are the consequence.

Not surprisingly, this dire picture was challenged by others, including those in charge of the convict establishment. But Carnarvon was speaking in the wake of a desperate convict rising aboard the Bermuda hulk *Medway* and again quoted Guilding, an eyewitness:

> The spectacle on board the Medway hulk upon the 1st of June last, when one prisoner was slain and twenty-four desperately wounded, would have appalled any humane heart. The hulk was a perfect shambles, and a frightful scene of uproar, excitement, and bloodshed. Suffice it to say, that a mere handful of warders was powerless to deal with the armed mob below decks. All that could be done was to fasten down the hatches, and when the work of butchery and carnage was over descend below to fetch up the dead and wounded.

Based on this evidence, Carnarvon observed that 'the Bermuda hulks were practically a repetition of Norfolk Island and all its abominations'.[21]

Around this time some were returned to English hulks. In 1861 it was decided that no more convicts would be sent to Bermuda, and all prisoners were withdrawn by the end of 1863. The first of two batches left for Western Australia in December 1862 aboard the *Merchantman*, and the last ship, carrying over 300 convicts, sailed out of Bermuda for Western Australia in March 1863.

DARK ISLAND

Lord Carnarvon's reference to the 'abominations' of Norfolk Island was well-founded. Even in the dark legendry of convictism, Norfolk was feared as a place of excessive tyranny, violence and lethal despair. It was meant to punish the worst of the worst. In sentencing to death the leader of Norfolk Island's first convict mutiny and escape attempt, the chief justice neatly summed up the purpose of the penal settlement there:

> With respect to the general harsh treatment of which you complain on Norfolk Island, what are men sent there for? It is within the knowledge of the Court that they are never sent except for crimes of the deepest dye; and is it then to be

supposed that they are sent there to be indulged, to be fed with the fruits of the earth and that they are not to work in chains? No, the object in sending men there is not only as a punishment for their past crimes, but to serve as a terror to others; and so far from it being a reproach, as you have stated it, it is a wise project of the Government in instituting that settlement for the punishment of the twice and thrice convicted felon, as a place of terror to evil doers, and in order to repress the mass of crime with which the Colony unhappily abounds.[22]

There would be many other desperate attempts to escape the dark isle. After the fates of those who led another failed attempt in 1834 had been determined, the Vicar General of New South Wales and Van Diemen's Land, the Very Reverend William Ullathorne, recalled: 'As I mentioned the names of those men who were to die, they one after another, as their names were pronounced, dropped on their knees and thanked God that they were to be delivered from that horrible place, whilst the others remained standing mute, weeping. It was the most horrible scene I have ever witnessed.'[23]

Norfolk Island's first penal settlement was established shortly after the founding of Sydney. It was abandoned in 1814, only to be reopened eleven years later as a punishment for 'the worst description of convicts'. These unfortunates, mainly reoffenders, came from many places and by the mid-1840s there were:

. . . prisoners from every part of the British dominions, and, indeed, from almost every part of the world. Besides English, Irish, Scotch, Frenchmen, Italians, and Germans, there were Chinamen from Hong Kong, Aborigines from New Holland, West Indian Blacks, Greeks, Caffres, and Malays. Among these were soldiers, for desertion, idiots, madmen, boys of seventeen, and old men of eighty. All these were indiscriminately herded together, without reference to age, crime, nation, or any other distinction.[24]

The brutality of the system at Norfolk Island was notorious. Men were flogged for minor offences, left in solitary confinement for lengthy periods, and driven to hard labour in an endless routine of back-breaking work. The only way off the island was by release at the end of a sentence, by escape or by death. It was said that convicts would deliberately attack each other, possibly fatally, in the knowledge that such acts would lead to their execution, so desperate were some to escape. There were rumours of a secret convict society that organized such extreme actions and generally ran the lives of the convicts and their keepers. These surfaced during the Molesworth Inquiry and were later transformed by writers like the pseudonymous 'Price Warung' (William Astley) and Marcus Clarke into a shadowy freemasonry known as 'The Ring'. This group was forty or more of the longest-serving prisoners who swore to be loyal to each other and take reprisals for punishments against them. They enforced a code of silence, not only among themselves, but obliging every prisoner to keep silent. Informing against any of the Ring's activities meant certain death.

From this basic prison gang the Ring was, over the years, inflated into a clandestine criminal cult with its own hierarchy, obligations, oaths and gory rituals. Its initiations involved drinking blood, accompanied by a dreadful oath of eternal loyalty. When the Ring decided to meet, word went through the prison that no non-member, including guards, should enter the prison yard. The leader, known as 'the One', entered the yard first and faced a corner of the wall. He was followed by the Threes, Fives, Sevens and Nines, each arrayed in a semicircle behind him. All were masked. Satanic prayers were intoned:

Is God an officer of the establishment?
And the response came solemnly clear, thrice repeated:
No, God is not an officer of the establishment.
He passed to the next question:
Is the Devil an officer of the establishment?
And received the answer – thrice:
Yes, the Devil is an officer of the establishment.
He continued:
Then do we obey God?
With clear-cut resonance came the negative –
No, we do not obey God!
He propounded the problem framed by souls that are not necessarily corrupt:
Then whom do we obey?

And, thrice over, he received for reply the damning perjury which yet was so true an answer:

The Devil – we obey our Lord the Devil!

And the dreaded Convict Oath was taken. It had eight verses:

Hand to hand,
On Earth, in Hell,
Sick or Well,
On Sea, on Land,
On the Square, ever.

And ended – the intervening verses dare not be quoted:

Stiff or in Breath,
Lag or Free,
You and Me,
In Life, in Death,
On the Cross, never.[25]

A cup of blood taken from the veins of each man was then drunk by all.

After these rites were performed, the Ring would conduct their business. Usually it was a trial and sentence of suspected collaborators among the convict population or of any of their gaolers who showed an inclination to be lenient to the prisoners.

The primary purpose of the Ring was to defy the authority of the gaolers and to reverse the power relations of the penal system, most completely played out on Norfolk Island. At first look the florid stories of the Ring seem more like a Masonic or occult order than a self-protection association of convicts on a remote Pacific island. Historians doubt that anything as luridly gothic as the Ring existed, though prison gangs are found in most gaol populations and it would be surprising if somewhere as brutal as Norfolk Island did not have some form of secret convict confederacy. Prisoners certainly spoke a secret language, or cant, among themselves.[26] It is also true that evidence for the existence of such an elaborate organization depends on a single documented mention of Norfolk Island convicts defying their gaolers, not in itself an uncommon event.

But despite the paucity of historical evidence, the story of the Ring lives on, along with the darker suspicions about the depravity, degradation and despair of Norfolk Island. Prison cliques and gangs are not unusual, though their aims and activities are far more mundane than those described by Warung and Clarke. Secret societies were also a feature of the nineteenth century. The Tolpuddle Martyrs were convicted and transported for making and taking oaths in a secret society and not, ostensibly at least, for forming a trade union. Some Irishmen, like John Boyle O'Reilly and his companions, were members of the semi-clandestine Fenian Brotherhood or similar nationalist entities. Because of their links with Irish and American groups, their members tended to stick together, though their interests were directed to the larger political world rather than the internal struggles of prison life. Others belonged to murky rural pre-trade union associations that produced the Swing Riots and other insurrections in Britain after the end of the Napoleonic Wars in 1815. Many of these rebels were transported to Australia and elsewhere, though it is unlikely that they were involved in any secret societies.[27]

But whether the Ring, or anything faintly like it, ever existed, the convict solidarity that it implied was no longer in evidence in 1846 when yet another rising involved some serious bloodletting. After the apprehension of the mutineers and their trial and sentencing, the twelve ringleaders were hanged a few days later, together with five other convicts. The gallows were in such demand that they required the services of two hangmen, both convicts. These were selected from twenty or more enthusiastic convicts who volunteered for the grisly privilege. One of the two men selected stated, in his written application, that having been a notorious offender and now deeply penitent for his past misconduct, he 'hoped to be permitted to retrieve his character by serving the Government on the present occasion'.[28]

A DEVIL'S CHOICE

Lying in the east Indian Ocean south of Burma, the Andaman Islands began their penal history in 1793 when the East India Company transported Bengali convicts there. Disease closed the establishment down after a few years, but the islands were reoccupied in the aftermath of the Indian Mutiny, or the Indian Revolt of 1857, as this bloody revolt against British colonialism is now usually known. The transportation of mutineers began in 1858,[29] and the Andamans evolved into a major site of penal and political punishment. Overall, around 80,000 individuals were transported for the usual array of crimes and around another 1,000 political prisoners spent shorter or longer periods there before the eventual closing of the penal settlement by the Japanese in 1942.[30]

Convict life in the Andamans echoed many of the practices in New South Wales and Van Diemen's Land. The indigenous Andaman people were displaced and 'pacified' in a process very similar to that which took place in Australia. As most of the transportees were men, there was an ongoing shortage of women, leading to practices such as 'the marriage parade' providing opportunities for relationships. The settlement even featured 'Female Factories' on the same lines as these infamous Australian establishments. As in Australia, the authorities were particularly concerned with what they perceived as the prevalence of 'unnatural offences'.[31] There were frequent clashes and forms of convict resistance, ranging from refusal to work up to full-scale revolt. A similar ticket-of-leave system operated in the Andamans and it was hoped to make the colony self-sufficient, the main motive for Governor Arthur Phillip's establishment at Port Jackson in New South Wales.

As was often the case, not only convicts and their keepers travelled the transportation routes of empire, but so did ideas. The reforming Alexander Maconochie's system of rewarding good conduct on Norfolk Island with possible remission of sentences through a system of 'marks' for good or bad behaviour was adopted in the Andamans and elsewhere.[32] Re-transportation to a secondary establishment for offences committed while serving out sentences was possible. In Australia these roles were provided mainly by Norfolk Island and Van Diemen's Land. In the Andamans it was the ominously named Viper Island. A 'convict stain' stigma much like that in Australia also developed. Escape attempts were also common,[33] with a myth developing that claimed the islands were somehow connected by road to the Burmese mainland. One escape had unusually significant consequences and also echoed the experiences of absconding convicts with indigenous people in Australia.

Dudhnath Tewari was a sepoy in the Bengal Native Infantry in Punjab when, along with many others, he deserted and joined the mutiny against British colonial rule. He was transported with others to Port Blair in the Andamans in 1858. A little more than six months later he was part of a mass escape. As in Australia, the fugitives met a harsh landscape and an enraged and dispossessed indigenous people. One by one they succumbed to either until Tewari himself was felled by the poisoned darts of the Andamanese. But instead of finishing him off, they nursed him back to health and allowed him to effectively join their community. He hunted with them, took part in their religious ceremonies and married two Andamanese women, one of whom, in due course, gave birth to a son.

Puzzled why he should be treated this way, yet grateful to be alive, Tewari followed his Andamanese life for a little over a year.[34] One day he heard excited talk among his hosts about plans to rid their homeland of the British. He quickly discovered that this involved a massacre of everyone in the islands, not only the British but his own countrymen and other convicts. 'Shocked to the hilt', he left the Andamanese and returned to Port Blair with news of the attack.

It came on 17 May[35] at a place the British had named 'Aberdeen'. Forewarned, British firepower easily repelled the determined attack by the poorly armed Andamanese, slaughtering them in their thousands and perpetrating what was effectively a genocide. It was the end of indigenous resistance and incited the British to consolidate their power throughout the Andaman and neighbouring Nicobar Islands.[36] For his treachery – or was it bravery? – Tewari was later given a full pardon and reportedly returned to his home in northern India. His actions, still controversial, were the result of a complicated conflict of interests, including the safety of his countrymen, his dislike of the British, and whatever obligations he must have felt towards the Andamanese.[37] A devil's choice.

The Indian Ocean penal islands were the location of an event that shook the empire and was perhaps propelled by the Muslim notion of *jihad*, or holy war, now fatally familiar throughout the world. Lord Mayo, Viceroy of India, visited the Andamans in February 1872. After completing his administrative and other duties he took a final walk before departing. As he approached his ship under supposedly strong security, an assassin hiding nearby seized an opportunity to plunge a knife into the Viceroy's briefly unguarded back. Lord Mayo died shortly after and his assassin surrendered.

The murderer's name was Shere Ali, a Pathan who had previously served in the British forces with distinction. He killed a man in a family feud and was sentenced to death. The sentence was changed to transportation for life and he was sent to the Andamans. His motives for the killing remain confused, though it is possible that he was inspired by a version of the Wahhabist interpretation of Islam that supports jihad and rewards those who die while following a fatwa with eternal life in para-dise.[38] Whether Shere Ali was motivated by religious dogma or a sense of personal injustice, or some of both, his actions ended the hopes of his fellow prisoners for any indulgences they might have received from the visit of so important a personage as the Viceroy of India.

During the 1920s there were official recommendations to abolish transporta-tion to the Andamans, based on previous investigations into the evils of Norfolk Island and other places of condemnation. A process was begun to repatriate pris-oners, but the returnees soon strained the capacity of Indian prisons and transpor-tation continued. Attempts were even made at this time to populate the colony with people who were not convicts, but who were considered criminal. The Hindu Bhantu tribe of Uttar Pradesh was registered by the British as a 'criminal tribe', their habitual methods of subsistence involving robbery and violence. Hundreds of Bhantu were more or less forcibly migrated in the hope that working in forestry would convince them to give up their previous habits. They were assisted in this rehabilitation experiment by the Salvation Army and not allowed to return to their homeland until the 1950s.[39]

ACROSS THE BLACK WATER

Elsewhere in the Indian Ocean the British developed their various possessions as they had done in the Atlantic and elsewhere. Between 1787 and 1857 the English East India Company made extensive use of transportation from and to India and other South Asian locations.[40] The number of individuals transported to a large number of colonial locations highlight the extent and functional effectiveness of the system.

Singapore, Penang and Malacca, known collectively as the Straits Settlements after 1823, received 20,000 transports from India between 1790 and 1857. Another 6,000 were sent to the Burmese regions of Arakan and Tenasserim between 1828 and 1857. Significant numbers went to Bencoolen in Sumatra (2,000), to Mauritius (1,500), and up to 1,500 were sent from Ceylon to Malacca between 1849 and 1873.[41] The Andamans, Aden and Amboyna[42] also received smaller human shipments at different times during this period. The Straits Settlements and Burma consigned perhaps 1,400 prisoners to the presidencies of Bengal, Bombay and Madras between 1836 and 1864. Sikh rebels were transported to Burma and to Singapore, as well as other penal establishments in the Straits colonies from the 1840s. Repeat offenders could also be re-transported to Cape Colony, New South Wales and Van Diemen's Land.[43] The Australian island prison also accepted a small batch of transports from the British colony of Hong Kong. Six Chinese, one European and three 'other' arrived in Hobart in 1844.[44]

After the Indian revolt of 1857, transportation continued to be used extensively. The files of the India Office Records at the British Library are thick with tables, statistics and reports on criminal trials and sentences of transportation, mostly for murder and dacoity, organized robbery, kidnapping and often murder of victims. Occasionally those sentenced to banishment across the seas petitioned the secretary of state for India for mercy after their appeals were rejected. In 1881 Singamala Chenchu Obigadu was confined in the Central Jail at Rajamundry, convicted, along with seventeen others, of dacoity. He and his accomplices had attacked the home of an elderly woman and her ailing son and 'very cruelly tortured and ill-used' her. Most of the attackers had confessed after their apprehension and although 'There seemed to be no reason to doubt the genuineness of the confessions', the officials saw no reason to make a recommendation,[45] effectively ensuring that Obigadu would become another statistic in the large numbers of those transported across the 'black water'.

Hong Kong pursued an active transportation policy of mainly Chinese between 1844 and 1858. Compared with the East India Company the numbers despatched were small, around 700. Almost 600 of these were sent to established operations like Singapore and 'the white man's grave', Penang (Prince of Wales Island), or to struggling colonies desperate for labour, including Sindh (now in

Pakistan) and Labuan (in modern Malaysia). The governor of Labuan was proud of the small profit delivered by the labour of his convicts.[46] Ceylon sent around 1,500 convicts to Malacca between 1849 and 1873.

In Chinese tradition, separation from homeland and family was considered equivalent to death. If sent abroad, their chances of return were slender, condemning them to a passing without the necessary religious and spiritual rituals. Consequently, many feared transportation almost as much as death, some even more, killing themselves in their cells, escaping or taking part in mutinies aboard transport ships. The British authorities welcomed the deterrent value of this form of punishment,[47] particularly as it gave them some leverage against the endemic piracy of the region. Hong Kong pirates were especially feared for their efficiency and brutality.

As on the Australian transportation runs, convict shipboard mutinies in British Asia were usually bloody, though relatively rare,[48] and few mutineers made good their escapes. In December 1839 the *Virginia* was transporting thirty-six convicts from Bombay, bound for life or other lengthy sentences in Singapore and Prince of Wales Island (Penang). The convicts mutinied, murdering the captain and first officer and sailing the ship to brief freedom. Some were recaptured, some executed and the remainder, once again, transported.[49]

The *General Wood* carried ninety-two convicts from Hong Kong to Penang in 1848. On the final stage of the voyage the convicts rose against the Lascar crew, throwing most overboard and murdering the captain and mates. A young lieutenant and his new wife, along with one other man, were the only Europeans left alive as the mutineers sailed towards an island in the South China Sea. Their plan was to kill the remaining passengers and crew and blow up the ship. But the local Malay people realized what was happening and rescued the three Europeans. Some of the convicts were recaptured, one of them bearing a written compact expressing their desire to stick together, support each other and return to China: 'We are to share alike in every thing, if we procure food we are to share alike . . . We all swear to assist and stand by one another to the last. God only besides ourselves shall know our actions and what is in our possession.'[50] This crude communitarianism gives another glimpse of the covert culture of transportees.

The vast majority of convicts served out their time or died before they did. Others with life sentences simply faded into the prison population of wherever they ended up. In 1864 Lee-afook (fifty-three), Wong-aung (forty-four) and Wong Poong-Neen (forty-nine) had served almost twenty years in Sindh, the last survivors of a group of thirty-two transports sent there in 1846. They were recommended for a pardon, though had forgotten most of the details of their trials for relatively minor offences. The Sindh authorities considered that the sentences of these men were disproportionate and that they had been the 'most laborious painstaking workmen, and are equally good tempered and amenable to discipline . . .' And they went even further in their commendations: 'It was by these three men and their fellow Chinese prisoners who were discharged on the expiry of their sentences, that all the different trades and manufactures now carried on so successfully in the Jail Factory were introduced and taught to the Sindee prisoners.' The men were released to work as paid labourers in the gaol's factory and garden, but they could never be allowed to go home to Hong Kong.[51]

Internal transportation contributed to colonization in unexpected ways. A group of Chinese men were sent from the Straits colonies to the Nilgiri Mountains area of southern India. Having no way, and perhaps no desire, to return to their homes after their release, they married Tamil women. Many years later the British ethnographer Edgar Thurston came across them squatting in the hills, describing them as 'a colony, earning an honest livelihood by growing vegetables, cultivating coffee on a small scale, and adding to their income from these sources by the economic products of the cow'. One of the Chinese men was reported as having no regrets, other than having to cut off his 'tail' or queue when he converted to the Christian faith of his Tamil Paraiyan wife.[52]

In the late 1780s convicts were transported from Bengal to Bencoolen, a sparsely populated and malarial area of Sumatra first occupied by the British in 1685. The East India Company planned to use the convict labour to develop the unpromising colony but, even with the thrusting reformer, Stamford Raffles, as Lieutenant-Governor resident between 1818 and 1824, the venture failed to thrive. When Raffles arrived, he found around 500 transportees languishing on the island and promptly sought permission to eventually free them to become productive members of island society. He proposed a three-tier arrangement in which the first class would become settlers after serving at least three years. The second class would work as labourers while the third class, the worst, would be set to hard labour and be confined at night. Raffles aimed for rehabilitation as a reward for good conduct and 'holding out the prospect of again becoming useful members of society'.[53]

By 1823 the numbers transported to Bencoolen from Madras as well as Bengal had climbed to around 900, and were gradually increasing. Raffles reported himself satisfied that his enlightened scheme was working well. But in 1825, after his return to England and the ceding of Bencoolen to the Netherlands in 1824, the Bencoolen convicts were re-transported to Penang, then to Malacca and Singapore. In these locations they were mostly deprived of the freedoms they had enjoyed under Raffles and were made to labour in work gangs.[54]

Conditions for Indian transports were much harder than for most Europeans. As the Singaporean penal administrator J.F.A. McNair recalled in his memoir:

> . . . for to be sent across the 'kala pani', or 'black water', in a convict ship or 'jeta junaza', or 'living tomb' as they called it, meant, especially to a man of high caste, whether of the right or left hand section, the total loss to him of all that was worth living for. He could never be received in intercourse again with his own people, and so strong are the caste ideas of ceremonial uncleanness that it would be defilement to his friends and relations even to offer to him sustenance of any kind, and he was in point of fact excommunicated and avoided.[55]

But it was even worse in the afterlife. Like the Chinese, the Indian convicts believed that their earthly separation from their society and consequent transportation meant that they would suffer even more in the afterlife.

However, in Singapore by the 1860s the Raffles approach had evolved into a ticket-of-leave system that at least held out the prospect of a kind of local redemption for these exiles. Dr Mouat, Inspector General of Jails in Bengal, visited Singapore in 1861 where he found:

> . . . a system of industrial training of convicts superior to anything we had at that time on the continent of India. It was said to have been inaugurated by the celebrated Sir Stamford Raffles in 1825, when Singapore was first selected for the transportation of convicts from India, and to have been subsequently

organized and successfully worked by General H. Man, Colonel MacPherson, and Major McNair. The ticket-of-leave system was in full and effective operation, and very important public works have been constructed by means of convict labour, chief amongst them St. Andrew's Cathedral, a palace for the Governor, and most of the roads. The ticket-of-leave convicts were said to be a well-conducted, industrious lot of men, who very rarely committed fresh crimes, who all earned an honest livelihood, and were regarded as respectable members of the community amongst whom they dwelt.[56]

Not all the transports were industrious members of society, despite the progressive administration of punishment in Singapore. Those with life sentences were murderers, bandits (dacoits) and thugs, professional murderers and robbers. The British made a determined effort to break up these gangs and by the 1860s most of their members had been hanged or transported to the Straits penal settlements. At this time some prisoners still bore the marks of hot-iron brandings on their foreheads, inflicted by the authorities in India[57], before the practice was ended. Some continued to commit crimes while serving their sentences but all had the chance to earn a ticket-of-leave if they wished.

Regardless of the cause of their transportation to the Straits, or elsewhere in the region, the rationale for their fates remained the same. In the context of an 1846 newspaper debate on the effect of convicts on the free labour market in Singapore, an unnamed writer concisely stated the justification for imperial penal transportation:

The object of the legislature is to employ convict labour in those operations [public works] which materially affect health and shorten life; and thus perform service which free labourers ought not to be called upon to do. Countries not possessing Colonies send their convicted felons to the mines, as Russia, Norway etc. where the period of life rarely exceeds 3 or 4 years. Such Kingdoms as possess Colonies always select for penal settlement a locality where the riches and resources are to be obtained only by a great sacrifice of human life, during the period of labour in clearing and draining the land, the formation of roads and construction of other public works. The end is considered sufficiently advantageous to justify the means.[58]

RUDRAPAH'S TALE

The British gained control of the almost deserted Straits of Malacca island of Penang in 1786. Six years later the population had reached 10,000, and was rapidly rising. Some of these were transports from various parts of India and in 1825 the convicts from Bencoolen were re-transported to the bustling island and set to work building roads through the jungle. Tigers and venomous snakes were a constant threat. Accommodation for the convicts was basic, with inadequate sanitation and the hospital poorly ventilated. Discipline was lax. The system was gradually improved with some trusted convicts themselves becoming warders. Many convicts earned a ticket-of-leave and found ways to support themselves and contribute to the community, including the discovery and development of the famous canes known as 'Penang Lawyers', exported in large numbers to Europe and the United States.

After a turbulent history of Malay, Dutch and Portuguese occupation, Malacca finally came into lasting British control in 1824. Soon after, convicts from Penang arrived and went to work on buildings in and around the town. More arrived from Penang around 1840. By 1860 the system had been refined to the point where the convicts were given useful skills. Some were able to use these for profit and success. During the early 1860s there was a convict revolt and escape from bad treatment during the building of the Cape Rachado lighthouse, which resulted in some loss of life. In 1873 the Straits penal settlements were closed and the inmates trans-ferred to the Andaman Islands, via Singapore.

Singapore was established as an East India Company trading hub in 1819 and six years later the brig *Horatio* deposited eighty Madras convicts from Bencoolen. Most of them had life sentences, including one woman. They were soon followed by larger shipments from India of prisoners who were 'manacled with light leg fetters' in which they had to work building infrastructure for a probationary period of three months.[59] The convicts were paid a monthly allowance and overseen by trustees from their ranks. Much of the labour went to reclaiming land from the sea, the basis of modern Singapore. Captain Stevenson of the 12th Madras Native Infantry, who held the position of superintendent, wrote in 1845 of the 'feeling of hopelessness that ever accompanies a sense of imprisonment and slavery for life'.[60] It was the opinion of the British that the low level of active resistance among prisoners was due to the mixture of castes, races and occupations among their charges, and that if any plot were fomented, one group or another would inform against it:[61]

> In the year 1857 there were 2,139 convicts from different parts of India, Burmah, and Ceylon in this jail; but upon an average, until the prison was broken up, there were 1,900 always under control. The men from India were Seikhs, Dogras, Pallis, or a shepherd race; Thugs and Dacoits from different parts of the Bengal presidency, and mostly from round about Delhi and Agra; felons from all parts of the Madras and Bombay presidencies, and a few from Assam and Burmah, chiefly Dacoits, and a sprinkling of Cingalese.[62]

By the mid-1880s Singapore was home to around 1,200 Indian convicts. Escapes were attempted, though the native Malays were so unsympathetic to the escapees that most of them gave up and returned to their gaol. Flogging on the buttocks at the triangle with the cat-o'-nine-tails was permitted. The usual minimum was a dozen lashes but up to six dozen could be inflicted.[63] As well as corporal punishment there were many other hazards faced by convicts and their gaolers. Tigers, crocodiles and venomous snakes were a continual threat. Tropical fevers were endemic, as were ulcers and sores caused by leg irons, Beri-Beri and Malay pirates could also be dangerous. While convicts were allowed to follow their own trades and businesses in the early years, by this time penal thinking had moved to punishment by hard labour as well as deprivation of liberty. Nevertheless, those who served out their time frequently did well for themselves as milk sellers, road contractors and cart owners, among other occupations, and contributed to the business and community development of the island, particularly if they had benefited from learning one of the many trades taught to amenable convicts. One of those was a Madras planter with a sad story of human frailty.

Rudrapah grew up in a village along with his great friend, Allagappen – 'we were like brothers'. When he reached manhood Rudrapah married a thirteen-year-old local girl, as was the custom, and they had a happy life together for five or six years. Allagappen remained a firm family friend throughout these years.

Rudrapah eventually managed to save enough money to buy a bandy, or dray, and a brace of bulls. He hired the vehicle and himself out and was often away for days on end. After one of these journeys he returned home in the early hours of the morning to find the door of his house unlocked. Wondering why the door was not latched, Rudrapah slipped quietly into his house and went straight to the bedroom: 'there I saw my wife laying asleep, and beside her was a man also asleep. On going close up to him that I might see who it was, to my great sorrow I found that it was my friend, Allagappen.'

Overcome with anger and grief, Rudrapah, by accident he improbably claimed, smashed his friend's skull in with a grinding stone:

My wife woke up, and seeing me, she screamed and ran away from the house. She went to the neighbours' house in whose charge I had left her. I followed her, and told them what I had done: that morning I was taken by the police and locked up, and after that I saw my house no more. I was tried by an English judge, and was sentenced to be sent away from my country for as long as I lived: such was my misfortune.

Rudrapah was considered to be contrite for his crime and a suitable subject for 'reclamation'. He was pardoned after twenty-five years, by then an old man.[64]

The Straits Settlements separated from British India in 1867. The Indian life convicts went to the Andaman Islands. Many of those who remained were pardoned, with the exception of those serving sentences for various forms of murder, including thuggee and dacoity. Around 20,000 convicts, at least 95 per cent male, were transported to the Straits Settlements. Some who committed further crimes were re-transported to New South Wales, Van Diemen's Land and Robben Island at the Cape Colony.

The internal and external links of penal settlements in British Asia and beyond were a vital aspect of the empire's global transportation strategy. As elsewhere, they allowed the removal of criminals and other outcasts to places where their labour built infrastructure and, in many places, new communities providing markets and trade resources. They were also convenient for the punishment and sequestration of political undesirables. This useful dimension of punishment and control became apparent early in the linked histories of the empire and transportation. In 1760 the slaves of Jamaica revolted against their British masters. In a bloody year and a half around 1,000 black and white lives were lost in the conflict, either in battle, through suicide, or some extremely unpleasant executions. Damage to property and produce was valued at around a quarter of a million pounds. Hundreds of surviving rebels were transported elsewhere for life.[65] This was an early case of internal transportation, a technique that increased in frequency and volume as the empire expanded and ever more severe punishments were deemed necessary.[66] The Bussa Revolt of Barbadian slaves resulted in over one hundred of the rebels being transported to Sierra Leone by way of Honduras in 1816.[67]

9

ONE VAST CHARNEL HOUSE

Now I lay my coat, vest, and shirt on the ground,
And to the triangles I am bound,
When the flagellator did behind me stand
With the cat-a'-nine-tails in his hand.
He flogged me till my back was raw
And painted with my crimson gore . . .

Charles Ashton, 'The Convict's Dream'[1]

In the 'vast charnel house' of New South Wales, many of the transported lived lives of varying misery and degradation. Some did not survive, while ordinary women, children and men, as well as rebels and other misfits, struggled to overcome their circumstances. Some succeeded. Some did not. Others found ways to twist the rules to suit illicit ends or fiercely refused to bend to the iron authority of the system. As these lives and deaths played out, so transportation was seen, at home and abroad, as both cruel and unsuccessful. After several official inquiries and the increasingly effective activities of the many who opposed it, the despatching of convicts to Australia was slowly wound down. Before the eventual demise of the system, thousands more would be caught in its many snares.

ARTFUL DODGERS

With no mother and an alcoholic father, fourteen-year-old Samuel Holmes was in trouble from an early age: '[I] used to play about in the streets, [my] father tried to keep me at home – has stripped me, taken away my clothes and tied me to a bed post – because the Boys used to come round the House at night and whistle and entice me to go out thieving again with them.' Two of the boys took Samuel to a house in Stepney:

> ... kept by a Jew and he agreed to board and lodge me for 2/6 [two shillings and sixpence] a week provided I brought and sold to him all that I might steal – He has about 13 boys in the house on the same terms ... The landlord has also the adjoining House and there is a communication into it from every room – The back kitchen is fitted up with a trap door to help escape – and in a corner of one of the back kitchens is a sliding floor underneath which property is hid.[2]

A coat was hung up in the kitchen 'and Boys practise how to pick the pockets, the men in the house show them how to manage'. Samuel was a quick learner: 'I was about a fortnight in training and afterwards went out to assist and screen the boys where they picked pockets – In a short time I went out on my own account as I soon saw how they did it.'

Young Samuel, known to his companions in crime as 'Smouchee', had fallen in with a character from a Charles Dickens novel and may have even been the basis for the fictional young thief, the 'Artful Dodger'. Dickens published *Oliver Twist* a couple of years later and may have come across Samuel's story in his work as a court reporter. We will probably never know, but it seems that the Samuel Holmes story of juvenile offending and learning the black arts required was hardly unique. He was only one of many 'wild and wicked youths' transported to Australia.

Samuel arrived in Van Diemen's Land in August 1836 and joined the other juvenile offenders at Point Puer. He was soon in trouble. His record shows an average of four punishments each year up to 1839. In the first year he spent thirteen days in the Black Hole on suspicion of pilfering buttons. In December he used blasphemous language on the Sabbath and was kept on bread and water for three days. The following January he was flogged for insolence to the superintendent and in April served another three days on bread and water. Three months later, for singing in his cell and other infractions, the boy was flogged again. Another twelve lashes were visited on him in August for resisting his overseer. There were various other visits to the Black Hole and starvation diets over the three-year period.

After fourteen years of this ill-treatment and defying the system that inflicted it upon him, Samuel Holmes at last gained his liberty. Where he went and what befell him after his poor start in life, nobody knows. He was just one of the barely known bodies shipped away to serve time in a penal purgatory that had never been previously imagined. There would be so many more. Some of these young offenders reached Australia through what was, for the time, a progressive transportation programme.[3]

Convicted juveniles held at London's Millbank and Pentonville prisons (and some from Parkhurst) were transported to Van Diemen's Land, New South Wales, and what would later become the colony of Victoria, from 1844 to 1849. In that period, over 1,700 boys from the age of eleven and young men with an average age of twenty-two served out sentences begun in England. They were there given some basic literacy training and trade skills. Unlike regular convicts, the boys and young men were pardoned on their arrival, as long as they did not return to Britain before the expiry of their original sentences. The scheme aimed to both reform and to provide much-needed labour for colonists at a time of economic depression in Britain and Australia.

There was strong local opposition to the 'Pentonvillains', as the press dubbed the group, particularly as transportation to New South Wales had by then been curtailed and the scheme was seen by many as a return to the practice by stealth. While the settlers who benefited from free labour on rural properties were unsurprisingly enthusiastic, Melbourne city dwellers were vocally against the 'taint' of convictism and mounted a strong political campaign against the Pentonvillains. By 1849 they had succeeded in refusing entry to a shipload of the boys and the British government suspended the programme.[4]

But among the boys were many unreformed characters who continued to commit crimes after their arrival. One of the most colourful was described by Chief Justice Sir William à Beckett as 'certainly no common criminal'. Owen Suffolk had the possibly unique distinction of having been exiled once from Britain when transported to Australia, and later being banished from Australia. A thief, conman, swindler, bigamist, bushranger and adventurer, Suffolk was a criminal conjuror, adept at deceit, illusion and evading capture. These wicked abilities landed him in a transport to Melbourne at the age of only seventeen. On arrival at

Geelong in 1847 he was granted a conditional pardon, as were all the 'Pentonvillains' transported to the Port Phillip district.

The following year Owen Suffolk was sentenced to five years hard labour in a road gang for horse stealing. From then on, he was in and out of various prisons and the hulk *Sacramento* for robbing a mail coach and horse stealing. His eloquence and intelligence usually earned him significant remittances. During one period of freedom he even managed to join the police corps, though his career in law enforcement was brief. He was soon in prison again for forgery. After several more collisions with the law, Suffolk was banished back to England with a full pardon.

Once there, his deep criminality reasserted itself and the eloquent exile from Australia quickly married a wealthy widow, and not for love. In 1868 he was tried with stealing and obtaining money by false pretences. He pleaded guilty and his appeal to the court was that he had care of his brother's nineteen-year-old daughter and her child. This time, though, Suffolk's silver tongue failed. The chief justice did not mince his words: 'Don't try and impose on me. I know your career. You were married to a widow, obtained all her property, deserted her, pretended by a fake report inserted in a newspaper that you were drowned, went away with your brother's child, who cannot therefore be your wife . . .' At this point Suffolk interrupted to insist 'She is my wife, my lord.' His lordship replied 'if you did marry her, you have added bigamy to your other offences, and I sentence you to a term of 15 years penal servitude'.[5]

Suffolk went to prison and seems never to have been heard of again.[6] Unless the odd account appearing in some Australian newspapers a few months after his last trial can be believed. According to this report, Suffolk engineered a boating accident involving his niece/wife and managed to fake his own drowning: '. . . it was ultimately discovered that he escaped to America with his wife's moneys, and the proceeds of the sale of his wife's furniture, which he sold before he left England. By the latest advices he was enjoying himself in New York.'[7]

Despite his crimes, and to some extent because of them, Owen Suffolk was a remarkable character. As well as educating himself from the proceeds of his youthful illicit activities, his experiences in many gaols and long associations with the underworlds of London and the colonies gave him the ability to walk, talk and write on both sides of society. His autobiography is full of racy information about thieves' cant, street life and surviving in the underbelly of his time, as in one of his less flowery poems celebrating one of many releases from gaol:

I'm out in the world once more,
And I mean to run the rig,
For I've learned from the prison lore
That the pauper fares worse than the prig.
I've shivered and starved in vain,
And been honest for months in rag,
So, if I'm convicted again,
I think it won't be on the vag [being a vagrant].

THE OUTSKIRTS OF HABITABLE CREATION

The French provinces of Quebec and Ontario rebelled against British rule in Canada in 1838. Often known as 'the Patriot War', the conflict was a combination of insurrection and cross-border invasion, drawing in volunteer fighters from America. The revolt was quickly and ruthlessly put down by the British with almost thirty of the Patriots executed and the death sentences against the rest commuted to transportation. The French Canadians were sent to New South Wales[8] and the Americans to Van Diemen's Land.

The French Canadians arrived in Sydney in February 1840, fearing the worst for themselves in a penal colony operating a regime of hard labour. They were sent to a derelict farm on the outskirts of the city, rebuilt as a stockade to hold them. Their status as political prisoners and their good conduct afforded them a privileged position, assisted by their Roman Catholic religion which gave them support from the Church. Father John Brady said mass for the prisoners and also looked out for their well-being. He wrote:

When I consider the courage of these prisoners, and their spirit of resignation, I cannot conceive how men so gentle, so modest and so good, whose conduct arouses the admiration of all those who are witnesses of it, can have deserved so terrible a punishment. They have had the misfortune to see themselves snatched

173

from the arms of their wives and children; they have seen their homes and their possessions given over to pillage and to destruction by fire and after months of anguish, fear and shattered hopes, spent in the depths of prison cells, they received the terrible sentence which is to separate them from all they held dear in the world, so as to cast them into banishment in a far distant soil, where they are suffering through being deprived of the most necessary things.

While the French Canadians avoided forced labour, their rations were the same as other convicts. Brady wrote that 'The food that they receive is so bad that the white Irish slave, accustomed to living on potatoes and salt could scarcely put up with it.'[9] The Patriots were fast-tracked to tickets-of-leave and within two years of their landing were assigned servants, enjoying the comparative liberty of that indulgence. By 1844 all had received free pardons. Most eventually returned home, though two died and one married in the colony.

The Americans were not so lucky. In the eyes of the British government they were traitors, despite their citizenship. Discrimination against them began from the moment they left Canada. The French were allowed to bring their clothes, belongings and money, whereas the Americans had to make do with whatever they had upon them. Massachusetts-born Samuel Snow wrote an account of their experience. The Americans and French Canadians had been given 'a sham court martial' by their captors but received no sentence which, as Snow wrote, 'left us in the dark as to the enormity of our crimes, and the penalty which we were doomed to suffer'.[10]

A hundred and thirty-six Patriots and four Canadian criminals shipped aboard the *Buffalo* in September 1839, 'bound to parts unknown'. One died shortly after and 'was relieved of future sufferings by death, a few weeks after leaving Quebec, and was thrown overboard'. The prisoners were un-ironed, but a false mutiny alarm off the American coast led to a closer guard. Food was minimal and, when they reached the tropics, so was water. Rio was the only port of call and by the time they entered the Indian Ocean via the Cape of Good Hope, the prisoners guessed their destination was the notorious Van Diemen's Land. More than four months after leaving Quebec, the Americans were landed in Hobart: 'Thus we finally found ourselves again on terra firma, on the celebrated as well as notorious Van Diemen's

Island; situated as I should think, without consulting geographers, on the very south-eastern outskirts of habitable creation.' The French continued the voyage to serve their sentences in New South Wales, while the Americans came under the indecisive Lieutenant-Governor John Franklin.

Sir John Franklin, later to disappear in the search for a Northwest passage, was preceded in his oversight of the prison island by Sir George Arthur. He had, some years before, been transferred to British Canada where he presided over retribution against Snow and his rebel companions. Arthur's governorship of Van Diemen's Land was one of cruel despotism, as Snow and his companions knew only too well:

> . . . during his governorship of thirteen years, he signed FIFTEEN HUNDRED AND EIGHT death warrants, and only EIGHT of these condemned persons were saved from the gallows, and these were sentenced to toil in irons the remainder of their days, a fate worse than death itself, so that his very acts of royal clemency were but the most aggravated specimens of his cruelty. Many of the citizens could not tell what were the crimes of these victims, for which they were executed; these were secrets with the Governor and his officers.

The gallows in Hobart were within sight of the governor's residence and were usually their busiest in the morning, 'and it was no uncommon sight for the citizens of Hobart Town to see a dozen convicts suspended at once, and their dead bodies left dangling the whole day, a spectacle for every eye. His Excellency seemed better to relish a good English breakfast of "beef and porter", after satiating his vision in the morning, by such horrid sights.'

Snow was also aware of the attempted extermination of the indigenous population of the island a few years earlier: 'Of the six thousand natives who used to live upon this island, the most of them were hunted down and exterminated during his residence there; only about eighty now remain of the whole number, and they are kept as prisoners on a small island in the vicinity.'

Arthur was an extreme version of the colonial governors who were the backbone of the empire, many of whom were intimately associated with transportation. After executing and banishing the Patriots in Canada, he continued his career in Bombay. Franklin, though, particularly through the influence of his wife, Lady

Jane Franklin, was a less despotic character, but he was getting old and had limited effective control of his subordinates. Nor was he getting much help from the British government. After being given their new convict uniforms, the prisoners were lined up and addressed by Franklin himself. He told them that their arrival was unprecedented and that he was not sure how long they were to be held or under what conditions. While he requested guidance from Lord John Russell back in England they would work on the roads. He warned them against speaking to the old lags, 'as they were a desperate and hardened class of individuals, and that the term of our servitude would be graduated by our good or bad behaviour'.

The Patriots went to work 'levelling DOWN hills, and levelling UP valleys, breaking stone and drawing them in hand carts to where they were wanted, for making and mending McAdamized roads'. Despite the hard labour they had to perform, the convicts' victuals were meagre. They received bread, water, flour, potatoes and mutton, the meat having already been picked over for the best pieces by the guards and administrators. With the water and flour they made a gruel, spiced with the two ounces of salt they received each week. To thicken it a little, men would scavenge potato skins and cabbage leaves and boil these up in the skilly. They received no tea, sugar, coffee or tobacco.

Some tried to escape but were captured and sent to Port Arthur for the remainder of their time. This notorious prison 'was named in honor of Sir George, that prince of land pirates, whom we have before mentioned, and is known as being the place where some of the forms of cruelty instituted by him are perpetuated'. The prison was guarded by the 'dogline': 'The town is situated on a point, which is connected to the main land by a narrow neck, and the escape of prisoners is prevented by chaining large savage dogs so close to each other across the neck, that a man cannot pass between them without being seized and torn in pieces. These dogs are provoked daily to aggravate their ferocious dispositions.'

The rest of the Patriots were punished for these attempted escapes by being sent further into the bush where the conditions and food were even worse: 'We remained at this place through the winter; our work was a mile and a half from the station, and frequently was it our lot, to return to our huts this distance, through the cold and rain after a hard day's toiling, and have to lay down for the night with our clothes drenched with water, and no fire allowed us to dry them.'

Despite these conditions, the Patriots were not made to wear irons, nor were they flogged, though the threat of both punishments hung continually over them. Some of their overseers treated them well and even allowed them to work for wages and to purchase extra food for themselves. But they were not in favour with officialdom. A well-meaning petition for the freedom of the Patriots irritated Franklin, who used it as a reason to delay granting tickets-of-leave. By now, the lieutenant-governor had received his instructions from Britain: 'give those political prisoners any indulgence you may think proper, with the exception of allowing them to return home, to endanger the safety and well-being of the North American colonies'.

While Franklin vacillated, the men laboured on the roads for almost another year under Captain Wright, 'an inhuman, overbearing, unprincipled, incarnate devil'. As well as working the men he declared that 'he would subdue that d----d independent Yankee spirit of ours if possible'. Wright withheld some of their rations, but the Patriots complained to the local magistrate who upheld their petition and had the rations restored, along with a reprimand for Wright.

Later, the Americans were separated for the first time into smaller groups and made to work alongside other convicts, something the governor had originally forbidden. The convicts were inveterate thieves, stealing food to supplement the miserable rations. When they were caught, they were flogged and made to work on the roads in irons. Not surprisingly, 'bolting', or attempting to escape, was a frequent occurrence. Most attempts eventually failed but while they were on the run, escaped convicts became bushrangers, preying on the isolated free settlers for food and other needs. Sometimes their raids were violent, leaving wounded and dead settlers or policemen in their wake. Those guilty of these crimes were invariably executed when caught, while less violent absconders were flogged and sent to work in the coal mines.

Early in 1842 the Patriots were finally given their promised tickets-of-leave: 'We received our tickets sooner than prisoners in general; their own convicts have to work on the road two years, and are then LOANED to the settlers for a number of years more, according to the nature of their sentence.' They were only allowed to go to certain parts of the colony well away from the deep-water port at Hobart. Although the men could now work for themselves, the colony was in an economic recession and wages were low. A number banded together to operate a farm but could not get high enough prices for their harvest to make a decent wage.

The men were still struggling to make ends meet when almost thirty suddenly received free pardons. They waited impatiently for two months until an American whaler arrived and took them aboard to work their passage back home or wherever else they fancied during a three-year whaling voyage across the Pacific and along the Northwest coast of the United States. Early in 1845 'we left the land with thankful hearts' and with a parting verse:

> Farewell, Van Dieman [*sic*], ruin's gate,
> With joy we leave they shore;
> And fondly hope our wretched fate,
> Will drive us there no more.

Samuel Snow concluded his narrative of suffering:

> We had seen misery in all of its varied forms; we had seen how prone man is to tyrannize over his brother, when clothed with 'brief authority', and we had learned to cherish the institutions of our own beloved country our native land. We had thought of the moral influence exerted upon the minds of children of the free population by being associated with, and surrounded by so many of the most vicious human beings the world ever saw; we had in countless instances seen TOTAL DEPRAVITY PERSONIFIED.

Other Patriots recalled their time in Van Diemen's Land with even more disgust than Snow. Linus Miller observed: 'We have been, de jure, free men for years and the abominable slavery we have endured was not only a wanton violation of the laws of justice and humanity, but even of Van Diemen's Land.'[11]

Most made it back to America, or at least to a better place, though they received no help from the British government. It was the government's practice to pay for the return fares of pardoned convicts. No such assistance was given to the Americans, who were compelled to earn their passages by working as sailors or trying to scrape the necessary money together from the poor wages in the depressed colonial economy. A few of the men were denied the opportunity to return home. Some Patriots lost their tickets-of-leave and were returned to serve their original sentences and simply forgotten by the system. The pardons process was a mess, with Patriots being left off lists, documents never delivered and general bureaucratic ineptitude. One man, John Berry, working in the back country as a shepherd, was actually pardoned in 1844 but was not informed for thirteen years. When he was, he went home on the first American ship he could find.[12]

SEE A FEMALE FACTORY ONCE

The few years most of the American Patriots spent in British captivity were hard, yet much easier than the lot of common convicts, especially women. The crime that brought Lydia Clay and her companions to the Cascades Female Factory in Hobart was one of the oldest of all. Young George Boothroyd's father sent him to cash a substantial cheque at the Yorkshire Bank in Huddersfield. George withdrew the money and began a pub crawl that ended the next day in the house of Ruth Richardson. Ruth and her friends Lydia Clay, Mary Anne Wentworth and Elizabeth Quarmby were 'nymphs of the pave', as the press often described women who needed to make their living on the streets in 1845.

The women soon got gullible George gambling and very drunk. With no difficulty, they knocked him down and took the money he was still carrying. George managed to stagger back to the public house where he was lodging and was eventually sober enough to report on his misadventure and identify his assailants. The four women were arrested, tried, convicted and sentenced to ten years each. They landed together in Van Diemen's Land in 1846 and entered the Cascades Female Factory in Hobart.

Established in 1826, the Cascades was a prison, a workhouse and a nursery for the children of convicts. Women laboured for up to twelve hours a day in summer and were subjected to severe regulation, as laid out in the rules of 1829: 'Females guilty of disobedience of orders, neglect of work, profane, obscene, or abusive language, insubordination, or other turbulent or disorderly or disrespectful conduct, shall be punished by the superintendent with close confinement in a dark or other cell, until her case shall be brought under consideration of the Principal Superintendent.'

At the Cascades, the four Huddersfield 'nymphs' were incorporated into the system like all the other female convicts. As well as their trade and place of origin, the state noted every personal detail – height, age, complexion, the size and shape of the head, hair colour, 'visage' or face shape, angle of the forehead, colour of eyes and eyebrows, size and shape of the nose and chin, as well as any marks, blemishes or other distinguishing bodily characteristics.

Lydia Clay was described as a 'house maid' of thirty-six years and five and a quarter inches tall (without shoes). Her complexion was dark and her hair black, as were her eyes. With oval face, low forehead, long nose, large mouth and round chin she was more than adequately catalogued as a creature of the state and easily identifiable. In case of any possible doubt, she had a mole on the inside of her right arm. Lydia quickly became a troublemaker who refused to buckle to the system. She was insolent, insubordinate and sometimes absent without leave. On one of these occasions she was 'found in bed with a man' and sentenced to six months' hard labour. She spent a good deal of time in solitary and at hard labour in the first few years of her sentence.

Elizabeth Quarmby caused almost no trouble and was free in December 1855. She was married by then and had produced three children by 1860. It seems that the grog got the better of her. There was a separation and although Elizabeth took her husband to court, he refused to pay to support her. She had some satisfaction though. Years later, her husband bigamously remarried and was gaoled for three months. Elizabeth lived a pauper's life until her death of 'senile decay' in 1893. She was seventy-two.

Mary Anne Wentworth and Ruth Richardson were well-behaved prisoners. Mary Anne married well while still serving her sentence and then again after her first husband died. She lived comfortably until her death at the age of ninety-one in 1911. Ruth married a farmer, dropping her age on the marriage certificate by about fifteen years to twenty-one. She died of consumption, or tuberculosis, in 1858.[13]

Cascades inmates were constantly in and out of the place, usually over minor infractions. Rebellious Lydia Clay from Huddersfield might have been among the women Colonel George Mundy saw at the Cascades Female Factory on New Year's Day 1851. Mundy was the senior military officer among a small group visiting Hobart's Cascades Female Factory, apparently as a kind of holiday sight-seeing excursion. The facility, accessible still today, is wedged into a gully at the foot of Mount Wellington, its buildings enclosed in a high wall. Its inmates were contained by barred gates and sharp-eyed turnkeys – 'it is, in short, a gaol in every respect,' wrote Mundy. The matron, 'a dignified lady who looked quite capable of maintaining strict discipline', greeted the visitors.

There were 730 women and 130 infants in the prison. A group of seventy or eighty women was lined up for inspection in one of the squares that make up the establishment. They were available for hire as servants and were 'the better conducted, and the pregnant women'. Elsewhere, Colonel Mundy saw 'more troublesome and notorious characters, who were under restraint and not permitted to go into service'. Their uniform was 'a very unbecoming one' consisting of 'a white mob cap and a dress of grey duffle'. As the visitors passed along the ranks 'the poor creatures saluted us with a running fire of curtseys, and a dead silence was everywhere observed'.

In the exercise yard were sixty or so women with babies from two days to two years old, all silent:

One would have thought them all deaf and dumb; – never was I before in so numerous a nursery; – I hope I never may again! The children were mostly healthy and pretty. As for their mothers—there must, I suppose, be a good deal in dress as an element of beauty – for I scarcely saw a tolerably pretty woman in seven hundred. Some of the females, I found, were the hired nurses of the establishment – not the mothers of the children. Of these latter many, it appears, merely enter the factory to deposit their 'kid forlorn,' and, when sufficiently recovered, return to service in the town or country within the district to which their ticket or pass extends, and not a few re-enter its walls as soon as it is possible for them to require again obstetric assistance.

Mundy knew that 'many of these poor brats will never know their own fathers – their mothers, perhaps, know them no better: and many of the wretched little ones, in the hands of the nurses, will never know either parent.'

The visiting doctor said that the more troublesome women had been put on half rations and dosed with an emetic to induce nausea and vomiting. This kept them quiet and prevented complaints from those with 'fiery temperaments'. Mundy then went to the solitary cells where women were carding and combing wool. The third cell he came to was dark and, he thought at first, empty:

> It looked like the den of a wolf, and I almost started back when from the extreme end of the floor I found a pair of bright, flashing eyes fixed on mine. Their owner arose and took a step or two forward; it was a small, slight, and quite young girl – very beautiful in feature and complexion – but it was the fierce beauty of the wild cat! I am a steady married man, of a certain age – but at no period of my life would I, for a trifle, have shared for half-an-hour the cell of that sleek little savage; for when she purred loudest I should have been most afraid of her claws!

The heavy cell door was slammed tight and the turnkey said the woman was one of the most unmanageable women in the prison. Mundy reflected that 'beauty is a sad distorter of man's perceptions! Justice ought to be doubly blindfolded when dealing with her. I fear me that the pang of pity that shot across my heart when that pretty prisoner was shut again from the light of day, might have found no place there had she been as ugly as the sins that brought her into trouble. I had no more stomach for solitary cells this day.'

Continuing the tour, they reached the laundry where 'Squads of women were up to their elbows in suds – carrying on the cruel process of wringing – or displaying their thick ankles as they spread the linen over the drying lines.' The women were doing the washing of the townspeople to earn money towards the upkeep of their prison. Mundy was 'pained to see so many very youthful creatures in this yard – delinquents in their earliest teens; debauched ere the pith had hardened in their little bones.'

The next stop was a room full of seamstresses, where most were busy at fine or detailed needlework. 'It was not impossible, the matron stated, that some of the elaborate shirt-fronts we should see at the Government-house ball this evening had been worked in this, and washed and "got up" in the last ward.' The convict women were making garments for the quality members of society.

Colonel Mundy was impressed with the cleanliness and discipline of the establishment, which he dutifully recorded in the matron's visitor book. But his final enjoinder was: 'See a Female Factory once, and don't do so again.'[14] The women of the Cascades were not at liberty to take Mundy's advice, though the feisty Lydia Clay did eventually settle down enough to be granted a ticket-of-leave in 1851 and a conditional pardon two years afterwards. She married in 1850 but was widowed in 1854. A year later she remarried but in 1858, at the age of forty-eight, she was dead – an 'abscess on the brain'.

THE CHARNEL HOUSE

The system established in New South Wales from 1788, and, within a few years its colonial offshoot, Van Diemen's Land, differed fundamentally from previous forms of convict transportation within the empire. From the seventeenth century, felons had been sent to the Americas and elsewhere through an ad hoc bureaucracy of government legislation, the whims of different courts, and the business interests of merchants who were often slave traders as well. The settlement founded at what became the city of Sydney was from the first a government operation. Indeed, it was a military establishment in which the rule applying for a very long time was purely martial law, tending to be perfunctory and favouring extreme punishments. Even as a more civil society evolved, the system remained in powerful domination, affecting all aspects of colonial life, free or bound. Convicts not required for government service or incarcerated for crimes committed in the colonies were mostly 'assigned' to free settlers requiring labour, or to officials to assist with running their households, the land grants they usually held or some aspects of their office, such as clerical or other work. Despite its laudable aims of providing labour for the colony and the opportunity for convicts to reform, learn new skills and, originally at least, to obtain a grant of land at the end of their sentences, the assignment system was ready-made for corruption and oppression, as noted by Charles White, an early historian of the convict days:

Under its operation New South Wales became one of the largest slave plantations the world has ever seen, the form of slavery being more degrading than that existing anywhere the wide world over in times either ancient or modern. I have only lightly touched some of the worst features of the system; they will not bear probing in public – the rottenness and corruption that would be revealed would be too offensive to look upon . . . For over fifty years New South Wales was one vast charnel house![15]

White went on to quote (unattributed) from the memoirs of the Irish rebel leader, Joseph Holt:

It would have been far more merciful to have hanged all who violated the laws of their country, than to have sent them out to New South Wales, subject to the unmerciful treatment of human tigers, who tortured or killed those within their power according to the caprice of the moment. I saw many a fine man die in misery, inch by inch, from the oppression he experienced – the most cruel of all deaths.[16]

Later historians have presented broader and more balanced interpretations of convictism in Australia, indicating the diversity and complexity of the overall experience. Nevertheless, the intent and, for many, the reality of convictism involved the minute control of almost every detail of daily life for convicts in government occupations – and their wives and children. The extent of this subjugation is reflected in some of a lengthy set of instructions issued by Governor Sir Ralph Darling in 1829.[17] Most convicts were to be set to agricultural production, their labour being both reforming and productive. The assumption was that the majority of the convict population were habitual criminals and loafers: 'As an aversion to honest industry and labour has been the chief cause of most of the convicts incurring the penalties of the law, they shall be employed at some species of labour of an [sic] uniform kind, which they cannot evade, and by which they will have an opportunity of becoming habituated to regular employment.' While carrying out this work: '. . . the use of the hoe and spade shall be as much as possible adopted; and where the number of men who can be employed in agriculture is sufficient to raise food for the settlement with these implements, the use of the plough shall be given up; and no working cattle are to be employed in operations which can be effected by men and hand-carts.'

Convicts were to be 'steadily and constantly employed at hard labour from sunrise to sunset, one hour being allowed for breakfast and one hour for dinner during the winter six months, but two hours will be allotted for dinner during the summer'. The commandant had complete control not only of convicts but also of free settlers, including the wives and children of convicts, who were to be employed by the government and paid in credits redeemable only at what was effectively a company store:

> The wives and children of convicts are not to be allowed to convey money or property of any kind to the settlement, nor to possess any live stock or poultry, and they are strictly to be prohibited from carrying on any trade or traffic in the Settlement; but they will be furnished with employment in spinning flax, making straw hats or bonnets, making up slops, and such other work as they may be capable of performing, the materials for which will be supplied from the Government store. They will receive credit in the books of the Settlement, at the market or factory prices, on such work being returned to the stores; and the amount of their earnings shall be annually placed in the Saving Bank at Sydney, to be received by them on their return from the Settlement, as a means of support on their arrival.

Convict families had to attend the Sunday musters and convicts were not allowed to send or receive letters except through the commandant who had the right to read them. Some rules were designed to protect convicts: 'The constables and overseers are not to strike or push the convicts, and no punishment is to be inflicted but by the express order of the commandant.' The evidence suggests that this rule was often broken, and the main tenor of the regulations was directed at ensuring the full subjugation of the convicts and anyone who might interfere with that control.

Conditions of this kind could be seen as a form of judicial slavery. Even a member of the executive government said so. The hated Sir George Arthur, perhaps surprisingly, wrote of the convict's lot as one 'deprived of liberty, exposed to all the caprice of the family to whose service he may happen to be assigned, and subject to the most summary laws. His condition in no respect differs from that of the slave, except that his master cannot apply corporal punishment by his own hands, or those of his overseer, and has a property in him only for a limited period. Idleness and insolence of expression or of looks, anything betraying the insurgent spirit, subject him to the chain-gang or the triangle, or hard labour on the roads.'[18]

According to Sir William Molesworth, chair of the inquiry that led to the cessation of transportation to New South Wales, the former Governor of New South Wales, Sir Richard Bourke, 'designated as a slave code the law which enabled a magistrate, invariably himself a master of convicts, to inflict 50 lashes on a convict for drunkenness, disobedience of orders, neglect to work, absconding, abusive language to his master or overseer, or any other disorderly or dishonest conduct.'[19]

The words of governors and British politicians were important and so were written down and preserved in official records. Few ordinary convicts left behind written evidence of their troubles in the 'charnel house' of New South Wales or the hell that was Van Diemen's Land. But Charles Ashton, transported to Van Diemen's Land with several hundred others on the *David Malcolm* in 1845, did so. Around thirty-three years old, he was convicted at Chester of stealing money and given a life sentence. Seven years later, while at Port Arthur, Ashton tried to escape, knocking down a constable. He received a sentence of fifty lashes and thirty days solitary confinement on bread and water in a darkened cell with only one blanket against the cold air. He also served a year in the 'light cells' wearing extra heavy chains weighing thirty-five pounds (nearly sixteen kilograms). 'Rather rough on a prisoner?' was his comment on this treatment, together with a poem graphically describing the living nightmare that he and his fellow sufferers endured:

I dreamt I saw some prisoners bound,
Standing in heavy chains on the parade ground,
'tis true as I do tell this tale,
They marched both in and out of the gaol;
On every morning when the first bell rings
Up from our beds we are forced to spring –
To wash ourselves and brush our hair,
Sweep out our cells we must not dare;
Nor we must not dare a word to speak
Or the silent system rules we break.

Then to the lamp-post we are dragged,

When our mouth is gagged, and our wrist is darbed. [handcuffed]

While laboring under a scorching sun

The sweat from off our brow does run;

And whatever labor we are at

We must not look this way nor that,

For the overseer says that will do,

And to the court we are forced to go.

Then the Commandant does at me stare,

'You are charged with idleness, I do declare,

It is true the overseer I must believe,

And fifty lashes you must receive.'

Now I lay my coat, vest, and shirt on the ground,

And to the triangles I am bound,

When the flagellator did behind me stand

With the cat-a'-nine-tails in his hand.

He flogged me till my back was raw

And painted with my crimson gore;

When I awoke with a frightful scream –

It was a reality, and not a dream.[20]

Little else is known of Charles Ashton, other than that he died in 1859 and is buried at Fingal, another faceless victim of the system whose voice nevertheless still speaks to us through his rough verse. Some other convicts also managed to tell their stories.

THE HERO OF VAN DIEMEN'S LAND

The man digging his own grave on the Isle of the Dead was tall and burly. As he cut deeper into the ground, he was careful to pat the back of the shovel against the earth walls. This would keep the worms out. Completing his work, the gravedigger returned to his crude hut to eat and sleep. That night he had an unwanted visitor. His Satanic Majesty spoke directly to Mark Jeffrey. Whatever Satan said, the frequently pugnacious but pious Mark was terrified. He rushed to the shore and hurriedly lit a signal fire to let his gaolers across the water know he wanted to be taken back to Port Arthur prison.

This was only one of many lurid stories told about the thief, cheapjack, pugilist, occasional fortune-teller and killer, Mark Jeffrey. He arrived in Van Diemen's Land in 1850 following a hard life of crime and violence in England. When sentenced for his sins, he recalled: 'fifteen years transportation appeared to me equal to being consigned to a living grave. What a vista of utter misery and torture stretched before me. Surely death itself would be thrice welcome before the enforcement of such a life.' Mark would one day beg to be put to death, but now he was so incensed that he threatened the life of his co-accused, John Hart, who he blamed for his predicament; 'Heedless of the consequences, as these despairing thoughts rushed through my mind, I showered a tirade of abuse upon the treacherous John Hart, and would there and then have committed some bodily injury upon him had not the warders come to his assistance.'

The court officials had a hard time subduing 'Big Mark', six foot tall, fifteen stone, and well able to use his 'fists to the best advantage'. He was dragged out of the court and later, along with his accomplices was to spend time in Millbank Prison. Here, he behaved himself until coming, apparently accidentally, face to face with John Hart. Big Mark now demonstrated his preternatural ability to instil terror. He told Hart 'you have signed your death warrant. You know how determined I am; you know that I am never thwarted in my wishes; and on the first opportunity, I shall surely put an end to your existence and so revenge myself.' His menacing tone and body language 'made such an impression on Hart that no sooner had I uttered them than his features grew swollen and discoloured, a spasm twisted his lips, and he fell speechless and motionless to the ground like a man stricken with apoplexy'.

Hart died three days later. Big Mark Jeffrey's apparent ability to kill a man by threat alone made him a legend to his felonious peers. This act, together with his large physique and bad temper, made him both feared and hated by other convicts. He was frequently involved in brawls and falsely implicated in escape plots. He refused to submit to any order or authority that offended his strong sense of what was right and just. But when well fed and not provoked, Mark was friendly and personable. Careening between these extremes of personality, Mark Jeffrey's long years of bondage in Van Diemen's Land were to be brutal and grinding.

After his initial apprehension, Jeffrey was transferred to the Woolwich hulks where 'Starvation, misery, and want beset me on every side. Day after day my life was horrible, and I cursed existence.' There was more trouble here, resulting in a charge of assault and a return to prison, this time Newgate, to await trial. Outraged by the unjust treatment of his captors, he continued to resist the system. When he was found guilty and sentenced to transportation for life, he begged to be hanged instead, declaring to the judge: 'Life in gaol is worse than torture to me, and I long for hanging, so as to be removed from such a cowardly, tyrannical mass of humanity as that in authority over the helpless prisoner.' He called on the judge to 'carry out the law to its fullest extent. It is your duty to do so, and if I had the means I would shoot you at the present moment and so make sure of what I most desire – the gallows.'

Back in his cell, Jeffrey continued his violent rebellion whenever provoked, which was frequently. At one point he feigned insanity, even managing to froth at the mouth, such was his determination to transgress. He was then transported to Norfolk Island, via Van Diemen's Land. On seeing the 'savage grandeur' of the rugged Van Diemen's Land, he recalled, 'I would rather be dead than be compelled to live in a savage country like this!' In time, Big Mark would suffer here, but his first Australian penance would be served on the dreaded Norfolk Island.

This tormented and savage man's island imprisonment began well. He was made a gardener, a relatively pleasant job. But soon there were hints of the terrors of Norfolk. He found out about the 'races' – not horses, but the regular Monday morning entertainment where around 150 'incorrigibles' were tried. Depending on the verdicts, 'Some of these were flogged, some spread-eagled and gagged, and others sentenced to solitary confinement.' After himself narrowly escaping a flogging on 'race day', Jeffrey was made a 'sub-constable', placing him in authority over other convicts, supervised by a gaoler. Apart from some minor incidents, this position suited Jeffrey well until his temper again triumphed. He threatened an official and was promptly sent to the bush to work as a gardener. Later he worked as a cook, another suitable occupation for a man of his appetite.

But the 'thraldom of my unruly temper' kept Jeffrey in almost perpetual trouble. Labouring in thirty six-pound chains in a quarry, he threatened the overseer with death. After a stretch in solitary, he saw an opportunity after being returned to the quarry chain gang: 'I was in a state bordering on frenzy, and one day when he had irritated me beyond endurance I seized a spade and rushed towards him with the full intention of splitting his head open. But I was heavily ironed, and he therefore had no difficulty in getting out of my way.' This failed attempt on the overseer's life earned Jeffrey fifty lashes and solitary confinement in fifty-six-pound chains.

By now the notoriously cruel commandant John Price, known to convicts as 'the demon', had taken an interest in the defiant Jeffrey, visiting him in his cell two or three times a week. On these occasions he would 'foppishly' raise his eyeglass and contemptuously ask the manacled convict how he liked his treatment. 'I never replied, but to show my unquenchable hatred and defiance, spat at him.' During another visit, Price tormented Jeffrey with his knowledge of convict cant:

'How do you like it now, my joker? I think I have taken all the flashness out of you!'

Then I found my tongue.

'You unnatural monster!' I shouted. 'What pleasure can it give you to witness the sufferings of your fellow-men? Come, take my place, and learn from experience how a man can enjoy such punishment.'

'What!' he exclaimed, 'Belly proud still! You are strong yet, my joker? I must see if I cannot take it out of you.'

He then left me once more to reflection and solitude.

The meagre diet of corncracker, the heavy manacles and dysentery took their toll and Jeffrey's health deteriorated. He was put in lighter irons but soon succumbed. Rescued just in time by the doctor, he lay for three months in hospital. When released to work he was frequently back there, suffering from recurring dysentery. These trials and troubles did not subdue his spirit. He continued his abrasive way through convict life, avoiding the informers who traded information about their fellow inmates for favours from the warders, including the notorious bushranger Martin Cash, who he called a coward.

Norfolk Island gaol was closed in 1855 and the prisoners were transferred to Van Diemen's Land. Here, Jeffrey seems to have taken to calling himself 'Newmarket John' to hide his true identity. It made no difference to his violent temper. He began working for a magistrate who was highly appreciative of his strength, skills and work ethic. As usual, everything went well for a while, with Jeffrey negotiating better conditions and food for himself in return for his labour. But eventually matters came to a head over the wages that the unnamed magistrate should pay him. Twelve pounds a year, said the magistrate, but Jeffrey demanded forty pounds. The magistrate pointed out that Jeffrey only needed to work for another six months before gaining his ticket-of-leave. Then he could marry the servant girl, rent one of the magistrate's farms, and receive a full free man's wage of forty pounds a year. You can 'make your fortune', said the magistrate. 'I told him that my future prospects had nothing to do with him. I wanted £40 a year, or I would not stay with him. Then my blood began to get hot at the thought of this man reaping the advantage of my superior strength and ability, and I told him my opinion of him, and demanded my discharge.'

Unable to control himself, Jeffrey went on to tell the man that his 'tyrannical conduct' was well known and that he had secured the property he now owned through the labours of the 'prisoners from Maria Island whom you ground down'. Then he drew the sword that he had secretly been preparing in the farm's smithy and 'brandishing it ominously over the magistrate's head declared "I have been the brave hero of England . . . and I am the brave hero of Tasmania! Write me my discharge, or I will give you what I have given others."' The magistrate's wife came into the room and seeing this screamed out 'James, James, for God's sake give him his discharge! I can see something desperate in the man's face.' Wisely, the magistrate did just that and Jeffrey went on his way.

There was another sentence of nine months at Port Arthur for attacking a magistrate. Here, Jeffrey resumed his campaign for proper rations and earned himself an extension to his original sentence, as well as solitary confinement and a stint in the Model Prison. This was the creation of nineteenth-century penal thinking and involved prisoners held in separate cells with no communication with others. Whenever they were out of the cells the men were 'compelled to wear masks with eyelet-holes, so that the only faces a prisoner saw were those of the constables and warders'. At Sunday service they sat in silence on seats with individual partitions to ensure they had no human contact.

Jeffrey was released from Port Arthur and resumed his wandering lifestyle with a ticket-of-leave. Like many convicts, alcohol was a problem and although he managed to keep working and receive good wages, the grog probably contributed to the decline in his health which began during this period. He also began to repent of his ways. Under the pain of his afflicted leg, life became a burden to him and 'Never previously had I more regretted my youthful follies and excesses, which had practically given birth to the miserable condition I was then in. Taverns and the haunts of ill-repute, spit [sic] of all watchfulness and self-control, have proved a continual source of wretchedness and suffering to me from that time until the present.' His leg became so painful that he pleaded with two doctors to amputate it. They refused, which was fortunate, as the limb made a partial recovery, though it would continue to trouble him for the rest of his still tumultuous life.

In 1872 Big Mark killed a man in a Hobart pub brawl. In drink, James Hunt unwisely called Jeffrey 'a Port Arthur Flagellator'. This ultimate convict insult cost him his life. A few days later he finally succumbed to the beating Jeffrey gave him. Jeffrey was returned to Port Arthur for life on a verdict of manslaughter. His existence resumed its familiar pattern of violent reactions to tyranny and injustice. He again suffered solitary confinement as he protested and complained about conditions, unfair treatment and, the issue that he particularly crusaded for, the deliberate dilution of rations by corrupt officials. So incorrigible and unruly had the violent man become that he was sent to the Isle of the Dead to dig graves. He was happy there, taking particular pleasure in excavating and maintaining what he intended to be his own final resting place, until his encounter with Satan.

Back in the Port Arthur prison again, his complaints and ill-tempered violence earned him few friends. His petitions for a pardon were ignored year after year until 1890, when 'at last, through the influence of some kind gentleman, who interceded for me, I was sent from the Hobart Gaol to the Launceston Invalid Depot, as a ticket-of-leave man, on the 23rd December, 1890'. Physically broken, with an ulcerated leg and shuffling around with the aid of sticks, the troublesome convict spent the last few years of his life here. He was, perhaps surprisingly, popular with the staff and other inmates and he was even given a position of authority in the establishment. His obituary summed up the life and death of the Hero of England and Van Diemen's Land, pointing out how he:

> . . . brought upon himself every kind of punishment inflicted upon refractory prisoners. His great enemy was his temper, which was of the most violent character, and when aroused he was exceedingly dangerous. He was essentially an egotist-physically and mentally strong but without balance, his animal nature dominating all that was good in him. He desired death, for his life had been a failure, and his sufferings during the past two years were very acute. Before he left England he was injured in the chest by a kick during a fight. Some time ago a swelling appeared in his chest, and the growth increased day by day. He regarded the swelling as his 'death warrant', and his favourite expression was, 'I have given my life; read it and see how I have suffered.'[21]

Big Mark was sixty-eight years old and had spent many of those years in one prison or another in England and in Australia. His almost pathological sense of fair play and a vague notion that he was a protector of the rights of other convicts, as well as his own, marked him out as an unusual individual. His volcanic temper and chilling presence gained him notoriety and a measure of respect, as he struggled against, as well as negotiated with, what he saw as oppression and humiliation. And there was one other thing that distinguished Big Mark Jeffrey from the vast body of human suffering he survived – he was able to tell his story.[22] Other surprising lives must be excavated from their traces in scattered archives.

THE MYSTERIES OF MINA

Her black hair, light hazel eyes and 'rather wide mouth' caused the Dublin press to describe Mina (Euphemia Mercevona) McCaulfield,[23] five feet five inches tall, as a 'pretty young woman'. The servant to the wife of a wealthy merchant, nineteen-year-old[24] Mina was unable to resist the jewels and fine fabrics of her mistress. In 1847 she was arrested for their theft and sentenced to seven years transportation.

In Van Diemen's Land she quickly mastered the vagaries of the penal system, caused no trouble and, with a 'very good' character, was by 1849 married to a free sailor named Frances Jury. The first of what would be many children began arriving and the seemingly rehabilitated Mina received her ticket-of-leave in 1851. After successfully running a guesthouse and early tourism business together with Mina in Hobart, Jury secured a government position in South Australia and the whole family moved to Adelaide in 1865.

But now Mina's success story turned very sour. After a few years, Jury died in a gun accident, leaving Mina with at least eleven children aged between two and sixteen years. The family soon became largely dependent on charity as Mina struggled to provide for her children and herself in Adelaide and then in Melbourne, where she was living with her children by 1868.[25] And then a distant family link to the perpetrator of the century's greatest ruse completely changed the course of Mina Jury's life.

In July 1865 the front page of the *Sydney Morning Herald* carried an unusual advertisement. 'A handsome reward will be given to any person who can furnish such information as will discover the fate of Roger Charles Tichborne.' Curious readers were informed that Tichborne had disappeared ten years earlier while sailing home from Rio de Janeiro aboard the ill-fated *La Bella*. Rumours of survivors being taken to Melbourne prompted his grieving mother to place the advertisement, which also pointed out that Tichborne was 'the son of Sir James Tichborne, Bart., now deceased and is heir to all his estates'.[26] And so began a very strange tale.

A few months later, Lady Tichborne heard from an Australian solicitor with the wonderful news that her son was alive. He was a butcher in the town of Wagga Wagga by the name of Tom Castro. Although the rotund Tom was larger than the slight Tichborne and spoke no French, in which language Tichborne was fluent, he insisted on the truth of his story. It was ten years since Tichborne's disappearance and his appearance might have changed. At least, Lady Tichborne thought this might be so and asked Castro to come to England. In December 1866 he arrived and met the family and their friends, convincing many that he was the missing heir. He was set up in splendour and lived in style with the English elite.

But there were sceptics. Even as the persuasive butcher from Wagga enjoyed his newfound luxury, investigations were made. Eventually it was discovered that Castro was, in fact, Arthur Orton from Wapping in East London. Lady Tichborne died in 1868 and some family members brought a civil case against Orton, as he was now known. The trial became a press and popular circus, lasting almost a year until March 1872. It was soon followed by criminal proceedings against Orton for perjury. For over six months a jury heard a procession of witnesses for the defence and the prosecution, including Mina.

Mina's connection by marriage to Orton's family made her a witness for the prosecution. She was paid to cross the seas to testify at the trial. She contributed her convincing evidence about Orton's identity to an already persuasive case against the butcher's audacious deception. She recalled how she met Orton in Hobart, where he claimed never to have been, and how she loaned him a substantial amount, only to lose her money when he disappeared the day repayment was due. Orton simply stared at Mina 'with an expression of mingled curiosity and amusement', but she persisted: '"He is Arthur Orton, sir, to whom I lent the money"; and nods familiarly to claimant, who does not reciprocate her friendly greetings.'[27]

Orton was found guilty and given fourteen years hard labour. Controversy continued as the claimant's supporters tried to have a royal commission look into the matter. They failed, and Orton served ten years before his release. Except on one occasion when he confessed to being an imposter, later withdrawn, he continued to insist on being the lost heir. The rest of his life was lived in poverty. He died in 1898 and was buried as 'Sir Roger Tichborne', the name appearing on his death certificate and on the coffin plate.

During the trial Mina received a grilling from the prosecution but handled herself with aplomb, refusing to be badgered. While in London, Mina met other witnesses, including a man she took up with. They lodged together briefly before breaking up. Now Mina, only once before convicted of a crime, began a remarkable life of thieving and confidence tricks. She and her lover stole from the owner of the Ship hotel as they left to go their separate ways. Mina travelled north with her share, surviving by thieving and, perhaps inspired by Orton's initial success, impersonating gentlewomen. She was often caught and served several lengthy prison terms, always returning to crime after her release.

Back in Australia, her many abandoned children[28] fended for themselves as best they could. Her oldest son, 'who was the principal support to me', died before Mina left for England. Some went into care or became wards of the state, several absconding when they got the chance. Those who survived into adulthood went on to various careers in the railways, farming and mining. As far as the records can tell, Mina and her surviving children were never reunited.[29]

Mina continued her precarious life of theft, deception and fraud. Perhaps her most daring crime was defrauding both the Earl of Kilmorey and the Duke of Edinburgh. Under another of her aliases, she wrote to the aristocrats with a confected but convincing sob story and managed to extract from them the then very substantial sum of twenty pounds. This earned her a year of hard labour,[30] a relatively short term compared with the usual seven-year sentences she received for most of her other infractions.

Mina's married name, together with the many aliases she adopted, kept her true identity from the authorities in the many different locations where she was apprehended. But she eventually became an officially registered 'habitual criminal', claiming her birthplace as Australia. In 1885 she was again in prison for more stealing and imposture, this time targeting the Freemasons and the mayor of Stoke-on-Trent. She was discharged just before Christmas in 1889. Her dark hair had turned to grey, her face and arms were scarred, and she was missing some teeth. Her occupation was entered in the discharge records as 'pianoforte teacher', though she seems to have preferred robbing to teaching and continued to offend. By 1890 she was wanted in her native country as well as for thefts in England.[31] But there are no further records of her apprehension or crimes.

What became of Mina? Perhaps she continued her colourful career of robbery more successfully than previously under yet another alias. Maybe she retired, perhaps with a partner who was able to support her in her final years. She may even have returned to Australia and her living children, though probably not. We will likely never know what became of this resourceful and capable woman whose talents were, sadly, lost to crime even after a considerable period of rehabilitation and respectability.

THE END OF THE SYSTEM?

Through the years from 1788, the transportation system's dual functions of social and political cleansing and colonial economic development ground on. Irish, English and Welsh rebels continued to grace the manifests of convict ships following famines, risings and ongoing disaffection. Those convicted of transportable crimes formed the bulk of the unwilling migrants to New South Wales, Norfolk Island and Van Diemen's Land, contributing to their growth. But the voices of those who opposed transportation grew louder in the places of power and influence.

Much of the public antagonism towards the system was based on graphic accounts of the mistreatment suffered by many prisoners, well ventilated by the Anti-Transportation League and a press always hungry for lurid stories and graphic details. There was no shortage of these. As well as loss of liberty and free will, convicts could be subjected to disciplinary measures that included imprisonment, solitary confinement, hard labour in chains on roads, public buildings and in mines, the dangers of the cruel treadmill and the crushing physical and psychological brutality of flogging. In 1840 the British government finally heard the growing din of disapproval from the general public, politicians and critics. An Order-in-Council declared that no more convicts were to be transported to New South Wales, though they could still be sent to Van Diemen's Land, Norfolk Island, Bermuda and other places in the empire.[32]

In 1842, 200 convicts were sent to repair public works in the strategic holding of Gibraltar. The *Owen Glendower* that brought them there was transformed from a once-proud frigate to a hulk where prisoners were kept until cells could be built ashore. Britain continued to dispatch convict labour to this destination, many serving two or three years there before moving on to Australia to complete their sentences. The 'Gib prisoners', as they called themselves, reached a peak of just over 900 by 1863,[33] spread between two hulks in the harbour and a wooden 'barracks' ashore.

They worked very hard. The prisoners began their labours at 4.30 a.m. either in their prison quarters or on the buildings and fortifications. They were marched to work in ankle chains or handcuffs. The hot work of quarrying stone was a major task and infractions of the rules were punished with severe floggings. The whip used was a heavy 'cat-o'-nine tails' of a type once common in the Royal Navy. A 'flogging mast' was the usual pinion post for these punishments.[34] The Gibraltar convict establishment was not closed until 1875 and proved a convenient substitute destination after the close of transportation to Western Australia.

It took some time for the juggernaut of exile to the Antipodes to wind down after the convict ships ceased their trade. Prisoners still had to serve out sometimes lengthy sentences, ensuring that the infrastructure and organization of the system remained in place for many years. In 1870 an observer, George Dunderdale, looked back over the human experiences of the bleak years in New South Wales from 1788 and compared them to the lot of black slaves:

> Many men who had been prisoners of the Crown, or seamen, lived on the islands in Bass' Straits, as well as on islands in the Pacific Ocean, fishing, sealing, or hunting, and sometimes cultivating patches of ground. The freedom of this kind of life was pleasing to those who had spent years under restraint in ships, in gaols, in chain-gangs, or as slaves to settlers in the bush, for the lot of the assigned servant was often worse than that of a slave, as he had to give his labour for nothing but food and clothing, and was liable to be flogged on any charge of disobedience, insolence, or insubordination which his master might choose to bring against him. Moreover, the black slave might be sold for cash, for five hundred to a thousand dollars, according to the quality of the article and the state of the market, so that it was for the enlightened self-interest of the owner to keep him in saleable condition. But the white slave was unsaleable, and his life of no account. When he died another could be obtained for nothing from the cargo of the next convict ship.

He allowed that some 'masters' did not ill-treat 'their men' but 'with regard to others, the exercise of despotic authority drew forth all the evil passions of their souls, and made them callous to the sufferings of their servants'.[35]

Transported convicts were not slaves, but the brutalities the system fostered were similar enough to those suffered by black slaves for commentators of the period, and convicts themselves, to frequently make the comparison. Perceptions of this kind gave rise to the attitude known as 'the convict stain', a belief that convictism was a dark blot on the founding of modern Australia and was best ignored and forgotten. This prejudice persisted for generations and has not been entirely erased.

Even as George Dunderdale wrote down his thoughts on 'prisoners of the Crown', there were convicts still serving out their sentences on the eastern shores of the country. Over on the western edge of the continent, another group of transported men were killing time.

10

RIVER OF TEARS

Have I no future left me?
Is there no struggling ray
From the sun of my life outshining
Down on my darksome way?

John Boyle O'Reilly[1]

Governor James Stirling's prime piece of Western Australian real estate began taking settlers in 1829. Unlike New South Wales and Van Diemen's Land, the Swan River was to be a free colony, developing on the bounty of its resources and the enterprise of the British yeoman farmers and respectable tradesmen it hoped to attract. But there were early signs that all might not proceed to plan. Two structures were quickly erected on the new land. As befitted a pious age, one was a church. The other was a twelve-sided stone building intended as a gaol, the Fremantle Roundhouse, its layout influenced by Jeremy Bentham's panopticon. And while the Swan River aspired to a better society than that of the convict east coast, it was not immune from the evils of transportation and would come to find the system useful in a number of ways.

Just after sunset on 4 March 1830 the 440 tons of teak, iron and copper-sheathing that was the sailing ship *Cumberland* ground into an unseen reef off Cape Leeuwin. Captain Steel ordered the boats lowered as the forty-nine crew and two passengers cast whatever they could into the sea to lighten the stricken vessel. But the pumps were unable to prevent the sea being sucked in. By three the next morning the hold was full of water. After an abortive attempt to reach the shore in the ship's cutter, Steel ordered 'Abandon ship' at 5 a.m. Two of the ship's four boats managed to reach Fremantle two days later, while the others remained in the area and were not rescued until it was too late for the three crewmen who died of exposure.

As well as a cargo of coal, the *Cumberland* was carrying the worldly goods of the pioneering Bussell family to their new home. Driven ashore by storms, she soon broke up, and it was five years before William Ledgard and his thieving companions discovered decayed bodies in the isolated sands of Cape Hamelin, along with the belongings of the Bussells, strewn along miles of beach and surf. Clothes, furniture and jewellery lay there for the taking. And so, the plunderers helped themselves. They were discovered attempting to sell off the loot and six were brought to trial in January 1835. The evidence against them was overwhelming and, as one of their number turned informant in return for a pardon, they had no choice but to plead guilty. Ledgard and one other were transported for seven years; three were transported for fourteen years, the extra time being punishment for another robbery they had committed. The youngest member of the gang received six months' hard labour.[2] Their sentences were to be served in Van Diemen's Land, where they were duly dispatched.[3]

Barely five years after its foundation, the 'free' colony on the Swan River, now officially Western Australia, was availing itself of the legal instrument of transportation to expel its convicted criminals. As it had been elsewhere in the Australian colonies, the same weapon was deployed against indigenous resisters and troublemakers. But in Western Australia, Aboriginal people received very special treatment.

A RATS' NEST

The local indigenous leader, Yagan, was involved in several fatal attacks on Swan River settlers, probably as part of the retributive code known as 'payback'. He was outlawed, captured and 'exiled' to Carnac Island in 1832, along with other Aboriginal prisoners. The group soon escaped, but Yagan was later shot dead. His body was decapitated, the head smoked, decorated, and sent to England as a colonial trophy.[4] Other indigenous troublemakers would soon find themselves transported to a different convenient island, just across the water from the mouth of the Swan River.

To the original inhabitants of the Perth region, now known collectively as Noongar, the nineteen square kilometres of rock lying just offshore from Fremantle was *Wadjemup*, 'a place across the water'. In local mythology it possessed negative spiritual significance. Early Dutch explorers named the island 'Rottnest', mistaking its small indigenous marsupial 'quokkas' for rats. From 1838 the island was used as a prison for Aboriginal men and boys condemned to be transported there from many different parts of the colony. Six of the men sent there in 1838 for various crimes against bodies and property were manacled by one leg each and 'were all made fast together by passing a trace chain through their irons and locking the end with a handcuff : the chain was placed round a cypress-tree.' In the stormy night they managed to burn through the tree and free themselves sufficiently to struggle down to the beach where a boat was moored, 'and there with some of the iron work contrived to break the handcuff, which united the two ends of the chain. They all got into the boat and pushed off, trusting to the open sea'. The boat capsized in the surf and one escapee drowned. The surviving fugitives robbed settler properties before they were apprehended, causing the newspaper to opine 'we are bound to regard the whole of the proceedings connected with this affair as affording a serious but useful lesson to the aborigines, who would set at defiance our institutions for their correction or instruction'.[5]

The following year Rottnest was made into an Aboriginal prison. The inmates were employed in quarrying and general labouring which built the lighthouse, and they also operated a salt works. In the 1850s they were taken back to the mainland to work road gangs. Aboriginal prisoners were also brought to the island from distant parts of Western Australia, long and hard journeys during which the prisoners were sometimes chained. A Nullarbor Mirning man named Benjamin told the 1883 Royal Commission inquiring into the treatment of Aboriginal prisoners:

I walked from Eyre Sand Patch to Albany naked, with a chain on my neck. My neck was sore from chain. I knocked up from the long walk. Policeman Truslove no good. He hit me for knocking up . . . I came with a bullock chain around my neck from Eyre Sand Patch to Albany. When it rained my neck was very sore from the chain . . . I had no clothes given to me from Eyre Sand Patch to Albany.[6]

Over the years Rottnest held a growing number of inmates, peaking at 170 during 1880. An influenza outbreak killed sixty prisoners. The resulting inquiry, conducted while a deadly measles epidemic raged through the prisoners, revealed the lack of clothing, bedding and warmth. Four prisoners were sleeping in the small cells, with each having only sixty centimetres of space. There were some improvements made to the poor conditions in which they were housed and treated and the octagonal Quod[7] prison was erected as part of these improvements, though it was inadequate for decent accommodation.

Incidents of intergenerational violence and probable murder by the father and son superintendents, Henry Vincent and William Vincent, were shoddily investigated. The Vincents were both tried for the killing of a prisoner in 1865. A coroner decided that his death was due to natural causes rather than William Vincent's vicious attack. He was given a sentence of three months' hard labour.

As Perth and Fremantle expanded, calls grew louder for the island to be opened up to holiday-makers. The prison was closed in 1904, though a number of inmates served out the remainder of their time, helping to establish the tourism industry that is now the island's main role. It has been estimated that possibly 4,000 indigenous men and boys were imprisoned on the island during its history as a gaol. For Aboriginal people from many parts of Western Australia the island is an especially unhappy place and still the subject of protest and dissent. As well as its history of incarceration, some 370, perhaps more, deceased inmates were buried in unmarked graves. Most died of disease, but at least five were hanged.[8]

THE CHILDREN'S FRIENDS

The morally and socially improving temper of the Victorian era saw some better treatment of orphaned and criminal juveniles. Instead of scooping them up from the streets and dockyards, destitute and homeless boys and girls were saved from lives of crime and depravity by well-meaning charitable societies of many kinds.

The Children's Friend Society was founded in 1830 to retrieve orphaned, destitute, vagrant and criminal children from usually appalling circumstances. Initially, the Society was for boys only, but soon it also accepted girls. As usual, the reformers sent the children to various parts of the empire to assist with local development and population growth. At first, they were taken to Cape Colony and Canada, then to Western Australia. Twenty-five boys and four girls aged between ten and sixteen were sent out in 1834. Over the next eight years the Society shipped another hundred or so to the west.

Jane Green, aged fourteen, arrived in 1837. She found work as a servant to Captain Whitfield, one of the commissioners appointed to look after the welfare of the Society's charges, in July 1839. The following year Jane gave birth to Whitfield's child, which died at or shortly after birth. She was charged with its murder, but when Whitfield's paternity was discovered she received legal help and was acquitted of the charge. But she was then sentenced to two years imprisonment for concealing the birth of a child.[9] Public opinion was sufficiently outraged to force Whitfield to leave the colony. After her punishment, Jane went on to marry and have eight children and helped to pioneer the Rockingham–Mandurah area south of Perth. She died in 1909 aged eighty-six.[10]

Another scheme also brought juveniles to Western Australia. The Parkhurst institution for juvenile offenders on the Isle of Wight officially began transporting boys in 1842, though it seems that some came earlier. An account of the prison written in 1840 notes that over 130 of the 180 boys then held at Parkhurst were under sentence of transportation.[11] Eight years later the practice of sending Parkhurst inmates to Australia came up as an issue in a debate on the budget for the juvenile establishment in the House of Commons. Mr V. Smith said that 'though not officially, that many of those convicts had been sent to Australia, and that the colonists would willingly take many more of them. No young men ever went out in such excellent condition as these convicts did [a laugh].' Another member, J. Graham, previously in the Home Office, said that, while there, he had authorized Parkhurst boys to be sent to Australia and that 'those boys, taken from the very refuse of society here, were sent out so much improved in character and conduct as to be well suited for service in the colonial establishments of the country, and enabled to earn an honest livelihood for themselves. If such a system was for the advantage of these youth, it was at the same time for the interest of the colonies well understood.'[12]

In July 1840 eight-year-old William Beale was sentenced at Lewes Assizes in Sussex to seven years transportation for larceny. He was described as a 'laborer' [sic]. He landed in Fremantle from the Isle of Wight in October 1843. Presumably eleven years old by now, he was thought to be too small and weak[13] to work as an apprentice and one of his employers said he had barely been able to carry half a bucket of water.[14] William was quickly in trouble for neglecting his work, sleeping rough in the bush, absconding, and 'working on his own account'. He was also described by two of his 'masters' as a good worker. Eventually, the boy was 'paid off', as the records put it, and was last reported to be earning good wages of two pounds a month as a shepherd.[15] Hopefully, his entrepreneurial character led him to prosper, although a 'William Beale' received three months' hard labour for perjury in 1876 and it is not impossible that this was the Parkhurst boy, by then aged in his mid-forties.[16]

Shortly after William Beale began his new life in Western Australia, fifteen-year-old John Gaven (or Gavin or Gavan) arrived at Fremantle from Parkhurst as an 'apprentice' in 1843. He was assigned to the Pollard family of rural Dandalup as a servant and all seemed to be going well at first. He formed a close friendship with George, the eldest of the three Pollard boys and the one who usually took John's side when he was in trouble for minor infractions or not performing his work well enough. George even saved John's life when they were swimming together.

One day in February 1844 Mrs Pollard was not feeling well. John was going about his chores in what she later described as an unusual manner and did not seem himself. At one point he appeared in her room with a length of wood. Mrs Pollard ordered him out and told him to leave the board somewhere else until her husband returned. She then tried to sleep but was disturbed by singing in the next room. The singing stopped and Mrs Pollard got up to find John in the kitchen drinking from a basin. She asked him what he was doing, and he said he was filling a barrow with straw at the door of George's bedroom. Mrs Pollard went on preparing her dinner and then wondered where her son might be as she had not seen or heard him for some time:

> I went out of the kitchen towards the deceased's door, when I saw the prisoner rush out of that door looking wild as if in distraction. He began to stoop, and look down and about him, I asked him what he was looking for, he said nothing; I said he could not look for less. He continued walking about in the same way for a minute or so, when I said, 'Why Gaven, you are like one losing your senses; are you losing your reason, or what ails you, boy?', he made no answer that I heard.

Mrs Pollard then stood at the door of George's room and saw him lying on his bed with his back towards her. She called his name but there was no answer, so she went into the room and shook him:

> There was a coat over, and tucked under his head, I removed the coat, and saw him in a gore of blood, and thought it might have been from bleeding at the nose. I put my left hand under his face, and my right hand under the back of his head, to raise it up, and my hand sunk into the back of his head. I raised his face a little, and he breathed a few times. I clapped my hands and said, 'my child is smothered in his own blood'. I screamed, 'George, my jewel, tell me your murderer.' I am sure he was not dead when I first raised his head.

Michael Pollard heard his mother's cry and came running to find her 'going in and out of the deceased's room. He saw an adze lying on the floor covered with hair, and blood and brains. 'I found it lying on the floor half-way between the bed and door.' Thomas Pollard arrived shortly after. His mother told him his brother George had been murdered and showed him the bloody weapon. He went for help to the nearest neighbours, two miles through the bush. 'All the time I had kept calling out, "murder! murder! Johnny Gaven! Johnny Gaven!"'

Mrs Pollard then saw John Gaven coming towards the house. He was wet and said he had gone to the river for a drink and fallen in. She accused him of killing George, but he denied it, saying perhaps a native had done it:

> He then said, perhaps he had murdered himself; I said, 'you murdering villain, why should you belie my dead child – he could not take an adze and murder himself on the back of the head'. He then went into deceased's room and said, George won't say I murdered him; I answered, you did not give him leave to breathe. He then called out 'George, George', and I went to push him away from the bed, he said 'don't put a drop of blood on me; you said I murdered your child, don't put a drop of blood on me.' I then took notice of his shirt being wet, and said, 'you villain, did you go and wash the blood of my dear child off your clothes?'

Mrs Pollard tied Gaven's hands together and took him into the only room with a single door, guarding him with a stick. There was a struggle, which she won, and then he suddenly 'knelt down and repeatedly said, "do forgive me, ma'am, and don't say I murdered your son, and I'll pray for George." ' Mrs Pollard answered that he had not given her son time to pray. Gaven continued to act erratically, asking 'do ma'am, blow my brains out', and then denying his guilt until the soldiers arrived and arrested him.

At the trial the committing magistrate described the scene he found at the Pollard house on the day of the murder:

> I found the head cleft to pieces, a continuation of wounds, quite a mash of skull, brains, and hair. I gave directions for the body to be washed. Early next morning I returned to Pollard's, and, with Sergt. Burrell, examined the body again. I found two wounds on face, one across the cheek bone and nose, the other across the temple, part of three fingers severed, one cut behind left ear, several blows on back of head, smashing the skull into a number of pieces, in a slanting direction, 9 inches long.

The boy pleaded not guilty and had the benefit of a lengthy defence by his counsel. Nevertheless, the jury took only half an hour to return a verdict of guilty. He subsequently confessed to planning to murder Mrs Pollard but had changed his mind when he realized that George would probably overpower him once the deed had been done. So, he decided to kill his friend. He claimed he went to the river not to wash the blood from his clothes but to drown himself, but his courage failed him. John Gaven was unable to state why he wanted to kill Mrs Pollard. He was sentenced to death.

Gaven was held in the Fremantle Round House the night before his execution. At 8 a.m. on 6 April 1844, 'The prison bell then began to toll, and the melancholy procession set out from the condemned cell to the scaffold: the Sheriff and his deputies and constables, the Rev. G. King, reading appropriate passages of Scripture, the prisoner, supported by Mr. Schoales, and lastly, more constables closed the train. The boy was deeply affected, and was assisted up the steps to the platform.' At 8.10 the cart beneath the scaffold was driven away and John Gaven was 'launched into eternity'. His small body was so light that heavy weights had to be tied to his legs to ensure he was strangled. The slight corpse swung in the air for an hour before they cut him down. As was customary at the time, a cast of the face and skull was made 'for the purpose of furthering the ends of science'. The boy's head was said to be 'of extraordinary formation; the anterior organs being very deficiently developed, while the posterior organs are of an enormous size.' A group of convicts carried the body to the sandhills where they buried him in an unmarked and unhallowed grave 'without rite or ceremony'.[17] The day was Easter Saturday.

Jane Green, William Beale and John Gaven were the forerunners of what would become a flood of unaccompanied children sent to Western Australia and to other parts of the continent, during and after the period of penal transportation. There were others, like John Dwyer, a nine-year-old, sentenced in County Cork (though he was English) to seven years transportation for stealing a watch. In New South Wales he tried to run away, was flogged and sent to the notorious Cockatoo Island in Sydney Harbour, then to Port Macquarie, where he died aged thirteen.[18] The abandonment of these unwanted children for the ostensible purpose of powering and populating the empire's colonies stemmed from the same remorseless logic that produced penal transportation. As that system wound down, so children would increasingly become its victims through an extensive and interlocking system of private charity and official confinement. In the meantime transportation continued to be an effective method of dealing with political dissent.

THE LAST REBELS

Western Australia was the location of the last great drama of convictism. The arrival and eventual escape of a group of Irish nationalists electrified the empire's political networks. The shock of these events was felt not only in Australia, but in Britain, Ireland, America and Canada.

In January 1868 the last convict ship to sail to Western Australia included sixty-two Irish rebels. These men had been involved in an abortive rising master-minded by a secret organization known as the Irish Republican Brotherhood, dedicated to overthrowing British rule by force. With support and funds from

Irish interests in the United States of America, the Fenians, as this group of insurrectionists became known, recruited tens of thousands of members, including significant numbers from British army regiments. One of the most effective recruiters was a young man in the 10th Hussars named John Boyle O'Reilly. He, and all those he convinced to join the rebellion, took a secret oath to fight against the British when the revolution was called. The call went out in 1866 but due to inadequate planning, lack of guns and money, as well as the informing of British infiltrators, it was quickly put down. Along with many other Fenians, O'Reilly was arrested and tried. He was convicted of mutinous conduct and sentenced to death, his actions being seen as especially treacherous because he was member of a British regiment. The sentence was commuted to transportation for twenty years though he spent time in several prisons, from which he tried to escape on several occasions, until he was transported aboard the *Hougoumont*.

He and his comrades arrived in a colony nearing the end of its active transportation era, though floggings, solitary confinement and related brutalities were still inflicted. The convict escaper and only Western Australian bushranger, the Welshman Joseph Bolitho Johns, known as 'Moondyne Joe', had felt its sting.

The Glamorganshire ironworker was twenty-two years of age when he arrived in Western Australia in 1853. He had a ten-year sentence for larceny but earned a conditional pardon in 1855. He took up the business of catching stray horses, returning them to their owners for the rewards offered on such valuable assets. Johns was eventually arrested on suspicion of causing the horses to leave their rightful owners and then helpfully 'catching' them in his horse-traps at a place called Moondyne Springs. He was arrested and now began a career punctuated by imprisonment, escape, recapture, harsher incarceration and ever more ingenious escapes from ever more secure cells. While in prison, he was subjected to hard labour in chains, as well as solitary confinement on bread and water. His last recapture was shortly after the arrival of the Fenians and his sentence was served during the same period as their Western Australian sojourn. Johns' escapes, general good nature and lack of a violent temperament made him a local hero. Despite the humorous aspect of his life and legend, he defied the convict system and carved out a life of his own within it. His celebrated escapes were also a model for others with similar ambitions,[19] the Fenians among them.

Bearing the brand 'D' for deserter on their chests, the *Hougoumont* prisoners were marched in chains to Fremantle's forbidding limestone prison. They were bathed, cropped, barbered and examined by a doctor. Their physical and personal details were recorded and they were issued with the regulation summer clothing: cap, grey jacket, vest, two cotton shirts, one flannel shirt, two handkerchiefs, two pairs of trousers, two pairs of socks and a pair of boots. O'Reilly and his companions were soon sent to work along with the convicts. Later in life O'Reilly would publish his novel, *Moondyne*, based on his convict experiences and dedicated to 'the interests of humanity, to the prisoner, whoever and wherever he may be'. In the book he describes the bush, working on road gangs and the work of the free sawyers:

During the midday heat not a bird stirred among the mahogany and gum trees. On the flat tops of the low banksia the round heads of the white cockatoos could be seen in thousands, motionless as the trees themselves. Not a parrot had the vim to scream. The chirping insects were silent. Not a snake had courage to rustle his hard skin against the hot and dead bush-grass. The bright-eyed iguanas were in their holes. The mahogany sawyers had left their logs and were sleeping in the cool sand of their pits. Even the travelling ants had halted on their wonderful roads, and sought the shade of a bramble.

He went on to contrast this with his own situation and that of other convicts toiling alongside him:

All free things were at rest; but the penetrating click of the axe, heard far through the bush, and now and again a harsh word of command, told that it was a land of bondmen. From daylight to dark, through the hot noon as steadily as in the cool evening, the convicts were at work on the roads – the weary work that has no wages, no promotion, no incitement, no variation for good or bad, except stripes for the laggard.

O'Reilly's education and literary skills soon earned him the job of clerical assistant to Henry Woodman, the overseer of the road gangs. In this capacity the young Irishman travelled with reports and messages to the Woodman family home and seems to have developed a romantic attachment to Jessie Woodman, the warder's daughter. This ended unhappily, perhaps before it really began. In the poetry he wrote O'Reilly expressed his despair:

> Have I no future left me?
> Is there no struggling ray
> From the sun of my life outshining
> Down on my darksome way?
>
> Will there no gleam of sunshine
> cast o'er my path its light?
> Will there no star of hope rise
> Out of this gloom of night?

Just after Christmas 1868 O'Reilly slit the veins of his left arm. He passed out but was found and saved from death just before it was too late. Despite his despair, all was not lost for this transported revolutionary. His case became a popular cause of the day, taken up by those with a political conscience about the activities of the British government in Ireland. A powerful coalition of Irish republicans in the United States of America, elements of the Roman Catholic Church and local sympathizers in Western Australia plotted to free the rebel. In February 1869 he was whisked away to freedom by an American whaler, the appropriately named *Gazelle*. O'Reilly celebrated his twenty-fifth birthday in the middle of the Indian Ocean on his secret voyage back to England. He played an influential part in the early planning of the plot to free his companions still labouring in the West Australian bush. They bore the indignities and sufferings described in O'Reilly's novel for five more years, while agitation about their plight and plots to end it slowly developed.

In 1869 and 1871 pardons for many of the imprisoned Fenians were granted by the British for some, but not for all, of those who had arrived with O'Reilly aboard the *Hougoumont*. Many, including James Wilson, Thomas Darragh, Martin Hogan, Michael Harrington, Thomas Hassett and Robert Cranston, were still labouring in Western Australian quarries, roads and buildings in 1874, when James Wilson penned a desperate letter to be secretly smuggled to the leader of the

American branch of the Irish Republican Brotherhood, now known as *Clan na Gael*:

> Dear Friend, remember this is a voice from the tomb. For is not this a living tomb? In the tomb it is only a man's body that is good for worms, but in the living tomb the canker worm of care enters the very soul. Think that we have been nearly nine years in this living tomb since our first arrest and that it is impossible for mind or body to withstand the continual strain that is upon them. One or the other must give way. It is in this sad strait that I now, in the name of my comrades and myself, ask you to aid us in the manner pointed out . . . We ask you to aid us with your tongue and pen, with your brain and intellect, with your ability and influence, and God will bless your efforts, and we will repay you with all the gratitude of our natures . . . our faith in you is unbound. We think if you forsake us, then we are friendless indeed.[20]

The leader of *Clan na Gael* was James Devoy, imprisoned, then exiled to America for his role in the abortive rising of 1866. He was also the man who had recruited many of the Fenians and felt a responsibility to do something to help them. He read the letter to a *Clan na Gael* gathering and gave his strong recommendation for the association to fund an escape bid. They agreed, and Devoy developed a plan to spring the Fenians from 'the convict establishment', as Fremantle Prison was known. A whale ship, the *Catalpa*, was purchased, a captain found for her and a Fenian agent, John Breslin, was sent to Fremantle to arrange the escape. It took the *Catalpa* many months to reach Western Australia, as equipment failures, bad weather and poor whale fishing slowed her down. During this time Breslin had plenty of opportunities to let the imprisoned men know they would soon be rescued and to identify local sympathizers. Two other Irishmen also turned up in response to requests for help from other Fenians; they soon became part of Breslin's escape plan.

Breslin's message reached the Fenians on Easter Sunday: 'We have money, arms and clothes, let no man's heart fail him.' The prisoners needed to be outside the prison walls the following morning for the breakout to succeed. Luckily, they were, or could easily contrive to be. The Irish recruits cut the Fremantle–Perth telegraph wire. Breslin met the fugitives with wagons and horses at the pre-arranged spot and they headed south for a rendezvous with a rowboat and crew ready to ferry them to the rescue ship waiting outside territorial waters. About half a mile offshore the well-laden rowboat saw a cutter and a steamer coming fast towards them. As they rowed ever harder towards the distant *Catalpa*, Breslin produced a copy of the sarcastic letter he had sent to the governor and read it out to the men:

> This is to certify that I have this day released from the clemency of Her Most Gracious Majesty Victoria, Queen of Great Britain, etc., etc., six Irishmen, condemned to imprisonment for life by the enlightened and magnanimous government of Great Britain for having been guilty of the atrocious and unpardonable crimes known to the unenlightened portion of mankind as 'love of country' and 'hatred of tyranny'; for this act of 'Irish assurance' my birth and blood being my full and sufficient warrant. Allow me to add that in taking my leave now, I've only to say a few cells I've emptied; I've the honor and pleasure to bid you good-day, from all future acquaintance, excuse me, I pray. In the service of my country . . .'[21]

Heartened, the crew continued rowing, bailing out the boat as a gale began to blow. With the cutter full of armed police in pursuit, the escapees miraculously made it through the night. Dawn found them within sight of the *Catalpa*, but with the cutter close behind. As they pulled away for freedom, the *Georgette* closed on the American whaler and demanded to be allowed aboard. The first mate reportedly replied, 'Not by a damn sight.'

The *Georgette* needed to return to harbour to refuel, leaving the cutter to capture the rowboat. The race for the *Catalpa* was barely won by the escapees. But as the whaleship made sail, the wind dropped and left the ship unable to sail. The *Georgette* returned and the Fenians and crew aboard the *Catalpa* got ready to fight. The steamer put a shot from its twelve-pound cannon across the bows of the whaleship and commanded her to heave to or have her masts blown out. Captain Anthony famously pointed to the Stars and Stripes and cried, 'This ship is sailing under the American flag and she is on the high seas. If you fire on me, I warn you that you are firing on the American flag.'

Once again the luck of the Irish came to the aid of the Fenians. The *Catalpa* was drifting towards Australian territorial waters, and if she entered them Anthony's defiance would be pointless. But the wind returned. Anthony had the sails raised and headed straight for the *Georgette*, barely missing the steamer as the American ship made for the open sea and freedom. The *Georgette* followed for an hour or so, but as the whaler was well into international waters, it did not fire again and eventually broke off the chase.

It was four months before the *Catalpa* arrived in New York, where thousands met the ship and her liberated heroes. The balladists had another rousing chapter to add to the already bulging annals of Irish rebellion, transportation and escape. Not surprisingly, the tone of these songs was jubilant:

Now boys if you will listen to the story I'll relate,
I'll tell you of the noble men who from the foe escaped.
Tho' bound with Saxon fetters in the dark Australian jail,
They struck a blow for freedom and for Yankee land set sail . . .[22]

As well as ballads like this produced within the international networks of Irish nationalism, local songs were produced in Western Australia. The best known is one that has lasted in the mouths of singers to the present day. It tells an inaccurate but racy version of the escape and features the rousing chorus:

So, come all you screw warders and jailers
Remember Perth regatta day
Take care of the rest of your Fenians
Or the Yankees will steal them away.

And ends triumphantly:

Now they've landed safe in America
And there will be able to cry
Hoist up the green flag and shamrock
Hurrah for old Ireland we'll die.[23]

The men were safe but, after a decade of the 'iron discipline of England's prison system', some were broken, as Devoy sadly observed.[24] O'Reilly went on with his glittering journalistic and political career in America. He remained deeply involved in Irish patriotic activities and is remembered by some in that country, in Australia and in the country of his birth as a great patriot, with several statues to his memory and an active international appreciation society.[25]

SEEDS OF EMPIRE

Western Australia's engagement with the criminal transportation system was in some ways unique. Only men were transported. It was the only Australian colony to move from a foundational freedom from convictism to embracing the institution as a necessary means of survival. Otherwise, it was simply the last large chapter of an epic story in which an imperial government hurled its unwanted across the planet to settle an unknown continent. The Australian gambit – and a gamble it was – came about through the dire need of the British government to continue expanding its empire and to maintain it through the deployment of labour, skills and populations. Western Australia was at the distant end of the very long and interconnected chain of trade, migration and strategic necessity, as well as social and political sanitization at home. Some of the worst evils had been removed by the time the colony asked for convicts, but the system remained an institution in which many lives were lived and lost. Few of those exiled to Western Australia rose above their original socio-economic status, while many sank lower.[26] As convictism faded slowly away, it was replaced by another mechanism for solving the old problem of the unwanted.

Efforts to stop criminal transportation reached a successful peak with the findings of the Molesworth Inquiry. With thousands still serving out their time, the Leviathan system lumbered on for years, initially in New South Wales and Van Diemen's Land and then for another few decades in Western Australia. But the empire still needed people and workers and the streets and workhouses of Britain's grim industrial cities were teeming with orphaned, abandoned or otherwise destitute children. Although it was no longer possible to transport criminals and political prisoners (from metropolitan Britain, at least), the first victims of the system once again became its favoured targets. As criminal transportation fell away, so a new version of the social-cleansing imperative developed. Non-state organizations began to fill the expanding people vacuum left by the contracting transportation system. Private charities and religious groups sent ever-increasing numbers of boys, girls and youths to various outposts of empire, beginning in the early nineteenth century and not ceasing until the 1980s. The state provided legislative, administrative and other support for these largely well-meaning activities and by the time this phase of transportation ended, hundreds of thousands of children had been dispatched to work in and populate Australia, Canada, Rhodesia (Zimbabwe) and New Zealand. Their stories, if possible, were often more harrowing than those of the transported criminals who preceded them.

Between 1848 and 1854, The Philanthropic Society at Redhill, Surrey, sent 300 boys to Australia. More were sent to New South Wales and South Australia from the Ragged Schools in approximately the same period. From 1833 the Barnardo homes began dispatching boys to Australia, beginning with an unofficial group of eleven. Many thousands of children were also sent to Canada, though unaccompanied child migrants were barred there from 1925, due to problems with boarding them out, rather than putting them in foster homes as was the usual Australian practice.[27] In the late 1840s and early 1850s the St Pancras Poor Law Guardians sent children to the British West Indian colonies, and from 1850 Poor Law Guardians were allowed to fund the emigration of children in their care. A number of charities in Canada, Britain and the United States, including The Children's Aid Society,[28] the Home of Industry at Spitalfields and the Orphan Homes of Scotland, sent unaccompanied children to various parts of Canada and America. By 1891 these private operations within the empire were placed on a legal basis by the Custody of Children Act (the 'Barnardo's Act'). Churches were also active over this period and Roman Catholic child migrant arrangements were centralized under the banner of the 'Crusade of Rescue' in 1899. In the early twentieth century a new body based on the same philosophy would send unaccompanied child migrants to work the empire's farms in Rhodesia, New Zealand, Canada and Australia. But before that, the system and its aftermath would devastate many more lives.

The more or less experimental beginnings of unaccompanied child migration over this period were founded on the developing principles of social and moral improvement. Many of the early organizations were inspired by ideals of Christian charity and social reform, which would become very much the spirit of the nineteenth century[29] and had also fuelled the fight against transportation.[30] These charities were soon joined by established religious entities, primarily Christian, both Roman Catholic and Protestant. By the beginning of the twentieth century there were a multitude of child migration organizations operating, especially between Britain, Australia and Canada. The Salvation Army began sending children to Canada and Australia in 1908, while other programmes sent children and youths from under fourteen years of age to Australia and New Zealand. Children, known as 'home children', were also conveyed from Britain to Canada from the 1860s until the late 1940s. On some estimates, more than 100,000 boys and girls were sent under the auspices of more than fifty organizations,[31] many being the same as those operating in Australia and New Zealand.

As with criminal transportation, private and public concerns about the abuses within these programmes began quite early. In the 1880s reports of mistreatment, abuse and suicides among Canadian 'home children' led to an investigation. The findings recognized the good intentions and often positive outcomes of the organizations investigated but was generally critical of the treatment of many child migrants. Little was done to investigate further, a failing that was to become a feature of the child migration story through to the relatively recent revelations and subsequent investigations, inquiries and consequences of institutional abuse. In the early 1920s a number of suicides among home children led to the British government's Bondsfield Commission investigation, which concluded that children were being used primarily as labour and so being denied educational opportunities. There was also popular concern that Britain was 'dumping its undesirables in Canada'.[32] In 1922 Britain passed the Empire Settlement Act. This legislation was designed to improve the ramshackle child migration arrangements that had grown up over the decades and to continue the population of the empire with Britain's lost children, survivors of poverty, neglect, disease and misfortune. There were many different approaches to child migration. One particularly ambitious programme was founded by an idealistic young man with 'a Vision Splendid' for the population of the empire, beginning in Western Australia.

Kingsley Fairbridge was born in South Africa in 1885 and from the age of eleven was brought up in Rhodesia. On a visit to England in late adolescence he was deeply disturbed by the extent and depth of poverty in the industrial cities and especially horrified at the wasted human resources of children born into such poverty. He returned home a year later determined to do something to help these children, developing a vision that would initiate the Child Emigration Society, later the Fairbridge Society, and lead to the establishment of settlements for orphaned and unwanted children in Rhodesia, New Zealand, Canada and Australia. The scheme that Fairbridge and his collaborators constructed was based on a vision he claimed to have experienced in which he saw 'great Colleges of Agriculture (not workhouses) springing up in every man-hungry corner of the Empire. I saw children shedding the bondage of bitter circumstances and stretching their legs and minds amid the thousand interests of the farm. I saw waste turned to providence, the waste of un-needed humanity converted to the husbandry of unpeopled acres.'[33]

To realize this 'Vision Splendid', Fairbridge determined that he needed to become a Rhodes scholar in order to provide himself with the education and contacts he correctly believed necessary to achieve his aims. After four attempts (his primary and secondary education had been sporadic) he became the first South African to be successful in winning this demanding scholarship and returned to England to study at Oxford University. On 19 October 1909 Kingsley Fairbridge addressed a meeting of forty-nine fellow undergraduates at the Colonial Club, Oxford, on the subject of child emigration, founding the Child Emigration Society, later to become the Fairbridge Society. In 1911 the premier of Western Australia met Kingsley Fairbridge in London. An offer of land was made by the state government and in 1912 Kingsley and his wife established the first Farm School, soon receiving the first thirteen orphans from Britain in January 1913. Seven years later the school was relocated to its current site north of Pinjarra, with the assistance of the Western Australian government.

The agreement formalized between Fairbridge (as the Child Emigration Society) and the Commonwealth in 1923 highlighted the close connection between empire, migration and the politics of child migration: 'Whereas the Society has established a Fairbridge School at Pinjarra in Western Australia (hereinafter called the 'Farm') for the purpose of training children of the poorer classes from the UK for settlement in the country districts of Australia.'[34]

These arrangements went ahead despite serious misgivings within the Commonwealth government. Officers in the Immigration Section, and the later Development and Immigration Commission (Melbourne), opposed any Commonwealth grant to the Child Emigration Society in 1922. A federal government bureaucrat signing only as 'L J H' wrote to the chairman of the commission on 26 May 1927, stating that:

Prior to the decision of the Commonwealth Government in 1922 to contribute £10,000 over a period of five years, I reported, as did my predecessor, that from the purely migration point of view the scheme was not economical and on a per capita basis would be more costly than any other migration scheme.

Despite such bureaucratic objections, the prime minister decided to continue the maintenance subsidy for a further year.[35]

Although Kingsley Fairbridge died in 1924 at the age of thirty-nine, his 'Vision Splendid' lived on in England, Rhodesia, New Zealand, Canada, elsewhere in Australia and, most persistently, in Western Australia. In 1937 two farm schools were founded in New South Wales and Victoria.[36] Two smaller schools were also established in South Australia and Tasmania in the 1950s. Canadian schools were established in the 1930s and there were also Fairbridge operations in Southern Rhodesia. The schools were generally modelled on similar lines, with a number of cottages or cabins grouped into small settlements within a working farm. Each dwelling had a 'cottage mother' and the boys were equipped with agricultural work skills, while the girls were trained in domestic chores, their labour also producing most of their food. Eating, worship, education and healthcare were communally provided. Children between six and fifteen years of age were catered for. The scheme also provided pre-school care for those under six, who were looked after in England until old enough to emigrate. When children left the schools there was also an after-care operation catering for individuals up to the age of twenty-one.

This arrangement generally operated until after World War II when, in response to changing circumstances in the Dominions and in Britain, ongoing administrative and managerial changes were made. Throughout these changes Fairbridge farm schools continued to send considerable numbers of boys and girls to their various operations. From the 1960s shifting attitudes to welfare and immigration, new arrangements for child welfare and a decreasing demand for agricultural skills increasingly rendered Kingsley Fairbridge's basic scheme unviable. The era of child migration had ended and the Fairbridge farm schools gradually closed down or were repurposed. In 1981 the first, and last, of the operations, Fairbridge Village at Pinjarra, ceased to operate as a farm school.[37]

The Fairbridge story, while but one of many similar well-intentioned schemes, perhaps most completely demonstrates the continued mindset of transportation. Take one perceived problem, in this case, orphans and otherwise destitute children, and move it to those parts of the empire where human resources were required for work and population. With Fairbridge farm schools in several Australian states, and elsewhere around the world, the Fairbridge Society created a miniature realm of forgotten children within the greater empire, making use of the existing routes of transportation and continuing the ideology of coerced migration beginning in the sixteenth century. But it was only the most perfectly conceived of such initiatives – there were many more.

These were variously governmental, private and secular, or religious. Government developed the 1921 Joint Commonwealth and States Scheme for migration, while secular, community and religious schemes were numerous. The first official group of Dr Barnardo's children arrived in New South Wales in 1921, urged on by the Millions Club, whose aim was to bring a million British settlers to work Australian farms.[38] In 1925 the Big Brother Movement began sending what would be a final total of 12,500 teenagers to Australia. The Roman Catholic Christian Brothers were active in Western Australia from the late 1920s. These arrangements continued unabated under the Empire Settlement Act, which was renewed for another fifteen years in 1937. During World War II the programmes were mostly suspended, but 600 children were evacuated from Britain to Australia, and another 200 to New Zealand. Canada and South Africa between them received several thousand more evacuees.

After the war, the Christian Brothers, Barnardo's and the Fairbridge schemes reopened and a number of Roman Catholic groups, notably the Sisters of Mercy and the Sisters of Nazareth, became involved in child migration. Almost 300 children went to the Fairbridge operation in Southern Rhodesia.[39] The 1950s saw a Home Office Fact-Finding Committee visit Australia and criticize some institutions in a secret report. Despite this the Empire Settlement Act, retitled as the Commonwealth Settlement Act, was again renewed in 1957, though the numbers of children dispatched continued to decline and faded almost completely by the late 1960s. Over 3,000 child migrants had by then been sent to Australia in the post-World War II period. Big Brother continued sponsoring youth migrants to Australia until 1983.[40]

It was not until later in the 1980s and into the following decade that the institutionalized abuse of unaccompanied child migrants was revealed as campaigner Margaret Humphreys and the Child Migrant Trust began to receive media coverage, followed by a number of revelatory books and documentary films.[41] These eventually led to *The Leaving of Liverpool*. Made and screened in the United Kingdom, this television mini-series brought the issue forcibly to public attention. Some organizations involved in unaccompanied child migration, such as the Christian Brothers, began to examine their practices and to make amends and offer apologies.[42]

The *Lost Innocents* report of 2001 documented the sexual, physical and psychological abuse and assault of many child migrants in Western Australia and elsewhere on that continent, with reference to the situation in British and Canadian institutions. The report quoted and endorsed the view of the earlier United Kingdom Health Committee report on the evidence it had received: 'It is impossible to resist the conclusion that some of what was done there was of a quite exceptional depravity, so that terms like "sexual abuse" are too weak to convey it.'[43] Priests, institutional staff and visitors, members of families where child migrants were sent for holidays and sometimes older institutionalized children, inflicted 'the humiliation and degradation of criminal sexual assault including extreme pain associated with sexual penetration and rape'. In many institutions, children were beaten 'often with specially made leather straps, belts, canes, pieces of wood or other weapons'. In some places, brutality was 'endemic' and 'at times descended into what can only be described as torture'. Former child migrants also recalled the depersonalizing processes in which they were ensnared, including name changes, removal of possessions, and being numbered rather than named. Various forms of psychological abuse included emotional deprivation, 'sustained cruelty', and the public shaming and other consequences of bed-wetting. Education was often neglected, children were frequently underfed or poorly nourished and inadequately clothed and shod. The consequences for them in later life were often calamitous, especially in relation to self-esteem, inability to form emotional relationships or disadvantage in competing for work.[44]

The extent to which this institutionalized abuse was part of a system originating in Britain and extending throughout the empire and Commonwealth was highlighted in many of the personal stories provided to the various inquiries. Some of the worst stories came from children condemned to institutions in Western Australia.

Michael O'Donoghue was two or three years old when he was placed in the care of Nazareth House nuns in Hampshire in England in 1942. He was beaten for wetting his bed, ill-fed, regularly raped and otherwise mistreated. He was told that he was an orphan, even though he knew he had a mother. He ran away and lived rough for a year before being taken back into care in Nazareth House, Hammersmith, where he was not abused. But that changed in 1953. He was sent to a Christian Brothers institution in Western Australia where he was again mistreated and continually raped by 'a sadistic paedophile' priest and others until he left the institution.[45]

Marcelle O'Brien was around four years old when she was sent to the Fairbridge Farm School at Pinjarra. She was physically and verbally abused by a cottage mother and sometimes locked in a dark cupboard. Sex education and female hygiene were neglected, bed-wetting publicly punished, and education less than rudimentary. She was sometimes so hungry she ate grain intended for the pigs. She was also sexually molested, though not raped, by the deputy principal. After she left Fairbridge she was molested at the farm where she was sent to work and at another placement was raped by three men. In later life Margaret was put back in touch with her family in England and Canada. She travelled to the United Kingdom to give her evidence to the independent inquiry '. . . to wake up the British government, the British people, to exactly what happened to us all'.[46]

Many more traumatic stories like these were aired and increasingly heard after decades of official and community neglect and denial.[47] In 1996 civil action by the Western Australian VOICES organization was settled out of court for 3.5 million Australian dollars, a Western Australian Parliamentary Committee investigated child migration activities in that state, and the Christian Brothers took further remedial measures. A 1997 United Kingdom Health Committee Inquiry into child migration was followed with a United Kingdom Parliamentary Committee on Child Migration, which took evidence in Australia and published a critical report in 1998. The Western Australian Legislative Assembly subsequently passed a motion of apology to child migrants,[48] while Prime Minister Gordon Brown made an apology to children sent to all empire-receiving countries on behalf of Her Majesty's Government in 2010, establishing a Family Restoration Fund to assist the reconciliation and related processes. This was followed with an apology in the House of Commons on 16 February 2017, specifically to the Canadian Home Children:

> That the House recognize the injustice, abuse and suffering endured by the British Home Children as well as the efforts, participation and contribution of these children and their descendants within our communities; and offer its sincere apology to the former British Home Children who are still living and to the descendants of these 100,000 individuals who were shipped from Great Britain to Canada between 1869 and 1948, and torn from their families to serve mainly as cheap labour once they arrived in Canada.

Child migration was an empire and post-empire practice, but it was especially prominent in Australia, a country where, unlike other affected destinations, transportation and its historical and contemporary consequences remains a controversial issue. In 2012 the Australian Royal Commission into Institutional Responses to Child Sexual Abuse was announced. Its findings revealed the chilling reality for many children ensnared in abusive state, private and religious institutions over very long periods. In the United Kingdom, the Independent Inquiry into Child Sexual Abuse reported on child migration programmes in 2018. The report was critical of the British government's role in child migration and recommended financial redress and apologies from those organizations that had not yet done so.[49]

In 2019 the government established an *ex-gratia* payment scheme for former British child migrants to Australia, New Zealand, Canada and Zimbabwe.[50] The consequences of these findings, which have merged with the larger issues of institutionalized abuse of children other than child migrants,[51] are still being worked out in legal systems and organizations around the old empire world and are the targets of calls for substantial reparations to the victims.[52]

Whatever their ideological inspiration, secular or religious, organizations involved in child migration operated on the assumption, explicit or not, that the children would contribute to the economic and social development of their destinations. In this sense they were direct descendants of the kidnappers of children in the first centuries of transportation and the later transportation of criminal youths, such as the Pentonvillains and Parkhurst inmates in the nineteenth century. While these children only rarely came in chains, they were bound by the state and vulnerable to the abuses of the penal system. In the child migration schemes their successors fell victim to institutional abuse.

The trajectories of the transported and the migrated also paralleled each other. Convicts were those who committed crimes, were apprehended, tried and sentenced, imprisoned, sent 'beyond the seas', deployed to useful tasks on arrival and, in theory at least, released into the community as, ideally, rehabilitated characters. The 'crime' of migrant children was to be without parents,[53] and so, procured by a state or quasi-state entity that made decisions about their placement and fate. They were then effectively imprisoned in institutions, sent across the seas, and usually deployed after their arrival to useful tasks or training for such tasks later in life. Eventually, they too were released into the community with the skills and attitudes needed to become productive members of society. But, as with time-served convicts, the institutions that evolved to ensure child migrants achieved these laudable aims often produced more of the problems they were intended to solve.

11

THE END OF THE CHAIN?

The duration and extent of transportation in its various phases and forms is not widely appreciated. It is estimated that Britain transported over 376,000 convicts between 1615 and 1940.[1] These included the vagrant poor; professional or other criminals; rebellious Irish, Scots and English; religious recalcitrants; sundry unrulies, including Gypsies, border reivers (raiders), pirates, military deserters and 'Superfluous multitudes' of unwanted children. To this figure can be added the unknown numbers of abducted as well as internally transported and re-transported peoples of the far-flung empire. Other than slavery, an institution with which it shared some features, the forced transportation of men, women and children – legally and illegally – 'beyond the seas' was one of history's most prolonged and brutal forms of oppression and punishment. Originating in ancient practices of banishment and exile, from the seventeenth century, transportation evolved into a system of coercion and punishment that allowed Britain to build and maintain a global empire. Many of the hundreds of thousands sent to various outposts of empire were convicted criminals or political prisoners; others were guilty only of being unwanted, while some were simply too slow to escape when government agents or private interests were scouring town and country for victims. Whether legally or illegally transported, these human beings were seen as sources of colonial labour, markets and procreation. Over four centuries the various public and private interests involved in this trade evolved into an extensive and large-scale 'system' of global labour transfer built on human misery, of individuals enmeshed in economic, political, strategic and commercial forces beyond their control. Many died. A few escaped. Some prospered. Most did their time and then got on with life. But almost all suffered.

The transportation system and its consequences became a major element of British and imperial experience, erupting in political division, imperatives of trade and commerce, grand global strategy, and even in eighteenth- and nineteenth-century popular culture. British consumers of broadside ballads, street literature and early newspapers and magazines hungered for usually lurid tales of transported felons, especially of escapes, trials and, particularly, executions. Audiences in America, Australia and elsewhere also provided a steady market for literature of this kind, closely related to that other form of sensationalist 'true crime' literature, the criminal biography. The ballads, reports and dying confessions energized an increasingly vociferous civil debate about the moral, penal and economic benefits and evils of the system. But too many interests, official and private, needed the transportation trade, regardless of its manifest evils. The fight to abolish transportation was long and hard-fought. And it was never completely won, remnants of the system lingering on almost until the empire was dismantled after World War II.

While the bureaucratic processes of transportation retired to the archives and its material elements decayed, the world view and ideology that had propelled the practice for centuries remained. The prisons, hulks, fortifications and docks, the army, the factory and the farms and penal stations had been the links in the empire of chains, held together by the seaways along which British ships traded, patrolled and transported the condemned.[2] Now they served a new purpose. Even as the system was winding down, the forced migration, incarceration and labour of unaccompanied children became an acceptable practice, even if wrapped in a cloak of Victorian paternalism and religious respectability. The same imperatives that fuelled penal and other forms of transportation encouraged the evolution of institutionalized child migration from the late nineteenth century until nearly the end of the twentieth.

Of course, the past never stays there. It is forever thrusting itself into our attention, not only in matters of great global consequence, but also in more intimate, familial and everyday interests. Britain's condemned built roads, bridges, buildings and much of the public infrastructure of early colonies in America, South Asia and Australia. They laboured in fields for the production of food and trade goods. In those places where the evidence of their bondage remains we can see the results of their work and now treat them as 'heritage'. Where there are few, if any traces left, the evidence of their presence can be found in archives, libraries and museums, in re-enactments, books, movies, language, and even in the occasional haunting.

Today, the best-preserved remains of the system can be seen and visited in Australia. The brooding beauty of Port Arthur is still an important Tasmanian site. It is accompanied by many other remaining public works, along with the ruins of female factories, Macquarie Harbour and elsewhere. There are few parts of the island where convictism cannot be sensed, even if not seen. In Western Australia the still grim bulk of Fremantle Prison hangs over the scrappy modern city and there are convict-built structures throughout the south of the state and on Rottnest Island. Sydney retains a few convict stone buildings, as do many towns throughout New South Wales. Much of what was once an extensive prison community remains now at Norfolk Island, including restored buildings, sombre ruins and a cemetery. They are the *memento mori* of a dark past, forced into sharp relief by the surrounding natural beauty.

Around the old empire, other vestiges can be found. Cape Coast Castle survives, as does Robben Island and the cellular gaol of the Andaman Islands. Elsewhere, there is little to satisfy the modern need for 'dark tourism', though the defences and other works erected on the sweat and blood of transported convicts can still be seen in the convict cemetery in Bermuda, Wellington Front in Gibraltar and Fort St Jago in Ghana, as well as other places with transportation associations. Brick and stone remain, but flesh is gone from all those places of condemnation and suffering. To retrieve the human dimension of transportation, even the fragments in this book, we must go to the ragged remnants of history, the dry but revealing official records; the letters, diaries, newspaper articles, street ballads, convict verse and occasional memoir from which we can extract and reconstruct the many small stories that make up the immense story of the condemned. The narrative is always expanding. A steady stream of books, film, television and other media feeds this popular interest, much like the print technologies of previous centuries. Historians are still drawn to the complexities and consequences of transportation, with a great deal of outstanding scholarship being published in print and digital formats over the last twenty years or so.

As well as building countries, the condemned populated them. Descendants are actively seeking out their ancestors' lives and deaths in the receding past. There is, it seems, a need to connect with the familial long-ago, a need that fuels a global family history movement, mostly energized by the digital availability of relevant records through the internet. Family history research has given descendants an enduring connection with the transportation system. Convict ancestors are now identified, tracked down through archives, libraries, family documents and oral tradition. They are effectively returned to life, coming to form part of the intergenerational family narrative. Romanticized, mythologized and sentimentalized though these recovered lives may sometimes be, they nevertheless form a strong link between the present and the past, connecting those in the present with whatever larger versions of local, national and global history they prefer.

Britons understand transportation and child migration through the rear-view mirror of empire. Through such lengthy and tumultuous history, even the brutalities and oppressions of coerced migration tend to meld into the overarching imperial narrative of exploration, discovery, conquests, colonialism and almost numberless wars.

When they consider it at all, Americans see transportation against, and fading into, the background of the far greater calamity of slavery. The existence of transported convicts was denied early, a sleight of history made possible by the unprecedented expansion and turmoils of America after independence. The uncertain status of the transported, of indentured servants and even murky lines between these and some aspects of black chattel slavery also contributed to these obfuscations. While there has been outstanding scholarship carried out into the American transportation experience, for the general public the topic is barely known.

Australia was the culminating malignity of a festering imperial tumour. Australians have execrated or celebrated penal transportation in relation to the founding of their nominally independent nation and as an aspect of national identity. In that country, the foundational nature of transportation and convictism was, for a long time, ignored, even suppressed, as the attitude known as 'the convict stain' developed. As the country developed, especially after the mid-nineteenth-century gold rushes, so people were less inclined to remember how many of their colonies had begun. This attitude persisted after the federation of the colonies into the modern Commonwealth of states and territories in 1901. It has not been until relatively recently that this stigma has begun to fade, stimulated by the growth of family history and the ameliorations of elapsing time. Today, many Australians are proud to declare a convict ancestor and historians generally argue that the establishment and initial development of the nation owed much to the men, women and children who were brought there in chains.

Wherever convicts, abductees, rebels or child migrants were banished in the old empire, they unwillingly contributed to its growth and persistence. The long centuries of condemnation engendered ways of seeing and doing that persist today. In 2001 Australia adopted the 'Pacific Solution', an ironic inversion of much that had come before in response to asylum seekers and unofficial refugees. Australia has used the old techniques of empire transportation. Those intercepted at sea have been banished to 'camps' on Nauru, Christmas and Manus islands. Now, asylum seekers and refugees transport themselves to Australia and are incarcerated in what are effectively offshore hulks. The convicts who founded modern Australia came there in chains. The asylum seekers came in hope. Their bondage is no different.

TIMELINE

1494	Vagabonds and Beggars Act
1530	The Vagabonds Act
1547	Vagrancy Act decreed idle persons given to masters and compelled to work for them, effectively as slaves (repealed 1550)
1572	Vagabonds Act
1577	Condemned men sent to join Martin Frobisher's second voyage to find Northwest Passage
1584	Richard Hakluyt's *Discourse of Western Planting* suggests transportation as labour source in colonies
1585	(1584) Jesuit priests could be banished instead of martyred
1593	Roman Catholic recusants and Protestant sectaries could be banished instead of martyred
1597	Act under Elizabeth I sanctioned transportation of rogues and vagabonds
1603	Royal decree on vagabondage identifies the East and West Indies, Newfoundland and mainland Europe as likely locations for transportees
1607	Jamestown established
1611	Colony of Virginia requests King James I to send condemned convicts to provide a workforce
c. 1613	Attempted transportation to Robben Island abandoned
1615	Legal system established to allow forced labour in colonies for misdemeanours and reprieves for felons, on condition they absent themselves to the colonies

from 1618	London's Old Bailey is transporting convicts
1619–20	City of London transports a 'superfluous multitude' of children to Virginia
1621	Another Act to enslave convicted criminals is drafted, though not presented to Parliament
1627	England establishes colony in Barbados
late 1620s – early 1630s	People possibly transported to Barbados, Bermuda and St Christopher's
1635	Sixteen intended to be transported to Guyana
1640	Thomas Verney has 100 Bridewell prisoners sent to Barbados to work his plantation
1642	English Civil War begins
1649–55	Civil War prisoners transported to Barbados and elsewhere
1655	Prisoners of Penruddock's failed rising transported to the West Indies
1650s	Irish transported in significant numbers to American and Caribbean colonies
1656	Council of State orders 'lewd and dangerous persons' transported to 'the English plantations in America'
1661	English and Scots courts transport people to Tangier until 1684. Also Algonquin Native Americans sent there from America following 1676–7 war in New England
1666	More Scots transported to America
1670	Bill to stop transportation without trial (became basis of Habeas Corpus Act of 1679)
1676–7	Bacon's Rebellion in Virginia and another in Maryland
1680	Christopher Jeaffreson travels to England to escort a group of convicts back to his St Kitts plantation
1685	Argyll's rebellion fails, Scots prisoners transported to Jamaica and New Jersey
1685–6	Monmouth's Rebellion prisoners transported to Jamaica, Barbados, Leeward Islands and perhaps Virginia
1689	First performance of Aphra Benn's *The Widow Ranter*

1705	'Benefit of clergy' extended to all first offenders if their offence had not been made a 'non-clergyable' and therefore, capital crime
1715	Jacobite Rebellion, 'the Fifteen'
1718	(1717) Transportation Act allows regular transportation to America though thousands transported during the previous century
1718–75	Scottish courts transport *c.* 800 to America
1722	*Moll Flanders* published
1730	Convicts transported to St John's, Newfoundland
1746	Battle of Culloden ends Jacobite cause
1752	Confinement at Hard Labour Bill provides alternative to transportation for those pardoned from a capital sentence
1752	(1751) Murder Act makes attempts to steal corpses of executed murderers punishable by transportation
1775	Transportation to America ceases, although English courts continue to send felons there
1775–6	746 felons transported to the island of Goree, Senegambia
1776	Parliament of Westminster extends 1718 Transportation Act provisions to Scotland (later repealed)
1776	First hulks established on River Thames
early 1780s	British transport soldier convicts to Cape Coast, West Africa
1783	American War of Independence ends
1783–4	Attempts to continue transportation to America fail
1784–5	Plans for transportation to Honduras stymied
1785	Plans for transportation to Gambia River abandoned
1786	Britain contemplates transportation to Madagascar and India
1787–8	Transportation to New South Wales (Australia) begins with the First Fleet
from 1787	Transportation to Bencoolen
1789	Shipload of Irish transported to Nova Scotia are refused and returned
1789	Shipload of Irish transported to Newfoundland
from 1790	Irish transported directly from Cork
1790–1806	Transportation to Penang

1790–1857 Transportation to and from India in the Straits Settlements

1793–9 English East India Company (EIC) experiments with transportation to the Andaman Islands

1795 British take control of Cape Colony from Dutch

1795–6 Fifty convicts experimentally transported to Corsica, but were withdrawn

1803–4 Van Diemen's Land (later Tasmania) settled

1804 Castle Hill ('Vinegar Hill') rising, New South Wales

1805 Transportation to Melaka (Malacca)

1806 British again take over Cape Colony

1814–37 Indians transported to Mauritius from Bengal and Bombay, as well as Ceylon (Sri Lanka); transportation to Mauritius later abandoned

1815 Convict ships begin to go straight to Van Diemen's Land

1820 Robben Island prisoners escape – some survivors sent to New South Wales

1820–30s Free migration increasing and eventually leads to anti-transportation agitation in New South Wales and Britain

1820–63 Transportation to Bermuda

1822–3 Bigge Report highly critical of Governor Macquarie's administration of New South Wales

1823 Act authorizes transportation to any colony designated by the monarch

from 1825 Transportation to Singapore

1827 Convicts with Major Lockyer to Western Australia

1828–57 Transportation to Burma

1833 Unofficial group of Dr Barnardo's 'home children' sent to Canada

1834 Children's Friend Society begins sending children to Western Australia

1835 Fledgling colony of Swan River (later Western Australia) transports convicts to Van Diemen's Land

1836–64 1,000 transported from Straits Settlements to British India

1837–8 Molesworth Committee recommends ending transportation to New South Wales and Van Diemen's Land

1838 (possibly 1837)	First indigenous Australians transported to Rottnest Island, Western Australia
1840	Order-in-Council removes New South Wales from list of places convicts could be transported; Van Diemen's Land remains on the list
1841–50	Transportation to Aden
1842	Transportation to Australia for Parkhurst boys introduced
1842–75	Transportation to Gibraltar
1844 (possibly earlier)	Transportation of juveniles to Australia from Pentonville and Millbank prisons begins
1844–58	Transportation from Hong Kong to Singapore, Penang, Sindh, Labuan (in modern Malaysia) and Van Diemen's Land
1845–51	Irish Potato famine and rebellion, Irish transported to Bermuda
1846	Robben Island prison closed (though some African political prisoners held there until 1880s); becomes hospital, lunatic asylum and leper colony and high-security prison for political prisoners
1846–50	Short-lived transportation to Port Phillip (Victoria)
1848	First cargo of free Irish orphan girls sent to Sydney
1849–50	Brief revival of transportation to New South Wales
1849–73	Transportation to Sumatra, Mauritius, and from Ceylon (Sri Lanka) to Malacca
1850	Transportation to Western Australia begins
1851–80	Transportation to Labuan (Malaysia) from Hong Kong
1853	Transportation to Tasmania abolished
1858	British reoccupy Andaman Islands and begin transportation from India
1858–9	Convicts from Indian Mutiny/First War of Independence sent to Singapore
1859	Irish convict rising aboard *Medway* hulk in Bermuda
1862	Transportation to Bermuda ceases and convicts from Bermuda begin to be sent to Western Australia
1867–8	End of transportation to Western Australia
1869	John Boyle O'Reilly escapes from Fremantle

1873	Straits penal stations closed in favour of Singapore; most convicts transferred to Andamans
1875	Home Children, Canada, inspection and report
1876	Escape of Fenians from Fremantle aboard *Catalpa*
1904	South Sea Islanders deported from Australia
1912	First Fairbridge Farm School established in Western Australia, followed by others elsewhere in Australia, New Zealand, Canada and Rhodesia (Zimbabwe)
1922	Empire Settlement Act
1923	Joint Australian-Commonwealth and States child migration scheme
1925	Big Brother Movement begins sending teenagers to Australia
late 1920s	Christian Brothers taking child migrants in Western Australia
1935	Prince of Wales Fairbridge Farm School established on Vancouver Island, closed 1951
1937	Empire Settlement Act renewed for fifteen years
1937	Transportation to the Andaman Islands ceases
1938	Death of last Australian transportee, Samuel Speed
1957	Commonwealth Settlement Act (UK), previously Empire Settlement Act, renewed
1992	*The Leaving of Liverpool* TV mini-series
1994	*Empty Cradles* published
1996	Robben Island prison closed
2001	Australian government adopts 'the Pacific Solution' for transporting asylum seekers to detention on Pacific island nations
2001	*Lost Innocents* report released
2010	Eleven Australian convict sites become UNESCO World Heritage Sites
2017	The Royal Commission into Institutional Responses to Child Sexual Abuse final report
2018	Independent Inquiry into Child Sexual Abuse, Child Migration Programmes investigation report (UK)
2019	British government establishes *ex gratia* payment scheme for empire child migrants

NOTES

INTRODUCTION: EMPIRE OF CHAINS

1. *The Sydney Gazette and New South Wales Advertiser*, 27 July 1806, p. 1 (Public Notice). Samuel Chace is sometimes spelled 'Chase'.
2. 'A Convict's Recollections of New South Wales' (Mellish's Book of Botany Bay), *The London Magazine*, vol. 2, 1825, p. 54. Obviously authored by a male, this document purportedly relates to around 1814. The author's identity is unknown, though the details of colonial life and environment are generally accurate; see Nathan Garvey, 'The Convict Voice and British Print Culture: The Case of "Mellish's Book of Botany Bay" ', *Australian Historical Studies*, vol. 44, issue 3, 2013, pp. 423–37.
3. *The Sydney Monitor*, 10 September 1834, p. 4, prints a ballad allegedly sung by the women of the Female Factory, projecting their image of casual defiance.
4. Kathleen Trevena, 'Charlotte Badger – Female Factory Inmate and Australia's First Female Pirate', *Riotous and Disorderly – The Women and their Stories from the Parramatta Female Factory*, https://riotousanddisorderly.com/index.php/2017/01/03/charlotte-badger-female-factory-inmate-australias-first-female-pirate, accessed August 2018.
5. *The Sydney Gazette and New South Wales Advertiser*, 13 July 1806, p. 4.
6. Elsbeth Hardie, 'Was Charlotte Badger a Colonial Renegade?', *Journal of New Zealand Studies* NS28 (2019), 84-97 https://doi.org/10.26686/jnzs.v0iNS28.5422.
7. V. Blomer, 'The Fate of the Brig *Venus* Seized in 1806', *Convict Connections Chronicle*, Convict Connections 2013, http://www.convictconnections.org.au/newsletterarticles.html, accessed March 2017; Mary Louise Ormsby, 'Badger, Charlotte', *Dictionary of New Zealand Biography. Te Ara – the Encyclopedia of New Zealand*, http://www.TeAra.govt.nz/en/biographies/1b1/badger-charlotte, accessed March 2017.
8. Also a feature of transportation in other empires; see Clare Anderson (ed.), *A Global History of Convicts and Penal Colonies*, London: Bloomsbury Academic, 2018, pp. 5–6.

CHAPTER 1: A HISTORY WITH MANY LINKS

1. Graham Seal, *The Outlaw Legend: A Cultural Tradition in Britain, America and Australia*, Cambridge: Cambridge University Press, 1996.
2. For a detailed study of the legislation relating to transportation, see Alan Brooks, 'Prisoners or Servants? A History of the Legal Status of Britain's Transported Convicts', PhD thesis, University of Tasmania, 2016.
3. 11 Henry VII c. 2. 1494.

4. *Vagrancy Act 1547* (1 Edward VI c. 3). Another proposal to enslave those 'convicted for cheaters or incorrigible rogues' was drafted in 1621; see Krista Kesselring, 'A Proposal to Enslave Petty Offenders (1621)', *Legal History Miscellany*, January 2017, https://legalhistorymiscellany.com/2017/01/10/a-proposal-to-enslave-petty-offenders-1621/, accessed September 2018.

5. 14 Elizabeth I c. 5. 1572.

6. Acts of Privy Council, XXV, 230, 1596, https://www.british-history.ac.uk/acts-privy-council/vol25.

7. Cynthia Herrup, 'Punishing Pardon: Some Thoughts on the Origins of Penal Transportation', in Simon Devereaux and Paul Griffiths (eds), *Penal Politics and Culture 1500–1900: Punishing the English*, London: Palgrave Macmillan, 2004.

8. Richard Hakluyt, *A Discourse Concerning Western Planting*, 1584, in Leonard Woods (ed.), *A Discourse Concerning Western Planting: Written in the Year 1584 by Richard Hakluyt, Now First Printed from a Contemporary Manuscript*, Cambridge, MA: J. Wilson and Son, 1877, p. 3.

9. *An Act for restraining Popish Recusants to some certain Places of Abode*, Stat. 35 Elizabeth c. 2, 1593.

10. Vagabonds Act 1597 (39 Elizabeth c. 4).

11. Hamish Maxwell-Stewart, 'Transportation from Britain and Ireland, 1615–1875', in Clare Anderson (ed.), *A Global History of Convicts and Penal Colonies*, London: Bloomsbury Academic, 2018, p. 189.

12. For an indication of the differences between English and Scottish law and their effect on individual cases of banishment and transportation through Scottish courts, see Cassie Watson, 'Execution Delayed: Some Scottish Examples', *Legal History Miscellany*, September 2018, https://legalhistorymiscellany.com/2018/09/23/execution-delayed-some-scottish-examples, accessed April 2019.

13. A.G.L. Shaw, *Convicts and the Colonies: A Study of Penal Transportation from Great Britain and Ireland to Australia and Other Parts of the British Empire*, London: Faber and Faber, 1966, p. 24.

14. Krista Kesselring, 'Star Chamber Stories: Felons' Labours', *Legal History Miscellany*, January 2018, https://legalhistorymiscellany.com/2018/01/02/felons-labours, accessed September 2018.

15. Maxwell-Stewart, 'Transportation from Britain and Ireland, 1615–1875', pp. 188–9.

16. Joyce Lee Malcolm, *Guns and Violence: The English Experience*, Cambridge, MA: Harvard University Press, 2009 (2002), p. 76, also observing that 'With the Restoration, Middlesex magistrates, for example, were again transporting vagabonds and idle and disorderly persons.'

17. The Conviction Politics project at https://www.convictionpolitics.net is studying eighteenth- and nineteenth-century radical politics in the empire.

18. 'Charles II, 1666: An Act to continue a former Act for preventing of Thefte and Rapine upon the Northerne Borders of England', in *Statutes of the Realm: Volume 5, 1628–80*, ed. John Raithby (s.l, 1819), p. 598. *British History Online*, http://www.british-history.ac.uk/statutes-realm/vol5/p598, accessed 17 November 2019.

19. The term 'system', as used in this book to denote transportation, means the connected legal, commercial and strategic processes through which human beings were moved to, between and within empire colonies, and the hegemonic and ideological imperatives supporting those activities.

20. Gwenda Morgan and Peter Rushton, *Banishment in the Early Atlantic World: Convicts, Rebels and Slaves*, London: Bloomsbury Academic, 2013.

21. It is not clear whether the Algonquin were prisoners of war, indentured servants or even 'judicially enslaved' – 'In the seventeenth-century Atlantic the line between servant, slave, convict and soldier was often paper-thin', Hamish Maxwell-Stewart, 'Transportation from Britain and Ireland, 1615–1875' in Anderson (ed.), *A Global History of Convicts and Penal Colonies*, p. 186.

22. Mathew Parker, *Willoughbyland: England's Lost Colony*, London: Hutchinson, 2015.

23. 4 Geo I, c. 11, effective from 1718.

24. Nick Robins, *The Corporation that Changed the World: How the East India Company Shaped the Modern Multinational*, 2nd edn, London: Pluto Press, 2012.

CHAPTER 2: KIDNAPPERS, SPIRITS AND SOUL DRIVERS

1. David Hackett Fischer, *Albion's Seed: Four British Folkways in America*, Oxford and New York: Oxford University Press, 1989.
2. *Acts of the Privy Council of England: Colonial Series*, vol. 1, AD 1613–1680. Liechtenstein: Kraus Reprint Ltd., 1966. First Published London: HMSO, 1908, pp. 10–13.
3. See Alan Brooks, 'Prisoners or Servants? A History of the Legal Status of Britain's Transported Convicts', PhD thesis, University of Tasmania, 2016, pp. 429–31, for use of royal prerogatives, 1614–1624, in the cases of over 100 individuals. One was Daniell Frank who, in 1622, was sent to Virginia under the custodianship of Sir Thomas Smythe and one 'Elianor [*sic*] Phillips who offered to pay for his passage if the Companie please to permit the said ffrancke to goe'. These cases were all examples of the flexibility of the system and the ability of some to manipulate it. Smythe had been deprived of his governorship by this time and was under investigation for corruptly enriching himself at the expense of the Virginia Company.
4. See Brooks, 'Prisoners or Servants?, pp. 426–8. For discussions of the numbers issue, see Christopher Tomlins, 'Indentured Servitude in Perspective: European Migration into North America and the Composition of the Early American Labor Force, 1600–1775', in Cathy D. Matson (ed.), *The Economy of Early America: Historical Perspectives and New Directions*, University Park, PA: Penn State University Press, 2006, pp. 146ff; Aaron S. Fogleman, 'From Slaves, Convicts and Servants to Free Passengers: The Transformation of Immigration in the Era of the American Revolution', *Journal of American History*, vol. 85, no. 1, June 1998, pp. 43–76, and estimates by other historians cited throughout.
5. J. M. Beattie, *Crime and the Courts in England, 1660–1800*, Princeton, NJ: Princeton University Press, 1986, chs 9, 10 in particular. In relation to the situation in London, see Robert Shoemaker and Tim Hitchcock, *London Lives: Poverty, Crime and the Making of the Modern City*, Cambridge: Cambridge University Press, 2015.
6. PROB 11/184 Coventry 117–173 Will of Anthony Abdy, Alderman of London 04 December 1640 at MRP: Anthony Abdy will, 'Marine Lives', http://www.marinelives.org/wiki/MRP: Anthony_Abdy_will, accessed August 2018.
7. Or 99, see Brooks, 'Prisoners or Servants?', p. 426.
8. 'America and West Indies: January 1620', in Calendar of State Papers Colonial, America and West Indies: Volume 1, 1574–1660, ed. W. Noel Sainsbury (London, 1860), p. 23. British History Online, http://www.british-history.ac.uk/cal-state-papers/colonial/america-west-indies/vol1/p23, accessed 22 May 2017.
9. *Flying Post*, 1 September 1698.
10. See Timothy J. Shannon, 'A "wicked commerce": Consent, Coercion, and Kidnapping in Aberdeen's Servant Trade', *The William and Mary Quarterly*, vol. 74, no. 3, July 2017, pp. 437–66, for a discussion of this trade.
11. Today, the preferred name for most of those people known as 'Gypsies' is generally, Roma or Rom.
12. Frances Hindes Groome, *Gypsy Folk Tales*, London: Hurst and Blackett, 1899, p. xviii.
13. Bruce P. Lenman, 'Lusty Beggars, Dissolute Women, Sorners, Gypsies, and Vagabonds for Virginia', *CW Journal*, Spring 2005, https://www.history.org/foundation/journal/spring05/scots.cfm, accessed April 2019.
14. Groome, *Gypsy Folk Tales*, p. xvi, citing the *Gypsy Lore Journal*, ii, 1890/1891, pp. 60–2.
15. Others were arrested and duly committed for criminal activity. In 1700 a man known as the 'King of the Gypsies' stole three gold rings and nine shillings from Rebecca Sellers. He was not convicted of robbery, but of a felony, because he had 'juggled' or shaken the goods out of Rebecca's possession. The king, under his proper name of Jacob Rewbury (also spelt 'Resbrey'), was sentenced to transportation. See 'Jacob Rewbrey. Violent Theft: highway robbery. 28th August 1700' (reference 't17000828-63') and 'Old Bailey Proceedings punishment summary. 28 August 1700' (reference s17000828-1'), available at *The Proceedings of the Old Bailey*, https://www.oldbaileyonline.org, accessed 2 November 2019.

16. Quoted in Rev. Edward D. Neill, 'Notes on American History', *New England Historical and Genealogical Register*, 30, 1876, p. 410.
17. Marcia Zug, 'The Mail-Order Brides of Jamestown, Virginia', *The Atlantic*, 31 August 2016, online at https://www.theatlantic.com/business/archive/2016/08/the-mail-order-brides-of-jamestown-virginia/498083/, accessed November 2018.
18. Neill, 'Notes on American History', p. 412.
19. Descendants of the indigenous peoples of Virginia refer to themselves as 'Indians', rather than Native Americans, see Jennifer Potter, *The Jamestown Brides: The Untold Story of England's 'Maids for Virginia'*, London: Atlantic Books, 2018, p. 3.
20. Kathleen M. Brown, *Good Wives, Nasty Wenches, and Anxious Patriarchs: Gender, Race and Power in Colonial Virginia*, Chapel Hill, NC: University of North Carolina Press, 1996, p. 94.
21. The same approach would be used in New South Wales, mainly through the approximately 4,000 Irish pauper girls, some as young as fourteen, who were sent out by the government from the 1840s.
22. Usually 'Guiana', at this time, and not necessarily correlating with the modern state of Guyana.
23. Krista Kesselring, 'Star Chamber Stories: Felons' Labours', *Legal History Miscellany*, January 2018, https://legalhistorymiscellany.com/2018/01/02/felons-labours, accessed September 2018.
24. Jeffrey A. Fortin and Mark Meuwese (eds), *Atlantic Biographies: Individuals and Peoples in the Atlantic World*, Leiden and Boston, MA: Brill, 2013, p. 178.
25. Hamish Maxwell-Stewart, 'Transportation from Britain and Ireland, 1615–1875', in Claire Anderson (ed.), *A Global History of Convicts and Penal Colonies*, London: Bloomsbury Academic, 2018, p. 189.
26. Some Scots were transported to France, see Walter Kendall Watkins, 'The Scotch Ancestry of Maj-Gen Sir David Ochterloney, Bart, A Native of Boston in New England', *The New England Historical and Genealogical Register*, vol. 56, 1902, New England Historic Genealogical Society, p. 181.
27. Arthur Hesilrige, A Letter from Sir Arthur Hesilrige, *To the Honorable Committee of The Councel of State For Irish and Scotish Affairs at White Hall, Concerning the Scots Prisoners*, 31 October 1650, available at https://digital.nls.uk/scotlandspages/timeline/1650.html, accessed 2 November 2019. See also news of the 2015 excavation of a mass grave of Scottish soldiers taken prisoner after the battle at 'Skeletons found in mass graves are 17th Century Scottish Soldiers', *Durham University News*, 2 September 2015, https://www.dur.ac.uk/news/newsitem/?id=25510&itemno=25510, accessed February 2018.
28. K.G. Davies, *The North Atlantic World in the Seventeenth Century*, Minneapolis, MI: University of Minnesota Press, 1974, p. 92. See also James Davie Butler, 'British Convicts Shipped to American Colonies', *American Historical Review*, vol. 2, no. 1, October 1896, pp. 12–33, https://www.jstor.org/stable/1833611, accessed 2 November 2019.
29. Anon, 'Scots Prisoners and their Relocation to the Colonies, 1650–1654', https://www.geni.com/projects/Scots-Prisoners-and-their-Relocation-to-the-Colonies-1650-1654/3465, accessed May 2017.
30. Davies, *The North Atlantic World*, p. 92.
31. See Lenman, 'Lusty Beggars'. Two Dumfries men were even transported to Shetland, apparently to provide labour for the governor's new castle. See 'Transportation Extracts from the records of the Edinburgh Tolbooth (*The Book of the Old Edinburgh Club*, vol. V, VI)', *The Reformation*, https://www.thereformation.info/transportations/, accessed June 2019.
32. 'Aprile 17th 1666', *The Reformation*, https://thereformation.info/wp-content/themes/twentyseventeen/Images/Slaves.jpg, accessed June 2019.
33. See Dane Love, *Scottish Covenanter Stories*, New York: Neill Wilson Publishing, 2011.
34. 'William Furbish' at *Geni*, https://www.geni.com/people/William-Furbish/4707973973080035946, accessed January 2019.
35. Anon, 'Scots Prisoners and their Relocation to the Colonies, 1650–1654' at https://www.geni.com/projects/Scots-Prisoners-and-their-Relocation-to-the-Colonies-1650-1654/3465, accessed July 2019.
36. Quoted in Lenman, 'Lusty Beggars'.
37. In 1649 the House of Commons resolved 'That an Act be brought in, for Transportation of some Felons, now in Newgate, beyond the Seas, by the Lord Mayor and Aldermen of London', see

'Transporting Felons', *Journal of the House of Commons*: vol. 6, 1648–1651 (London, 1802), pp. 243–4. British History Online, http://www.british-history.ac.uk/commons-jrnl/vol6/pp243–244, accessed August 2018.

38. Davies, *The North Atlantic World*, p. 92.

39. A.G.L. Shaw, *Convicts and the Colonies: A Study of Penal Transportation from Great Britain and Ireland to Australia and Other Parts of the British Empire*, London: Faber and Faber, 1966, p. 24.

40. See Liam Hogan, 'England's "Irish Slaves" Meme: The Numbers', *Global Research*, 4 November 2015, http://www.globalresearch.ca/englands-irish-slaves-meme-the-numbers/5529851?utm_campaign =magnet&utm_source=article_page&utm_medium=related_articles, accessed September 2016; 'White Slavery, what the Scots already know', *The Douglas Archives*, http://www.douglashistory.co. uk/history/Histories/slavery/whiteslavetrade.htm#.WSJbFhir2yE, accessed May 2017 and February 2020; Jerome S. Handler and Matthew C. Riley, 'Contesting "White Slavery" in the Caribbean: Enslaved Africans and European Indentured Servants in Seventeenth-Century Barbados', *New West Indian Guide*, 91, 2017, pp. 30–55, and Liam Hogan, Laura McAtackney and Matthew C. Reilly, 'The Irish in the Anglo-Caribbean: Servants or Slaves?', *History Ireland*, March–April 2016, pp. 18–22.

41. Robert Dunlop (ed.), *Ireland under the commonwealth; being a selection of documents relating to the Government of Ireland from 1651 to 1659*, vol. II, Manchester: Manchester University Press, 1913, pp. 374–5, Orders A/84. 44. Ff. 663–4.

42. In 1640 the Barbados planter Thomas Verney wrote home to his father in England for a hundred prisoners, see Larry Dale Gragg, *Englishmen Transplanted: The English Colonization of Barbados, 1627–1660*, Oxford: Oxford University Press, 2003, p. 142.

43. 'The Diary of Thomas Burton: 25 March 1658–9', in Diary of Thomas Burton Esq: Volume 4, March–April 1659, John Towill Rutt (ed.), London, 1828, pp. 254–73. British History Online, http://www.british-history.ac.uk/burton-diaries/vol4/pp254–73, accessed 22 May 2017. See also Lorena S. Walsh, 'The Hoe, the Plow, and the Whip: Gang Labour and Agricultural Improvement in Plantation Economics', Washington Area Economic History Seminar, 5 December 2014, p. 4, http://www.american.edu/cas/economics/upload/Walsh-Paper-12-5. pdf, accessed May 2017.

44. Alan Atkinson, 'The Free-Born Englishman Transported: Convict Rights as a Measure of Eighteenth-Century Empire', *Past and Present*, vol. 144, issue 1, 1994, pp. 88–115.

45. Carla Gardina Pestana, *The English Atlantic in an Age of Revolution, 1640–1661*, Cambridge, MA: Harvard University Press, 2004, pp. 209–10.

46. Ibid, p. 209.

47. Gragg, *Englishmen Transplanted*, pp. 142–3.

48. John Harrower, *The Journal of John Harrower, An Indentured Servant in the Colony of Virginia, 1773–1776*, New York: Holt, Rinehart, and Winston, 1963, entry for 16 May 1774.

49. W. G. [William Green], *The sufferings of William Green: being a sorrowful account, of his seven years transportation, wherein is set forth the various hardships he underwent, with his parting and meeting again in that Country, with his intimate Friend Anthony Atkinson, with their joyful arrival in England, after being absent ten Years. Likewise an Account of their manner of Living; the Climate of the Country, and in what it principally abounds. Written by W. Green, the unhappy Sufferer. Who returned on the second of June, 1774.* With the Place of his Birth and Parentage, and the Manner of his Life, Whitechapel: J. Long, 1775? See also Edith M. Ziegler, *Harlots, Hussies and Poor Unfortunate Women: Crime, Transportation, and the Servitude of Female Convicts, 1718–1783*, Tuscaloosa, AL: University of Alabama Press, 2014, pp. 67ff, for details of sale transactions.

50. Salem Quarterly Court. Salem, Massachusetts, 25 June 1661. Records and Files of the Quarterly Courts of Essex County, Massachusetts, vol. II, 1656–1662, pp. 298ff, https://archive.org/stream/recordsandfiles00dowgoog#page/n307/mode/2up, accessed 20 December 2017. Welch's proper forename was Phillip, as noted in the court records. Some references to these records claim that the youths were referred to as 'slaves' – they were not, see note 41 above, and also Jennie Jeppesen, 'Within the protection of law': debating the Australian convict-as-slave narrative', *History Australia*, vol. 16, issue 3, 2019, https://www.tandfonline.com/eprint/TYGCVFDNDUFDAY5NSGNN/full?target=10.1080%2F14490854.2019.1636674&, accessed November 2019.

CHAPTER 3: TRAITORS AND DECEIVERS

1. David Harris Sacks, *The Widening Gate: Bristol and the Atlantic Economy, 1450–1700*, Berkeley, CA: University of California Press, 1991, p. 299.
2. Robert Wodrow, *The History of the Sufferings of the Church of Scotland from the Restoration to the Revolution* (first published 1721–2), Glasgow: Blackie Fullerton & Co., 1828, vol. 3, pp. 130–1, https://archive.org/stream/sufferingsofchur03wodr/sufferingsofchur03wodr_djvu.txt, accessed May 2017.
3. 'America and West Indies: November 1697, 22–25', in *Calendar of State Papers Colonial, America and West Indies*, vol. 16, 1697–8, J. W. Fortescue (ed.), His Majesty's Stationery Office, London, 1905), pp. 30–7. British History Online, accessed March 2016, http://www.british-history.ac.uk/cal-state-papers/colonial/america-west-indies/vol16/pp30–37.
4. A.G.L. Shaw, *Convicts and the Colonies: A Study of Penal Transportation from Great Britain and Ireland to Australia and Other Parts of the British Empire*, London: Faber and Faber, 1966, pp. 24–5.
5. Ernest Bernbaum, *The Mary Carleton Narratives 1663–1673: A Missing Chapter in the History of the English Novel*, Cambridge, MA: Harvard University Press; and Humphrey Milford, London: Oxford University Press, 1914.
6. Anonymous, *The Arraignment, Tryal and Examination of Mary Moders, Otherwise Stedman, Now Carleton, (Stiled, the German Princess)*, London, 1663, p. 13, quoted in Kate Lilley, 'Mary Carleton's False Additions: The Case of the "'German Princess"'', *Humanities Research*, vol. XVI, no. 1, 2010, p. 80.
7. Quoted in Charles Whitehead, *Lives and Exploits of the Most Noted Highwaymen, Robbers and Murderers of All Nations: Drawn from the Most Authentic Sources, and Brought Down to the Present Time*, Hartford, CT: E. Strong, and London, 1836, p. 65.
8. 'J G' [John Goodwin], *The Memoires of Mary Carleton: Commonly stiled [sic], the German Princess. Being a Narrative of her Life and Death*, London, 1673, p. 6.
9. Anon., *An Exact and True Relation of the Examination, Trial and Condemnation of the German Princess, otherwise called Mary Carleton, at Justice Hall in the Old Bailey, January 17, 1672*.
10. Mihoko Suzuki (ed.), *Mary Carleton: Printed Writings 1641–1700*: Series II, Part Three, vol. 6, Abingdon: Routledge, 2017, pp. xivff.
11. Lilley, 'Mary Carleton's False Additions', p. 80, note 2.
12. Jennett Humpheys, 'Mary Carleton', *Dictionary of National Biography, 1885–1900*, vol. 9, pp. 95ff., accessed online May 2018, and Bernbaum, *The Mary Carleton Narratives 1663–1673*.
13. For some indications of how randomness played out in the Scottish justice system, see Cassie Watson, 'Execution Delayed: Some Scottish Examples' at Legal History Miscellany, https://legalhistorymiscellany.com/2018/09/23/execution-delayed-some-scottish-examples, accessed June 2018.
14. 'Richmond (Va.), *Enquirer*, of the 1st, 5th, and 8th September 1804, from an exact copy of the original manuscript, made by Mr. Jefferson, then President of the United States, in Tracts and Other Papers, relating principally to the Origin, Settlement and Progress of the Colonies, from the Discovery of the Country to the Year 1776, Peter Force, Washington, 1886', available at https://books.google.com.au/books?id=tHwBAAAAMAAJ&pg=RA2-PA55&lpg=RA2-PA55&dq=Enquirer,+of+the+1st,+5th,+and+8th+of+September+1804&source=bl&ots=rBmZeMcMvY&sig=ACfU3U2KaXrGUzepR0OJfRcDJS4L5sTIvA&hl=en&sa=X&ved=2ahUKEwik5JuPgdXlAhX66nMBHYFXDgAQ6AEwAXoECAcQAg#v=onepage&q=Enquirer%2C%20of%20the%201st%2C%205th%2C%20and%208th%20of%20September%201804&f=false, accessed November 2019.
15. David Hackett Fischer, *Albion's Seed: Four British Folkways in America*, Oxford and New York: Oxford University Press, 1989, pp. 9, 11, 125, 310, 340, 526, 687 and 708.
16. For estimates of numbers transported to the American colonies, see Hamish Maxwell-Stewart, 'Convict Labour Extraction and Transportation from Britain and Ireland, 1615–1870', in Christian Giuseppe De Vito and Alex Lichtenstein (eds), *Global Convict Labour*, New York: Brill, 2015, p. 169.

17. James Douglas Rice, 'Bacon's Rebellion 1676–1677', *Encyclopedia Virginia*, https://www. encyclopediavirginia.org/Bacon_s_Rebellion_1676–1677#start_entry, accessed November 2019, and Emily Jones Salmon, 'Convict Labor during the Colonial Period', *Encyclopedia Virginia*, https://www.encyclopediavirginia.org/Convict_Labor_During_the_Colonial_Period, accessed November 2019.

18. Aphra Behn, *The Widdow Ranter, or, The History of Bacon in Virginia*, London: James Knapton, 1690, available in Paul Royster (ed.), 'Electronic Texts in American Studies', *Digital Commons@ University of Nebraska – Lincoln*, p. 230, http://digitalcommons.unl.edu/etas/45/, accessed December 2016.

19. Mathew Parker, *Willoughbyland: England's Lost Colony*, London: Hutchinson, 2015, pp. 147ff.

20. Richard B. Sheridan, *Sugar and Slavery: An Economic History of the British West Indies, 1623– 1775*, Baltimore, MD: The Johns Hopkins University Press, 1974, pp. 151–4.

21. Abigail L. Swingen, *Competing Visions of Empire: Labor, Slavery, and the Origins of the British Atlantic Empire*, New Haven, CT and London: Yale University Press, 2015, pp. 20–8.

22. All quotations from John Cordy Jeaffreson (ed.), *A young squire of the seventeenth century: From the papers (A.D. 1676–1686) of Christopher Jeaffreson*, vol. 1, London: Hurst and Blackett, 1878.

23. Lists of rebels to be transported at 'Addenda: October 1685', in J. W. Fortescue (ed.), *Calendar of State Papers Colonial, America and West Indies: Volume 12 1685–1688 and Addenda 1653– 1687*, London, 1899, p. 651, accessible at British History Online, http://www.british-history. ac.uk/cal-state-papers/colonial/america-west-indies/vol12/p651, accessed May 2017.

24. John Coad, *A Memorandum of the Wonderful Providences of God to a poor un-worthy Creature, during the time of the Duke of Monmouth's Rebellion and to the Revolution in 1688. By John Coad, one of the Sufferers*, London: Longman, Brown, Green, 1849, pp. 19–20.

25. Macaulay's *History of England*, vol. 1, London: J. M. Dent, 1906, p. 470, https://archive.org/ stream/macaulayshistory01maca/macaulayshistory01maca_djvu.txt, accessed July 2018.

26. See 'Addenda: October 1685', in *Calendar of State Papers Colonial, America and West Indies, Volume 12, 1685–1688 and Addenda 1653–1687*, J. W. Fortescue (ed.), London: Her Majesty's Stationery Office, 1899, p. 651. *British History Online*, accessed April 2016, http://www. british-history.ac.uk/cal-state-papers/colonial/america-west-indies/vol12/p651.

27. Coad, p. 141. Coad's family held the record of his trials secret until the nineteenth century when they came to the attention of the historian Lord Macaulay.

28. K. G. Davies, *The North Atlantic World in the Seventeenth Century*, Minneapolis, MI: University of Minnesota Press, 1974, p. 92.

29. Henry Pitman, *A Relation of the Great Sufferings and Strange Adventures of Henry Pitman, Chyrurgion to the late Duke of Monmouth etc.*, London: Andrew Sowle, 1689, pp. 454–5.

30. Cindy Vallar, 'Captain Blood: The History Behind the Novel', http://www.cindyvallar.com/ captainbloodhistory.html, accessed November 2019.

31. Davies, *The North Atlantic World*, p. 92.

32. Stephen Mullen, 'Scots and Caribbean Slavery: Victims and Profiteers', *A Glasgow-West India Sojourn*, 6 March 2014, https://glasgowwestindies.wordpress.com/tag/jacobites, accessed May 2017.

33. For a list of Scots 'banished', mainly through transportation, to the American colonies see David Dobson, *Directory of Scots Banished to the American Plantations, 1650–1775*, Baltimore, MD: Clearfied Publishing Company, 1990, and subsequent reprints.

CHAPTER 4: THE BODY TRADE

1. William A. Shaw (ed.), 'Treasury Books and Papers: April 1739', *Calendar of Treasury Books and Papers, Volume 4, 1739–1741*, London: Her Majesty's Stationery Office, 1901, pp. 17–21, available at *British History Online*, http://www.british-history.ac.uk/cal-treasury-books-papers/vol4/ pp17-21, accessed October 2016.

2. A. Roger Ekirch, *Bound for America: The Transportation of British Convicts to the Colonies, 1718– 1775*, Oxford: Clarendon Press, 1987, p. 23.

3. Carl E. Swanson, '"The unspeakable Calamity this poor Province Suffers from Pyrats": South Carolina and the Golden Age of Piracy', *Northern Mariner/Le Marin du Nord*, vol. 21, no. 2, 2011, p. 124, and *Original Weekly Journal*, 24 January 1719.

4. 'Old Bailey Proceedings: Accounts of Criminal Trials, 16 January 1723', *London Lives 1690 to 1800: Crime, Poverty and Social Policy in the Metropolis*, https://www.londonlives.org/browse.jsp?id=t17230116-23-defend131&div=t17230116-23#highlight, accessed August 2018.

5. 'Order authorizing payment to Jonathan Forward', *Recent Antiquarian Acquisitions: The Lewis Walpole Library, Yale University*, https://lewiswalpole.wordpress.com/2018/12/12/order-authorizing-payment-to-jonathan-forward/, accessed February 2019.

6. 'Ordinary's Account: 3rd March 1737' (Ref. OA17370303), *The Proceedings of the Old Bailey-London's Central Criminal Court, 1674 to 1913*, https://www.oldbaileyonline.org/browse.jsp?div=OA17370303, accessed 13 March 2018.

7. Philip Gaskell, 'Henry Justice, a Cambridge book thief', *Transactions of the Cambridge Bibliographical Society*, vol. 1, no. 4, 1952, pp. 348–57, JSTOR, www.jstor.org/stable/41336971.

8. Richard Coulton, Matthew Mauger and Christopher Reid, *Stealing Books in Eighteenth-Century London*, London: Palgrave Macmillan, 2016, p. 2. The authors found 721 cases of book theft tried at the Old Bailey between 1674 and 1820.

9. 'Henry Justice. Theft; grand larceny, Theft; other. 5th of May 1736' (t17360505-88), *Old Bailey Proceedings Online*, https://www.oldbaileyonline.org/browse.jsp?div=t17360505-88, accessed June 2019; *London Evening Post*, 11 May 1736.

10. Peter Rushton and Gwenda Morgan, *Banishment in the Early Atlantic World: Convicts, Rebels and Slaves*, London: Bloomsbury Academic, 2013, pp. 121–3.

11. He died at the age of eighty in 1760. For an account of his business and of the convict transportation trade in general, see Anthony Vaver, *Bound With an Iron Chain: The Untold Story of How the British Transported 50,000 Convicts to Colonial America*, Westborough MA: Pickpocket Publishing, 2011, pp. 61–87 and *passim*.

12. The real wage or real wealth value of that income or wealth might be be £40,600 in 2018, https://www.measuringworth.com.

13. Robert Walpole, 'Order authorizing payment to Jonathan Forward for transporting convicts to the American plantations', 7 March 1723, at *Recent Antiquarian Acquisitions: The Lewis Walpole Library, Yale University*, https://lewiswalpole.wordpress.com/2018/12/12/order-authorizing-payment-to-jonathan-forward/, accessed February 2019.

14. James Davie Butler, 'British Convicts Shipped to American Colonies', *American Historical Review*, vol. 2, no. 1, October 1896, p. 23.

15. Ekirch, *Bound for America*, p. 21.

16. Some sources say 1721.

17. Ekirch, *Bound for America*, pp. 184–5.

18. George Ely Russell, *Maryland Magazine of Genealogy*, vol. 4, no. 2, Fall 1981.

19. David Waldstreicher, *Runaway America: Benjamin Franklin, Slavery, and the American Revolution*, New York: Farrar, Straus and Giroux, 2005, p. 67.

20. 'Proceedings and Acts of the General Assembly of Maryland, October 1724', in Clayton Colman Hall (ed.), *Proceedings and Acts of the General Assembly of Maryland, October 1724–Juiy [sic] 1726, Published by Authority of the State under the Direction of the Maryland Historical Society*, available at *Internet Archive*, https://archive.org/stream/archivesmarylan01archgoog/archivesmarylan01archgoog_djvu.txt, accessed April 2018.

21. '1727/28 MD Last will & testament of William Vanhaes Cornwi[a]llis alias Riddlesden Naming William and John Cornwell', *Ancestry*, https://www.ancestry.co.uk/boards/thread.aspx?mv=flat&m=3110&p=surnames.cornwell, accessed November 2019; see also https://www.genealogy.com/forum/surnames/topics/cornwallis/39/ and Provincial Court Land Records, 1731–1737, vol. 698, p. 209, Maryland State Archives, https://www.ancestry.co.uk/boards/thread.aspx?mv=flat&m=3110&p=surnames.cornwell. The documents refer to Riddlesden as 'Thomas'.

22. The exact date of Moll's birth, under the name Elizabeth Adkins, is not known. 'Moll King' was also an extremely common name and it is not impossible that the 'Moll King' of the pamphlet about her life (published in 1747) is a composite, deliberate or not, of the lives and criminal careers of several women.

23. Anon., *The Life and Character of Moll King, Late Mistress of King's Coffee House in Covent Garden, who Departed this Life . . . The 17th of September, 1747*, London: W. Price, 1747?

24. 'America and West Indies: November 1736, 21–30', in *Calendar of State Papers Colonial, America and West Indies, Volume 42, 1735–1736*, London: Her Majesty's Stationery Office, 1953, pp. 335–54, available at *British History Online*, http://www.british-history.ac.uk/cal-state-papers/colonial/america-west-indies/vol42/pp335-354, accessed September 2016; see also 'Governor's Letter-Book, Annapolis 1719–1742', pp. 158ff, in *The Records of British Government at Annapolis Royal, 1713–1749*, available at the *Nova Scotia Archives*, https://novascotia.ca/archives/heartland/archives.asp?Number=Two&Page=103&Language=English, accessed September 2016, and 'Buckler Family' at *Rootsweb*, http://www.rootsweb.ancestry.com/~kyrobert/family/bucklerfamily.html, accessed November 2019.

25. See also Gwenda Morgan and Peter Rushton. 'Fraud and Freedom: Gender, Identity and Narratives of Deception among the Female Convicts in Colonial America', *Journal for Eighteenth-Century Studies*, vol. 34, no. 3, 2011, pp. 335–55.

26. Silvio A. Bedini, *At the Sign of the Compass and Quadrant: The Life and Times of Anthony Lamb*, Philadelphia, PA: American Philosophical Society, 1984, p. 79.

27. Charles E. Smart, *The Makers of Surveying Instruments in America Since 1700*, New York: Regal Art Press, 1962.

28. Bedini, *At the Sign of the Compass and Quadrant*, p. 78.

29. Robert Sutcliff, *Travels in some parts of North America, in the years 1804, 1805, & 1806*, York: Printed by C. Peacock for W. Alexander, 1811, p. 115.

30. The legal proceedings were followed in *The Gentleman's Magazine*, vol. XIV, 1744. See also James Annesley, *Memoirs of an Unfortunate Young Nobleman, Return'd from a Thirteen Years Slavery in America, Where he had been Sent by the Wicked Contrivances of his Cruel Uncle*, 2 vols, London: J. Freeman, 1743, and Roger Ekirch, *Birthright: The True Story that Inspired* Kidnapped, New York: W. W. Norton & Company, 2010.

31. He claimed to have been only eight years old in his autobiography.

32. Peter Williamson, *French and Indian Cruelty, exemplified in the Life and various Vicissitudes of Fortune of Peter Williamson, who was carried off from Aberdeen in his Infancy, and sold as a slave in Pennsylvania . . .*, Edinburgh, 1787, p. 148.

33. Peter's sensational memoir was first published in 1757 and went through many subsequent editions. Some aspects are considered dubious, particularly his account of his sojourn with the Cherokee, though his initial kidnapping and transportation experience is credible. Subsequent editions included the story of his legal battles and what was effectively a manifesto against the trade of kidnapping.

34. Quoted in Edith Zeigler 'The Transported Convict Women of Colonial Maryland, 1718–1776', *Maryland Historical Magazine*, vol. 97, no. 1, Spring 2002, p. 12. Elizabeth Sprigs [*sic*] to John Sprigs, 22 September 1756, High Court of Admiralty Papers, HCA30/258, no. 106, PRO. Historians have thrown some doubt on the authenticity of this letter and it is not clear if Betty Spriggs was a convict or an indentured servant, not that such legal distinctions were often observed in practice. See Peter W. Coldham, *Settlers of Maryland*, vol. 3, 1731–1750, Baltimore, MD: Genealogical Publishing Company, 1995–6, and Kevin Young, 'Macaulay's Mirror: Myths, Martyrs, and White Slaves in the Early Atlantic World', graduate thesis in world history, Monmouth University, 2011.

35. Zeigler, 'The Transported Convict Women', pp. 21, 30.

36. *Maryland Gazette*, 28 May 1752 and 13 November 1751.

37. Edith M. Ziegler, *Harlots, Hussies, and Poor Unfortunate Women: Crime, Transportation, and the Servitude of Female Convicts, 1718–1783*, Tuscaloosa, AL: University of Alabama Press, 2014, pp. 3, 13, 14.

38. Ibid, p. 137.

CHAPTER 5: A RACE OF CONVICTS

1. George Birkbeck, Norman Hill and L. F. Powell (eds), *Boswell's Life of Johnson*, vol. 3: *The Life (1776–1780)*, Oxford: Oxford University Press, 1934, pp. 200–1.

2. 'By His Excellency Samuel Shute, Esq. Captain Ganeral and Govenour in chief in and over His Majesty's Province of the Massachusetts-Bay in New-England. &c. a proclamation [to apprehend seven escaped transported felons] Given under my hand . . .', *Library of Congress*, http://hdl.loc. gov/loc.rbc/rbpe.03305800, accessed August 2018.

3. Franklin's words appeared in *The Pennsylvania Gazette*, 9 May 1751, https://founders.archives. gov/documents/Franklin/01-04-02-0040, accessed October 2019.

4. See Gwenda Morgan and Peter Rushton, *Eighteenth-Century Criminal Transportation: The Formation of the Criminal Atlantic*, New York: Palgrave Macmillan, 2004, p. 139.

5. *The Universal Magazine of Knowledge and Pleasure*, vol. 8, June 1751, p. 283.

6. J. Hector St John Crevecoeur, *Letters from an American farmer, reprinted from the original ed., with a prefatory note by W. P. Trent and an introduction by Ludwig Lewisohn*, New York: Fox, Duffield, 1904, p. 88.

7. *The Cave and Lundy Review, and Critical Revolving Light*, Barnstaple 1824; A. F. Langham, 'Thomas Benson's Convict Slaves on Lundy', *Rep. Lundy Fld. Soc.* p. 40, http://www.lundy.org. uk/download/ar40/LFS_Annual_Report_Vol_40_Part_14.pdf, September 2016.

8. Stanley Thomas, *The Nightingale Scandal: The Story of Thomas Benson and Lundy*, Bideford, 1959; republished with additional notes by Myrtle Ternstrom, Appledore, Devon: Lazarus Press, 2001.

9. R. J. Clarke, *Impostress: The Dishonest Adventures of Sarah Wilson*, Cheltenham: The History Press, 2019.

10. *London Magazine or Gentleman's Monthly Intelligencer*, June 1773, p. 311.

11. Advertisement dated 11 October 1771, *Pennsylvania Gazette*.

12. *Gentleman's Magazine*, vol. 43, July 1773, 'Historical Chronicle for July 1773', p. 357.

13. A number of contemporary newspapers inaccurately reported that Sarah had worked for Miss Caroline Vernon, Queen Charlotte's maid of honour, from whom she had stolen clothes and jewellery, see Clarke, *Impostress*, pp. 79–81.

14. http://www.mysteriouspeople.com/princess_hoax.htm, November 2016. She died in Maine in 1780.

15. Gwenda Morgan and Peter Rushton, 'Fraud and Freedom: Gender, Identity and Narratives of Deception among the Female Convicts in Colonial America', *Journal for Eighteenth-Century Studies*, vol. 34, no. 3, 2011, p. 345 and n. 42.

16. *The Providence, Rhode Island Gazette and Country Journal*, January 1774, quoted in Daniel Rolph, 'The Remarkable Career of Sarah Wilson: Convict, Princess, and Marchioness of Colonial America', Historical Society of Pennsylvania, August 2014, https://hsp.org/blogs/history-hits/ the-remarkable-career-of-sarah-wilson-convict-princess-and-marchioness-of-colonial-america, accessed June 2018.

17. Morgan and Rushton, 'Fraud and Freedom', p. 349.

18. John Poulter, *The discoveries of John Poulter, alias Baxter; who was apprehended for robbing Dr. Hancock of Salisbury, on Clarken Down, near Bath; and thereupon discovered a most numerous gang of villains, many of which have been already taken*, Sherborne, 1754 (10th edn.), p. 28.

19. Morgan and Rushton, *Eighteenth-Century Criminal Transportation*, p. 107 and *passim*.

20. There was a perception that many were returning and that transportation was failing as an effective punishment or deterrent to crime. The Confinement at Hard Labour Act 1752 was introduced as an official response to that public concern. The legislation provided an alternative to transportation for those pardoned from a capital sentence.

21. Christopher Texiera, 'The Crime of Coming Home: British Convicts Returning from Transportation in London, 1720–1780', MA thesis, University of Central Florida, 2010; Morgan and Rushton, *Eighteenth-Century Criminal Transportation*, pp. 98ff.

22. 'Ordinary's Account. 1st June 1752' (OA17520601), *The Proceedings of the Old Bailey*, https:// www.oldbaileyonline.org/browse.jsp?div=OA17520601, accessed June 2019.

23. Joseph Derbin, 'Miscellaneous: returning from transportation', 12 September 1764'(t17640912-13), *The Proceedings of the Old Bailey*, https://www.oldbaileyonline.org/browse.jsp?div= t17640912–13, accessed January 2018.

24. 'Ordinary's Account. 4 June 1770' (OA17700604), *The Proceedings of the Old Bailey*, https:// www.oldbaileyonline.org/browse.jsp?div=OA17700604, accessed 12 March 2018.

25. *Virginia Gazette*, 12 August 1773.

26. Jennifer Lodine-Chaffey, 'From Newgate to the New World: A Study of London's Transported Female Convicts, 1718–1775', https://www.varsitytutors.com/earlyamerica/early-america-review /volume-14/newgate-new-world#_ftn54, accessed April 2018.

27. Morgan and Rushton, *Eighteenth-Century Criminal Transportation*, p. 63.

28. 'James Hancock. Miscellaneous: returning from transportation. 3rd June 1772' (t17720603-43), *The Proceedings of the Old Bailey*, https://www.oldbaileyonline.org/browse.jsp?div=t17720603-43, accessed November 2019.

29. Carleton Sprague Smith, 'Broadsides and their Music in Colonial America', Colonial Society of Massachusetts, https://www.colonialsociety.org/node/2012, accessed June 2018.

30. 'The Lads of Virginia' (Bod 2213), *Broadside Ballads Online from the Bodleian Libraries*, http:// ballads.bodleian.ox.ac.uk/search/roud/1488, accessed February 2018.

31. Various versions, see this one at 'The trappan'd maiden: or, The distressed damsel (Bod 23881)', *Broadside Ballads Online from the Bodleian Libraries*, http://ballads.bodleian.ox.ac.uk/search/ subject/Virginia/?query=&d=1650, accessed February 2018.

32. John Melville Jennings, who discovered and introduced this work in the *Virginia Magazine of History and Biography*, vol. 4 (1896–7), pp. 218–21, identifies a historical seventeenth-century 'James Revel', transported to Virginia between 1656 and 1671. However, later historians have doubted his existence; Morgan and Rushton, *Eighteenth-Century Criminal Transportation*, pp. 89–92 and 188–9, where the notes gloss the complex history of the song and its dated issues. See also Edith M. Ziegler, *Harlots, Hussies, and Poor Unfortunate Women: Crime, Transportation, and the Servitude of Female Convicts, 1718–1783*, Tuscaloosa, AL: University of Alabama Press, 2014, p. 188, and James Egan, 'James Revel (1640s?–?)', in *The Heath Anthology of American Literature*, 5th edn., http://college.cengage.com/english/lauter/heath/4e/students/author_pages/ colonial/revel_ja.html, accessed September 2016.

33. *Maryland Gazette*, 16 July 1767, p. 10

34. Special Committee on Transportation, House of Commons journals, vol. 37, 1 April 1779, also known as the Bunbury Committee; see Andrew Tink, 'The Role of Parliamentary Committee Witnesses in the Foundation of Australia', *Australasian Parliamentary Review*, vol. 20, no. 2, Spring 2005, pp. 33–8.

35. Emma Christopher, *A Merciless Place: The Lost Story of Britain's Convict Disaster in Africa*, Oxford: Oxford University Press, 2011, pp. 253–74; Don Jordan and Michael Walsh, *White Cargo: The Forgotten History of Britain's White Slaves in America*, New York: Random House, 2011; *Maryland Gazette*, 13 November 1783; Dan Byrnes, 'The Blackheath Connection', http://www. merchantnetworks.com.au/blackheath/thebc28.htm, accessed 24 May 2017.

36. Despite these disasters, it is estimated that 1,000 transportees were sent to the American colonies between 1776 and 1800; Hamish Maxwell-Stewart, 'Convict Labour Extraction and Transportation from Britain and Ireland, 1615–1870', in Christian Giuseppe De Vito and Alex Lichtenstein (eds), *Global Convict Labour*, New York: Brill, 2015, p. 169.

37. Quoted in Christopher, *A Merciless Place*, p. 205.

38. *Public Advertiser*, 12 January 1787, in 'EARLY NEWS FROM A NEW COLONY: BRITISH MUSEUM PAPERS. By Various, Unknown' [Newspaper Extracts Concerning the Colony of New South Wales, 1785–1795]. Source: 'APPENDIX E, Historical Records of New South Wales', Series 1; vol. II: Grose-Paterson, pp. 735–820, http://gutenberg.net.au/ebooks13/1300291h .html#ch-01, accessed January 2017.

CHAPTER 6: THIS SOLITARY WASTE

1. 'Proper Objects for Botany Bay', printed by J. Pitts, London, 1802–19, Bodleian Library (Bod 17034) at *Broadside Ballads Online from the Bodleian Libraries*, http://ballads.bodleian.ox.ac.uk/ search/title/Proper%20objects%20for%20Botany%20bay (but composed and published 1787 as 'Botany Bay: A New Song').

2. All quotations are from *Historical Records of New South Wales*, vol. 1, part 2, Phillip 1783–1792, Sydney 1892, pp.85ff. The instructions were drafted by Lord Sydney, Secretary of State.

3. The document contains a drafting error with regard to the deployment of male and female convicts; the intention is clearly to instruct Phillip to balance men with women whenever establishing further settlements.

4. See also Alan Frost, *Botany Bay and the First Fleet: The Real Story*, Melbourne: Black Inc., 2019.

5. Ralph Clark, 'The Journal and Letters of Lt. Ralph Clark 1787–1792', entry for 7 February 1788, http://setis.library.usyd.edu.au/ozlit/pdf/clajour.pdf, accessed November 2016.

6. Barrett's executioner may have been his co-condemned and friend, the reprieved John Ryan, who was exonerated from the 400 lashes to which he had been sentenced in return for performing the office of executioner, 'Jacob Nagle His Book A.D. One Thousand Eight Hundred and Twenty Nine May 19th. Canton. Stark County Ohio, 1775–1802'; compiled 1829, New South Wales State Library, entry for 22–26 January 1788 (but written after the events described), available at *New South Wales State Library*, https://www.sl.nsw.gov.au/collection-items/jacob-nagle-memoir-titled-jacob-nagle-his-book-ad-one-thousand-eight-hundred-and, accessed November 2019. Nagle was an American seaman.

7. Arthur Bowes Smyth, *A Journal of a Voyage from Portsmouth to New South Wales and China*, State Library New South Wales, https://www.sl.nsw.gov.au/collection-items/arthur-bowes-smyth-illustrated-journal-1787-1789-titled-journal-voyage-portsmouth, accessed November 2019.

8. Though Bowes Smyth gives the date as 26 February, James Scott gives the 27th, see NSW Capital Convictions Database at http://research.forbessociety.org.au/record/1; also John White, *Journal of a Voyage to New South Wales* [1790], entry for 27 February 1788 at https://ebooks.adelaide.edu.au/w/white/john/journal/index.html, accessed May 2019.

9. Bowes Smyth, pp. 107ff. Thomas Barrett also left a legacy. A skilled engraver and forger, he was commissioned by Surgeon-General John White to craft a medal commemorating the arrival of the transport ship *Charlotte* at Botany Bay. Today, 'The Charlotte Medal' (also known as the 'Botany Bay Medallion') is in the collection of the National Museum of Australia. It is considered to be the country's earliest colonial work of art.

10. John White, *Journal*, entry for 30 February 1788.

11. 'Letter from a female convict, Port Jackson, 14 November 1788', given in Hugh Anderson, *Farewell to Judges & Juries: The Broadside Ballad and Convict Transportation to Australia, 1788–1868*. Red Rooster Press: Hotham Hill, Victoria, 2000, p. 216 (from the *Public Advertiser*, 14 June 1793, and *Historical Records of New South Wales*, vol. 2, pp. 806–7). The letter also noted that 'All our letters are examined by an officer, but a friend takes this for me privately . . .'

12. Bowes Smyth, 22 March 1787–12 August 1789.

13. Robert Hughes, *The Fatal Shore: A History of the Transportation of Convicts to Australia, 1787–1868*, New York: Alfred A. Knopf, 1986, gives a particularly florid, though not the only version of this scene.

14. See Grace Karskens, 'The Myth of Sydney's Foundational Orgy', 2011, at the *Dictionary of Sydney*, http://dictionaryofsydney.org/entry/the_myth_of_sydneys_foundational_orgy, accessed August 2016.

15. The writer arrived on the *Lady Juliana* and wrote this letter in July 1790, published in the *Morning Chronicle*, 4 August 1791; see Hugh Tranter, 'The mystery convict correspondent of Lady Juliana and Lord George Gordon', https://www.academia.edu/1646389/The_mystery_convict_correspondent_of_Lady_Juliana_and_Lord_George_Gordon, accessed March 2020.

16. This and other extracts from Johnson's correspondence compiled in George Mackaness (comp. and ed.), *Some Letters of Rev. Richard Johnson, B.A. First Chaplain of New South Wales*, Part 1, vol. XX (New Series), George Mackaness (comp. and ed.), Sydney: D. S. Ford, 1954.

17. Charles Bateson, *The Convict Ships, 1787–1868*, Glasgow: Brown, Son & Ferguson, 1969; Siân Rees, *The Floating Brothel: The Extraordinary Story of the Lady Julian and its Cargo of Female Convicts Bound for Botany Bay*, Sydney: Hodder Headline Australia, 2001; Hughes, *The Fatal Shore*.

18. Michael Flynn, *The Second Fleet: Britain's Grim Convict Armada of 1790*, Sydney: Library of Australian History, 2001; Joy Damousi, *Depraved and Disorderly: Female Convicts and Gender in Colonial Australia*, New York: Cambridge University Press, 1997; Anne Summers, *Damned Whores and God's Police: The Colonisation of Women in Australia* [1975], Kensington, New South Wales: New South Books, 2016.

19. Anna Josepha King, 'Journal of a voyage from England to Australia in the ship "Speedy"', 19 November 1799–15 April 1800', Mitchell Library, State Library of New South Wales, C 185, http://acms.sl.nsw.gov.au/_transcript/2015/D33322/a1163.html, accessed November 2019. All quotations from this source.

20. It is estimated that around 15 per cent of all convicts to New South Wales were women; Clare Anderson (ed.), *A Global History of Convicts and Penal Colonies*, London: Bloomsbury Academic, 2018, p. 21.

21. 'George Barrington. Theft: grand larceny. 15th September 1790' (ref t17900915-10), *The Proceedings of the Old Bailey*, https://www.oldbaileyonline.org/browse.jsp?div=t17900915–10, accessed 20 August 2018.

22. Several volumes of Barrington's alleged autobiography were published and he was, probably inaccurately, credited with writing some early Australian theatrical works, see Suzanne Rickard (ed.), *George Barrington's Voyage to Botany Bay: Retelling a Convict's Travel Narrative of the 1790s*, London: Leicester University Press, 2001.

23. *The Argus*, 8 December 1956, p. 16.

24. *Freeman's Journal* (Dublin), 31 January 1801.

25. *Sydney Gazette*, 11 March 1804, p. 3.

26. Ibid.

27. Some were not Irish, but presumably joined the rising in sympathy or with the hope of escape – where to mattered little.

28. Quoted in Sarah Murden, 'A new life in Australia for prisoner Sarah Bird (1763-1842)', *All Things Georgian*, https://georgianera.wordpress.com/2015/06/11/a-new-life-in-australia-for-prisoner-sarah-bird-1763-1842/, accessed November 2018.

29. No marriage records have been found.

30. *The Sydney Gazette and New South Wales Advertiser*, 11 March 1804, p. 3.

31. Quoted in Sarah Murden, *All Things Georgian*, accessed November 2018.

32. Probably on a conditional pardon, as he petitioned for a free, or full, pardon in 1822. His petition was either denied, or he committed more crimes and was still on a conditional pardon in 1825.

33. Also known by other names, including Etherington, her birth name, and Astell.

34. The records of the investigation are in *Historical Records of Australia* for June and July 1820, pp. 200ff.

35. *Historical Records of Australia*, Report of the Bench of Magistrates [Enclosure no. 5.1], p. 322

36. Astell (or Esden), Lydia [398] utter, Suss., PB Suss. spring ass. 1819, 14 yrs trspn, £5 to sail on *Janus*, October 1819 [M5/321–2: 18 March, 14 April, 14 October 1819]', *Prisoners Letters to the Bank of England, 1781–1827*, London Record Society, London, 2007, available at British History Online, https://www.british-history.ac.uk/london-record-soc/vol42/pp245-268, accessed November 2019.

37. 'Individual Page: Lydia Broomfield/Etherington', *Rootsweb*, https://wc.rootsweb.ancestry.com/cgi-bin/igm.cgi?op=GET&db=platt&id=226129228, accessed November 2019.

CHAPTER 7: CRUEL TYRANNY

1. Geoffrey C. Ingleton (ed.), *True Patriots All, or News From Early Australia*, Rutland/Vermont/Tokyo: Charles Tuttle, 1988 (facsimile of 1st edn., 1952), p. 129.

2. Convicts, often soldiers, as well as indigenous people, were frequently transported to the Australian penal colonies from India and Ceylon (now Sri Lanka), see *Convicts to Australia*, http://members.iinet.net.au/~perthdps/convicts/india.html, accessed June 2019. Over the eighteenth and early nineteenth centuries, 15,000 or more convicts were recruited into the British Army, Hamish Maxwell-Stewart, 'Transportation from Britain and Ireland, 1615–1875', in Clare Anderson (ed.), *A Global History of Convicts and Penal Colonies*, London: Bloomsbury Academic, 2018, p. 196. See also Peter Lines, *The York Chasseurs: A Condemned Regiment of George III*, London: Francis Bootle, 2010.

3. All quotations from Stephan Williams (ed.), *A soldier's punishments, or, autobiography of a Botany Bay Hero by Michael Keane & two other tales of 1826*, Stephan Williams (ed.), Canberra: Popinjay Publications, 1994. Keane's 'Autobiography of a Botany Bay Hero', was first published in *The Australian*, 11 November 1826, p. 4.

4. *The Sydney Monitor*, 30 June 1830, p. 3, reprinted from the London *Observer*, 28 September 1829 with an editorial note: 'We vouch for the truth of this representation, at least as a general one, since Governor Darling came to the Government. It is the only correct representation made in the English papers that we ever read.' It is possible that the letter is not from a convict but a fabrication by opponents of transportation, though the hardships of convict life related are well attested in other sources.

5. James Backhouse, *A Narrative of a Visit to the Australian Colonies*, London: Hamilton, Adams and Co., 1843, p. 19.

6. They had plenty, as the *Cyprus* was provisioned to supply the penal station.

7. 'William Swallow', Convict records at https://convictrecords.com.au/convicts/swallow/william/119608, accessed April 2019, citing Australian Joint Copying Project. Microfilm Roll 89, Class and Piece Number HO11/6, p. 538.

8. Joshua Robertson, 'Australian Convict Pirates in Japan: Evidence of 1830 Voyage Unearthed', *Guardian*, 28 May 2017, https://www.theguardian.com/australia-news/2017/may/28/australian-convict-pirates-in-japan-evidence-of-1830-voyage-unearthed, accessed August 2018.

9. John Mulvaney, *The Axe Had Never Sounded: Place, People and Heritage of Recherche Bay, Tasmania*, Canberra: ANU Press, 2007.

10. Stephan Williams, *Johnny Troy*, Canberra: Popinjay Publications, 2001 (revised from original 1993 edn.), is the basis for this account.

11. At least three versions of this ballad have been collected in America, see Library of Congress for a version collected in California prior to World War I at 'Johnny Troy', *Library of Congress*, https://www.loc.gov/item/2017701036/, accessed May 2019. The opening stanza quoted here, slightly edited for scansion, is from southern Michigan, see Stephan Williams, *Johnny Troy*, Canberra: Popinjay Publications, 2001, pp. 35-41.

12. 'Account of Thomas Mathews', *Sydney Monitor*, 27 March 1830, p. 2. Mathews was said to have left this testimony in his cell the morning he was hanged and also made a dying speech referring to Moreton Bay as 'a state of suffering worse than death'. See also Rob Willis, *Alias Blind Larry: The Mostly True Memoir of James Laurence the Singing Convict*, Melbourne: Australian Scholarly Publishing, 2016, pp. 263–5.

13. *Sydney Gazette and New South Wales Advertiser*, 21 August 1832, p. 3.

14. 'Shameful Proceedings at the Funeral of Troy and Smith', *Sydney Herald*, 23 August 1832, p. 3.

15. For a thorough overview of Frank's life and legend, see Mark Gregory's research at https://frankthepoet.blogspot.com, accessed October 2018.

16. Williams, *Johnny Troy*, p. 38.

17. See Hugh Anderson, *A Rebecca in Tasmania: The Lamentations of David Davies, Welsh Convict 'In the Land of the Black Negro'*, North Melbourne: Red Rooster Press, 2009, for some insight into the radical Welsh underculture of the Rebecca movement in Australia and back into Wales, particularly through song and verse.

18. See Éva Guillorel, David Hopkin and William G. Pooley (eds), *Rhythms of Revolt: European Traditions and Memories of Social Conflict in Oral Culture*, Abingdon: Routledge, 2018, for an indication of the potency of oral traditions, as well as the problems of using them as historical evidence. In the specific context of Australian convictism, see Nathan Garvey, ' "Folkalising" Convicts: A "Botany Bay" Ballad and its Cultural Contexts', *Journal of Australian Studies*, vol. 38, no. 1, 2014, pp. 32–51.

19. MS 13361, State Library of Victoria, http://digital.slv.vic.gov.au/view/action/nmets.do?DOCCHOICE=2825096.xml&dvs=1557112609686-700&locale=en_AU&search_terms=&adjacency=&VIEWER_URL=/view/action/nmets.do?&DELIVERY_RULE_ID=4&divType=&usePid1=true&usePid2=true, accessed April 2019.

20. See Dorice Williams Elliott, 'Transported to Botany Bay: Imagining Australia in Nineteenth-Century Convict Broadsides', *Victorian Literature and Culture*, vol. 43, 2015, pp. 235–59; Ron Edwards, *The Convict Maid: Early Broadsides Relating to Australia*, Kuranda, Queensland: The

Rams Skull Press, 1985, and Hugh Anderson, *Farewell to Judges & Juries: The Broadside Ballad and Convict Transportation to Australia, 1788–1868*, Hotham Hill, Victoria: Red Rooster Press, 2000.

21. James Porter autobiography, 1840–1844, Mitchell Library, State Library of New South Wales, DLMSQ 604, p. 26.

22. See Vic Gammon, 'The Grand Conversation: Napoleon and British Popular Balladry', *RSA Journal*, vol. CXXXVII, no. 5398, September 1989, http://www.mustrad.org.uk/articles/boney. htm, accessed June 2019.

23. National Library of Scotland, 'The Grand Conversation of Napoleon' at National Library of Scotland: English Ballads, https://digital.nls.uk/english-ballads/archive/74893438?&mode= transcription, accessed June 2019.

24. George Rudé, *Protest and Punishment: The Story of the Social and Political Protesters Transported to Australia 1788–1868*. Oxford: Clarendon Press, 1978; Tony Moore, *Death or Liberty: Rebels and Radicals Transported to Australia 1788–1868*, Sydney: Murdoch Books, 2010.

25. See Theo Simon, 'Mr Lud's Song', *The Land: An Occasional Magazine about Land Rights*, issue 10, Summer 2011, www.thelandmagazine.org.uk/articles/mr-luds-song, accessed April 2019.

26. Graham Seal, *The Lingo: Listening to Australian English*, Kensington, New South Wales: University of New South Wales Press, 1999, pp. 32–8, 118, 142, 160.

27. From reports and other papers relating to a visit to the Australian colonies and South Africa, 1832–1840, by J. Backhouse & G. W. Walker. MLB706, Section 2, Report on Macquarie Harbour, p. 108. Microfilm CY1697 171-2.

28. James Porter autobiography, Mitchell Library, State Library of New South Wales, DLMSQ 604, composed between 1840 and 1844.

29. Hamish Maxwell-Stewart, 'Seven Tales for a Man with Seven Sides', in Lucy Frost and Hamish Maxwell-Stewart (eds), *Chain Letters: Narrating Convict Lives*, Carlton South, Victoria: Melbourne University Press, 2001, pp. 64–76.

30. All quotations are from Ian Duffield, (ed.), '"Jack Bushman": Passages from the Life of a '"Lifer"', http://iccs.arts.utas.edu.au/narratives/duffieldintro.html, accessed July 2018. 'Jack Bushman' was the pen name of the editor/transcriber of the *Passages*, presumably dictated by Brooks himself. There is some uncertainty over the identity of the author.

31. James Loveless, James Brine, R. Hartwell (of Dorchester.), John Standfield (a Dorsetshire labourer) and Thomas Standfield, *Narrative of the sufferings of J. Loveless, J. Brine, and T. & J. Standfield, four of the Dorchester Labourers; displaying the horrors of transportation, written by themselves*, London: John Cleave, 1838.

32. The sad details of Musquito's life and death are traced through the pages of *The Sydney Gazette*, 19 May 1805, p. 2; 30 June 1805, p. 2; 7 July 1805, p. 2; 4 August 1805, p. 2; 12 January 1806, p. 1; 19 January 1806, p. 2; 2 February 1806, p. 2; and the *Hobart Town Gazette*, 14 February 1818; 16 July 1824; 6 August 1824; 3 December 1824; 25 February 1825.

33. *The Sydney Gazette and New South Wales Advertiser*, 15 February 1831, p. 3.

34. Naomi Parry, '"Hanging no good for blackfellow": Looking into the Life of Musquito', in Ingereth Macfarlane and Mark Hannah (eds), *Transgressions: Critical Australian Indigenous Histories*, Canberra: ANU E- Press/Aboriginal History Incorporated, 2007, pp. 153ff.

35. Kristyn Harman, *Aboriginal Convicts: Australian, Khoisan, and Maori Exiles*, Kensington, New South Wales: University of New South Wales Press, 2012.

36. An account of the action is in *The Australian*, 19 September 1846, p. 3.

37. 'The Kanaka Labour Traffic', *The Argus*, 22 December 1892, p. 5.

38. Fiona Pepper et al., 'The Boys from Tanna who Never Came Home', 21 February 2020, https:// www.abc.net.au/news/2020-02-21/blackbirding-legacy-haunts-tanna-vanuatu/11764586, accessed February 2020.

CHAPTER 8: THE DEVIL'S ISLES

1. *The Straits Times*, 25 April 1846, p. 2.

2. Clare Anderson, 'Penal Transportation in the East India Company, 1787–1863', in *Convict Voyages: A Global History of Convict and Penal Colonies*, http://convictvoyages.org/expert-essays/

penal-transportation-in-east-india-company-asia-and-colonial-mauritius, accessed May 2017; Clare Anderson, *Convicts in the Indian Ocean: Transportation from South Asia to Mauritius, 1815–53*, Basingstoke: Palgrave Macmillan, 2000, p. 6. See also Anoma Pieris, *Hidden Hands and Divided Landscapes: A Penal History of Singapore's Plural Society*, Honolulu: University of Hawaii Press, 2009, pp. 59–60.

3. Charles Darwin, *Voyage of the Beagle* (first published as *Journal and Remarks*, 1839), 2nd edn., London: John Murray, 1845, chapter 21.

4. While Foucault's metaphorical formulation of 'carceral archipelagoes' referred to sequestered spaces of confinement, surveillance and control in mainly urban contexts, the insights contained in his *Discipline and Punish: The Birth of the Prison* are relevant to penal islands. See Katherine Roscoe, 'A Natural Hulk: Australia's Carceral Islands in the Colonial Period, 1788–1901', *International Review of Social History*, vol. 63, issue S26, August 2018, pp. 45–63.

5. *The Derby Mercury*, 20 October 1752, at Bahamianology, https://bahamianology.com/british-transport-109-irish-convicts-to-settle-abaco-1785, accessed February 2020.

6. See Estherine Adams, 'Early History of Penal Settlement Mazaruni 1842–1853', *Stabroek News*, 14 April 2011, https://www.stabroeknews.com/2011/features/history-this-week/04/14/early-history-of-penal-settlement-mazaruni-1842-1853, accessed February 2019.

7. IOR 'Board's Collections' 87352 to 87473, 1842–1845, vol. 1,984, F4 1984, pp. 207, 283.

8. William Sydes, 'Account of Life on the Convict Hulks by William Sydes, alias Jones, One of the Prisoners', *Bermuda Historical Quarterly*, vol. 8, 1951, pp. 28–39. For an overview of everyday life aboard British hulks, see Anna McKay, 'A Day in the Life: Convicts on Board Prison Hulks', Carceral Archipelago, https://staffblogs.le.ac.uk/carchipelago/2017/10/10/a-day-in-the-life-convicts-on-board-prison-hulks, accessed April 2019.

9. *The Royal Gazette*, vol. 3, no. 17, 1830, p. 2, http://cdm16347.contentdm.oclc.org/cdm/landingpage/collection/BermudaNP02, accessed July 2017.

10. Christopher Addams, 'Counterfeiting on the Bermuda Convict Hulk *Dromedary*', *Journal of the Numismatic Association of Australia*, vol. 18, 2007, http://www.numismatics.org.au/pdfjournal/Vol18/Vol%2018%20Article%201.pdf, accessed July 2017.

11. Clare Anderson, 'Bermuda 1823–1863 Convict Voyages', http://convictvoyages.org/expert-essays/convicts-in-bermuda, accessed October 2017.

12. John Mitchel, *Jail Journal, or, Five Years in British Prisons*, Office of the "Citizen", New York, 1854, 3 February 1849.

13. Ibid, 20 July 1848.

14. Ibid, 23 November 1848.

15. Ibid, 3 February 1849.

16. Ibid.

17. In 1866 the Sydney *Freeman's Journal* republished an article on the – decidedly treasonous – power of popular balladry compared with the more literary writings of the Young Irelanders, *Freeman's Journal*, 14 April 1866, https://folkstream.com/reviews/irishballads.html, accessed July 2018.

18. Songs on Irish rebel transportation are a distinct sub-genre of convict balladry and follow a different set of conventions that emphasize British tyranny, injustice without the moralistic warnings usually found in commercial broadsides; see Dorice Williams Elliott, 'Transported to Botany Bay: Imagining Australia in Nineteenth-Century Convict Broadsides', *Victorian Literature and Culture*, vol. 43, 2015, pp. 235–59, and a Wikipedia entry that makes the same point at https://en.wikipedia.org/wiki/Transportation_Ballads, accessed May 2019.

19. Texts and sources of these ballads all in Hugh Anderson, *Farewell to Judges and Juries: The Broadside Ballad and Convict Transportation to Australia, 1788–1868*, Hotham Hill, Victoria: Red Rooster Press, pp. 354–77.

20. Anthony Trollope, 'Aaron Trowe' (1860).

21. 'The Convict Establishment at Bermuda', Hansard, HL Deb 26 July 1860, vol. 160, cc181–3.

22. *The Sydney Gazette and New South Wales Advertiser*, 24 September 1827, p. 2.

23. Ullathorn was quoted in the Report from the Select Committee on Transportation chaired by Sir William Molesworth, in the seventeen-volume *Reports from Committees, Session 15 November–16 August 1838*, vol. XXII, p. xvi, 2019. See also Hilary M. Carey, *Empire of Hell: Religion and the*

Campaign to End Convict Transportation in the British Empire, 1788–1875, Cambridge: Cambridge University Press, 2019, pp. 123–54.

24. William Moy Thomas, 'Transported for Life', *Household Words*, vol. V, no. 124, 7 August 1852, pp. 482–9, being the account of William Barber who was on Norfolk Island at the time of the events described.

25. Marcus Clarke, *For the Term of His Natural Life*, first published in serial form in the *Australian Journal* between 1870 and 1872. 'Price Warung' (William Astley) wrote a number of related stories based on interviews with convicts, beginning with 'The Liberation of the First Three' in his *Tales of the Convict System*, Sydney: Bulletin Newspaper Company, 1892.

26. Ullathorn's evidence *in Reports from Committees, Session 15 November–16 August 1838*, p. xvi.

27. George Rudé, *Protest and Punishment: The Story of the Social and Political Protesters Transported to Australia 1788–1868*, Oxford: Clarendon Press, 1978; Tony Moore, *Death or Liberty: Rebels and Radicals Transported to Australia 1788–1868*, Sydney: Murdoch Books, 2010.

28. Thomas, 'Transported for Life', pp. 482–9.

29. A. Valdik, *Imperial Andamans: Colonial Encounter and Island History*, Basingstoke: Palgrave Macmillan, 2010, p. 35; *East India (Jails Committee) Report of the Indian Jails Committee, 1919–20*, London: HMSO, 1921, p. 274.

30. Robert Aldrich and Kirsten McKenzie, *The Routledge History of Western Empires*, London: Routledge, 2013, p. 111.

31. Manju Ludwig, ' "Murder in the Andamans": A Colonial Narrative of Sodomy, Jealousy and Violence', *South Asia Multidisciplinary Academic Journal* [Online], Free-Standing Articles, Online since 17 October 2013, http://journals.openedition.org/samaj/3633, accessed July 2019; *East India (Jails Committee) Report of the Indian Jails Committee, 1919–20*, pp. 278–9.

32. Clare Anderson, 'Transnational Histories of Penal Transportation: Punishment, Labour and Governance in the British Imperial World, 1788–1939', *Australian Historical Studies*, vol. 47, issue 3, 2016, pp. 381–97.

33. Twenty-six runaways were recaptured by the indigenous Andamanese in the year 1881–2 alone; M. V. Portman, *A History of our Relations with the Andamanese*, vol. 2, Calcutta: Superintendent of Government Printing, 1899, p. 651.

34. Rajni Sharma, 'The Statement of Mutiny Prisoner Doodnath Tewarry: An Ethnographic Study', MA dissertation, National Institute of Technology, Rourkela, 2014.

35. Or 14 May, sources differ.

36. O. N. Jaiswal, 'The Battle of Aberdeen in Retrospect', Press Information Bureau, Government of India, 5 December 2002, http://pib.nic.in/feature/feyr2002/fdec2002/f051220021.html, accessed 8 May 2017.

37. For the ongoing consequences of colonialism, including transportation, see Clare Anderson, Madhumita Mazumdar and Vishvajit Pandya, *New Histories of the Andaman Islands: Landscape, Place and Identity in the Bay of Bengal, 1790–2012*, Cambridge: Cambridge University Press, 2016.

38. Helen James, 'The Assassination of Lord Mayo: The "First" Jihad?', *International Journal of Asia Pacific Studies*, vol. 5, no. 2, July 2009, pp. 1–19.

39. Kailash [*sic*], 'Peaceful Coexistence: Lessons from Andamans', *Economic and Political Weekly*, vol. 35, no. 32, 5–11 August 2000, pp. 2,859–65.

40. On the relationship between the British EIC and British government transportation in the Indian Ocean, see Clare Anderson, 'Convicts, Commodities, and Connections in British Asia and the Indian Ocean, 1789–1866', *International Review of Social History*, vol. 64, issue S27, April 2019, pp. 205–27. It is estimated that at least 30,000 people were internally transported around British Asia by the EIC.

41. Stephen Nicholas and Peter R. Shergold, 'Convicts as Migrants', in Stephen Nicholas (ed.), *Convict Workers: Reinterpreting Australia's Past*, Cambridge: Cambridge University Press, 1988, p. 30.

42. Anderson, 'Transnational Histories of Penal Transportation', pp. 381–97.

43. Clare Anderson, 'Asia and Mauritius: Penal Transportation in East India Company 1787–1863', in *Convict Voyage*, http://convictvoyages.org/expert-essays/penal-transportation-in-east-india-company-asia-and-colonial-mauritius, accessed October 2017.

44. Christopher Munn, 'The Transportation of Chinese Convicts from Hong Kong, 1844–1858', *Journal of the Canadian Historical Association*, vol. 81, 1997, pp. 113–45.

45. British Library IOR/L/PJ/6/45, File 1053: 16 June 1881. At least two other similar petitions for mercy for the murderers of women had the same result in 1882.

46. Munn, 'The Transportation of Chinese Convicts', p. 125.

47. Ibid, p. 122; also Clare Anderson, 'Execution and its Aftermath in the Nineteenth-Century British Empire', https://lra.le.ac.uk/bitstream/2381/31686/6/AndersonCriminalCorpseFORMATTED. pdf, accessed February 2019.

48. See Clare Anderson, ' "The Ferringees are Flying – the ship is ours!": The Convict Middle Passage in Colonial South and Southeast Asia, 1790–1860', which investigates convict ship mutinies and also provides numbers for those transported in the period studied, https://lra.le.ac.uk/ bitstream/2381/9841/1/%5B10%5D%20IESHR%20article,%20convict%20ship%20 mutinties.pdf, accessed July 2018.

49. IOR 'Board's Collections' 87352 to 87473, 1842–1845, vol. 1984, F4 1984, pp. 1–9 and *passim*; also Clare Anderson, '"The Ferringees are Flying"'.

50. Clare Anderson, Niklas Frykman, Lex Herma van Voss and Marcus Rediker, *Mutiny and Maritime Radicalism in the Age of Revolution*, Cambridge: Cambridge University Press, 2013, p. 241.

51. Quoted in Munn, 'The Transportation of Chinese Convicts', p. 126.

52. Sarat C. Roy (Rai Bahadur), ed., *Man in India, Volume 39*, A. K. Bose, 1959, p. 309, referring to the ethnography of Edgar Thurston.

53. Major J.F.A. McNair assisted by W. D. Bayliss, *Prisoners Their Own Warders: A Record of the Convict Prison at Singapore in the Straits Settlements Established 1825, Discontinued 1873, Together With a Cursory History of the Convict Establishments at Bencoolen, Penang and Malacca From the Year 1797*, Westminster: Archibald Constable and Co., 1899, p. 4. McNair became Superintendent of Convicts in 1857.

54. Though *The Straits Times*, 25 March 1846, p. 2, carried an anonymous article claiming that 'the convicts in the Straits are better treated than at any other penal settlement'.

55. McNair, *Prisoners Their Own Warders*, p. 8.

56. Quoted in ibid, pp. 10–11.

57. Though not in Bengal.

58. *The Straits Times*, 25 April 1846, p. 2.

59. McNair, *Prisoners Their Own Warders*, p. 40.

60. Ibid, p. 49.

61. Ibid, pp. 53–4.

62. Ibid, p. 89.

63. Ibid, p. 88.

64. Ibid, pp. 117ff.

65. See Vincent Brown, ' "The Revolt", Slave Revolt in Jamaica, 1760–1761: A Cartographic Narrative', http://revolt.axismaps.com/project.html, accessed October 2018, and 'Slaves Transported to America and West Indies: December 1687', in Calendar of State Papers Colonial, America and West Indies: Volume 12, 1685–1688 and Addenda, 1653–1687, ed. J.W. Fortescue, London, 1899, pp. 474–85. British History Online, https://www.british-history.ac.uk/ cal-state-papers/colonial/america-west-indies/vol12/pp474-485.

66. Other examples of rebellious slave transportation from the British Caribbean to Sierra Leone in the late eighteenth and early nineteenth centuries in Clare Anderson (ed.), *A Global History of Convicts and Penal Colonies*, London: Bloomsbury Academic, 2018, p. 14. See also Clare Anderson, *Subaltern Lives: Biographies of Colonialism in the Indian Ocean World, 1790–1920*, Cambridge: Cambridge University Press, 2012, for individual experiences of transportation and re-transportation. This 'focuses on life histories as a route towards understanding the colonial repertoire of punishment and labour, of centring the experiential dimension of life in penal settlements and colonies, of understanding colonial identity formation, and of bringing to the fore networks of Empire in the Indian Ocean and beyond,' p. 22.

67. Hamish Maxwell-Stewart, 'Transportation from Britain and Ireland, 1615–1875', in Anderson (ed.), *A Global History of Convicts and Penal Colonies*, p. 189.

CHAPTER 9: ONE VAST CHARNEL HOUSE

1. *Critic* (Hobart), Friday 8 May 1914, p. 3.
2. Select Committee, Parliamentary Papers (1835), 4 and 5, vol. XII, p. 508, evidence of Mr William Augustus Miles.
3. See Heather Shore, 'Transportation, Penal Ideology and the Experience of Juvenile Offenders in England and Australia in the Early Nineteenth Century', *Crime, Histoire & Sociétés/Crime, History & Societies*, vol. 6, no. 2, 2002, pp. 81–102.
4. See Colleen Wood, 'Great Britain's Exiles Sent to Port Phillip, Australia, 1844–1849: Lord Stanley's Experiment', PhD thesis, University of Melbourne, 2014.
5. *The Times*, 11 August 1868, p. 9.
6. David Dunstan, 'Introduction' in David Dunstan (ed.), *Owen Suffolk, Days of Crime and Years of Suffering*, Melbourne: Australian Scholarly Publishing, 2000.
7. *Southern Argus*, 3 October 1868, p. 4. Another version of the story in *The McIvor and Rodney Advertiser*, 2 October 1868, p. 4 (from *The Evening Star*, 17 September 1868).
8. Except four who were convicted of civil crimes, they went to Van Diemen's Land with the Americans.
9. Quoted in Gregory Blaxell, 'A Slice of Canada in Australia', *Afloat*, 2007, http://www.afloat.com.au/afloat-magazine/archive/2007_December2007_AsliceofCanadainSydneybyGregoryBlaxell.htm#.WNi6RTtBVds, accessed March 2017.
10. Samuel Snow, ed. Cassandra Pybus, *The Exile's Return: Narrative of Samuel Snow who was banished to Van Diemen's Land, for participating in the Patriot War in Upper Canada in 1838*, Cleveland, 1846, at Convict Narrative, http://iccs.arts.utas.edu.au/narratives/snow.html#footnote15, accessed March 2017, all quotations from this source. See also T. P. Dunning, 'Convict Leisure and Recreation: The North American Experience in Van Diemen's Land, 1840–1847', https://pdfs.semanticscholar.org/65f9/879902d254f32a99a431e4b3da071f68d955.pdf, accessed October 2018.
11. Linus Wilson Miller, *Notes of an Exile to Van Diemen's Land*, Fredonia, NY: W. McKinstry, 1846, p. 352.
12. Snow, *The Exile's Return*. A number of other men from this group also wrote or otherwise recorded their mostly unpleasant memories, including Robert Marsh, Benjamin Wait, Daniel D. Heustis and Stephen Wright.
13. Based on T. C. Creaney, *The Huddersfield Four*, Female Convicts Research Centre, September 2015, http://www.femaleconvicts.org.au/docs/convicts/TheHuddersfieldFour.pdf, accessed February 2017.
14. Godfrey Charles Mundy, *Our Antipodes: or Residence and Rambles in the Australasian Colonies, with a glimpse of the Gold Fields*, 3rd edn., London: R. Bentley, 1855.
15. Charles White, 'Parts I and II: The Story of the Ten Governors, and the story of the Convicts', *Early Australian History'. Convict Life in New South Wales and Van Diemen's Land*, Bathurst, 'Free Press' Office, 1889, http://gutenberg.net.au/ebooks12/1204081h.html, accessed November 2019. Van Diemen's Land was part of New South Wales until 1825. White's comments applied as much, and even more, to Van Diemen's Land.
16. T. Crofton Croker (ed.), *Memoirs of Joseph Holt, General of the Irish Rebels, in 1788*, vol. 2, London: Henry Colburn, 1838, p. 220.
17. 'Instructions Issued by the Governor of New South Wales for the Regulation of the Penal Settlements, 1st July 1829', in *Acts and Ordinances of the Governor and Council of New South Wales, 1829–30*, printed by Order of the House of Commons, 15 February 1832, pp. 1–7, https://books.google.com.au/books?id=U2xbAAAAQAAJ&pg=RA1-PA71&lpg=RA1PA71&dq=As+an+aversion+to+honest+industry+and+labour+has+been+the+chief+cause+of+most+of+the+convicts+incurring&source=bl&ots=_tSyw0i4sg&sig=QFJyJWZkHxVejRoBM9neIQ_ryCs&hl=en&sa=X&ved=0ahUKEwjqhPDQ27SAhUJW5QKHXJWDXMQ6AEIHzAB#v=onepage&q=As%20an%20aversion%20to%20honest%20industry%20and%20labour%20has%20been%20the%20chief%20cause%20of%20most%20of%20the%20convicts%20incurring&f=false, accessed November 2019. All the following quotations are from this source.

18. Quoted in Hugh Anderson, *Farewell to Judges and Juries*, p. xxx, from J. B. L. and B. Hammond, *The Village Labourer*, London: Longmans, Green, 1948, vol. 1, p. 203.

19. Sir William Molesworth, *Speech of Sir William Molesworth Bart., on Transportation: Delivered in the House of Commons on the 5th May, 1840*, London: H. Hooper, 1840, p. 10.

20. From the Hobart newspaper the *Critic*, Friday 8 May 1914, p. 3.

21. *Launceston Examiner*, 19 July 1894, p. 6.

22. All quotations, unless otherwise noted, are from Mark Jeffrey, *Tales of the Early Days: A Burglar's Life or the Stirring Adventures of the Great English Burglar Mark Jeffrey*, Melbourne: Alexander McCubbin, 1900. Jeffrey's ghostwritten memoir was first published as *A burglar's life, or, The stirring adventures of the great English burglar, Mark Jeffrey: a thrilling history of the dark days of convictism in Australia*, Hobart: J. Walch & Sons, 1893.

23. Mina went by the surname of Caulfield prior to her marriage and as Jury in widowhood, in addition to her numerous criminal aliases.

24. Some records give her birth date as 1834, also 1836 and 1837. See Lucy Williams, 'Jury, Mina b. *c.*1828–1890', *Digital Panopticon*, https://www.digitalpanopticon.org/Jury,_Mina_b._c.1828–1890, accessed November 2019, for records and commentary. She was most likely born in 1827 or 1828.

25. *Victoria Police Gazette*, 13 October 1868.

26. *The Sydney Morning Herald*, 26 July 1865, p. 1.

27. Ibid, 1 August 1873, p. 3.

28. In her trial evidence, Mina claimed to have eleven living children in Australia, 'seven unprovided for', though genealogical records, not fully reliable, suggest there may have only been eight living. The relevant Australian sources are Birth Index, 1788–1922; Births, Deaths and Baptisms, 1792–1981; and Marriage Index, 1788–1950, accessed through Ancestry, November 2018.

29. Ancestry search for Euphemia Mercevina (Mina) Caulfield, November 2018.

30. *Old Bailey Proceedings Online* (www.oldbaileyonline.org, version 8.0, 22 November 2019), December 1883, trial of MINA JURY (46) (t18831210-145).

31. *Police Gazette* (Ireland), 2 May 1890, p. 5.

32. Order-in-Council ending transportation of convicts, 22 May 1840, https://www.foundingdocs. gov.au/resources/transcripts/nsw8_doc_1840.pdf, accessed June 2019.

33. Clare Anderson, 'Gibraltar', *Convict Voyages*, http://convictvoyages.org/statistic/gibraltar, accessed February 2019. These figures include local prisoners as well as those transported from England and Ireland.

34. Katy Roscoe, 'Convicts and the Sea: The Naval Influence on Gibraltar Convict Establishment' at Carceral Archipelago, https://staffblogs.le.ac.uk/carchipelago/2018/07/25/convicts-and-the-sea-the-naval-influence-on-gibraltar-convict-establishment, accessed February 2019.

35. George Dunderdale, *The Book of the Bush*, London: Ward, Lock & Co., 1870, beneath the subtitle 'White Slaves', http://gutenberg.net.au/ebooks/e00014.html, accessed August 2017.

CHAPTER 10: RIVER OF TEARS

1. 'Night Thoughts' quoted in Anthony G. Evans, *Fanatic Heart: A Life of John Boyle O'Reilly 1844–1890*, Perth: University of Western Australia Press, 1997, p. 195.

2. *The Perth Gazette and Western Australian Journal*, 17 January 1835, pp. 426–8.

3. The relevant records of this little-known incident were discovered and kindly provided by former Port Arthur historian, Peter MacFie.

4. Neville Green, *Broken Spears: Aborigines and Europeans in the Southwest of Australia*, Perth: Focus Education Services, 1984, p. 79; Sylvia Hallam and Lois Tilbrook (eds), *Aborigines of the Southwest Region, 1829–1840*, Nedlands, Western Australia: University of Western Australia Press, 1990, p. 333. Yagan's head was not repatriated until 1997.

5. *The Perth Gazette and Western Australian Journal*, 1 September 1838, pp. 138–9.

6. Peter Gifford, 'Murder and "the Execution of the Law"' on the Nullarbor', *Aboriginal History*, vol. 18, no. 2, 1994, p. 114.

7. Criminal cant meaning 'prison'. The Quod was based on the panopticon design of the Fremantle Roundhouse, but was much larger.

8. Rottnest Island Authority, 'Aboriginals on Rottnest Island', http://www.rottnestisland.com/the-island/about-the-island/our-history, accessed February 2019; see also Eversley Ruth Mortlock, *An Island Solution: Rottnest Reveals Our Colonial Secrets*, 4th edn., Perth: Gwelup Creative Life Writing Press, 2018, which documents the ongoing trauma of these events for the Noongar community.

9. *Inquirer* (Perth), 14 October 1840, p. 43.

10. Alan Gill, *Orphans of the Empire: The Shocking Story of Child Migration to Australia*, Alexandria, New South Wales: Millennium Books, 1997, p. 46.

11. *The Perth Gazette and Western Australian Journal*, 27 August 1842, p. 4. The article had been written two years earlier and was taken from *Chamber's Edinburgh Journal*. The fact that it was reprinted in a colonial newspaper suggests that the issue was already a live one in Western Australia.

12. *Sydney Morning Herald*, 20 October 1848, p. 4, reporting a Commons debate of 26 May 1848. The Parkhurst scheme ended with the cessation of transportation to New South Wales and Tasmania, by which time around 1,100 boys had been sent to Australia and around 90 to New Zealand.

13. Thomas E. Jordan, 'Transported to Van Diemen's Land: The Boys of the "Frances Charlotte" (1832) and "Lord Goderich" (1841)', *Child Development*, vol. 56, no. 4, August 1985, pp. 1092–9. Jordan's study of the physical development of this sample of juvenile convicts bound for Tasmania concluded that 'By both current and contemporary standards, the convict boys were a pitiful group' (p. 1096).

14. Andrew Gill, 'Forced Labour in the West: "Parkhurst Apprentices"' in Western Australia, 1842–1852', in Charlie Fox and Michael Hess (eds), *Papers in Labour History*, no. 6, November 1990, p. 7. The date usually given for the beginning of transportation from Parkhurst is 1842 but, as so often seen in the history of transportation, what was supposed to happen officially was rarely the full story.

15. Beale's record is at the Western Australian Genealogical Society pages on Parkhurst Boys, at '410. William Beale', https://membership.wags.org.au/members-data/public-data/parkhurst-boys, *Family History WA*, accessed November 2018.

16. *The Inquirer and Commercial News* (Perth), 11 October 1876, p. 3.

17. *The Perth Gazette and Western Australian Journal*, 6 April 1844, p. 3; *Inquirer* (Perth), 10 April 1844, pp. 2–3.

18. Gill, *Orphans of the Empire*, pp. 49–50.

19. I. Elliot, *Moondyne Joe: The Man and the Myth*, Perth: University of Western Australia Press, 1979; 2nd edn., Perth: Hesperian Press, 1998; Graham Seal, *The Outlaw Legend: A Cultural Tradition in Britain, America and Australia*, Cambridge: Cambridge University Press, 1996, p. 144; M. Tamblyn, 'Johns, Joseph Bolitho (1827–1900)', *Australian Dictionary of Biography*, National Centre of Biography, Australian National University, http://adb.anu.edu.au/biography/johns-joseph-bolitho-3859/text6139, published first in hardcopy 1972, accessed December 2016. For an account of one of Joe's spectacular escapes see *The Perth Gazette and West Australian Times*, 15 March 1867, p. 2.

20. Philip Fennell and Marie King (eds), *John Devoy's Catalpa Expedition*, New York: New York University Press, 2006, p. 3 (slightly edited). Other members of the Fenian group also wrote to Devoy asking for help.

21. *The Herald* (Fremantle), 18 November 1876, p. 3.

22. In Hugh Anderson, *Farewell to Judges & Juries: The Broadside Ballad and Convict Transportation to Australia, 1788–1868*, Hotham Hill, Victoria: Red Rooster Press, 2000, p. 409, from C.O. Lochlainn (ed.), *More Irish Street Ballads*, Dublin: The Three Candles, 1968.

23. Collected by historian Russel Ward from West Australian journalist Victor Courtney in the 1950s, in Russel Ward (ed.), *Three Street Ballads*, (The Black Bull Broadsides, no. 5), Ferntree Gully, Victoria: Rams Skull Press, 1957. See also the *West Australian*, 5 February 1902, p. 3.

24. Fennell and King, *John Devoy's Catalpa Expedition*, p. 125.

25. Evans, *Fanatic Heart*, p. 98. See also C.W. Sullivan (ed.), *Fenian Diary: Denis B. Cashman Aboard the Hougoumont, 1867–1868*, Dublin: Wolfhound Press, 2001; State Records Office of

Western Australia, 'Correspondence Entry Books of Letters from Secretary of State. Despatches 1856–73', CO 397/28 (part 2); John Boyle O'Reilly, *Moondyne*, published by P. J. Kennedy in Boston in 1879, in Australia the following year, and frequently reprinted since; Alexandra Hasluck, *Unwilling Emigrants*, Melbourne: Oxford University Press, 1959, p. 75.

26. Rica Erickson (ed.), *The Brand on His Coat: Biographies of some Western Australian Convicts*, Nedlands, Western Australia: University of Western Australia Press, 1983.

27. The Fairbridge Society was able to send boys and girls to Canada after this date because their model placed children in supervised groups on farm schools, rather than dispatching them to private homes.

28. For an overview of the Australian situation up to the late 1990s, see Barry Coldrey, *Good British Stock: Child and Youth Migration to Australia*, National Archives of Australia, Canberra, 1999 National Archives of Australia, http://guides.naa.gov.au/good-british-stock/index.aspx, accessed November 2018.

29. See Shurlee Swain and Margot Hillel, *Child, Nation, Race and Empire. Child Rescue Discourse, England, Canada and Australia, 1850–1915*, Manchester: Manchester University Press, 2010; Ellen Boucher, *Empire's Children: Child Emigration, Welfare, and the Decline of the British World, 1869–1967*, Cambridge: Cambridge University Press, 2014, and Shirleene Robinson and Simon Sleight (eds), *Children, Childhood and Youth in the British World*, London: Palgrave Macmillan, 2016.

30. Hilary M. Carey, *Empire of Hell: Religion and the Campaign to End Convict Transportation in the British Empire, 1788–1875*, Cambridge: Cambridge University Press, 2019.

31. British Home Children in Canada Advocacy and Research Association, https://canadianbritishhomechildren.weebly.com, accessed May 2019. As the House of Commons Health Committee Third Report, 1998, noted of child migration statistics, 'Exact statistics are difficult to come by'. This committee also concluded that 'In total it is estimated that some 150,000 children were dispatched over a period of 350 years', online at https://publications.parliament.uk/pa/cm199798/cmselect/cmhealth/755/75503.htm#note2, accessed July 2019.

32. Boucher, *Empire's Children*, p. 86.

33. V. F. Boyson (ed.), *The Autobiography of Kingsley Fairbridge*, London: Oxford University Press, 1927; Ruby Fairbridge, *Fairbridge Farm: The Building of a Farm School*, Perth: Paterson Press, 1948.

34. Prime Minister's Department, 'Migration agreement between the Secretary of State and the Child Immigration Society', CP103/11, 388), 15 August 1923, National Archives of Australia, Canberra, https://recordsearch.naa.gov.au/SearchNRetrieve/Interface/DetailsReports/ItemDetail.aspx?Barcode=449882&isAv=N, accessed November 2019.

35. Fairbridge Farm School. File 1, 1927–28, (A436, 1946/5/597, Part 1C), National Archives of Australia, Canberra, http://guides.naa.gov.au/good-british-stock/chapter3/fairbridge-farms.aspx, accessed October 2003.

36. In 1937 another farm school was established in Victoria through the bequest of Lady Northcote, an admirer of Kingsley Fairbridge.

37. Geoffrey Sherrington and Chris Jeffery, *Fairbridge, Empire and Child Migration*, Perth: University of Western Australia Press, 1998.

38. Barnardos Australia, 'Child Migration Program', https://www.barnardos.org.au/about-us/history/child-migration-program, accessed June 2019.

39. Independent Inquiry Child Sexual Abuse, Child Migration Programmes Investigation Report, March 2018, (2017) p. 7, https://www.iicsa.org.uk/key-documents/4265/view/child-migration-programmes-investigation-report-march-2018.pdf, accessed November 2019.

40. Though the 2018 Child Migration Programmes Investigation Report, March 2018, claims the last child migrant reached Australia in 1970, p. 9.

41. Including Philip Bean and Joy Melville, *Lost Children of the Empire*, London: Unwin Hyman, 1990; John Lane, *Fairbridge Kid*, Fremantle: Fremantle Arts Centre Press, 1990; Margaret Humphreys, *Empty Cradles*, London: Doubleday, 1994.

42. Senate Community Affairs Reference Committee Inquiry into Child Migration, *Lost Innocents: Righting the Record – Report on Child Migration*, Canberra, 2001, 4.18, is careful to point out that 'from the evidence it received the allegations of regular sexual assault involved children in the care

of only a small number of institutions'. Of the thirty-eight episodes of sexual assault reported 'almost two-thirds were from the Christian Brothers institutions in Western Australia', https://www.aph.gov.au/Parliamentary_Business/Committees/Senate/Community_Affairs/Completed_inquiries/1999-02/child_migrat/report/index, accessed November 2019.

43. *Lost Innocents*, 4.17, referencing Report of UK Health Committee, para. 51.

44. *Lost Innocents*, 4.7.

45. Independent Inquiry Child Sexual Abuse, Child Migration Programmes Investigation Report, March 2018, p. iii, https://www.iicsa.org.uk/key-documents/4265/view/child-migration-programmes-investigation-report-march-2018.pdf, accessed May 2019, pp. iv–v.

46. Independent Inquiry Child Sexual Abuse, Child Migration Programmes Investigation Report, March 2018, pp. ii–iii, accessed May 2019.

47. Over 300 Maltese children were sent to Western and South Australia after World War II. Although families were often involved in the decision to send them away from their homes, many reported abuse and other consequential disadvantage in Australia; see *Lost Innocents*, Supplementary Information 'Former Child Migrants – Malta' and *passim*.

48. Antonio Buti, 'British Child Migration to Australia: History, Senate Inquiry and Responsibilities', *Murdoch University Electronic Journal of Law*, vol. 9, no. 4, December 2002; Andrew Murray, 'Child Migration Schemes to Australia: A Dark and Hidden Chapter of Australian History Revealed', http://andrewmurray.democrats.org.au/Issues/congressbasedarticle.pdf (accessed October 2003, no longer available, but see Marilyn Rock, 'Child Migration Schemes to Australia: A Dark and Hidden Chapter of Australia's History Revealed' [online], *The Australian Journal of Social Issues*, vol. 38, no. 2, May 2003, pp. 149–67), and the Senate Community Affairs References Committee Inquiry into Child Migration and its report *Lost Innocents: Righting the Record* (2001), https://www.aph.gov.au/Parliamentary_Business/Committees/Senate/Community_Affairs/Completed_inquiries/1999-02/child_migrat/report/index.

49. Independent Inquiry Child Sexual Abuse, Child Migration Programmes Investigation Report, March 2018, pp. 150ff.

50. 'Ex-Gratia Payment Scheme for Former British Child Migrants', *Child Migrants Trust*, https://www.childmigrantstrust.com/iafcmf-news-archive, 31 January 2019, accessed May 2019.

51. The final report of the Royal Commission into Institutional Responses to Child Sexual Abuse, 2017, dealt with the broader issue of institutional child sexual abuse, but included further evidence relating to the abuse of children brought to Australia by many of the organizations previously investigated. See Commonwealth, Royal Commission into Institutional Responses to Child Sexual Abuse, 'Final Report', 15 December 2017, https://www.childabuseroyalcommission.gov.au/final-report, accessed November 2019.

52. Gordon Lynch, 'Britain Sent Child Migrants Overseas – It's Running out of Time to Make Reparations', *The Conversation*, 23 October 2018, http://theconversation.com/britain-sent-child-migrants-overseas-its-running-out-of-time-to-make-reparations-105447, accessed May 2019.

53. Though many did in fact, have one or both parents, but were either not told about them or were informed their parents were dead.

CHAPTER 11: THE END OF THE CHAIN?

1. Clare Anderson and Hamish Maxwell-Stewart in Robert Aldrich and Kirsten McKenzie (eds), *The Routledge History of Western Empires*, London: Routledge, 2013, p. 112.

2. On this network, see Hamish Maxwell-Stewart in Clare Anderson (ed.), *A Global History of Convicts and Penal Colonies*, London: Bloomsbury Academic, 2018, p. 204, and the depiction of the 'Atlantic proletariat' in Peter Linebaugh and Marcus Rediker, *The Many-Headed Hydra: Sailors, Slaves, Commoners, and the Hidden History of the Revolutionary Atlantic*, Boston, MA: Beacon Press, 2000, pp. 332–3 and *passim*.

SELECT BIBLIOGRAPHY

PRIMARY SOURCES

Anderson, Hugh, *A Rebecca in Tasmania: The Lamentations of David Davies, Welsh Convict 'In the Land of the Black Negro'*, North Melbourne: Red Rooster Press, 2009.

Anderson, Hugh, *Farewell to Judges & Juries: The Broadside Ballad and Convict Transportation to Australia, 1788–1868*, Hotham Hill, Victoria: Red Rooster Press, 2000.

Annesley, J., *Memoirs of an unfortunate young nobleman, Return'd from a thirteen years slavery in America, where he had been sent by the wicked contrivances of his cruel uncle*, 2 vols, London: J. Freeman, 1743.

Anon., 'A Convict's Recollections of New South Wales' (Mellish's *Book of Botany Bay*), *The London Magazine*, vol. 2, 1825.

Anon., *An Exact and True Relation of the Examination, Trial and Condemnation of the German Princess, otherwise called Mary Carleton, at Justice Hall in the Old Bailey, January 17, 1672*.

Anon., *The Life and Character of Moll King, Late Mistress of King's Coffee House in Covent Garden, who Departed this Life . . . The 17th of September, 1747*, London: W. Price, 1747.

Backhouse, James, *A Narrative of a Visit to the Australian Colonies*, London: Hamilton, Adams and Co., 1843.

Bernbaum, Ernest, *The Mary Carleton Narratives 1663–1673: A Missing Chapter in the History of the English Novel*, Cambridge, MA: Harvard University Press; and Humphrey Milford, London: Oxford University Press, 1914.

Bladen, F. M., Alexander Britton and James Cook, *Historical Records of New South Wales*, Sydney: Government Printer, 1892, http://nla.gov.au/nla.obj-343230396.

Carew, Bampfylde Moore, *The Life and Adventures of Bampfylde Moore Carew, the Noted Devonshire Stroller and Dog-Stealer, as related by himself during his Passage to the Plantations of America*, Printed by the Farleys, for Joseph Drew, Exeter, 1745.

Clark, Ralph, 'The Journal and Letters of Lt. Ralph Clark 1787–1792', University of Sydney Library, 2003, at http://setis.library.usyd.edu.au/ozlit/pdf/clajour.pdf.

Coad, John, *A Memorandum of the Wonderful Providences of God to a poor un-worthy Creature, during the time of the Duke of Monmouth's Rebellion and to the Revolution in 1688. By, one of the Sufferers*, London: Longman, Brown, Green, 1849.

Collins, David, *An Account of the English Colony in New South Wales*, vol. 2, London: T. Cadell and W. Davies, 1802.

Crevecoeur, J. Hector St John, *Letters from an American farmer, reprinted from the original ed., with a prefatory note by W. P. Trent and an introduction by Ludwig Lewisohn*, New York: Fox, Duffield, 1904.

Croker, T. Crofton (ed.), *Memoirs of Joseph Holt, General of the Irish Rebels, in 1788*, vol. 2, London: Henry Colburn, 1838.

Duffield, Ian (ed.), *'Jack Bushman': Passages from the Life of a 'Lifer'*, http://iccs.arts.utas.edu.au/narratives/duffieldintro.html.

Dunlop, Robert (ed.), *Ireland under the commonwealth; being a selection of documents relating to the government of Ireland from 1651 to 1659*, vol. II, Manchester: Manchester University Press, 1913.

Dunstan, David (ed.), 'Introduction', *Owen Suffolk, Days of Crime and Years of Suffering*, Melbourne: Australian Scholarly Publishing, 2000.

Eddis, William, *Letters from America, Historical and Descriptive, Comprising Occurrences from 1769 to 1777, Inclusive*, London: William Eddis, 1792.

Edwards, Ron, *The Convict Maid: Early Broadsides Relating to Australia*, Kuranda, Queensland: Rams Skull Press, 1985.

Edwards, Ron, *The Transport's Lament: Early Broadsides Relating to Australia*, Kuranda, Queensland: Rams Skull Press, 1986.

Gates, William, *Recollections of Life in Van Diemen's Land*, Lockport, NY, 1850.

Gragg, Larry Dale, *Englishmen Transplanted: The English Colonization of Barbados, 1627–1660*, Oxford: Oxford University Press, 2003.

Green, William, 'W. G.', *The sufferings of William Green: being a sorrowful account, of his seven years transportation, wherein is set forth the various hardships he underwent, with his parting and meeting again in that Country, with his intimate Friend Anthony Atkinson, with their joyful arrival in England, after being absent ten Years. Likewise an Account of their manner of Living; the Climate of the Country, and in what it principally abounds. Written by W. Green, the unhappy Sufferer. Who returned on the second of June, 1774. With the Place of his Birth and Parentage, and the Manner of his Life*, Whitechapel: J. Long, 1775?

Hakluyt, Richard, *A Discourse Concerning Western Planting: Written in the Year 1584 by Richard Hakluyt, Now First Printed from a Contemporary Manuscript*, Leonard Woods (ed.), Cambridge, MA: J. Wilson and Son, 1877. (Written, in secret, 1584).

Harrower, John, *The Journal of John Harrower, An Indentured Servant in the Colony of Virginia, 1773–1776*, New York: Holt, Rinehart and Winston, 1963.

Ingleton, Geoffrey C. (ed.), *True Patriots All, or News From Early Australia*, Rutland/Vermont/Tokyo: Charles Tuttle, 1988 (facsimile of 1st edn. 1952).

'Instructions Issued by the Governor of New South Wales for the Regulation of the Penal Settlements, 1st July 1829' in *Acts and Ordinances of the Governor and Council of New South Wales, 1829–30*, printed by Order of the House of Commons, 15 February 1832.

Jeaffreson, John Cordy (ed.), *A young squire of the seventeenth century: From the papers (A.D. 1676–1686) of Christopher Jeaffreson*, vol. 1, London: Hurst and Blackett, 1878.

Jeffrey, Mark, *A burglar's life, or, The stirring adventures of the great English burglar, Mark Jeffrey: a thrilling history of the dark days of convictism in Australia*, Hobart: J. Walch & Sons, 1893.

Johnson, Richard, *Some Letters of Rev. Richard Johnson, B.A. First Chaplain of New South Wales*, Part 1, vol. XX (New Series), George Mackaness (comp. and ed.), Sydney: D. S. Ford, 1954.

Keane, Michael, *A soldier's punishments, or, autobiography of a Botany Bay hero by Michael Keane & two other tales of 1826*, Stephan Williams (ed.), Canberra: Popinjay Publications, 1994.

Kelly, Edward ('Ned'), 'The Jerilderie Letter', MS 13361, State Library of Victoria.

King, Anna Josepha, 'Journal of a voyage from England to Australia in the ship "Speedy"', 19 November 1799–15 April 1800, Mitchell Library, State Library of New South Wales, C 185, http://acms.sl.nsw.gov.au/_transcript/2015/D33322/a1163.html

Loveless, James, James Brine, R. Hartwell (of Dorchester), John Standfield (a Dorsetshire labourer) and Thomas Standfield, *Narrative of the sufferings of Jas. Loveless, Jas. Brine, and Thomas & John Standfield, four of the Dorchester Labourers; displaying the horrors of transportation, written by themselves*, London: Cleave, 1838.

Mackaness, George (comp. and ed.), *Some Letters of Rev. Richard Johnson, B.A. First Chaplain of New South Wales*, Part 1, vol. XX (New Series), Sydney: D. S. Ford, Printers, 1954.

McNair, Major J.R.A. assisted by W. D. Bayliss, *Prisoners Their Own Warders: A Record of the Convict Prison at Singapore in the Straits Settlements Established 1825, Discontinued 1873, Together With a Cursory History of the Convict Establishments at Bencoolen, Penang and Malacca From the Year 1797*, Westminster: Archibald Constable and Co, 1899.

Miller, Linus Wilson, *Notes of an Exile to Van Diemen's Land*, Fredonia, NY: W. McKinstry, 1846.

Mitchel, John, *Jail Journal, or, Five Years in British Prisons*, Office of the *Citizen*, New York, 1854.

Molesworth, Sir William, *Speech of Sir William Molesworth Bart., on Transportation: Delivered in the House of Commons on the 5th May, 1840*, London: H. Hooper, 1840.

Moraley, W., *The Infortunate: The Voyage and Adventures of William Moraley, an Indentured Servant*, Susan E. Klepp and Billy Smith (eds), Pennsylvania, PA: Pennsylvania State University Press, 1992.

Mundy, Geoffrey Charles, *Our Antipodes: or Residence and Rambles in the Australasian Colonies, with a glimpse of the Gold Fields*, 3rd edn., London: R. Bentley, 1855.

Nagle, Jacob, 'Jacob Nagle His Book A.D. One Thousand Eight Hundred and Twenty Nine May 19th. Canton. Stark County Ohio, 1775–1802'; compiled 1829, *New South Wales State Library*, https://www.sl.nsw.gov.au/collection-items/jacob-nagle-memoir-titled-jacob-nagle-his-book-ad-one-thousand-eight-hundred-and-two.

Pitman, Henry, *A Relation of the Great Sufferings and Strange Adventures of Henry Pitman, Chyrurgion to the late Duke of Monmouth etc.*, London: Andrew Sowle, 1689.

Porter, James, *James Porter autobiography, between 1840–1844*, Mitchell Library, State Library of New South Wales, DLMSQ 604.

Poulter, John *The discoveries of John Poulter, alias Baxter; who was apprehended for robbing Dr. Hancock of Salisbury, on Clarken Down, near Bath; and thereupon discovered a most numerous gang of villains, many of which have been already taken*, 10th edn., London, 1754; 14th edn., London, 1761.

Smyth, Arthur Bowes, 'A Journal of a Voyage from Portsmouth to New South Wales and China', State Library New South Wales, https://www.sl.nsw.gov.au/collection-items/arthur-bowes-smyth-illustrated-journal-1787-1789-titled-journal-voyage-portsmouth.

Snow, Samuel and Cassandra Pybus (eds), *The Exile's Return: Narrative of Samuel Snow who was banished to Van Diemen's Land, for participating in the patriot War in Upper Canada in 1838*, Cleveland, 1846.

State Records Office, Western Australia, 'Correspondence Entry Books of Letters from Secretary of State. Despatches 1856 – 73', CO 397/28 (part 2).

Sutcliff, Robert, *Travels in some parts of North America, in the years 1804, 1805, & 1806*, York: Printed by C. Peacock for W. Alexander, 1811.

Sydes, William, 'Account of Life on the Convict Hulks by William Sydes, alias Jones, One of the Prisoners', *Bermuda Historical Quarterly*, vol. 8, 1951, pp. 28–39.

Thomas, William Moy, 'Transported for Life', *Household Words*, vol. V, no. 124, 7 August 1852.

Wilkes, G. A. and A. G. Mitchell (eds), *Experiences of a Convict Transported for Twenty-One Years*, Sydney: Sydney University Press, 1965.

Williamson, Peter, *French and Indian Cruelty, exemplified in the Life and various Vicissitudes of Fortune of Peter Williamson, who was carried off from Aberdeen in his Infancy, and sold as a slave in Pennsylvania*, Edinburgh, 1787.

PERIODICALS

Chamber's Edinburgh Journal
Colonial Times
Critic (Hobart)
Durham University News
Flying Post
Freeman's Journal (Sydney)
Hobart Town Gazette
Inquirer (Perth)
Launceston Advertiser
Launceston Examiner
London Evening Post
London Magazine
Maryland Gazette
Mirror (Perth)
Morning Chronicle

Original Weekly Journal
Pennsylvania Gazette
Police Gazette (Ireland)
Public Advertiser
Richmond Enquirer (Virginia)
Southern Argus
Stabroek News
Sunday Times (Perth)
Sydney Gazette
Sydney Herald
The Argus
The Australian
The Cave and Lundy Review, and Critical Revolving Light
The Gentleman's Magazine
The Herald (Fremantle)
The Inquirer and Commercial News (Perth)
The McIvor and Rodney Advertiser
The Observer (London)
The Perth Gazette and West Australian Times
The Perth Gazette and Western Australian Journal
The Providence, Rhode Island Gazette and Country Journal
The Royal Gazette
The Scone Advocate
The Straits Times
The Sydney Gazette and New South Wales Advertiser
The Sydney Monitor
The Sydney Morning Herald
The Times (London)
The Universal Magazine of Knowledge and Pleasure
Victoria Police Gazette
Virginia Gazette
West Australian

ARTICLES AND BOOK CHAPTERS, OCCASIONAL PAPERS

Addams, Christopher, 'Counterfeiting on the Bermuda Convict Hulk *Dromedary*', *Journal of the Numismatic Association of Australia*, vol. 18, 2007.

Anderson, Clare, 'Convicts, Commodities, and Connections in British Asia and the Indian Ocean, 1789–1866', *International Review of Social History*, vol. 64, issue S27.

Anderson, Clare, 'Transnational Histories of Penal Transportation: Punishment, Labour and Governance in the British Imperial World, 1788–1939', *Australian Historical Studies*, vol. 47, issue 3, 2016.

Atkinson, Alan, 'The Free-Born Englishman Transported: Convict Rights as a Measure of Eighteenth-Century Empire.' *Past and Present*, vol. 144, issue 1, 1994.

Bailyn, Bernard, *The Peopling of the British Peripheries in the Eighteenth Century*, Esso Lecture, 1988, Canberra, Australian Academy of the Humanities, Occasional Paper no. 5, 1988.

Bradley, James and Hamish Maxwell-Stewart, 'Embodied Explorations: Investigating Convict Tattoos and the Transportation System', in Ian Duffield and James Bradley (eds), *Representing Convicts: New Perspectives on Convict Forced Labour Migration*, Leicester: Leicester University Press, 1997.

Breen, T. H., 'A Changing Labor Force and Race Relations in Virginia, 1660–1710', *Journal of Social History*, vol. 7, no. 1, Fall 1973.

Buti, Antonio, 'British Child Migration to Australia: History, Senate Inquiry and Responsibilities', *Murdoch University Electronic Journal of Law*, vol. 9, no. 4, December 2002.

Butler, James Davie, 'British Convicts Shipped to American Colonies', *American Historical Review*, vol. 2, no. 1, October 1896, pp. 12–33.

Craig, Scott, 'Women, Crime and the Experience of Servitude in Colonial America and Australia', *Limina*, vol. 19, issue 1, 2013.

Duffield, Ian, 'From Slave Colonies to Penal Colonies: The West Indian Convict Transportees to Australia', *Slavery & Abolition: A Journal of Slave and Post-Slave Studies*, vol. 7, issue 1, 1986.

Dunning, T. P., 'Convict Leisure and Recreation: The North American Experience in Van Diemen's Land, 1840–1847', https://pdfs.semanticscholar.org/65f9/879902d254f32a99a431e4b3da071f68d955.pdf.

Ekirch, A. Roger, 'Great Britain's Secret Convict Trade to America, 1783–1784', *The American Historical Review*, vol. 89, issue 5, 1984.

Elliott, Dorice Williams, 'Transported to Botany Bay: Imagining Australia in Nineteenth-Century Convict Broadsides', *Victorian Literature and Culture*, vol. 43, 2015.

Fogleman, Aaron S., 'From Slaves, Convicts and Servants to Free Passengers: The Transformation of Immigration in the Era of the American Revolution', *Journal of American History*, vol. 85, no. 1, June 1998.

Gammon, Vic, 'The Grand Conversation: Napoleon and British Popular Balladry', *RSA Journal*, vol. CXXXVII, no. 5398, September 1989, http://www.mustrad.org.uk/articles/boney.htm.

Garvey, Nathan, '"Folkalising" Convicts: A "Botany Bay" Ballad and its Cultural Contexts', *Journal of Australian Studies*, vol. 38, issue 1, 2013.

Garvey, Nathan, 'The Convict Voice and British Print Culture: The Case of "Mellish's Book of Botany Bay"', *Australian Historical Studies*, vol. 44, issue 3, 2013.

Gifford, Peter, 'Murder and "the Execution of the Law" on the Nullarbor', *Aboriginal History*, vol. 18, no. 2, 1994.

Gill, Andrew, 'Forced Labour in the West: "Parkhurst Apprentices" in Western Australia, 1842–1852', in Charlie Fox and Michael Hess (eds), *Papers in Labour History*, no. 6, November 1990.

Gilliam, Charles Edgar, 'Jail Bird Immigrants to Virginia', *The Virginia Magazine of History and Biography*, vol. 52, no. 3, July 1944.

Grubb, Farley, 'The Transatlantic Market for British Convict Labor', *The Journal of Economic History*, vol. 60, issue 1, 2000.

Grubb, Farley, 'The Market Evaluation of Criminality: Evidence from the Auction of British Convict Labor in America, 1767–1775', *American Economic Review*, vol. 91, no. 1, March 2001.

Hardy, J. D., 'The Transportation of Convicts to Colonial Louisiana', *Louisiana History*, vol. 7, 1966.

Harman, Kristyn, *Aboriginal Convicts: Australian, Khoisan, and Maori Exiles*, Kensington, New South Wales: University of New South Wales Press, 2012.

Herrup, Cynthia, 'Punishing Pardon: Some Thoughts on the Origins of Penal Transportation', in Simon Devereaux and Paul Griffiths (eds), *Penal Politics and Culture 1500–1900: Punishing the English*, London: Palgrave Macmillan, 2004.

Jaiswal, O. N., 'The Battle of Aberdeen in Retrospect', Press Information Bureau, Government of India, 5 December 2002.

Jeppesen, Jennie, 'Searching for the Hidden Convict in Virginia's Servant Laws', *ANZLHS E-Journal*, 2013.

Johnson, R. C., 'The Transportation of Vagrant Children from London, 1618–1622', in H. S. Reinmuth (ed.), *Early Stuart Studies*, Minneapolis, MN: University of Minnesota Press, 1970, pp. 137–51.

Jordan, Thomas E., 'Transported to Van Diemen's Land: The Boys of the "Frances Charlotte" (1832) and "Lord Goderich" (1841)', *Child Development*, vol. 56, no. 4, August 1985, pp. 1092–9.

Keneally, Meg, 'Australia was Born out of a Gulag. Not Much has Changed', The *Guardian* (Australia), 18 March 2017, https://www.theguardian.com/commentisfree/2017/mar/17/australia-was-born-out-of-a-gulag-not-much-has-changed

Kupperman, Karen Ordahl, 'The Founding Years of Virginia – and the United States', *The Virginia Magazine of History and Biography*, vol. 104, no. 1, 1996.

Langham, A. F., 'Thomas Benson's Convict Slaves on Lundy', *Rep. Lundy Fld. Soc.*, p. 40, https://lfs-resources.s3.amazonaws.com/ar40/LFS_Annual_Report_Vol_40_Part_14.pdf.

Lenman, Bruce P., 'Lusty Beggars, Dissolute Women, Sorners, Gypsies, and Vagabonds for Virginia', *CW Journal*, Spring 2005.

Lilley, Kate, 'Mary Carleton's False Additions: The Case of the "German Princess"', *Humanities Research*, vol. XVI, no. 1, 2010.

Lynch, Gordon, 'Britain Sent Child Migrants Overseas – It's Running out of Time to Make Reparations', *The Conversation*, 23 October 2018.

Maxwell-Stewart, Hamish, 'Convict Labour Extraction and Transportation from Britain and Ireland, 1615–1870', in Christian Giuseppe De Vito and Alex Lichtenstein (eds), *Global Convict Labour*, New York: Brill, 2015.

Maxwell-Stewart, Hamish, 'Seven Tales for a Man with Seven Sides', in Lucy Frost and Hamish Maxwell-Stewart (eds), *Chain Letters: Narrating Convict Lives*, Carlton South, Victoria: Melbourne University Press, 2001.

Maxwell-Stewart, Hamish, 'Transportation from Britain and Ireland, 1615–1875', in Clare Anderson (ed.), *A Global History of Convicts and Penal Colonies*, London: Bloomsbury Academic, 2018.

Morgan, Gwenda and Peter Rushton, 'Fraud and Freedom: Gender, Identity and Narratives of Deception among the Female Convicts in Colonial America', *Journal for Eighteenth-Century Studies*, vol. 34, no. 3, 2011, pp. 335–55.

Morgan, Gwenda and Peter Rushton, 'Running Away and Returning Home: The Fate of English Convicts in the American Colonies', *Crime, History and Societies*, vol. 7, no. 2, 2003.

Munn, Christopher, 'The Transportation of Chinese Convicts from Hong Kong, 1844–1858', *Journal of the Canadian Historical Association*, vol. 81, 1997, pp. 113–45.

Neill, Rev. Edward D., 'Notes on American History', *New England Historical and Genealogical Register*, 30, 1876.

Parry, Naomi, '"Hanging no good for blackfellow": Looking into the Life of Musquito', in Ingereth Macfarlane and Mark Hannah (eds), *Transgressions: Critical Australian Indigenous Histories*, Canberra: ANU E- Press/Aboriginal History Incorporated, 2007.

Robertson, Joshua, 'Australian Convict Pirates in Japan: Evidence of 1830 Voyage Unearthed', *Guardian*, 28 May 2017, https://www.theguardian.com/australia-news/2017/may/28/australian-convict-pirates-in-japan-evidence-of-1830-voyage-unearthed.

Roscoe, Katherine, 'A Natural Hulk: Australia's Carceral Islands in the Colonial Period, 1788–1901', *International Review of Social History*, vol. 63, issue S26.

Seal, Graham, 'The Wild Colonial Boy Rides Again and Again: An Australian Legend Abroad', in Ian Craven (ed.), *Australian Popular Culture*, Cambridge: Cambridge University Press, 1994.

Shore, Heather, 'Transportation, Penal Ideology and the Experience of Juvenile Offenders in England and Australia in the Early Nineteenth Century', *Crime, Histoire & Sociétés/Crime, History & Societies*, vol. 6, no. 2, 2002, http://chs.revues.org/416; DOI: 10.4000/chs.416.

Simon, Theo, 'Mr Lud's Song', *The Land: An Occasional Magazine about Land Rights*, issue 10, Summer 2011.

Smith, Abbot Emerson, 'The Transportation of Convicts to the American Colonies in the Seventeenth Century', *The American Historical Review*, vol. 39, no. 2, 1934, pp. 232–49. *JSTOR*, www.jstor.org/stable/1838721.

Starr, Fiona, 'An Archaeology of Improvisation: Convict Artefacts from Hyde Park Barracks, Sydney 1819–1848', *Australasian Historical Archaeology*, vol. 33, 2015, pp. 37–54.

Swanson, Carl E., '"The unspeakable Calamity this poor Province Suffers from Pyrats": South Carolina and the Golden Age of Piracy', *Northern Mariner/Le Marin du Nord*, vol. 21, no. 2, 2011.

Tomlins, Christopher, 'Indentured Servitude in Perspective: European Migration into North America and the Composition of the Early American Labor Force, 1600–1775', in Cathy D. Matson (ed.), *The Economy of Early America: Historical Perspectives and New Directions*, University Park, PA: Penn State University Press, 2006.

Tranter, Hugh, 'The mystery convict correspondent of Lady Juliana and Lord George Gordon', https://www.academia.edu/1646389/The_mystery_convict_correspondent_of_Lady_Juliana_and_Lord_George_Gordon, accessed March 2020.

Wyatt, J. W., 'The Transportation of Criminals from Gloucestershire 1718–1773', *Gloucestershire Historical Studies*, vol. 3, 1969.

Zeigler, Edith, 'The Transported Convict Women of Colonial Maryland, 1718–1776', *Maryland Historical Magazine*, vol. 97, no. 1, Spring 2002.

Zug, Marcia, 'The Mail-Order Brides of Jamestown, Virginia', *The Atlantic*, 31 August 2016.

BOOKS

Anderson, Clare, *Convicts in the Indian Ocean: Transportation from South Asia to Mauritius, 1815–53*, Basingstoke: Palgrave Macmillan, 2000.

Anderson, Clare, *Subaltern Lives: Biographies of Colonialism in the Indian Ocean World, 1790–1920*, Cambridge: Cambridge University Press, 2012.

Anderson, Clare (ed.), *A Global History of Convicts and Penal Colonies*, London: Bloomsbury Academic, 2018.

Anderson, Clare, Niklas Frykman, Lex Heerma van Voss and Marcus Rediker, *Mutiny and Maritime Radicalism in the Age of Revolution*, Cambridge: Cambridge University Press, 2013.

Anderson, Clare, Madhumita Mazumdar and Vishvajit Pandya, *New Histories of the Andaman Islands: Landscape, Place and Identity in the Bay of Bengal, 1790–2012*, Cambridge: Cambridge University Press, 2016.

Anderson, Hugh, *A Rebecca in Tasmania: The Lamentations of David Davies, Welsh Convict 'In the Land of the Black Negro'*, North Melbourne: Red Rooster Press, 2009.

Anderson, Hugh, *Farewell to Judges & Juries: The Broadside Ballad and Convict Transportation to Australia, 1788–1868*, Hotham Hill, Victoria: Red Rooster Press, 2000.

Bailyn, Bernard, *Voyagers to the West: A Passage in the Peopling of America on the Eve of the Revolution*, New York: Vintage, 1988.

Bateson, Charles, *The Convict Ships, 1787–1868*, Glasgow: Brown, Son & Ferguson, 1969.

Bean, Philip and Joy Melville, *Lost Children of the Empire*, London: Unwin Hyman, 1990.

Beattie, J. M., *Crime and the Courts in England, 1660–1800*, Princeton, NJ: Princeton University Press, 1986.

Beckles, Hilary Mcd., *White Servitude and Black Slavery in Barbados, 1627–1715*, Knoxville, TS: University of Tennessee Press, 1989.

Bedini, Silvio A., *At the Sign of the Compass and Quadrant: The Life and Times of Anthony Lamb*, Philadelphia, PA: American Philosophical Society, 1984.

Blumenthal, Walter and Stephen R. Berry, *Brides from Bridewell: Female Felons Sent to Colonial America*, Rutland, VT: Charles E. Tuttle Publishing, 1962.

Boucher, Ellen, *Empire's Children: Child Emigration, Welfare, and the Decline of the British World, 1869–1967*, Cambridge: Cambridge University Press, 2014.

Boyson, F. (ed.), *The Autobiography of Kingsley Fairbridge*, London: Oxford University Press, 1927.

Breen, T. H., *Tobacco Culture: The Mentality of the Great Tidewater Planters on the Eve of Revolution*, Princeton, NJ: Princeton University Press, 1985.

Brown, Kathleen M., *Good Wives, Nasty Wenches, and Anxious Patriarchs: Gender, Race and Power in Colonial Virginia*, Chapel Hill, NC: University of North Carolina Press, 1996.

Carey, Hilary M., *Empire of Hell: Religion and the Campaign to End Convict Transportation in the British Empire, 1788–1875*, Cambridge: Cambridge University Press, 2019.

Christianson, Scott, *With Liberty for Some: 500 Years of Imprisonment in America*, Boston, MA: Northeastern University Press, 1998.

Christopher, Emma, *A Merciless Place: The Lost Story of Britain's Convict Disaster in Africa*. Oxford: Oxford University Press, 2011.

Christopher, Emma, Cassandra Pybus and Marcus Rediker (eds.), *Many Middle Passages: Forced Migration and the Making of the Modern World*, Berkeley, CA: University of California Press, 2008.

Coldham, Peter W., *Emigrants in Chains: A Social History of Forced Emigration to the Americas of Felons, Destitute Children, Political and Religious Non-Conformists, Vagabonds, Beggars and Other Undesirables, 1607–1776*, Baltimore, MD: Genealogical Publishing, 1992.

Coldham, Peter W., *Settlers of Maryland*, vol. 3, 1731–1750, Baltimore, MD: Genealogical Publishing Company, 1995–6.

Damousi, Joy, *Depraved and Disorderly: Female Convicts and Gender in Colonial Australia*, New York: Cambridge University Press, 1997.

Davies, K.G., *The North Atlantic World in the Seventeenth Century*, Minneapolis, MN: University of Minnesota Press, 1974.

Dobson, David, *Directory of Scots Banished to the American Plantations, 1650–1775*, Baltimore, MD: Clearfied Publishing Company, 1990, and subsequent reprints.

Ekirch, A. Roger, *Birthright: The True Story that Inspired* Kidnapped, New York: W. W. Norton & Company, 2010.

Ekirch, A. Roger, *Bound for America: The Transportation of British Convicts to the Colonies, 1718–1775*, Oxford: Clarendon Press, 1987.

Elliot, I., *Moondyne Joe: The Man and the Myth*, Perth: University of Western Australia Press, 1979; 2nd edn., Perth: Hesperian Press, 1998.

Erickson, Rica (ed.), *The Brand on His Coat: Biographies of some Western Australian Convicts*, Nedlands, Western Australia: University of Western Australia Press, 1983.

Evans, Anthony G., *Fanatic Heart: A Life of John Boyle O'Reilly 1844–1890*, Perth: University of Western Australia Press, 1997.

Fairbridge, Ruby, *Fairbridge Farm: The Building of a Farm School*, Perth: Paterson Press, 1948.

Faller, L. B., *Turned to Account: The Forms and Functions of Criminal Biography in Late Seventeenth- and Early Eighteenth-Century England*, Cambridge: Cambridge University Press, 1987.

Fennell, Philip and Marie King (eds), *John Devoy's Catalpa Expedition*, New York: New York University Press, 2006.

Fischer, David Hackett, *Albion's Seed: Four British Folkways in America*, Oxford and New York: Oxford University Press, 1989.

Flynn, Michael, *The Second Fleet: Britain's Grim Convict Armada of 1790*, Sydney: Library of Australian History, 2001.

Fortin, Jeffrey A. and Mark Meuwese (eds), *Atlantic Biographies: Individuals and Peoples in the Atlantic World*, Leiden and Boston, MA: Brill, 2013.

Foucault, Michel, *Discipline and Punish: The Birth of the Prison*, Paris: Gallimard, 1975; English edn. New York: Pantheon, 1977.

Frost, Alan, *Botany Bay and the First Fleet: The Real Story*, Melbourne: Black Inc., 2019.

Gill, Alan, *Orphans of the Empire: The Shocking Story of Child Migration to Australia*, Alexandria, New South Wales: Millennium Books, 1997.

Gragg, Larry Dale, *Englishmen Transplanted: The English Colonization of Barbados, 1627–1660*, Oxford: Oxford University Press, 2003.

Green, Neville, *Broken Spears: Aborigines and Europeans in the Southwest of Australia*, Perth: Focus Education Services, 1984.

Guigné, Anna Kearney, *The Forgotten Songs of the Newfoundland Outports: Taken from Kenneth Peacock's Newfoundland Field Collection, 1951–1961*, Ottawa: University of Ottawa Press, 2016.

Guillorel, Éva, David Hopkin and William G. Pooley (eds), *Rhythms of Revolt: European Traditions and Memories of Social Conflict in Oral Culture*, Abingdon: Routledge, 2018.

Hallam, Sylvia and Lois Tilbrook (eds.), *Aborigines of the Southwest Region, 1829–1840*, Nedlands, Western Australia: University of Western Australia Press, 1990.

Hill, David, *The Forgotten Children: Fairbridge Farm School and its Betrayal of Britain's Child Migrants to Australia*, Sydney: Random House, 2008.

Howell, Professor and Dr Xie, *Memoirs and Narratives of Canadian and American Convicts Sent to Australia*, Palmer Higgs, 2013 epub.

Hughes, Robert, *The Fatal Shore: A History of the Transportation of Convicts to Australia, 1787–1868*, New York: Alfred A. Knopf, 1986.

Jordan, Don and Michael Walsh, *White Cargo: The Forgotten History of Britain's White Slaves in America*, New York: Random House, 2011.

Kent, David and Norma Townsend, *Convicts of the Eleanor: Protest in Rural England, New Lives in Australia*, London: Merlin Press, 2002.

Linebaugh, Peter and Marcus Rediker, *The Many-Headed Hydra: Sailors, Slaves, Commoners, and the Hidden History of the Revolutionary Atlantic*, Boston, MA: Beacon Press, 2013.

Lynch, Gordon, *Remembering Child Migration: Faith, Nation-Building and the Wounds of Charity*, London: Bloomsbury Academic, 2015.

SELECT BIBLIOGRAPHY

Martin, Robert Montgomery, *History of the Colonies of the British Empire in the West Indies, South America, North America, Asia, Austral-Asia, Africa and Europe . . . From the Official Records of the Colonial Office*, London: W. H. Allen, 1843.

McKenzie, Kirsten, *Imperial Underworld: An Escaped Convict and the Transformation of the British Colonial Order*, Cambridge: Cambridge University Press, 2016.

Moore, Tony, *Death or Liberty: Rebels and Radicals Transported to Australia 1788–1868*, Sydney: Murdoch Books, 2010.

Morgan, Gwenda and Peter Rushton, *Eighteenth-Century Criminal Transportation: The Formation of the Criminal Atlantic*, New York: Palgrave Macmillan, 2004.

Mulvaney, John, *The Axe Had Never Sounded: Place, People and Heritage of Recherche Bay, Tasmania*, Canberra: ANU Press, 2007.

Nicholas, Stephen and Peter R. Shergold, 'Convicts as Migrants', in Stephen Nicholas (ed.), *Convict Workers: Reinterpreting Australia's Past*, Cambridge: Cambridge University Press, 1988.

O'Reilly, John Boyle, *Moondyne*, Boston, MA: P. J. Kennedy, 1879.

Parker, Mathew, *Willoughbyland: England's Lost Colony*, London: Hutchinson, 2015.

Pestana, Carla Gardina, *The English Atlantic in an Age of Revolution, 1640–1661*, Cambridge, MA: Harvard University Press, 2004.

Pieris, Anoma, *Hidden Hands and Divided Landscapes: A Penal History of Singapore's Plural Society*, Honolulu, HI: University of Hawaii Press, 2009.

Potter, Jennifer, *The Jamestown Brides: The Untold Story of England's 'Maids for Virginia'*, London: Atlantic Books, 2018.

Rees, Siân, *The Floating Brothel: The Extraordinary Story of the Lady Julian and its Cargo of Female Convicts Bound for Botany Bay*, Sydney: Hodder Headline Australia, 2001.

Robinson, Shirleene and Simon Sleight (eds), *Children, Childhood and Youth in the British World*, London: Palgrave Macmillan, 2016.

Robson, L. L., *The Convict Settlers of Australia: An Inquiry into the Origin and Character of the Convicts Transported to New South Wales and Van Diemen's Land 1787–1852*, Carleton, Victoria: Melbourne University Press, 1965.

Rudé, George, *Protest and Punishment: The Story of the Social and Political Protesters Transported to Australia 1788–1868*, Oxford: Clarendon Press, 1978.

Rushton, Peter and Gwenda Morgan, *Banishment in the Early Atlantic World: Convicts, Rebels and Slaves*, London: Bloomsbury Academic, 2013.

Sacks, David Harris, *The Widening Gate: Bristol and the Atlantic Economy, 1450–1700*, Berkeley, CA: University of California Press, 1991.

Seal, Graham, *The Lingo: Listening to Australian English*, Kensington, New South Wales: University of New South Wales Press, 1999.

Seal, Graham, *The Outlaw Legend: A Cultural Tradition in Britain, America and Australia*, Cambridge: Cambridge University Press, 1996.

Shaw, A.G.L., *Convicts and the Colonies: A Study of Penal Transportation from Great Britain and Ireland to Australia and Other Parts of the British Empire*, London: Faber and Faber, 1966.

Sheridan, Richard B., *Sugar and Slavery: An Economic History of the British West Indies, 1623–1775*, Baltimore, MD: Johns Hopkins University Press, 1974.

Sherrington, Geoffrey and Chris Jeffery, *Fairbridge, Empire and Child Migration*, Perth: University of Western Australia Press, 1998.

Shoemaker, Robert and Tim Hitchcock, *London Lives: Poverty, Crime and the Making of the Modern City*, Cambridge: Cambridge University Press, 2015.

Smart, Charles E., *The Makers of Surveying Instruments in America Since 1700*, New York: Regal Art Press, 1962.

Smith, Abbot Emerson, *Colonists in Bondage: White Servitude and Convict Labor in America, 1607–1776*, Gloucester, MA: University of North Carolina Press, 1947.

Smith, Lacey Baldwin, *This Realm of England 1399–1688*, Boston, MA: Houghton Mifflin Company, 2001.

Steele, I. K., *The English Atlantic, 1675–1740: An Exploration of Communication and Community*, New York and Oxford: Oxford University Press, 1986.

Sullivan, C. W. (ed.), *Fenian Diary: Denis B. Cashman Aboard the Hougoumont, 1867–1868*, Dublin: Wolfhound Press, 2001.

Summers, Anne, *Damned Whores and God's Police: The Colonisation of Women in Australia* [1975], Kensington, New South Wales: New South Books, 2016.

Swain, Shurlee and Margot Hillel, *Child, Nation, Race and Empire: Child Rescue Discourse, England, Canada and Australia, 1850–1915*, Manchester: Manchester University Press, 2010.

Swingen, Abigail L., *Competing Visions of Empire: Labor, Slavery, and the Origins of the British Atlantic Empire*, New Haven, CT, and London: Yale University Press, 2015.

Thomas, Stanley, *The Nightingale Scandal: The Story of Thomas Benson and Lundy*, Bideford, 1959; republished with additional notes by Myrtle Ternstrom, Appledore, Devon: Lazarus Press, 2001.

Valdik, A., *Imperial Andamans: Colonial Encounter and Island History*, Basingstoke: Palgrave Macmillan, 2010.

Vaver, Anthony, *Bound with an Iron Chain: The Untold Story of How the British Transported 50,000 Convicts to Colonial America*, Westborough, MA: Pickpocket Publishing, 2011.

Waldstreicher, David, *Runaway America: Benjamin Franklin, Slavery, and the American Revolution*, New York: Farrar, Straus and Giroux, 2005.

White, Charles and G.S. White, *Convict Life in New South Wales and Van Diemen's Land*, C. Free Press Office, Bathurst, 1889.

Wodrow, Robert, *The History of the Sufferings of the Church of Scotland from the Restoration to the Revolution* (first published 1721–2), Glasgow: Blackie Fullerton & Co., 1828.

Ziegler, Edith M., *Harlots, Hussies, and Poor Unfortunate Women: Crime, Transportation, and the Servitude of Female Convicts, 1718–1783*, Tuscaloosa, AL: University of Alabama Press, 2014.

REPORTS AND INQUIRIES

Commonwealth, Royal Commission into Institutional Responses to Child Sexual Abuse, 'Final Report', 15 December 2017, https://www.childabuseroyalcommission.gov.au/final-report, accessed November 2019.

Independent Inquiry Child Sexual Abuse, 'Child Migration Programmes: Investigation Report, March 2018', https://www.iicsa.org.uk/key-documents/4265/view/child-migration-programmes-investigation-report-march-2018.pdf.

Molesworth, William, *Report from the Select Committee of the House of Commons on Transportation: Together with a Letter from the Archbishop of Dublin on the Same Subject: and Notes by Sir William Molesworth*. Great Britain. Parliament. House of Commons. Select Committee on Transportation, London: Henry Hooper, 1838.

Report of Inspection of Home Children [1875, 1886], Archives of Ontario, RG 11-7, http://ao.minisisinc.com/scripts/mwimain.dll/144/ARCH_DESC_FACT/FACTSDESC/REFD%2BRG%2B11%2B7?SESSIONSEARCH.

Senate Standing Committee on Community Affairs, 'Lost Innocents: Righting the Record – Report on Child Migration', Australian Senate, 30 August 2001, https://www.aph.gov.au/Parliamentary_Business/Committees/Senate/Community_Affairs/Completed_inquiries/1999-02/child_migrat/report/index.

DATABASES, WEBSITES AND BLOGS

Ancestry, Ancestry.com, https://www.ancestry.com.au.

Anderson, Clare, 'Execution and its Aftermath in the Nineteenth-Century British Empire', https://lra.le.ac.uk/bitstream/2381/31686/6/AndersonCriminalCorpseFORMATTED.pdf

Australian Dictionary of Biography, National Centre of Biography, Australian National University, http://adb.anu.edu.au.

Blaxell, Gregory, 'A Slice of Canada in Australia', *Afloat*, 2007, http://www.afloat.com.au/afloat-magazine/archive/2007_December2007_AsliceofCanadainSydneybyGregoryBlaxell.htm#.WNi6RTtBVds.

Blomer, V., 'The Fate of the Brig Venus Seized in 1806', *Convict Connections Chronicle*, Convict Connections 2013, http://www.convictconnections.org.au/newsletter_articles.html

British History Online, University of London, https://www.british-history.ac.uk.

Broadside Ballads Online, Bodleian Library, Oxford, http://ballads.bodleian.ox.ac.uk.

Brown, Vincent, *Slave Revolt in Jamaica, 1760–1761: A Cartographic Narrative*, http://revolt.axismaps.com/project.html.

Byrnes, Dan, 'The Blackheath Connection', https://www.danbyrnes.com.au/blackheath.

Creaney, T. C., *The Huddersfield Four*, Female Convicts Research Centre, September 2015, http://www.femaleconvicts.org.au/docs/convicts/TheHuddersfieldFour.pdf.

The Digital Panopticon: Tracing London Convicts in Britain and Australia, 1780–1925, https://www.digitalpanopticon.org.

Dunae, Patrick A., 'Fairbridge Farm School, Cowichan Station, British Columbia', *British Home Children in Canada*, 2007, https://canadianbritishhomechildren.weebly.com/fairbrige-farm-vancouver.html

Eighteenth Century Collections Online, Gale, https://www.gale.com/intl/primary-sources/eighteenth-century-collections-online.

Encyclopedia Virginia, Virginia Humanities, https://www.encyclopediavirginia.org.

Encyclopedia of New Zealand, https://teara.govt.nz/e.

The Geography of Slavery in Virginia, http://www2.vcdh.virginia.edu/gos/index.html.

Gregory, Mark, *Frank the Poet – Francis MacNamara – 1811–1861*, https://frankthepoet.blogspot.com.

Hogan, Liam, 'England's Irish Slaves Meme: The Numbers', *Global Research*, 4 November 2015, http://www.globalresearch.ca/englands-irish-slaves-meme-the-numbers/5529851?utm_campaign=magnet&utm_source=article_page&utm_medium=relatedarticles.

Jeppesen, Jennifer, 'Searching for the Hidden Convict in Virginia's Servant Laws', *Australian and New Zealand Law and History E-Journal*, 2013, http://classic.austlii.edu.au/au/journals/ANZLawHisteJl/2013/2.pdf.

Karskens, Grace, 'The Myth of Sydney's Foundational Orgy', 2011, *Dictionary of Sydney*, http://dictionaryofsydney.org/entry/the_myth_of_sydneys_foundational_orgy.

Legal History Miscellany, https://legalhistorymiscellany.com.

Maryland State Archives, http://aomol.msa.maryland.gov/html/index.html.

Morgan, Matthew, *British Museum Project – Group 6*, https://sites.google.com/site/britishmuseumproject2/home/object-3.

Mullen, Stephen, 'Scots and Caribbean Slavery: Victims and Profiteers', *A Glasgow-West India Sojourn*, 6 March 2014, https://glasgowwestindies.wordpress.com/tag/jacobites.

Murray, A., 'Child Migration Schemes to Australia: A Dark and Hidden Chapter of Australian History Revealed', http://andrewmurray.democrats.org.au/Issues/congressbasedarticle.pdf (accessed October 2003), no longer available, but see Marilyn Rock, 'Child Migration Schemes to Australia: A Dark and Hidden Chapter of Australia's History Revealed' [online], *The Australian Journal of Social Issues*, vol. 38, no. 2, May 2003, pp. 149–67, https://search.informit.com.au/documentSummary;dn=772174054848704;res=IELFSC;type=pdf.

The Proceedings of the Old Bailey: London's Central Criminal Court, 1674–1913. The Digital Humanities Institute, http://www.oldbaileyonline.org.

Records and Files of the Quarterly Courts of Essex County, Massachusetts, vol. II, 1656–62, https://archive.org/stream/recordsandfiles00dowgoog#page/n307/mode/2up.

Rootsweb: Finding our roots together, https://www.rootsweb.com.

Roscoe, Katy, 'Convicts and the Sea: The Naval Influence on Gibraltar Convict Establishment' at *Carceral Archipelago*, https://staffblogs.le.ac.uk/carchipelago/2018/07/25/convicts-and-the-sea-the-naval-influence-on-gibraltar-convict-establishment.

Smith, Carleton Sprague, 'Broadsides and their Music in Colonial America', *Colonial Society of Massachusetts*, https://www.colonialsociety.org/node/2012.

Trevena, Kathleen, 'Charlotte Badger – Female Factory Inmate and Australia's First Female Pirate',

Riotous and Disorderly – The Women and their Stories from the Parramatta Female Factory, https://riotousanddisorderly.com/index.php/2017/01/03/charlotte-badger-female-factory-inmate-australias-first-female-pirate.

Walsh, Lorena S., 'The Hoe, the Plow, and the Whip: Gang Labour and Agricultural Improvement in Plantation Economics', Washington Area Economic History Seminar, 5 December 2014, p. 4, http://www.american.edu/cas/economics/upload/Walsh-Paper-12-5.pdf.

THESES

Brooks, Alan, 'Prisoners or Servants? A History of the Legal Status of Britain's Transported Convicts', PhD thesis, University of Tasmania, 2016.

Edgar, W. J., 'The Convict Era in Western Australia: Its Economic, Social and Political Consequences', PhD thesis, Murdoch University, 2014.

Jeppesen, Jennie, 'Necessary Servitude: Contrasting Experiences of Convicts in Virginia 1615–1775 and Australia 1800–1840', PhD thesis, University of Melbourne, 2014.

Parrott, Jennifer, 'For the Moral Good? The Government Scheme to Unite Convicts with their Families, 1818–1843', MA thesis, University of Tasmania, 1994.

Schmidt, Frederick Hall, 'British Convict Servant Labor in Colonial Virginia', PhD thesis, College of William and Mary, 1976.

Sharma, Rajni, 'The Statement of Mutiny Prisoner Doodnath Tewarry: An Ethnographic Study', MA dissertation, National Institute of Technology, Rourkela, 2014.

Teixeira, Christopher, 'The Crime of Coming Home: British Convicts Returning from Transportation in London, 1720–1780', MA thesis, University of Central Florida, 2010.

Wood, Colleen, 'Great Britain's Exiles Sent to Port Phillip, Australia, 1844–1849: Lord Stanley's Experiment', PhD thesis, University of Melbourne, 2014.

Young, Kevin, 'Macaulay's Mirror: Myths, Martyrs, and White Slaves in the Early Atlantic World', graduate thesis in world history, Monmouth University, 2011.

INDEX

Abdy, Anthony, London Alderman 15
Aberdeen, kidnappers 63, 65
Aboriginal peoples 135
    raids against settlers 139–40
    transportation and exiling of 139–42
Africa
    early colonies 11
    see also Cape Castle; Gold Coast
Allen, Tom, murder by 132–3
American colonies
    crimes committed by convicts in 69–71
    factors 49
    labour shortages 14–15
    rebels sent to 24–5
    see also Maryland; United States of America;
        Virginia
American War of Independence 47
    effect on transport trade 86
Americans
    and Canadian Patriot War 173, 174
    as race of convicts 68
    view of transportation 227
Andaman Islands, penal colony 156–9, 226
    assassination of Lord Mayo 158–9
    closure (1942) 157
    escapes from 157, 158
    Female factories 157
    indigenous people 157, 158
    Viper Island 157
Annapolis, Maryland 53
Annapolis Royal, Nova Scotia 57
Anne, transport ship 104–5
Annesley, James, kidnapped and sent to
    Delaware 63
Anti-Transportation League 197
apprenticeship 6
Argyll, Archibald, 9th Earl of, supporter of
    Monmouth 47
Armestrong, Robert (aka Hethersgill), sent to
    Barbados 23

Armstrong, Lawrence, Lieutenant Governor of
    Nova Scotia 57–8
Arthur, Sir George, Lieutenant Governor of
    Van Diemen's Land 175, 185–6
Ashton, Charles, The Convict's Dream 169,
    186–7
Asia transport ship 120
Astley, William, on the Ring 154
Australia 169–73
    child evacuees (World War II) 219
    construction of infrastructure by convicts
        225
    early convicts in 92–112
    established as colony 11–12, 92–3
    First Fleet (1787) 91, 96–7
    modern attitudes to transportation 227–8
    modern heritage sites 225
    and response to asylum seekers and refugees
        228
    Royal Commission into Institutional Responses
        to Child Sexual Abuse (2012) 222
    Second Fleet (1790) (women only) 97
    Third Fleet 97
    transportation records 11–12
    see also New South Wales; Norfolk Island;
        Queensland; Van Diemen's Land; Western
        Australia

Backhouse, James, Quaker missionary 117
Bacon, Nathaniel, Virginia 38
Badger, Anny 2, 3
Badger, Charlotte, convict 1–3
Bahamas, transportation to 143
ballads 68–9, 225
    'The Convict's Tour to Hell' 122
    'The Cyprus Brig' 113, 119–20
    on Fenians' escape from Fremantle 213
    'The Grand Conversation on Napoleon'
        124–5
    'John Mitchel's Address' 149

'John Mitchel's Escape' 150
'John Mitchel's Return' 150
'The Lads of Virginia' 81
The Poor Unhappy Felon's Sorrowful Account (James Revel) 82–5
subversive 124–5
Baltimore, brigantine 57
Barbados
  Bussa slave revolt (1816) 168
  Monmouth's rebels transported to 45–7
  prisoners of war sent to 22
  slave plantations 26–8
  Thomas Verney's plantation 21
Barnardo homes, and child migration 215, 219, 220
Barret, James, felon 69
Barrett, Thomas, hanged in New South Wales 94
Barrington, George, pickpocket 99–104
  to New South Wales 103–4
  trials 99–101, 102–3
Beagle, voyage of 142–3
Beale, William, transported to Fremantle 203–4
Beckett, Sir William à, Chief Justice 171
Beckford, Elizabeth, convict 96
Behn, Aphra
  on Bacon's Rebellion in Virginia 39
  The Dutch Lover 37
  on Mary Carleton 37
  The Widdow Ranter 32
Belcher, Jonathan, governor of Massachusetts 57
Bencoolen, Sumatra, penal colony 160, 162–3
benefit of clergy, immunity from death penalty 47–8
Bengal, convicts transported to Andaman Islands 156–7, 158
Bennett, John, hanged in New South Wales 94
Benson, Thomas, convict colony on Lundy Island 71–4
Bermuda 144–52
  convict cemetery 226
  convicts from North America 146
  convicts transferred from 149, 152
  prison hulks 145, 146–7, 148, 151–2
  reputation 150–1
  Royal Naval Dockyard 145
  slaves sent to 145
  yellow fever 145–6
Berry, John, American rebel 179
Bhantu tribe, Uttar Pradesh 159
Big Brother Movement, child migration 219, 220
Bird, Ann, proprietor of *Sydney Gazette* 110
Bird, Sarah, to New South Wales 108–10
Blewit, William, return from transportation 51

bonded labour *see* indentured labour
Bondsfield Commission, on child migration 216
Boothroyd, George 179
Boston, Scottish prisoners of war 22
Botany Bay 91, 93
Bothwell Bridge, Battle of (1679) 23
Bourke, Sir Richard, Governor of New South Wales 186
Boyer, Hannah 67
Brady, Father John 173–4
branding, by Indian authorities 164
Breslin, John, Fenian agent, and escape of convicts from Fremantle to America 211–13
Brine, James, Tolpuddle martyr 137–8, 139
British army, and penal colonies in West Africa 89
British empire 224–5
  and child migration 214–23
  need for settlers 214–15
  and penal colonies 148–9
  see also colonies
British Guiana *see* Guyana
Brooks, Thomas, convict 130–6
  escapes 131, 132, 133–4
  floggings 131–2, 134
  reminiscences 135–6
Brown, Gordon, prime minister 222
Brown, John, master of brigantine 69
Browne, John, felon, to East Indies 15
Buckler, Andrew 57
Buckler, Susanna(h) 57–8
Buffalo, transport ship 174
Burma *see* Myanmar
Bussell family, settlers 200
Butler, Mary, convict 98

Campbell, Duncan, overseer of convicts 85–6
Canada 11
  child migrants to 215, 216
  Patriot War (1838) 173–4, 178–9
Canadian Home Children, 2017 apology to 222
cant (secret language) 126
  the Ring (Norfolk Island) 155–6
Cape Castle, West Africa, penal colony 86, 89–90, 226
  mutinies 89
Cape Colony, South Africa 11
Carleton, John 34, 36
Carleton, Mary (née Moders) ('the counterfeit lady') 34–7
  return and execution 36–7
  transportation to Jamaica 35–6

Carnarvon, 4th Earl of, on Bermuda prison
    hulks 151–2
Cash, Martin, bushranger 190
Castle Hill, Sydney, 1804 uprising 105–8
Castro, Tom, Wagga Wagga 194–5
Catalpa, whale ship 211, 212–13
Chace, Samuel, captain of *Venus* 1, 2
chains and shackles, use of 98, 127, 145, 197–8
    Aboriginals 141, 201
    Bermudan prison hulks 147, 151
    in prison 103, 129–30, 133
    road gangs 177
    work gangs 116, 131, 132, 147, 196, 208
Charles I, King 10, 20
Charles II, King, Restoration 23
Charlotte, Queen, wife of George III 74
Charming Nancy, American convict ship 72–3
Chartists 125, 139
Child Emigration Society 217
Child Migrant Trust 220
child migration schemes (from 1840s) 215–23
    farm schools 218–19
    investigations into 216, 221–3
    mistreatments 216, 220–1, 223
    suicides of children 216
children
    abduction 16, 25–6, 28, 62–5
    'ill-disposed' 14–17
    Irish 25–6
    transported to Australia 12
    see also juvenile offenders
Children's Aid Society, and child migration 215
Children's Friend Society, and resettlement of
    juveniles and orphans 202–3
Chile, *Frederick* mutineers in 128–9
China, *Cyprus* brig in 119
Chinese, transported from Hong Kong 160–2
Christian Brothers, and child migration 219,
    220, 221, 222
City of London, and removal of vagrant
    children to Virginia 16
Clan na Gael, American Branch of Irish
    Republican Brotherhood 211
Clark, Ralph, on Second Fleet to Australia 97
Clarke, Marcus, on the Ring 154
Clay, Lydia, Hobart 179, 180, 183
Coad, John
    to Jamaica 42–5
    petition for freedom and return 44–5
coins, counterfeit 145
colonies
    commodity trade with 12
    crimes committed by convicts in 69–71
    early 10–11
    growing resistance to transportation 52

links between 13
need for labour 24–5
need for wives for settlers 17–19
Commonwealth Settlement Act (1957) 220
Company of Merchants Trade to Africa, and
    Gold Coast 88–9
Company for the Plantation of Guyana 20
Connelly, Philip, Catholic priest 111
Connor, Elizabeth, pickpocket 77
Conventicle Act (1664) 32
convicts, transported 3–4
    backgrounds 123–4
    compared with slaves 6, 26, 117, 198
    culture of 124–5
    mutinies 89, 113, 152–3, 156
    pardoned 33
    payments to gaolers for 40–2
    rehabilitation 126
    resistance and defiance 125–6
    sold as slaves 23, 28–9, 43, 63
    successful careers in colonies 61–2, 126
Cook, Captain James 93
Council of Trade 33
Cranston, Robert, Fenian rebel 210
Creagh, James, surgeon on *Janus* 111
Crevecoeur, J. Hector St John 71
criminals
    banishment 5
    outlawry 5
    proposals for useful employment in colonies
        7–8
    temporary ejection 5
    see also convicts, transported
Cromwell, Henry, and transportation of Irish
    children 25
Cromwell, Oliver 22, 24
cruelty, treatment of Scottish Covenanters 32–3
Culloden, Battle of (1746) 47
Cumberland, sailing ship, wrecked (1830)
    199–200
Cunningham, Philip, Irish rebel 104–8
    and 1804 Castle Hill uprising 105–7, 108
Custody of Children Act (1891), and child
    migration 215
Cyprus brig, mutiny 117–20

Dalton, Michael, attorney 75
Darling, Sir Ralph, Governor of New South
    Wales 184
Darragh, Thomas, Fenian rebel 210
Darwin, Charles, in Mauritius 143–4
David Malcolm, transport ship 186
Davis, Mary, hanged in New South Wales 94
death penalty, transportation as alternative
    47–8

Defoe, Daniel, *Moll Flanders* 54–7
Derbin, Joseph, purchase of freedom 78–9
Devall, Mr W. 75
Development and Immigration Commission (Melbourne) 218
Devoy, James, leader of *Clan na Gael* 211, 214
disease
  cholera 121
  epidemics in Western Australia 202
  Singapore 166
  on voyage 33, 60, 85, 96
  yellow fever in Bermuda 145–6
Downing, William, indentured convict 29–31
Dromedary, Bermudan prison hulk 146
Dunbar, Battle of (1650) 22
Dunderdale, George, on New South Wales convicts 198
Dutton, Magdalene, transportation to Guyana 19–21
Dwyer, John, transported child 207

Eagle, transport ship 50
East India Company
  and British expansion in India 11
  pardoned convicts for 9
  and Singapore 165
  transportation of Indian convicts 143, 159–60, 162
  use of Andaman Islands for transportation 156–7
East Indies 8
Elizabeth I, Queen 10
Emmett, Robert, Dublin uprising (1803) 105
Empire Settlement Act (1922) 216, 219, 220
English Civil Wars 22
Esden, Lydia, convict in Australia 111, 112
Europe, banishment to 8, 17
Evelyn, Richard, Sheriff 20

factors (agents for indentured labour), America 49, 51
Fairbridge, Kingsley, 'Vision Splendid' child migration scheme 217, 218, 220
Fairbridge Society 217–19, 220
family history, modern popular interest in 226–7
fees 51
  payment to gaolers 40–2, 49–50
Female factories 226
  Andamans 157
  Cascades (Hobart) 179–83
  Parramatta 1–2
Fenian Brotherhood 156, 207–14
  escape of convicts from Fremantle to America 211–14
  pardons (1869, 1871) 210

flogging tree 136
floggings 89, 114–17
  Australia 93, 98
  Bermudan prison hulks 147–8
  Moreton Bay 121–2
  Norfolk Island 110, 153, 189
  Port Macquarie 131–2, 134
  rules on 147–8
  Singapore 166
  women 96
Flying Post newspaper 16
Forward, Jonathan, trader 49–52
Forward, transport ship 60
Foyle, Oxenbridge 14, 26–8
Franklin, Benjamin
  exchange of rattlesnakes for convicts 69–70
  and Riddlesden 54
Franklin, Jane, Lady 176
Franklin, Sir John, Lieutenant Governor of Van Diemen's Land 175–7
Frederick, brig, mutiny 128, 129
Freeman, James, as public executioner in New South Wales 94
Fremantle, Western Australia 119, 202
  escape of Fenians to America 211–13
  Roundhouse gaol 199, 226
Frobisher, Martin, voyage to find Northwest Passage 7
Furbush, William 23
Fynes, Captain, commandant 135

Gadigal people, New South Wales 95
Gambia 11
Gaven, John
  execution 206–7
  in Fremantle 204–7
General Wood, transport ship 161
Georgette, steam ship 212, 213
Georgia, colony 11
Ghana
  Fort St Jago 226
  see also Gold Coast
Gibraltar 11
  convict labour in (1842–75) 197
  Wellington Front 226
Gilbert, Humphrey 10
Glorious Revolution (1688) 23, 44, 47
Gold Coast, West Africa 226
  slave forts 88–9
  see also Cape Castle
Goodfellow ship 25, 29
Gordon, Roderick, ship's surgeon 24
Graham, J., MP 203
Green, Jane, to Western Australia 203
Green, William, convict 29

Guilding, Revd J.M., on Bermuda prison hulks 151, 152
Guyana (British Guiana) 9, 143
  first settlement 10
  transportees from West Indies 143
  women transported to 20–1
Gypsies (Roma people, 'Egyptians'),
  banishment 17

Habeas Corpus Act (1679) 33
Hakluyt, Richard, *Discourse of Western Planting*
  (1584) 5, 7–8, 9
Ham, Cornelia, married to Anthony Lamb 61
Hammett, James, Tolpuddle martyr 137
Hancock, James, returned transportee 80
hard labour
  agricultural 184–5
  bush clearing 131–2
  as further punishment 153, 166
  in mines 108, 177
  quarries 147, 190, 197
  road gangs 98, 172, 177, 186, 209
  in sugar mills 27
  tree-felling 127
  see also chains; indentured labour
Harrington, Michael, Fenian rebel 210
Harrison, Colonel William, Maryland 79
Harrower, John, on indenture 28–9
Hart, John 188
Harvey, Peter, ship's master 69
Hassett, Thomas, Fenian rebel 210
Hegarty, Kitty, convict 1, 2
'Hell's Gate' (Macquarie Harbour) 127–8
Henry VIII, King 6
Hitcham, Justice 19, 20
Hobart, Tasmania, Cascades Female Factory
  179–83
Hogan, Martin, Fenian rebel 210
Holmes, Samuel, to Van Diemen's Land
  169–71
Holt, Joseph, Irish rebel 184
Home of Industry, Spitalfields, and child
  migration 215
Honduras Bay, South America 87–8
Hong Kong
  as Crown Colony 11
  transportations from 160–1
Horatio, transport brig 165
Hougoumont, transport ship 208, 209
Humphreys, Margaret, Child Migrant Trust
  220
Hunt, James, in Hobart 192
Hunter, John, governor of New South Wales
  103
Hutcheson, George, Edinburgh merchant 17

Immigration Restriction Act (1904) 142
indentured labour 23
  blackbirding 141–2
  economics of 49
  legal appeals against 30–1
  as slavery 26
  transportees as 14, 15–16
  treatment of servants 66–7
  see also hard labour
India 11
  Chinese transportees in 162
Indian Mutiny (1857) 11, 157, 160
Indians, tranported to Mauritius 142
Ireland 10
  1798 Rebellion 104, 113
  1803 Dublin uprising 105
  Fenian rebellion (1866) 208
  Scottish prisoners of war 22
Irish
  children to New England and Virginia 25–6
  as convicts 113
  rebels 104–5, 125, 207–14
  transported to Leeward Islands 24
Irish Catholics, transportation 9, 104–8,
  110–11
Irish Republican Brotherhood
  Clan na Gael (American branch) 211
  see also Fenian Brotherhood
irons *see* chains

Jacobite Revolts 47
Jamaica 25, 28
  Monmouth's rebels sent to 42–5
  slave revolt (1760) 168
James I, King, and penal banishment 9
James II, King, deposed 44, 47
Jamestown
  Bacon's Rebellion 38
  colony at 10
  convicts as labourers 14
Janus, transport ship 110–11
Japan, *Cyprus* brig in 117–19
Jeafferson, Christopher 39–42
  and St Kitts sugar plantation 39–40
  and trade in convicts 40–2
Jeffrey, Mark 187–93
  at Port Arthur 191–2
  transported to Norfolk Island 189–91
Jeffreys, George, Judge, and Bloody Assizes 42,
  43
Jennings, Catharine 67
Jesuits priests, banishment 8
Johns, Joseph Bolitho (Moondyne Joe), escapes
  208
Johnson, Samuel 68

Johnston, Major George 104
  and Castle Hill uprising (1804) 106–7
Joint Commonwealth and States Scheme
  (1921), for migration 219
Jury, Francis, marriage to Mina McCaulfield
  194
Justice, Henry, payment for freedom 52
juvenile offenders
  from London (Pentonvillains) 171
  sent to Australia 12, 202–7
  see also children

Katenkamp, George, and Cape Castle colony
  89
Keane, Michael, soldier and convict, floggings
  114–17
Kelly, Ben, first mate on *Venus* 1, 2
Kibble, Richard, returned transportee 80
kidnapping
  of children 16, 25–6, 63–5
  'spiriting' 28–31
King, Anna, diary 98–9
King, Revd G. 206
King, Moll (Adkins), 'Moll Flanders' based on
  55–7
King, Philip Gidley, RN, governor of New
  South Wales 98
  and Castle Hill uprising (1804) 106
King, Tom 56

La Trobe, Charles, Lieutenant Governor in
  Hobart 141
Lady Juliana, only women convicts on 97
Lady Penrhyn, transport ship to Australia 96
Lamb, Anthony, instrument-maker
  career in New York 61–2
  transported to Maryland 59–60
Lancey, John, Captain of the *Nightingale* 72, 73
Laud, William, Archbishop of Canterbury 21
Leader, Mr, partner of David Selleck 25
The Leaving of Liverpool (documentary) 220
Ledgard, William, sent to Van Diemen's Land
  200
Leeward Islands
  Irish in 24
  Monmouth's rebels sent to 45
Life and Character of Moll King (pamphlet) 55
Logan, Captain, commandant at Moreton Bay
  121
Long, Mary, convict in Australia 111, 112
Lost Innocents report (2001) 220–1
Loveless, George and James, Tolpuddle martyrs
  137
Luddites 125, 139
Lundy Island, Benson's convict colony 71–4

McCaulfield, Mina (Euphemia Mercevona)
  children 195–6
  and trial of Arthur Orton 195
  in Van Diemen's Land 193–6
Mackenzie, Captain Kenneth, and Cape Coast
  Castle 89–90
McNair, J.F.A., Singapore penal administrator
  163
MacNamara, Francis, poet 122
Maconochie, Captain, commandant at Norfolk
  Island 130
Macquarie Harbour 226
  'Hell's Gate' 127–8
Macquarie, Lachlan, governor of New South
  Wales 111
Malacca 165
  Indian convicts sent to 160, 161
Malaya 11
Mary Fortune, ship 32
Maryland
  anti-transportation laws 52
  convicts to 49, 86–7
  Riddlesden in 54
Maryland Gazette, advertisement 85–6
Mathews, Mrs 58–9
Mauritius 143–4
  Indian convicts sent to 160
Maxwell, Alexander, in America 24
Mayo, Lord, Viceroy of India, assassination
  (1872) 158–9
Medway, Bermudan prison hulk 152
Melbourne, Australia 171
Merchantman, transport ship 152
Mercury, transport ship 87–8
Miller, Linus 178
Millions Club, immigration scheme in Australia
  219
Mitchel, John, Irish nationalist 146–50
  on convict underworld 148–9
  descriptions of Bermudan prison hulks 146–8
  election to Parliament as member for
    Tipperary 150
  escape to New York 150
  transfer to Hobart 149–50
Molesworth Inquiry 186, 214
  into Norfolk Island 154
Molesworth, Sir William 186
Monmouth, Duke of 42, 43
Monmouth's Rebellion 42–3, 45
Moore, George, convict trader 86–7
Moore, Sergeant of Police, Parramatta 121
Moreton Bay penal colony, near Brisbane 121,
  131
Morris, John (aka John Morris Stephens),
  attack on Sarah Bird (Sydney) 109–10

Mosquito Shore, South America 88
Mowat, Captain Thomas, *Janus* 111–12
Mundy, Colonel George, on Cascades Female
    Factory, Hobart 180–3
Murray, William, convict 89
'Musquito', Aboriginal man, exiled to Norfolk
    Island 140
mutinies 89, 113
    Cyprus brig 117–20
    Frederick brig 128, 129
    Norfolk Island 152–3, 156
    ships 86, 87, 105, 161
Myanmar (Burma) 11
    Indian convicts sent to 160
Mysore, India 11

Natal, South Africa 11
National Covenant (1631), Scotland 21
Native Americans 19
    and Bacon's Rebellion in Virginia 38–9
Neptune, transport ship 149
New Caledonia 141
New South Wales, Australia 91
    attempted escapes from 105
    convict mutinies 113
    discipline in colony 93–5
    end of transportation (1840) 197
    French Canadian rebels 173–4
    organisation of convict settlement 183–7
New South Wales Corps 106–7
New York, Anthony Lamb in 61–2
New York Tribune 150
New Zealand
    child evacuees (World War II) 219
    child migrants to 216
    first female convicts 2–3
    Maoris exiled from 140–1
Newcastle, New South Wales, penal colony
    115–16, 130–1
Newfoundland 8
    claimed as colony 10
Newgate Gaol, payments for convicts for
    plantation owners 40–1
Nicol, John, steward on *Lady Juliana* 97
Nightingale, Thomas Benson's ship 72–3
Noongar people, Perth 201
Norfolk Island 110, 189–91
    closure (1855) 191
    convict mutinies 152–3, 156
    escape attempts 153
    as heritage site 226
    penal colony 105, 130
    reputation for violence and brutality 151,
    152–6, 189–91
    the Ring (secret society) 154–6

Nova Scotia 57, 87

Obigadu, Singamala Chenchu, transported 160
O'Brien, Marcelle, child migrant 221
O'Donoghue, Michael, child migrant 221
Oliver, Daniel, ship merchant 69
Ontario, French province 173
O'Reilly, John Boyle 156
    escape 210, 214
    and Fenian rebellion 208
    Moondyne (novel) 209
Orlov, Count 102
Orphan Homes of Scotland, and child
    migration 215
Orton, Arthur 194–5
Owen Glendower, prison hulk in Gibraltar 197

Pacific Islanders, transported to Queensland
    141–2
Pacific Islanders Protection Act (1872) 141
pamphlets (and street literature) 68–9
    see also ballads
pardons, for transported convicts 33, 46
Parkhurst prison, Isle of Wight 203
Parkinson, Jane, convict 96
Parliament, opposition to enslavement of
    convicts 27
Parramatta, New South Wales 103
    Female Factory 1–2
paupers, transported 21
penal transportation, Act (1597) 8
Penang 165
    Indian convicts sent to 143, 160, 161
Pennsylvania, tax on transported convicts 52
Pennsylvania Gazette 61, 69
Penruddock's Rising, Cornwall (1655) 24
    rebels from 26–8
Pentland Rising (1666) 23
'Pentonvillains' 171
Pepys, Samuel, on Mary Carleton 34
Perth, Western Australia 202
Philanthropic Society, and child migration
    215
Phillip, Arthur, first Governor of New South
    Wales 92–4, 95, 157
Pinjarra, Western Australia, Fairbridge Farm at
    217–18, 219, 221
pirates
    attacks on transport ships 46, 50
    transportation 9
Pitman, Henry
    escape 46
    return 46–7
    sent to Barbados 45–6
Pobjoy, William, convict 118, 119

Pollard, George, murdered in Fremantle 204–6
Pollard, Michael 205
Pollard, Mrs 204–6
Pollard, Thomas 205
Poor Law Guardians, and child migration 215
Port Arthur, Tasmania 191–2
    as heritage site 226
Port Jackson, New South Wales 95, 157
    Female Orphan Institution 99
Port Macquarie, penal colony 131
Port Royal, Jamaica 35–6
Porter, James
    escape from 'Hell's Gate' (Macquarie
        Harbour) 124–5, 126–30
    mutiny on *Frederick* 128–9
Pott, Anthony, sent to Barbados 23
Poulter, John, *The Discoveries of John Poulter*
    (account of illegal return) 76–7
poverty, criminalization of 6–7, 21
Preston, Battle of (1648) 22
Price, John, commandant on Norfolk Island
    190
Prince of Wales Island, Indian convicts sent
    to 143
prison hulks (decommissioned ships) 88
    Bermuda 145, 146, 148, 151–2
    coin forging in 145
    Gibraltar 197
    Phoenix 121
    Woolwich 102
prisoners of war
    Scottish 22
    transportation 9
prisons
    Fremantle Roundhouse 199, 226
    and payment for convicts for plantation
        owners 40–1, 49–50
    Rottnest Island 201–2
    use of chains 103, 129–30, 133
    see also prison hulks
privateers, and convicts 46
Providence ship 25
public opinion 68
    interest in stories of transportation 124–5
    opposition to enslavement of convicts 27
punishments, in Australia 107–8
    floggings 114–17, 131–2, 134
    women 96
punishments, Singapore 164

Quakers 32
Quarmby, Elizabeth, sent to Hobart 179, 180
Quebec, French province 173
Queensland, Australia, Pacific Islanders in
    141–2

Raffles, Stamford, and Bencoolen colony,
    Sumatra 162–3
Ragged Schools, and child migration 215
Raleigh, Walter, and Roanoke settlement 10
Read, John (aka Miller), escaped transportee 79
Reardon, Margaret, transported from New
    Zealand to Tasmania 141
rebels 9
    American (Canadian Patriot War) 173,
        174–9
    French Canadians 173–4, 178–9
    Irish 104–8, 125
    Monmouth's 42–7
    political (agricultural) 137–9
    Scottish 21–3
    to slave plantations 26–8
Reformation, and religious dissidents 8
reivers (English–Scottish border raiders),
    transportation 9–10
religious dissidents 8, 32–3
    Scottish Covenanters 32–3
Revel, James, ballad of 82–5
Richardson, Ruth, sent to Hobart 179, 180
Rickard, Anne, to Virginia 18
Riddlesden, William, lawyer and swindler 53–4
Ring (secret society), Norfolk Island 154–6
    initiation rituals 154–5
    secret language 155–6
Rivers, Marcellus 14, 26–8
Roanoke settlement 10
Robben Island, South Africa 9, 226
Roman Catholic church, and child migration
    215–16, 219, 220
Roman Catholics, banishment 8
Ross, David, convict consignee in Maryland 79
Rottnest Island 226
    Aboriginal prison 201–2
Rudrapah, transported from Madras to
    Singapore 166–7
Rullion Green, Battle of (1666) 23
Russell, Lord John, prime minister 176

Sabatini, Rafael, *Captain Blood* 47
Sacramento, prison hulk 172
St Kitts, sugar plantations 39–40, 41
St Pancras Poor Law Guardians, and child
    migration 215
Salisbury, Maurice, escaped transportee 77–8
Salmon, George, convict trader 86–7
Salvation Army
    in Andaman Islands 159
    and child migration 216
Sandys, Sir Edwin, Virginia Company 17
Sarah Island, Macquarie Harbour, penal colony
    127–8

Scotland
  children from 17, 63, 65
  and English Civil Wars 22
  Presbyterian Church 22, 23
Scots
  in colonies 23–4
  rebels 21–3, 47
Sea Venture(r), Virginia Company ship 144–5
Selleck, David, and transportation of Irish
  children to New England and Virginia 25
sexual relations, with female convicts (Australia)
  96, 97, 98–9
Sheehy, Marcus, Irish rebel and mutineer 105
Sheppard, Jack, thief 59–60
Shere Ali, Pathan, assassination of Lord Mayo
  159
ships
  conditions aboard 43, 85, 96, 97, 98
  mutinies 86, 87, 105, 161
  treatment of prisoners on 33
  see also prison hulks
Shute, Samuel, Governor of Massachusetts 69
Sierra Leone 11
  Barbadian slave rebels sent to 168
Simonds, John, felon 69
Sind (now Pakistan), transportations to 161,
  162
Singapore 165–6
  escape attempts 166
  Indian convicts sent to 143, 160, 161
  industrial training of convicts 162–4
  ticket-of-leave system 163–4
Sir John Byng brig 130
Sisters of Mercy, and child migration 220
Sisters of Nazareth, and child migration 220,
  221
slave traders 51
slavery
  abolition (1834) 145
  black chattel 14, 227
  Gold Coast 88–9
  plantation 26–8
  see also indentured labour
slaves
  Barbadian rebels 168
  to Bermuda 145
  convicts sold as 23, 28–9, 43, 63
Smith, Michael, convict and bushranger 121
Smith (Smythe), Sir Thomas 15
Smith, V., MP 203
Smyth, Arthur Bowes, ship's surgeon 96
Smyth, P.J., Irish correspondent for *New York
  Tribune* 150
Snow, Samuel, American rebel 174–5, 178–9
Somers Isles Company 145

songs *see* ballads
Speedy, transport ship 98
'spiriting' (abduction, kidnapping) 28–31
Spriggs, Betty 49, 66–7
Sri Lanka (Ceylon) 11
  transportations from 160, 161
Standfield, Thomas and John, Tolpuddle
  martyrs 137
Steel, Captain, of the *Cumberland* 199–200
Stevenson, Captain, superintendent of
  Singapore 165–6
Stevenson, Robert Louis, *Kidnapped* 63
Stewart, Captain, of the *Anne* 105
Stirling, James, Governor of Western Australia
  199
Straits Settlements (Singapore, Penang,
  Malacca) 160–1, 162–4, 165–7
  retransportation from 167
street literature *see* ballads; pamphlets
Suffolk, Owen, 'Pentonvillain' 171–3
  autobiography 172–3
Sumatra, Indian convicts sent to 160
Sutcliff, Robert, in Maryland 62
Sutton, George, sent to Virginia 51
Swallow, William (Walker) 118–20
Swan River, Western Australia
  free colony 199–200
  Rottnest Island 201–2
  treatment of Aboriginal prisoners 200–2
Swift, transport ship 86–7
Swift, Jeremiah, murder in Maryland 70
Swing Riots 125, 137, 156
Sydney, heritage sites 226
Sydney Gazette 110
Sydney Morning Herald 194
Sydney, New South Wales 91
Symonds, Samuel, indenture-master 29–31

Tangier, as English possession 10
Tasmania *see* Van Diemen's Land
Te Umuroa, Maori rebel 140–1
Tewari, Dudhnath, escape from Andamans 158
Therry, John, Catholic priest 111
Thompson, John, convict 127–8
Thornton, transport ship 85–6
'Three Jolly Settlers', first legal pub in Australia
  109
Thurston, Edgar, ethnographer 162
Tichborne, Roger Charles, disappearance
  194
ticket-of-leave system 135, 157, 163–4, 181–2,
  191–2
  Patriots 174, 177, 178–9
tobacco traders 49, 50, 51
Tolpuddle Martyrs 137–9

transportation
   avoidance 76–7
   colonial laws against 52
   criticism of 186, 197, 214, 225
   decline of 214–15
   duration and extent 224
   end of to New South Wales (1840) 197
   escapes and (illegal) return 53–4, 55–7, 68, 75
   fees 51
   first Act (1597) 8
   first proposals 7–8
   to islands 143
   in lieu of death penalty 47–8
   modern popular interest in 226–7
   and opposition to enslavement of convicts 27
   popular view of 68–9
   profits 85
   records 11–12, 226
   see also child migration; convicts
Transportation Act (1717) 10–11, 48, 49
Trollope, Anthony, on Bermuda 150–1
Troy, John, convict and bushranger 120–3
   ballads about 122–3

Ullathorne, Very Revd William, Vicar General
   of New South Wales and Tasmania 153
United Irishmen 104
United Kingdom
   Health Committee Inquiry into child
      migration (1997) 222
   Independent Inquiry into Child Sexual
      Abuse, and Child Migration programmes
      222
   see also British empire
United States of America
   Australian folk songs in 122–3
   Irish interests in 207–8
   see also American colonies
Unity, transport ship 22

vagabondage, Royal Decree on (1603) 15
vagabonds
   legislation against 5–7
   rounded up for transportation 17
Vagabonds Act (1572) 6–7
Vagrancy Acts (1530, 1547) 6
Van Diemen's Land (Tasmania) 1–2, 91
   American rebels in 174–9
   brutality of Arthur's governorship 175–6
   indigenous people 175
   Launceston Invalid Depot 192
   Maori rebels sent to 140–1
   Mark Jeffrey in 187–93
   Recherche Bay 118
   see also Hobart

Vanuatu 141
Venus, cargo ship 1, 2
Verney, Thomas, plantation in Barbados 21
The Veteran, transport ship 47
Vincent, Henry, superintendent of Rottnest
   prison 202
Vincent, William, superintendent of Rottnest
   prison 202
Vinegar Hill, Battle of (Irish rebellion 1798)
   113
Virginia
   anti-transportation laws 52
   Bacon's Rebellion 38–9
   banishment to 9
   children removed to 16, 25
   need for wives for settlers 17–19
   omens (1675) 37–8
Virginia Company
   and Bermuda 144–5
   costs for passage of women settlers
      18–19
Virginia, transport ship 161
VOICES organization, Western Australia,
   civil action on child migration 222

Wales, Rebecca riots 125, 139
Walker, Alice, twice transported 79–80
Walpole, Robert, prime minister 52
Waterloo, Battle of (1815) 139
Welch, Phillip, indentured convict 29–31
Welsteed, William, ship merchant 69
Wentworth, Mary, sent to Hobart 179,
   180
West Indies 8, 9
   child migrants sent to 215
   see also Barbados; Bermuda; Guyana
Western Australia 91, 199–200
   child migration schemes 216–19
   investigations into child migration 222
   and progress to settlement 214
   see also Fremantle; Swan River
White, Charles, on New South Wales
   183–4
White, John, medical officer 94
Whitfield, Captain, Western Australia 203
Wild, Jonathan, thief-taker 53, 56
William III, King 44, 47
Williamson, Peter
   kidnapped in Aberdeen and sent to
      Philadelphia 63–5
   return to Edinburgh 65
Willoughby, Francis 10
Wilson, Hugh, master in America 64
Wilson, James, Fenian rebel 210–11
Wilson, Sarah, imposter 74–5

women
    abducted ('spirited') 28
    at Cascades Female Factory, Hobart 179–83
    convicts in New South Wales 95–9
    emigration to Virginia 18–19
    need for settlers in New South Wales 92
    new lives in colonies 67
    punishments in Australia 96
    sexual relation on ship *Janus* 111–12
    survival on ships 85
    'the counterfeit lady' (Mary Carleton) 34–7
    transported 66–7
    'virtuous maids' 17–19
    see also Buckler, Susanna; King, Moll
Woodman, Henry, overseer 209–10
Woolwich, prison hulks at 102
Worcester, Battle of (1651) 22
World War II, children evacuated to Australia
    and New Zealand 219
Worley, Richard, captain of *Eagle* 50
Wynn, Elizabeth, transportation to Guyana
    19–21

Yagan, Noongar Aboriginal leader 200